# YOU'RE READING THE

# **WRONG WAY!**

**PLATINUM END**
reads from right to left,
starting in the upper-right
corner. Japanese is read
from right to left, meaning
that action, sound effects
and word-balloon order
are completely reversed
from English order.

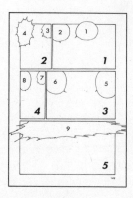

# PLATINVM END

VOLUME 10
SHONEN JUMP Manga Edition

STORY **T s u g u mi  Oh b a**

ART Ta **k e sh i**  O b a **ta**

TRANSLATION Stephen Paul
TOUCH-UP ART & LETTERING James Gaubatz
DESIGN Shawn Carrico
EDITOR Alexis Kirsch

ORIGINAL COVER DESIGN Narumi Noriko

PLATINUM END © 2015 by Tsugumi Ohba, Takeshi Obata
All rights reserved.
First published in Japan in 2015 by SHUEISHA Inc., Tokyo.
English translation rights arranged by SHUEISHA Inc.

Printed in the U.S.A.

Published by VIZ Media, LLC
P.O. Box 77010
San Francisco, CA 94107

10 9 8 7 6 5 4 3 2 1
First printing, December 2019

viz.com

shonenjump.com

ART
Takeshi Obata

STORY
Tsugumi Ohba

Platinum End

# PLATINVM END

**10**

## CHARACTERS

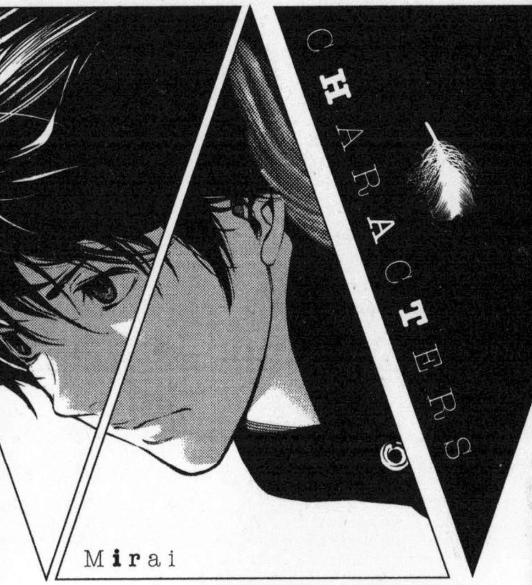
Mirai

**Mirai Kakehashi**

First-year high school student. His parents and brother died in an accident when he was seven. After a painful life with his abusive relatives, he attempts to commit suicide and survives through Nasse's help.

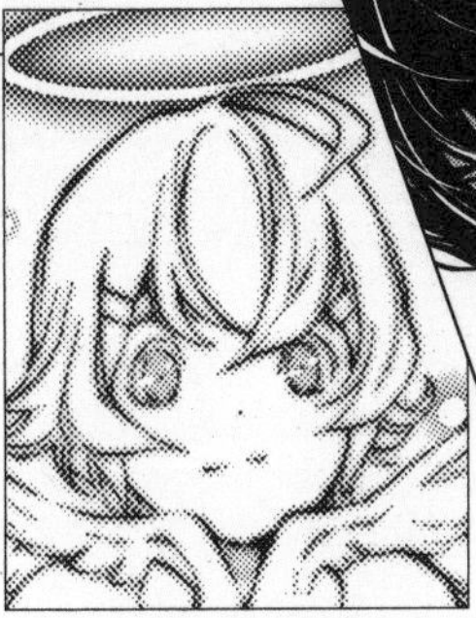

**Nasse**

A special-rank angel who wants to bring happiness to Mirai's life. Bright and bubbly.

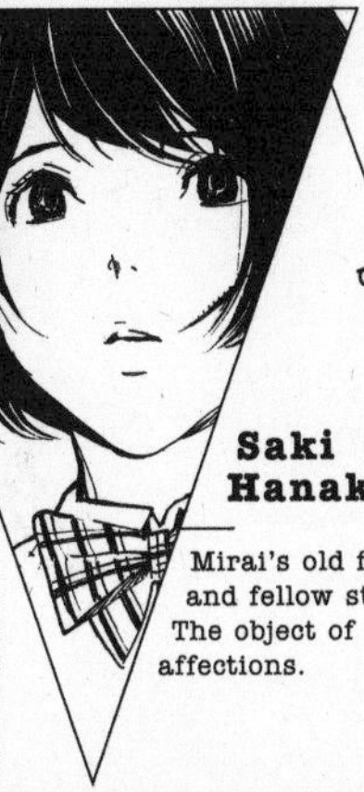
Saki

**Saki Hanakago**

Mirai's old friend and fellow student. The object of his affections.

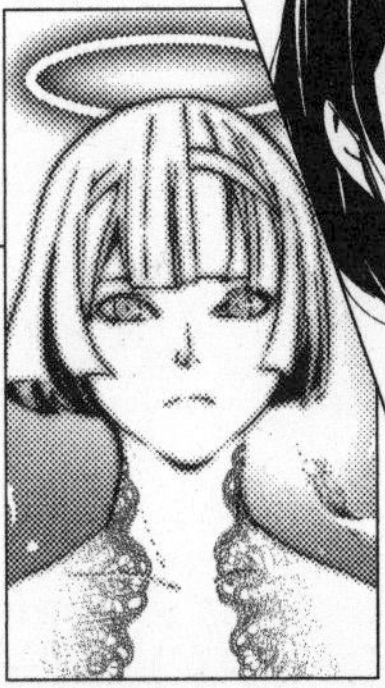

**Revel**

Promoted to the first-rank Angel of Emotion.

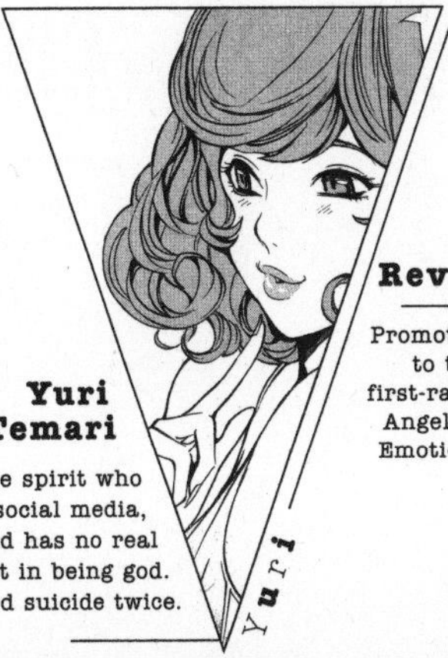
Yuri

**Yuri Temari**

Free spirit who enjoys social media, and has no real interest in being god. Attempted suicide twice.

## Story

"My time has come. I leave the seat of god to the next human. To a younger, fresher power.

The next god shall be chosen from the 13 humans chosen by you 13 angels. When the chosen human is made the next god, your angelic duty is finished, and you may live beside that god in peace

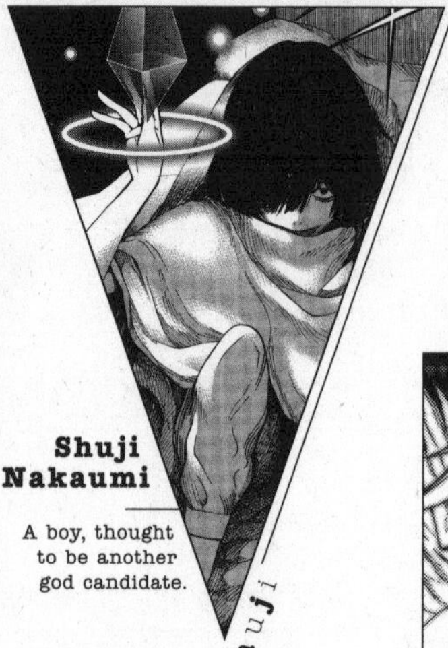

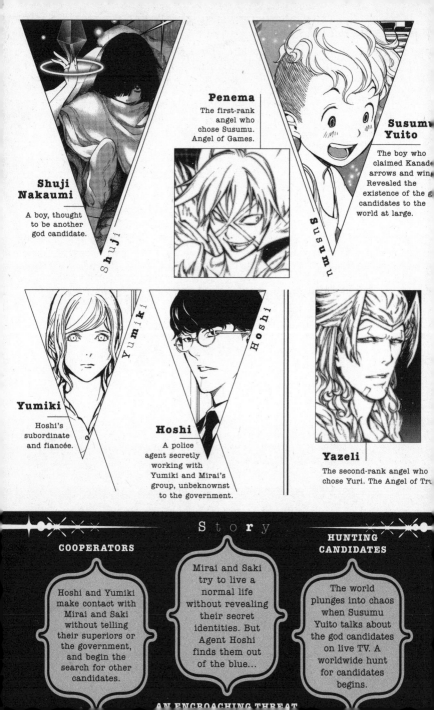

**Shuji Nakaumi**

A boy, thought to be another god candidate.

Shuji

**Penema**

The first-rank angel who chose Susumu. Angel of Games.

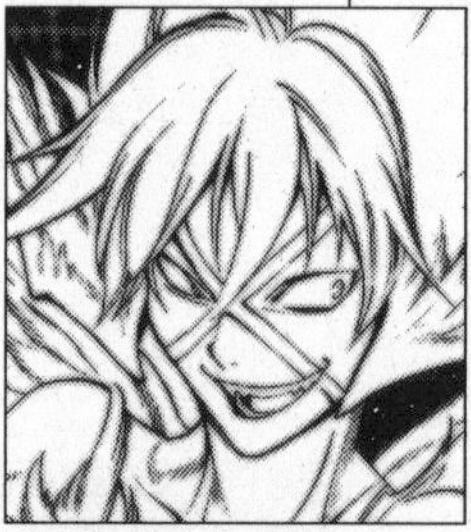

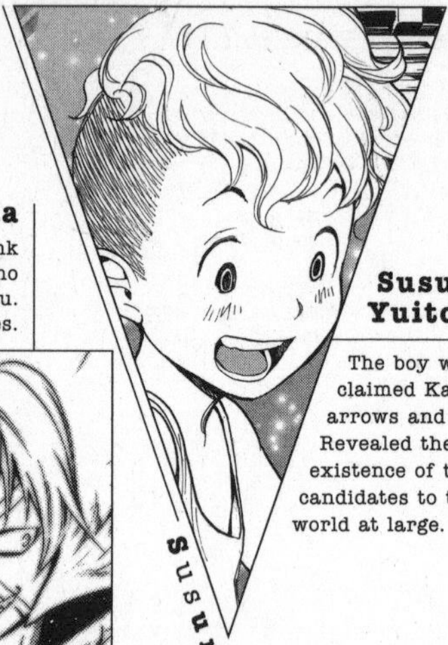

**Susum Yuito**

The boy who claimed Kanad arrows and win Revealed the existence of the g candidates to the world at large.

Susumu

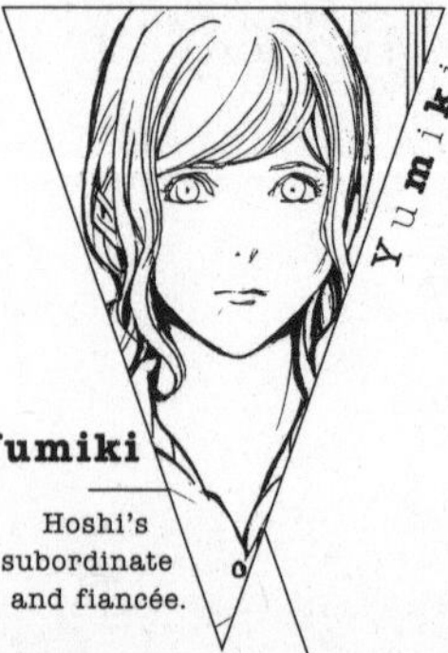

Yumiki

**Yumiki**

Hoshi's subordinate and fiancée.

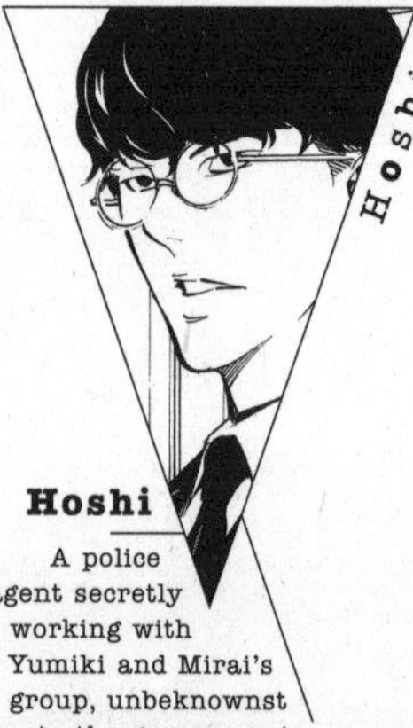

Hoshi

**Hoshi**

A police agent secretly working with Yumiki and Mirai's group, unbeknownst to the government.

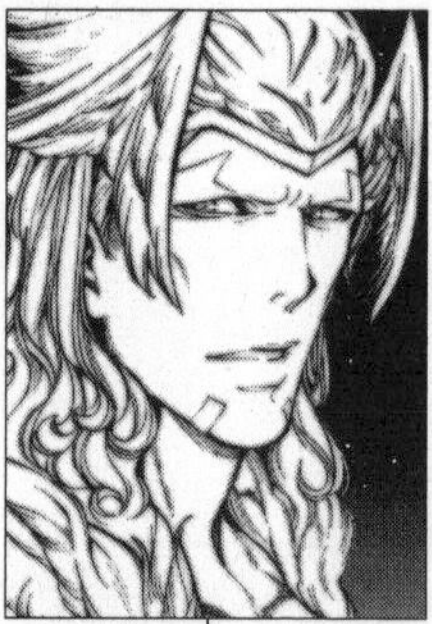

**Yazeli**

The second-rank angel who chose Yuri. The Angel of Tru

## Story

**COOPERATORS**

Hoshi and Yumiki make contact with Mirai and Saki without telling their superiors or the government, and begin the search for other candidates.

Mirai and Saki try to live a normal life without revealing their secret identities. But Agent Hoshi finds them out of the blue...

**HUNTING CANDIDATES**

The world plunges into chaos when Susumu Yuito talks about the god candidates on live TV. A worldwide hunt for candidates begins.

**AN ENCROACHING THREAT**

# CONTENTS

10

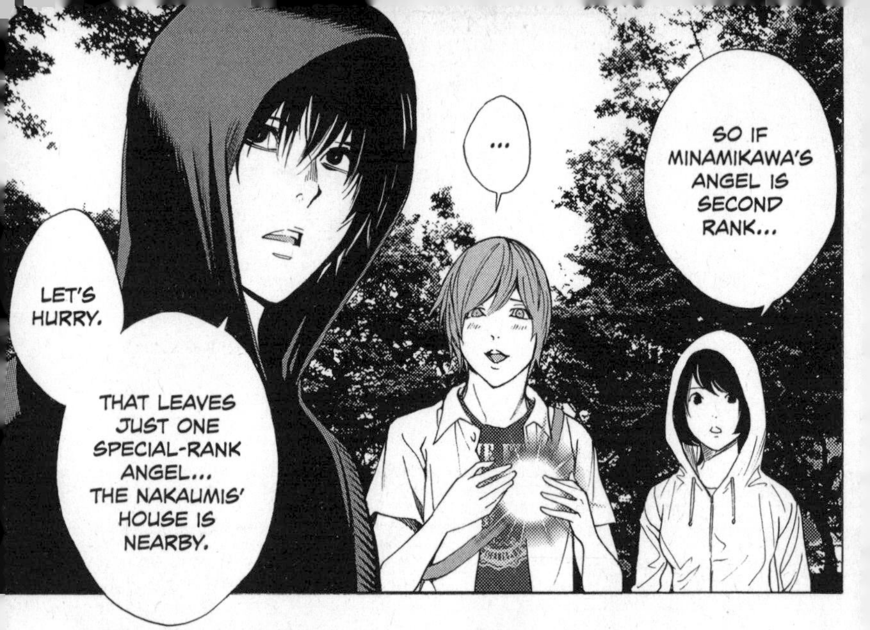
SO IF MINAMIKAWA'S ANGEL IS SECOND RANK...
...
THAT LEAVES JUST ONE SPECIAL-RANK ANGEL... THE NAKAUMIS' HOUSE IS NEARBY.
LET'S HURRY.

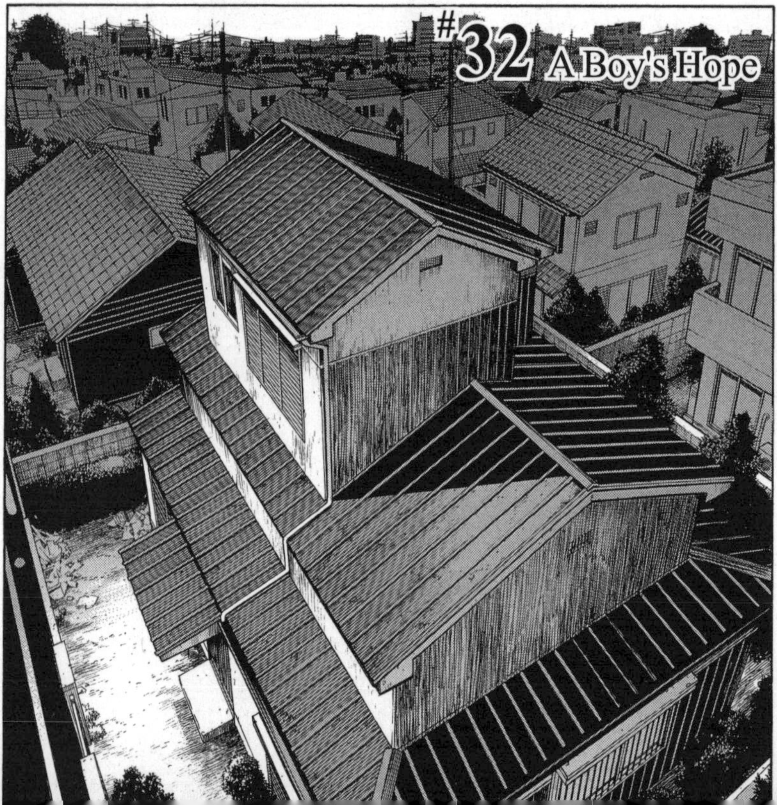
#32 A Boy's Hope

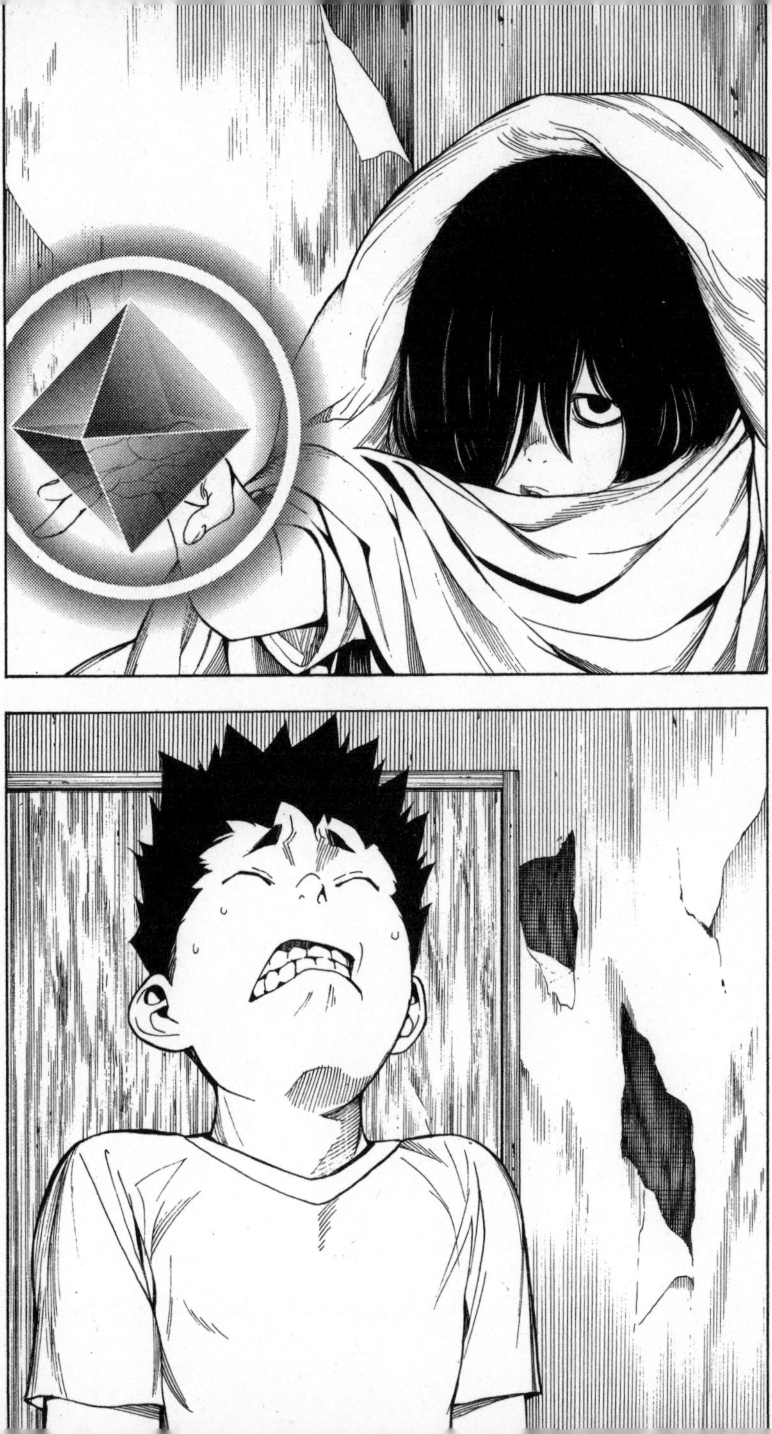

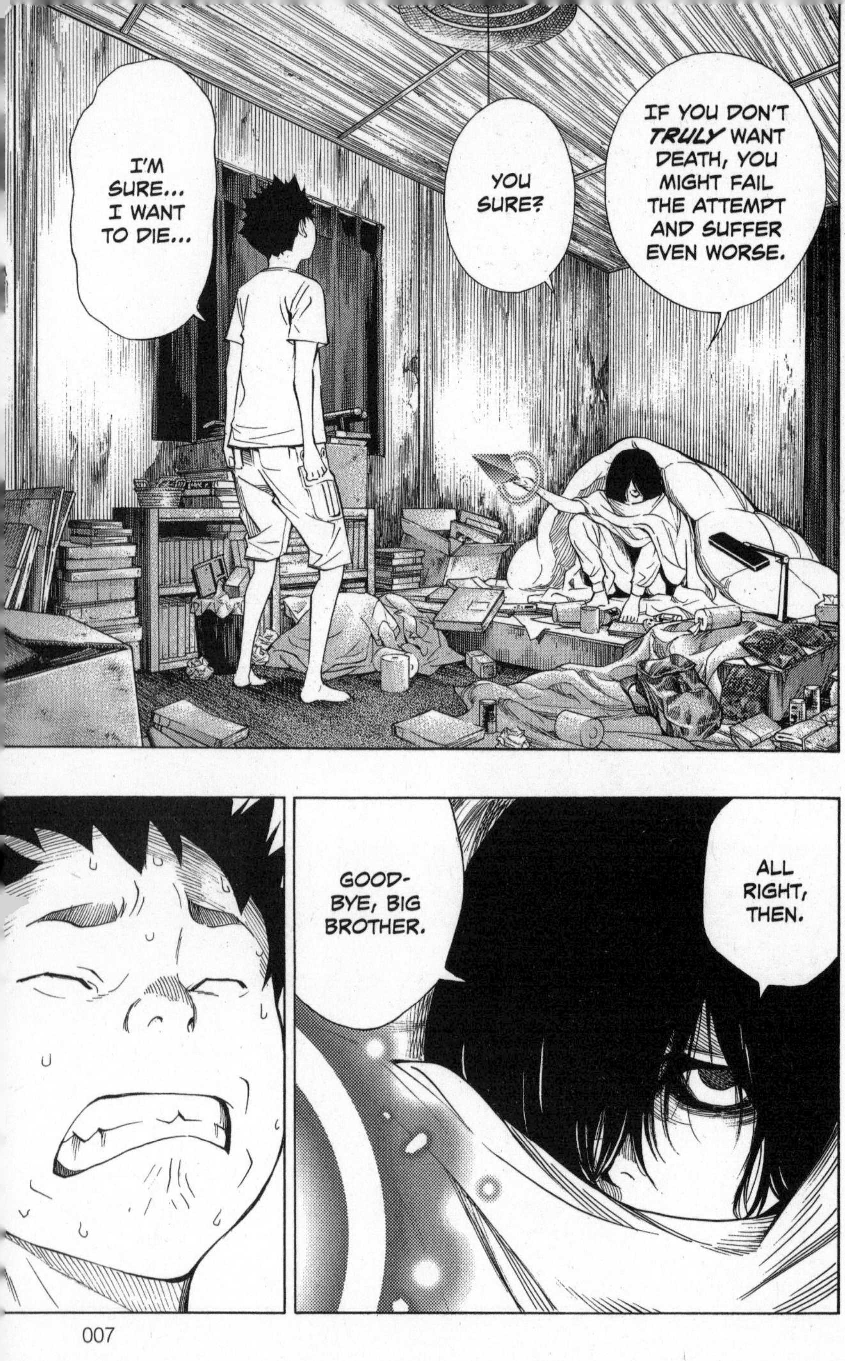
IF YOU DON'T *TRULY* WANT DEATH, YOU MIGHT FAIL THE ATTEMPT AND SUFFER EVEN WORSE.
YOU SURE?
I'M SURE... I WANT TO DIE...
ALL RIGHT, THEN.
GOOD-BYE, BIG BROTHER.

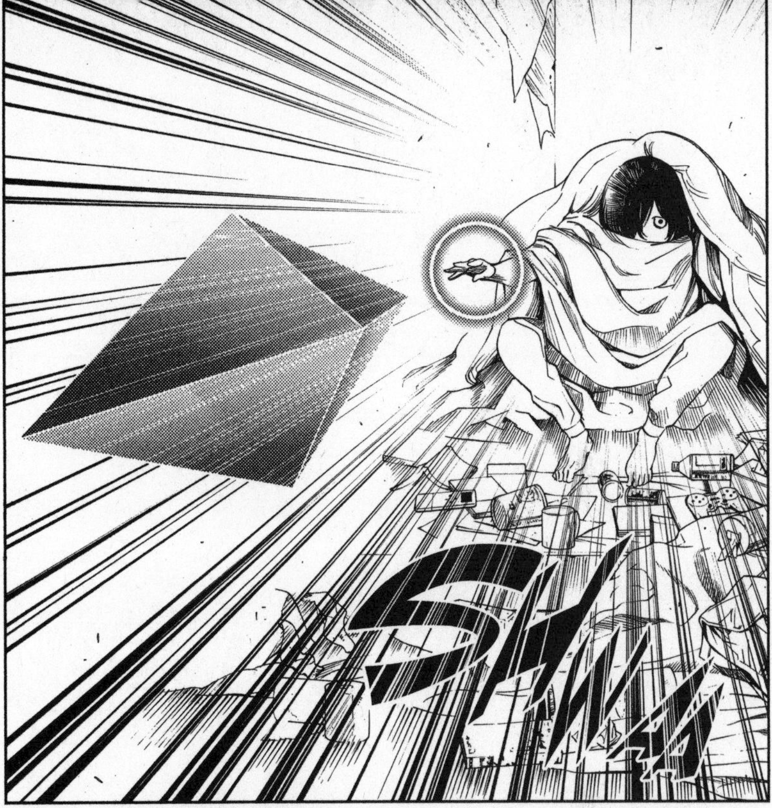
SHWA
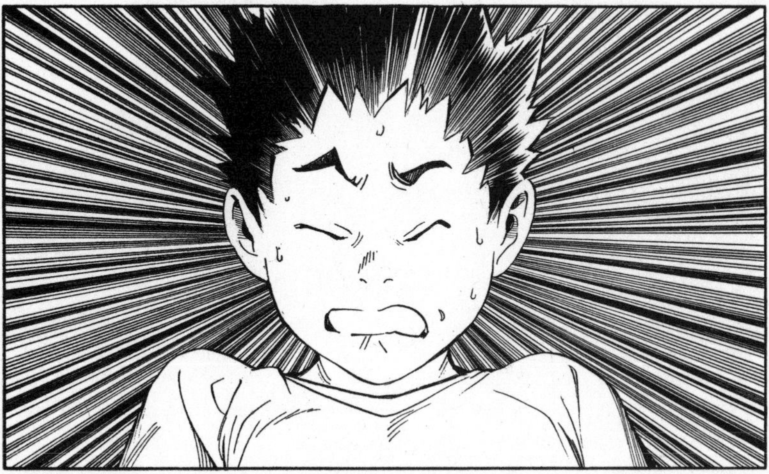

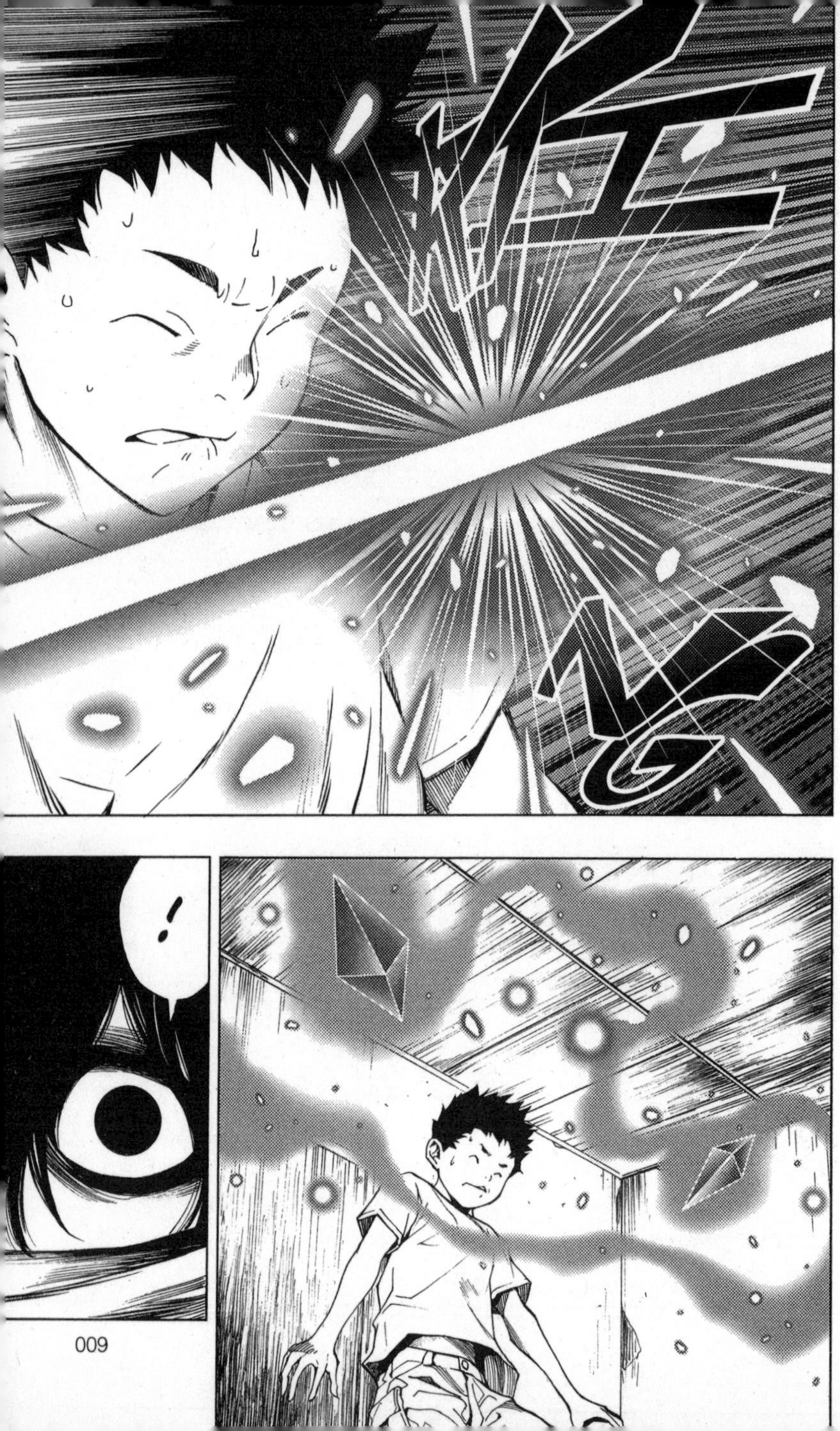
!

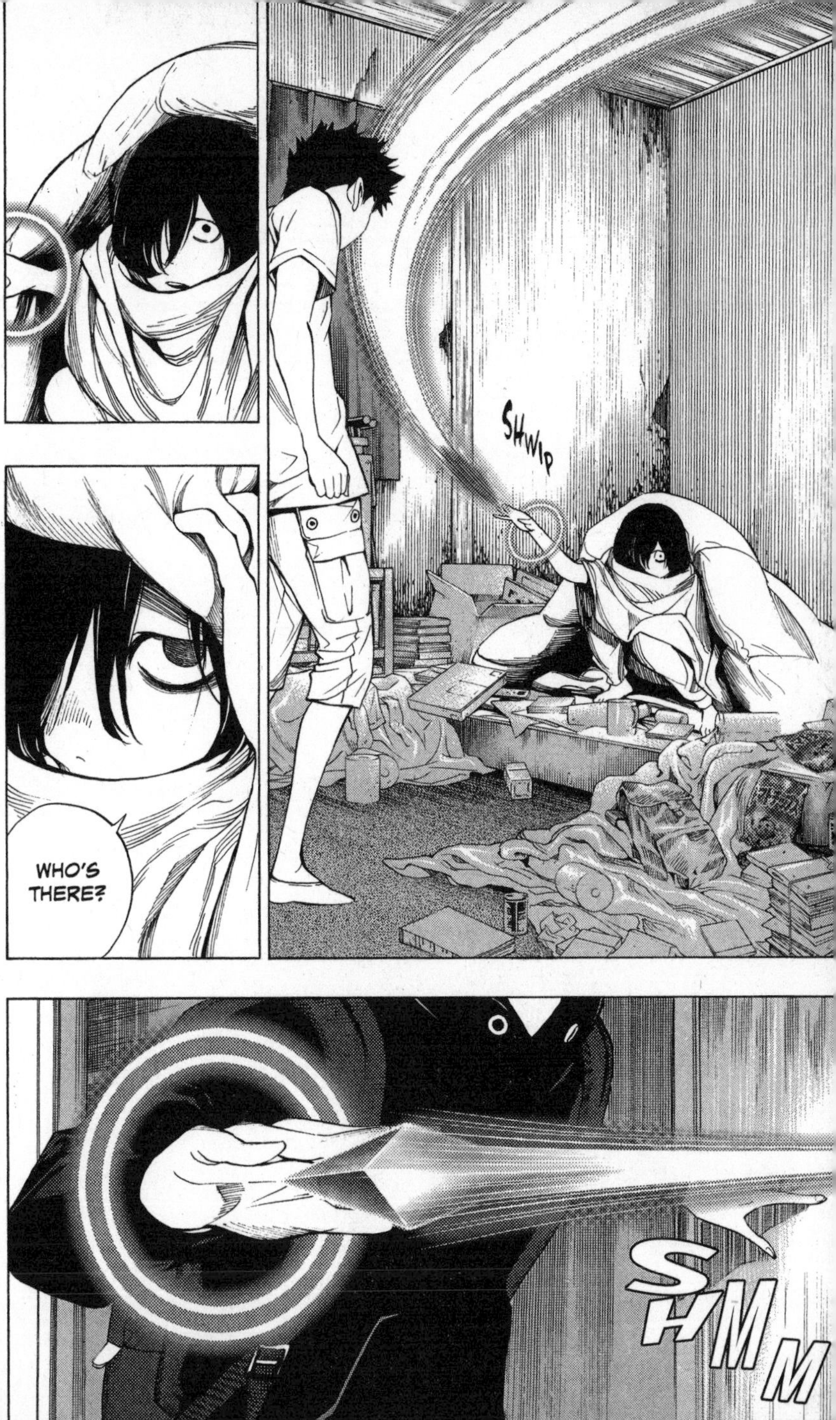
SHWIP
WHO'S THERE?
SHMM

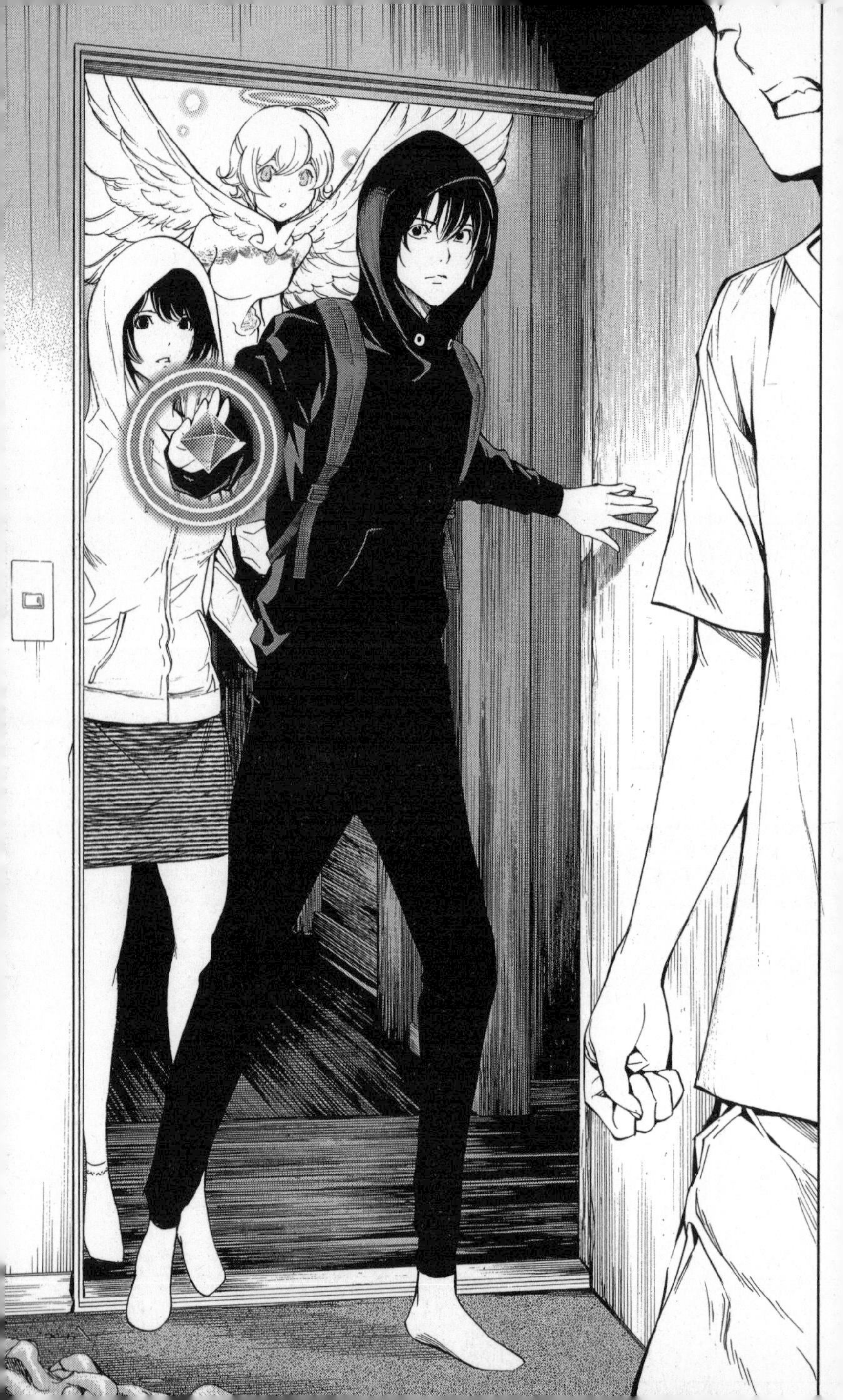

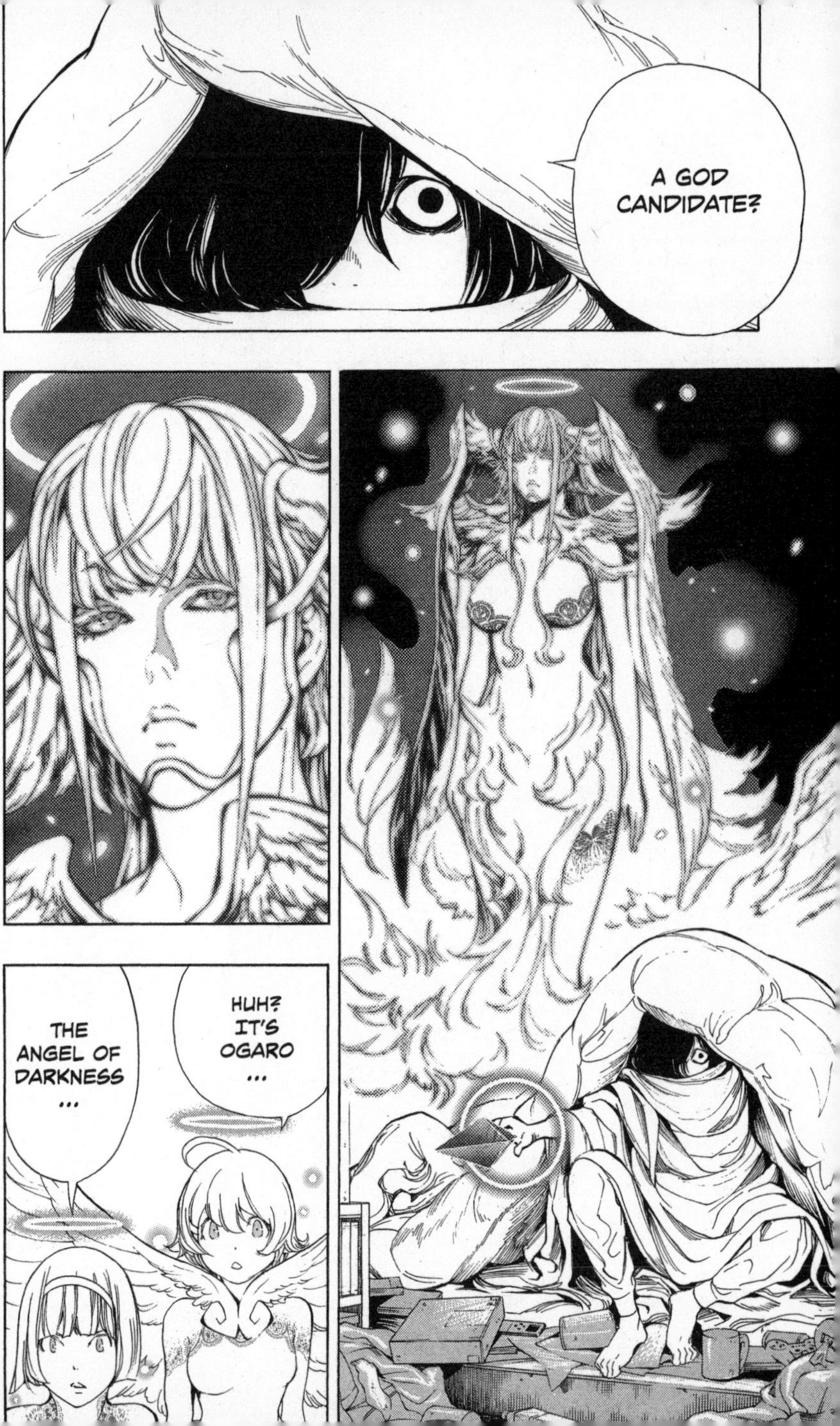
A GOD CANDIDATE?
HUH? IT'S OGARO ...
THE ANGEL OF DARKNESS ...

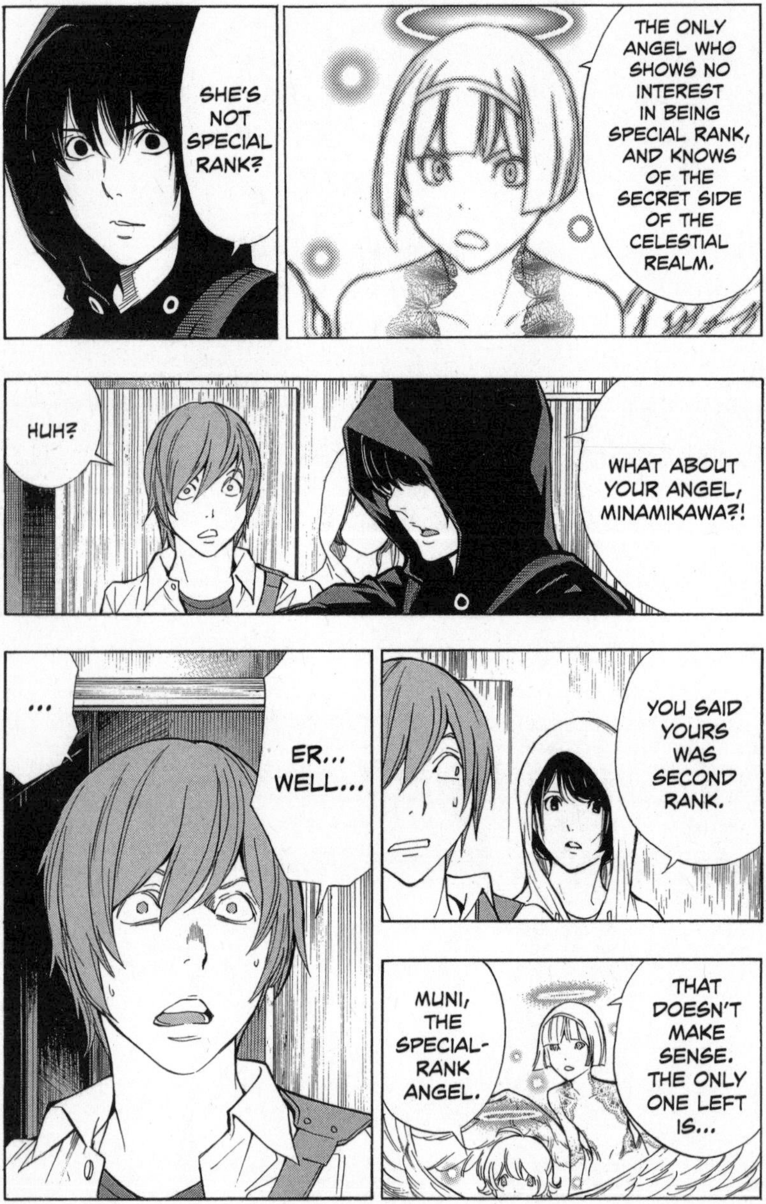
THE ONLY ANGEL WHO SHOWS NO INTEREST IN BEING SPECIAL RANK, AND KNOWS OF THE SECRET SIDE OF THE CELESTIAL REALM.
SHE'S NOT SPECIAL RANK?
WHAT ABOUT YOUR ANGEL, MINAMIKAWA?!
HUH?
YOU SAID YOURS WAS SECOND RANK.
THAT DOESN'T MAKE SENSE. THE ONLY ONE LEFT IS...
MUNI, THE SPECIAL-RANK ANGEL.
ER... WELL...
...

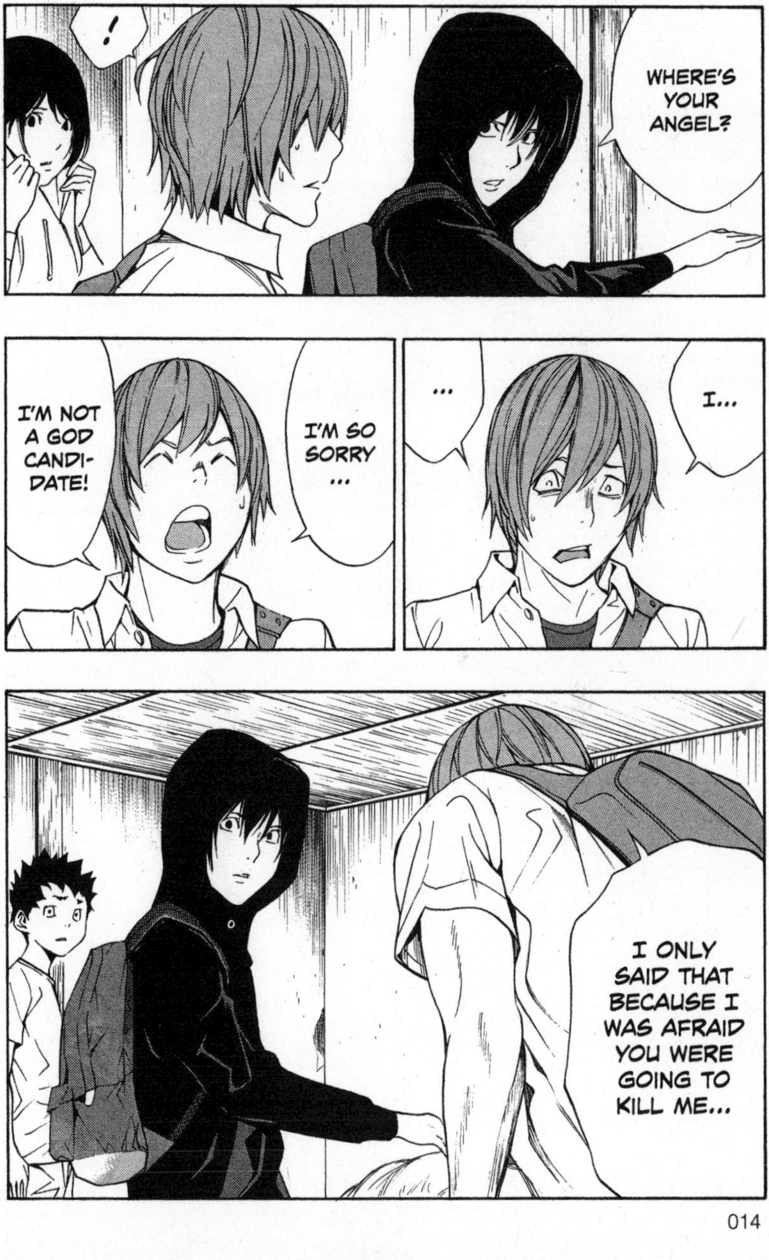
WHERE'S YOUR ANGEL?
!
I...
...
I'M SO SORRY ...
I'M NOT A GOD CANDI-DATE!
I ONLY SAID THAT BECAUSE I WAS AFRAID YOU WERE GOING TO KILL ME...

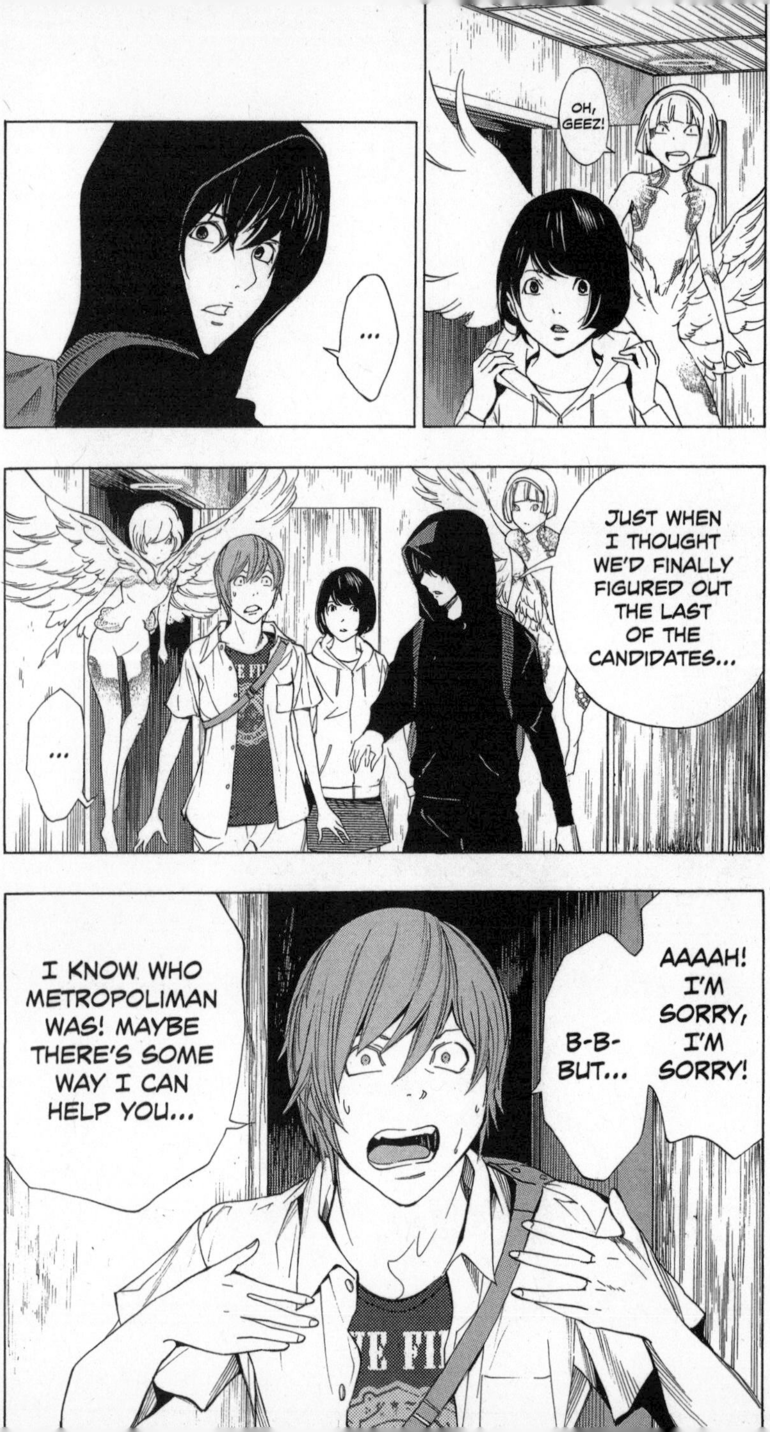
OH, GEEZ!
...
JUST WHEN I THOUGHT WE'D FINALLY FIGURED OUT THE LAST OF THE CANDIDATES...
...
AAAAH! I'M SORRY, I'M SORRY!
B-B-BUT...
I KNOW WHO METROPOLIMAN WAS! MAYBE THERE'S SOME WAY I CAN HELP YOU...

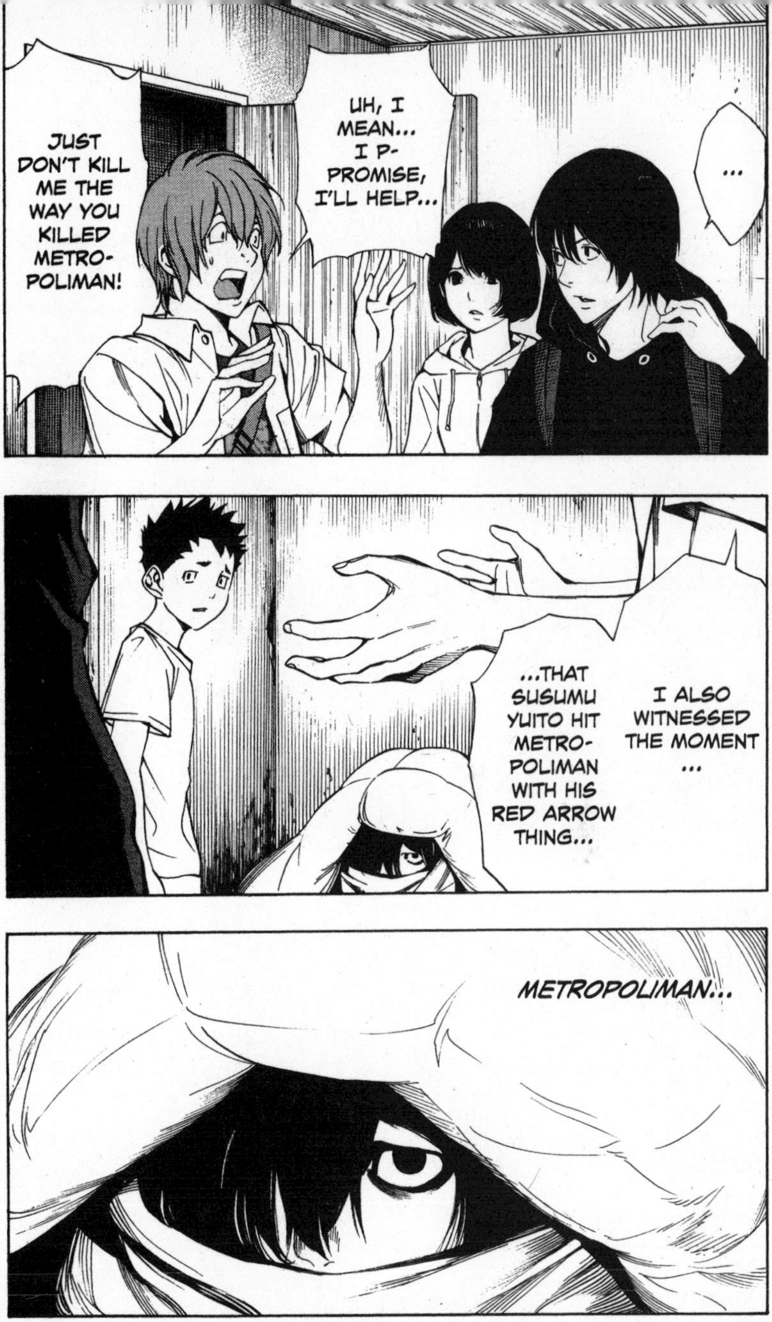
...
UH, I MEAN... I P-PROMISE, I'LL HELP...
JUST DON'T KILL ME THE WAY YOU KILLED METRO-POLIMAN!
I ALSO WITNESSED THE MOMENT...
...THAT SUSUMU YUITO HIT METRO-POLIMAN WITH HIS RED ARROW THING...
METROPOLIMAN...

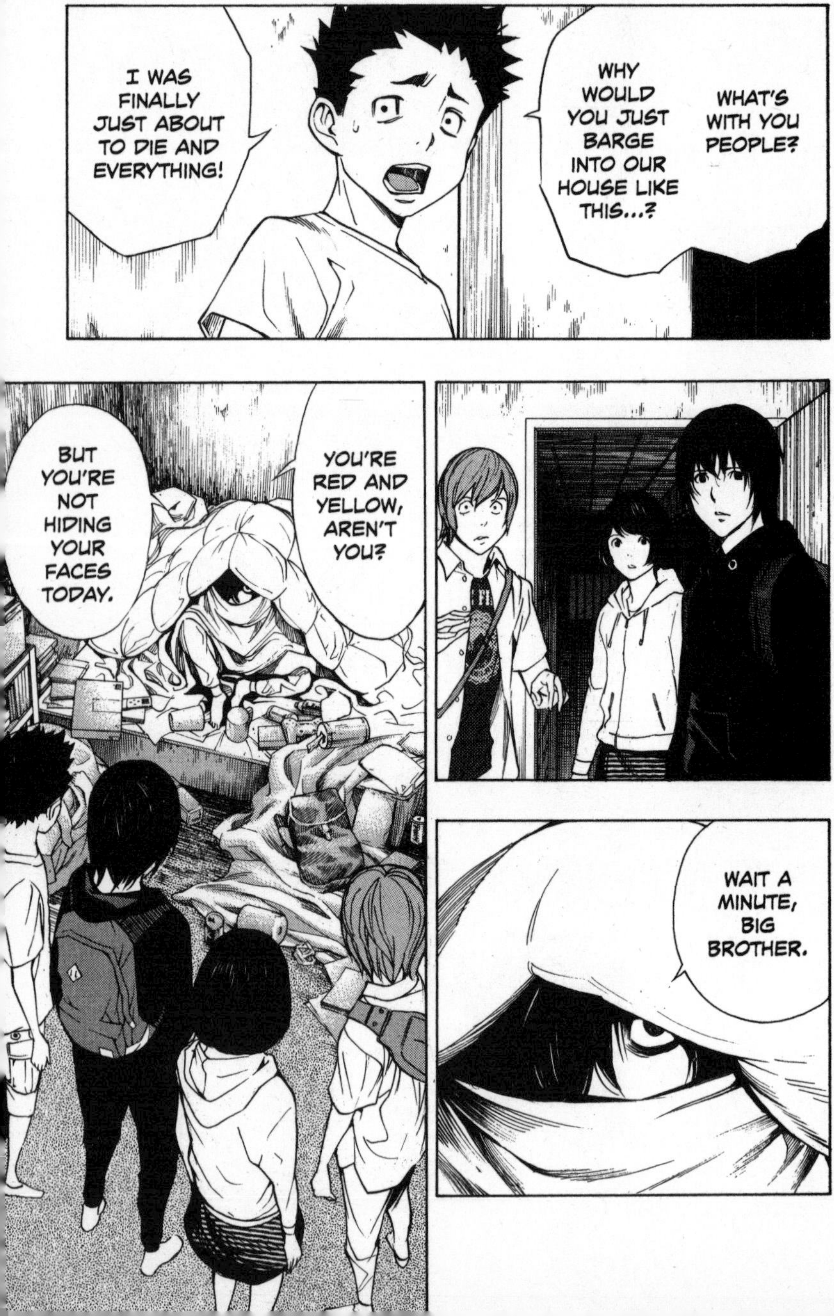
WHAT'S WITH YOU PEOPLE?
WHY WOULD YOU JUST BARGE INTO OUR HOUSE LIKE THIS...?
I WAS FINALLY JUST ABOUT TO DIE AND EVERYTHING!
WAIT A MINUTE, BIG BROTHER.
YOU'RE RED AND YELLOW, AREN'T YOU?
BUT YOU'RE NOT HIDING YOUR FACES TODAY.

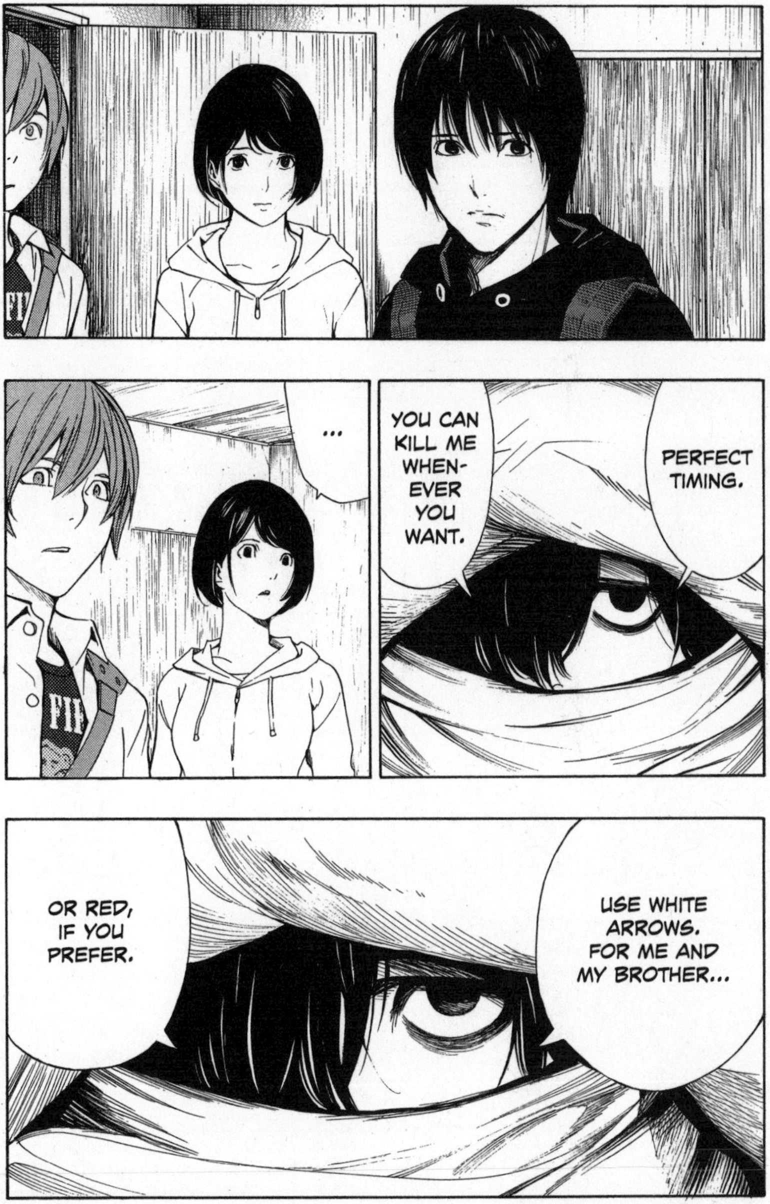
PERFECT TIMING.
YOU CAN KILL ME WHEN-EVER YOU WANT.
...
USE WHITE ARROWS. FOR ME AND MY BROTHER...
OR RED, IF YOU PREFER.

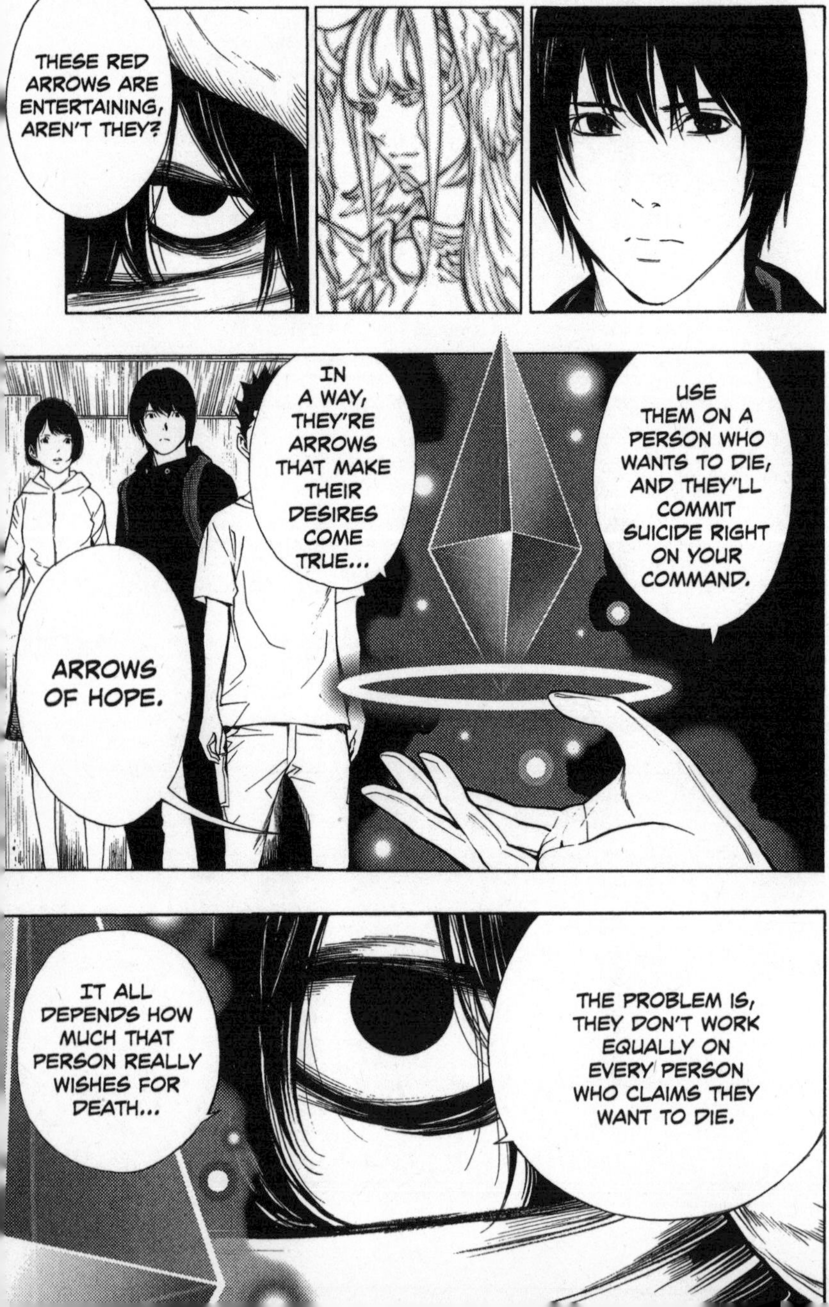
THESE RED ARROWS ARE ENTERTAINING, AREN'T THEY?
USE THEM ON A PERSON WHO WANTS TO DIE, AND THEY'LL COMMIT SUICIDE RIGHT ON YOUR COMMAND.
IN A WAY, THEY'RE ARROWS THAT MAKE THEIR DESIRES COME TRUE...
ARROWS OF HOPE.
THE PROBLEM IS, THEY DON'T WORK EQUALLY ON EVERY PERSON WHO CLAIMS THEY WANT TO DIE.
IT ALL DEPENDS HOW MUCH THAT PERSON REALLY WISHES FOR DEATH...

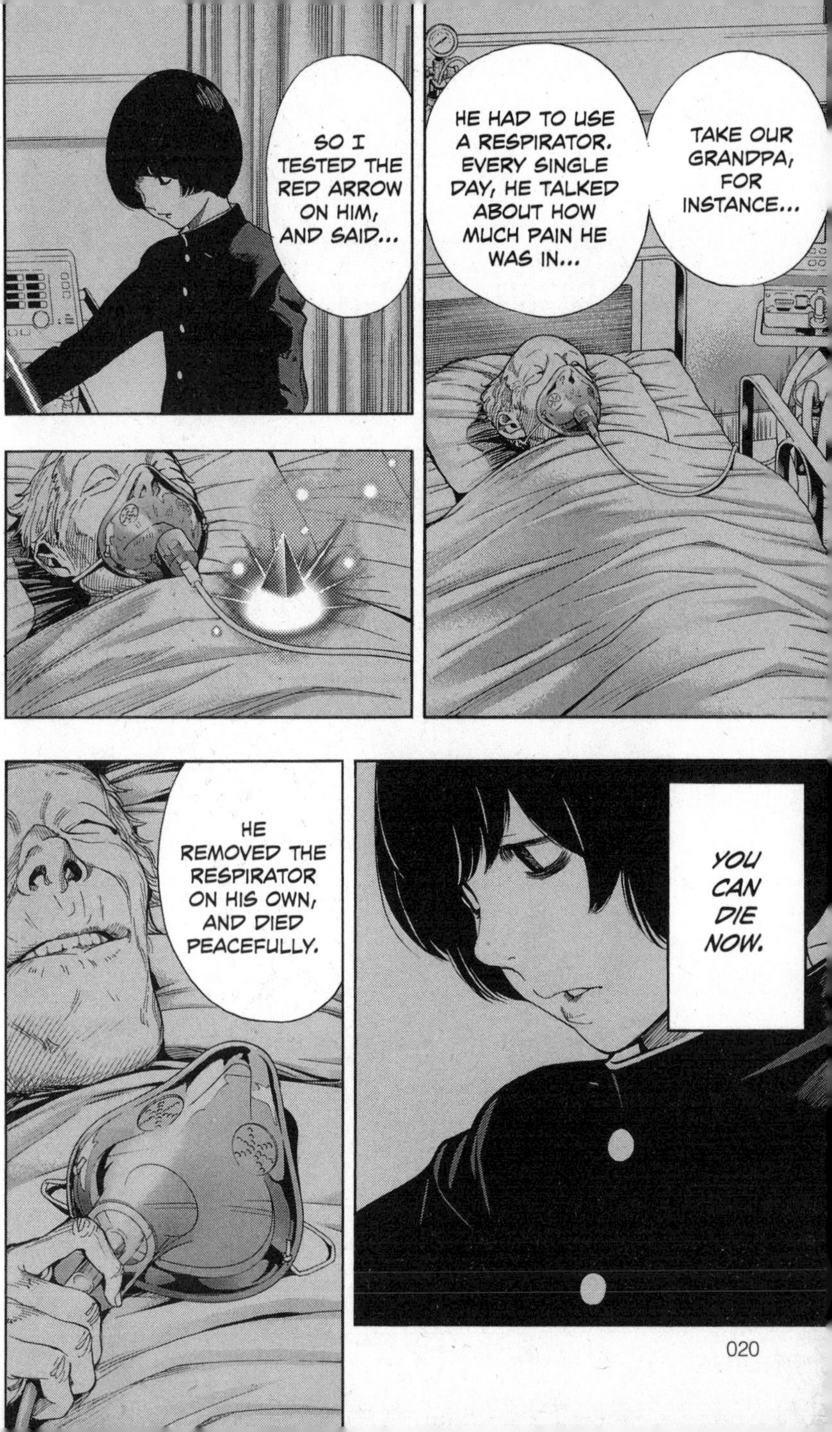
TAKE OUR GRANDPA, FOR INSTANCE...
HE HAD TO USE A RESPIRATOR. EVERY SINGLE DAY, HE TALKED ABOUT HOW MUCH PAIN HE WAS IN...
SO I TESTED THE RED ARROW ON HIM, AND SAID...
YOU CAN DIE NOW.
HE REMOVED THE RESPIRATOR ON HIS OWN, AND DIED PEACEFULLY.

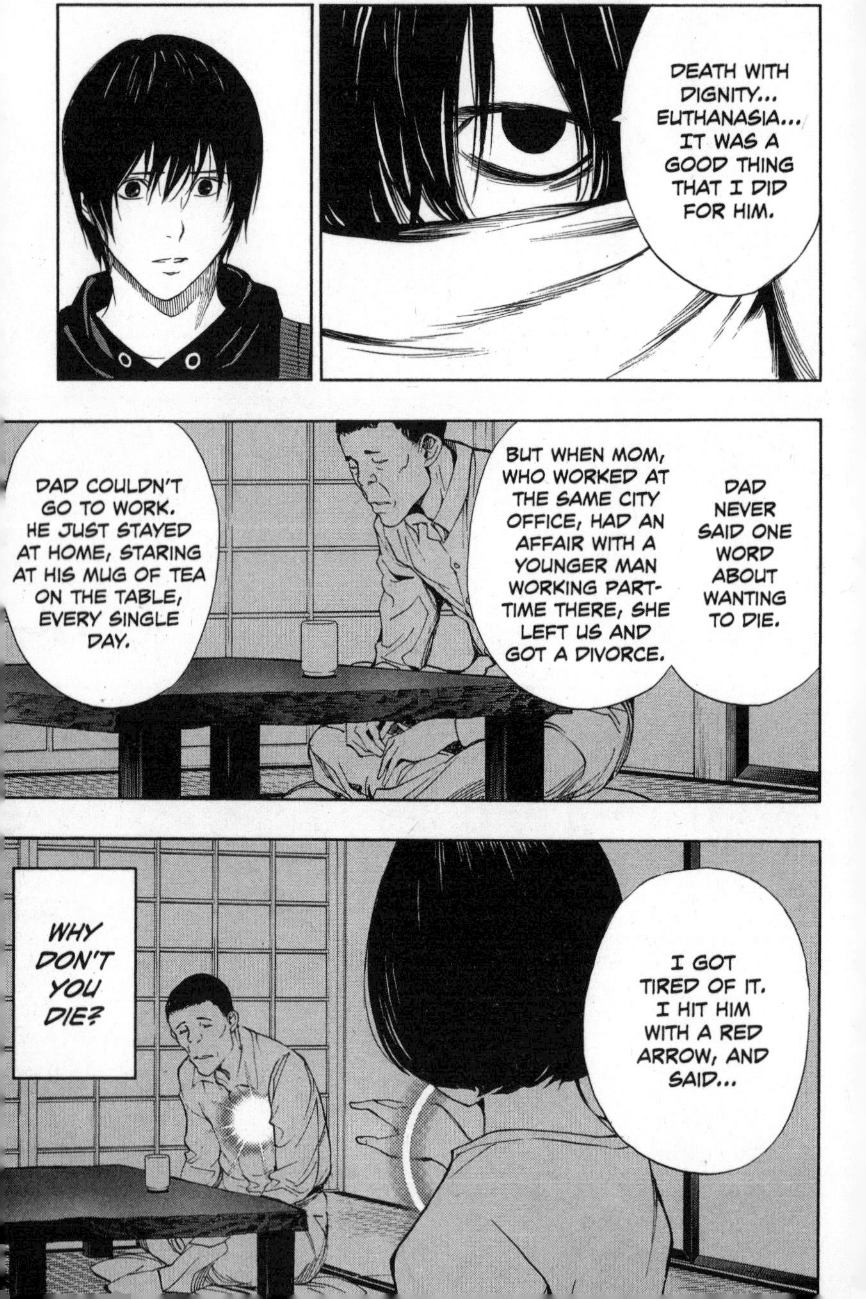
DEATH WITH DIGNITY... EUTHANASIA... IT WAS A GOOD THING THAT I DID FOR HIM.
DAD NEVER SAID ONE WORD ABOUT WANTING TO DIE.
BUT WHEN MOM, WHO WORKED AT THE SAME CITY OFFICE, HAD AN AFFAIR WITH A YOUNGER MAN WORKING PART-TIME THERE, SHE LEFT US AND GOT A DIVORCE.
DAD COULDN'T GO TO WORK. HE JUST STAYED AT HOME, STARING AT HIS MUG OF TEA ON THE TABLE, EVERY SINGLE DAY.
I GOT TIRED OF IT. I HIT HIM WITH A RED ARROW, AND SAID...
WHY DON'T YOU DIE?

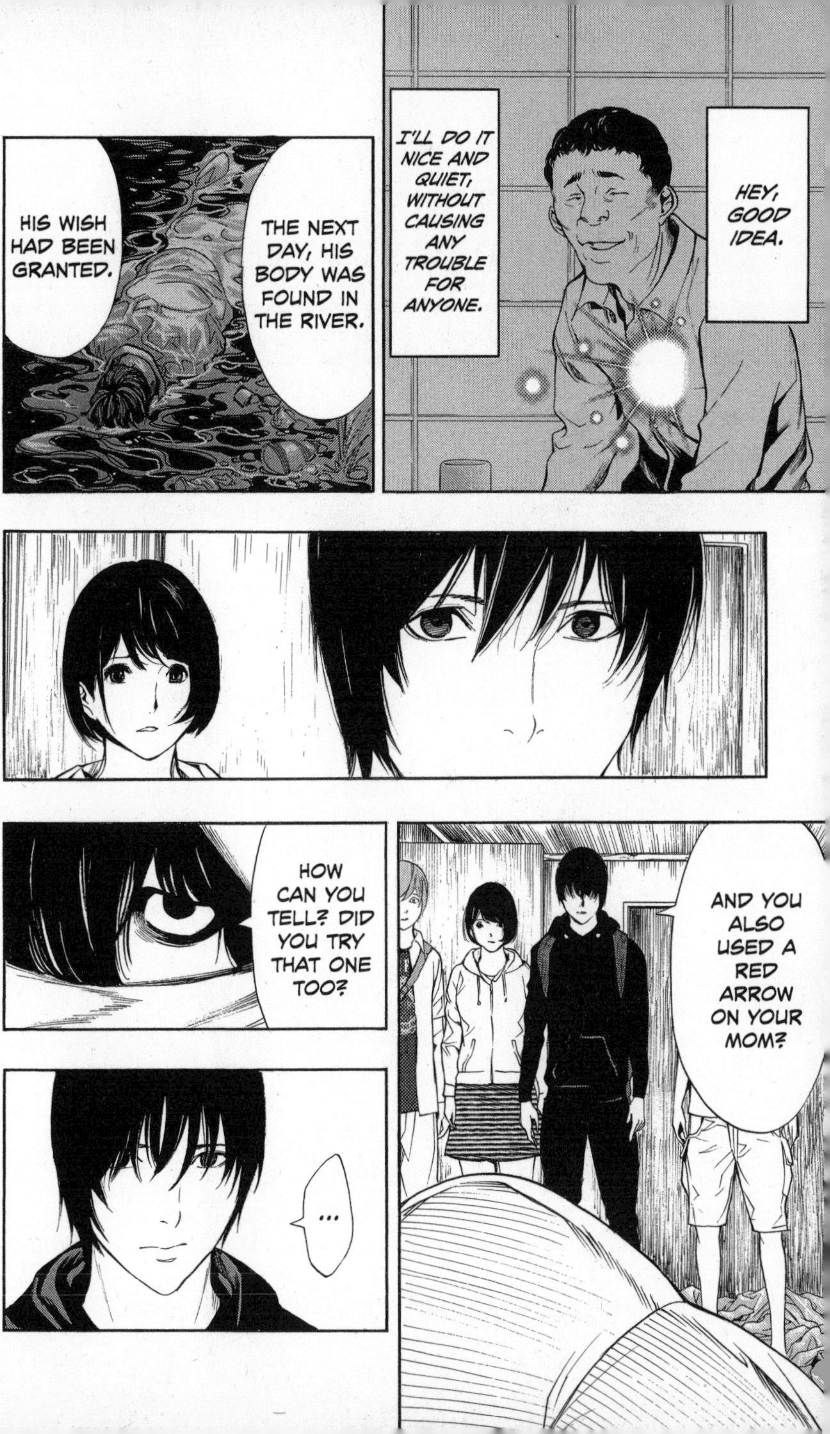
HEY, GOOD IDEA.
I'LL DO IT NICE AND QUIET, WITHOUT CAUSING ANY TROUBLE FOR ANYONE.
THE NEXT DAY, HIS BODY WAS FOUND IN THE RIVER.
HIS WISH HAD BEEN GRANTED.
AND YOU ALSO USED A RED ARROW ON YOUR MOM?
HOW CAN YOU TELL? DID YOU TRY THAT ONE TOO?
...

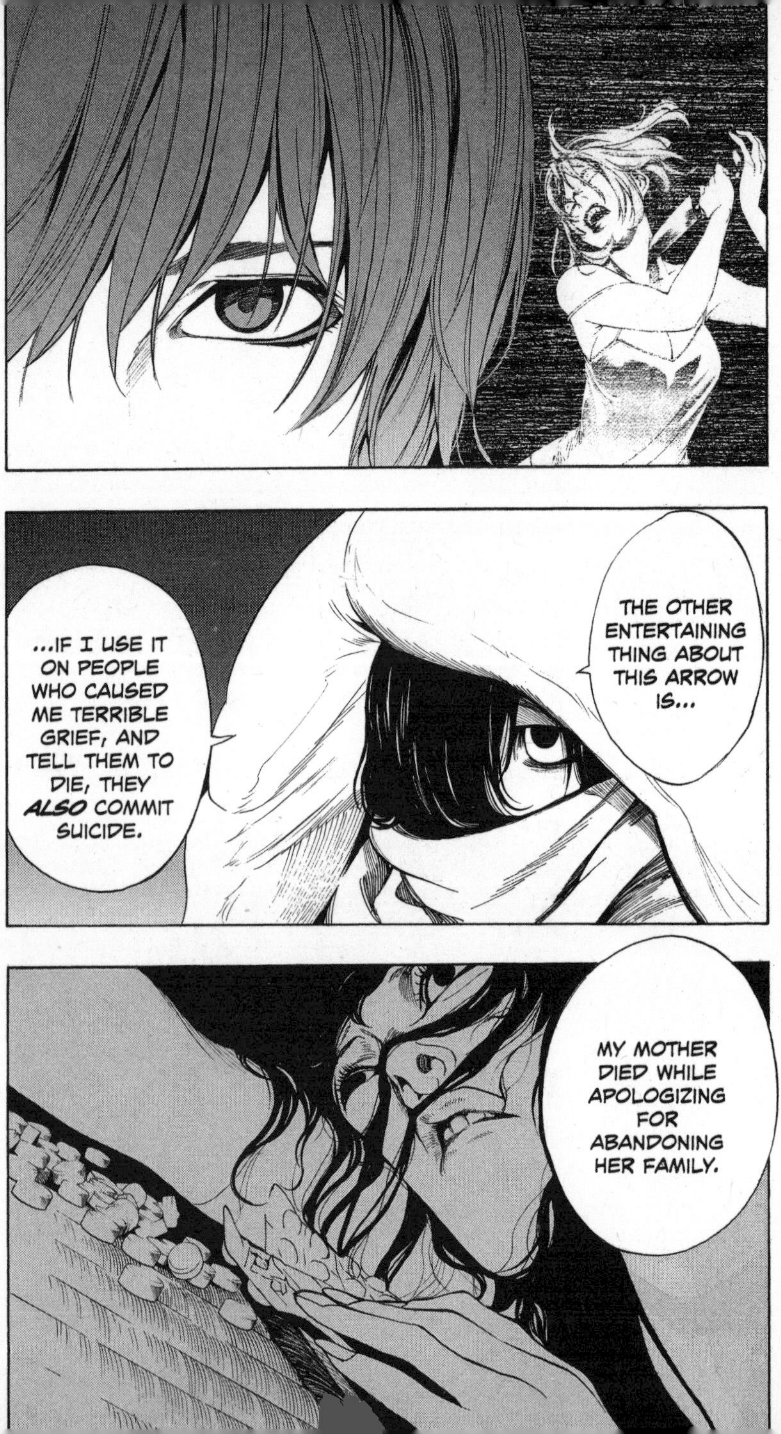
THE OTHER ENTERTAINING THING ABOUT THIS ARROW IS...
...IF I USE IT ON PEOPLE WHO CAUSED ME TERRIBLE GRIEF, AND TELL THEM TO DIE, THEY *ALSO* COMMIT SUICIDE.
MY MOTHER DIED WHILE APOLOGIZING FOR ABANDONING HER FAMILY.

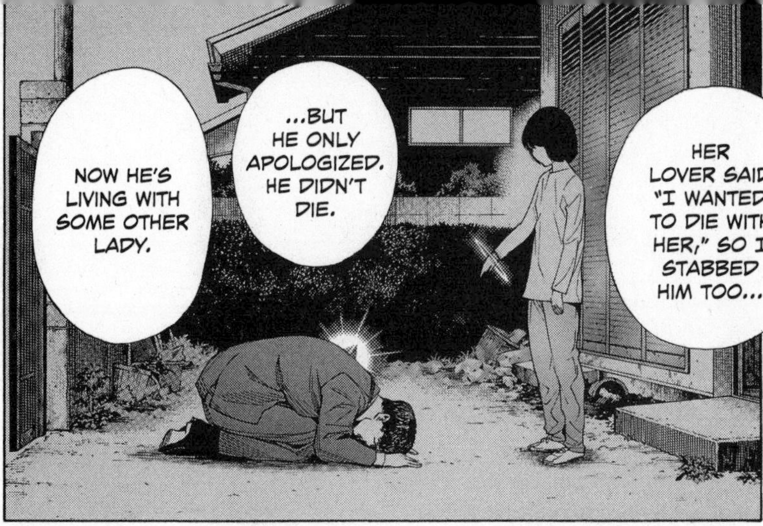
HER LOVER SAID "I WANTED TO DIE WITH HER," SO I STABBED HIM TOO...
...BUT HE ONLY APOLOGIZED. HE DIDN'T DIE.
NOW HE'S LIVING WITH SOME OTHER LADY.

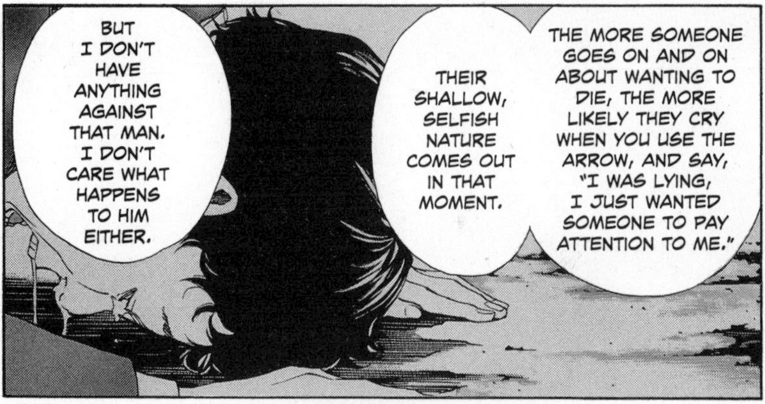
THE MORE SOMEONE GOES ON AND ON ABOUT WANTING TO DIE, THE MORE LIKELY THEY CRY WHEN YOU USE THE ARROW, AND SAY, "I WAS LYING, I JUST WANTED SOMEONE TO PAY ATTENTION TO ME."
THEIR SHALLOW, SELFISH NATURE COMES OUT IN THAT MOMENT.
BUT I DON'T HAVE ANYTHING AGAINST THAT MAN. I DON'T CARE WHAT HAPPENS TO HIM EITHER.

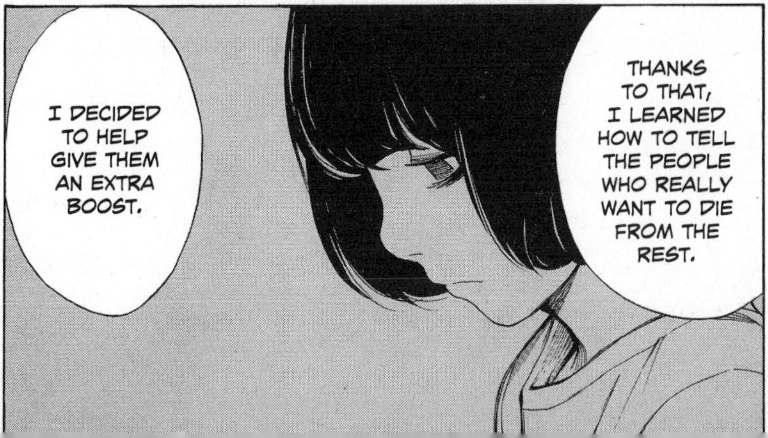
THANKS TO THAT, I LEARNED HOW TO TELL THE PEOPLE WHO REALLY WANT TO DIE FROM THE REST.
I DECIDED TO HELP GIVE THEM AN EXTRA BOOST.

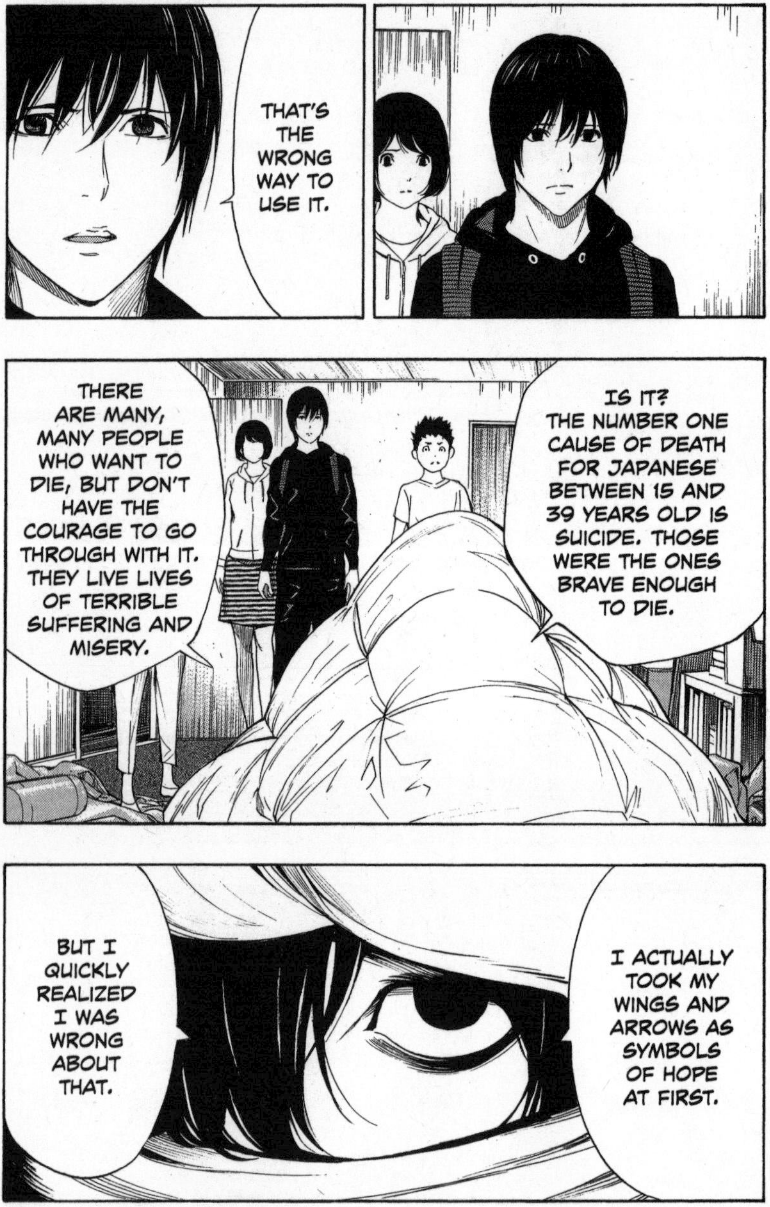
THAT'S THE WRONG WAY TO USE IT.
IS IT? THE NUMBER ONE CAUSE OF DEATH FOR JAPANESE BETWEEN 15 AND 39 YEARS OLD IS SUICIDE. THOSE WERE THE ONES BRAVE ENOUGH TO DIE.
THERE ARE MANY, MANY PEOPLE WHO WANT TO DIE, BUT DON'T HAVE THE COURAGE TO GO THROUGH WITH IT. THEY LIVE LIVES OF TERRIBLE SUFFERING AND MISERY.
I ACTUALLY TOOK MY WINGS AND ARROWS AS SYMBOLS OF HOPE AT FIRST.
BUT I QUICKLY REALIZED I WAS WRONG ABOUT THAT.

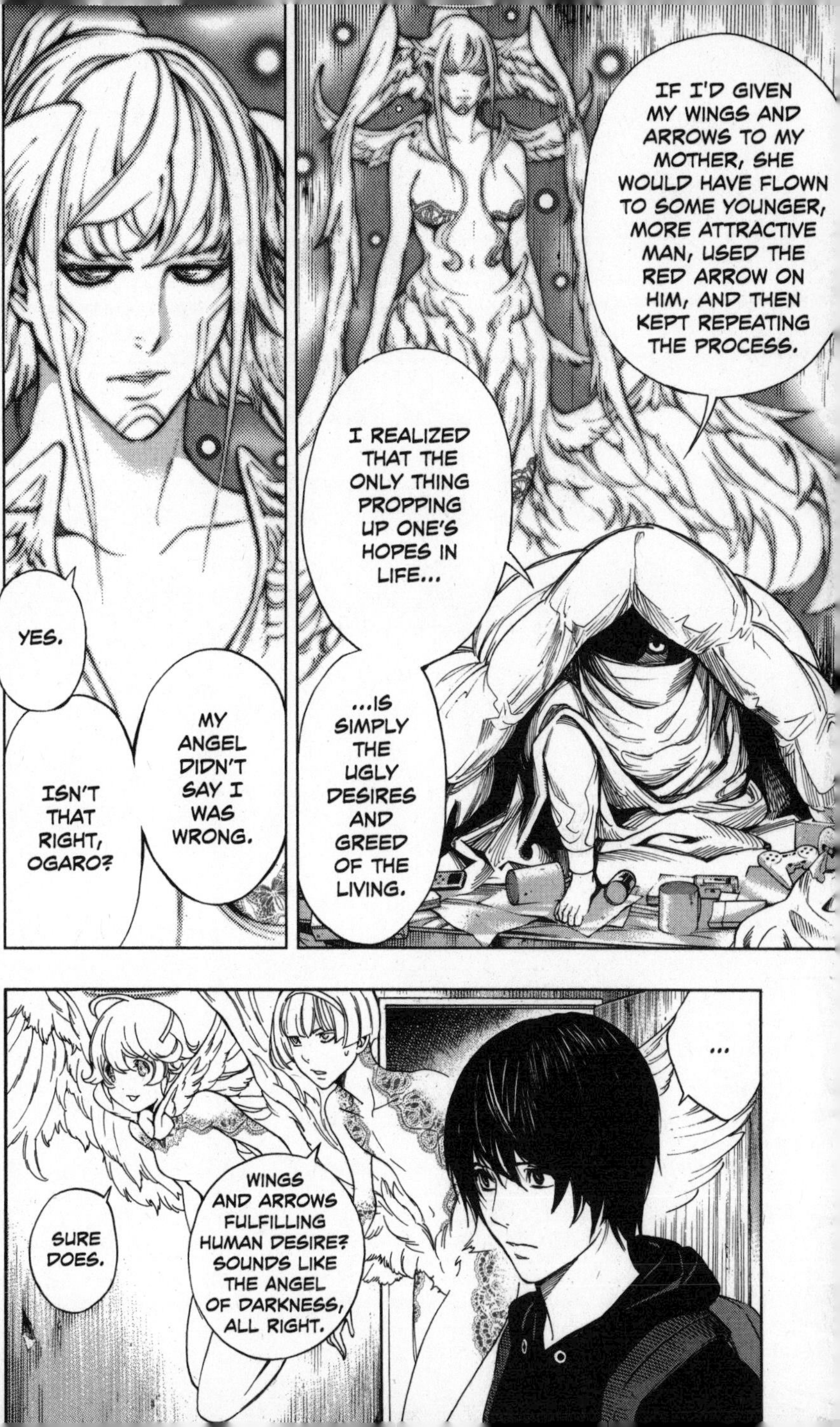
IF I'D GIVEN MY WINGS AND ARROWS TO MY MOTHER, SHE WOULD HAVE FLOWN TO SOME YOUNGER, MORE ATTRACTIVE MAN, USED THE RED ARROW ON HIM, AND THEN KEPT REPEATING THE PROCESS.
I REALIZED THAT THE ONLY THING PROPPING UP ONE'S HOPES IN LIFE...
...IS SIMPLY THE UGLY DESIRES AND GREED OF THE LIVING.
MY ANGEL DIDN'T SAY I WAS WRONG.
ISN'T THAT RIGHT, OGARO?
YES.
...
WINGS AND ARROWS FULFILLING HUMAN DESIRE? SOUNDS LIKE THE ANGEL OF DARKNESS, ALL RIGHT.
SURE DOES.

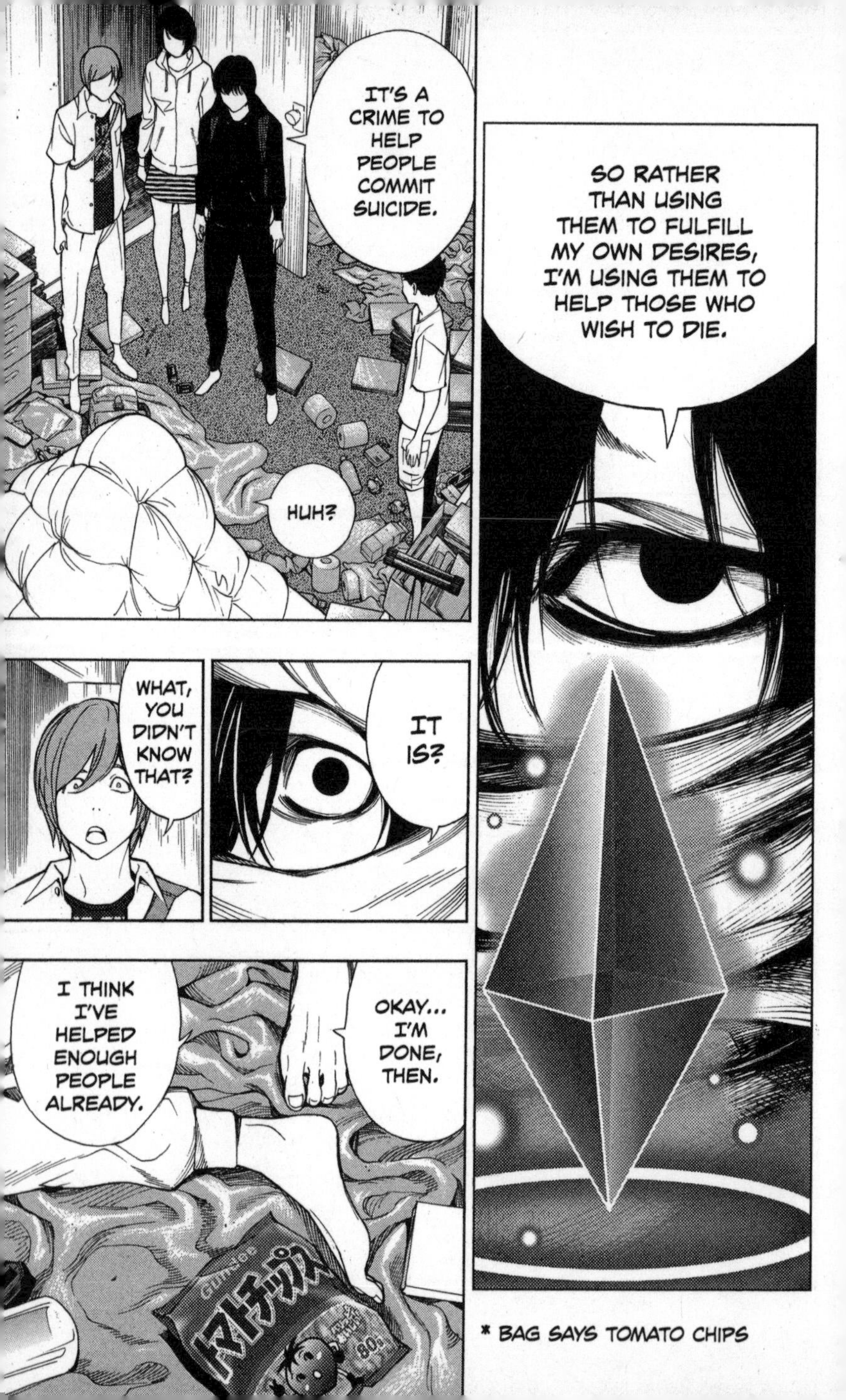
SO RATHER THAN USING THEM TO FULFILL MY OWN DESIRES, I'M USING THEM TO HELP THOSE WHO WISH TO DIE.
IT'S A CRIME TO HELP PEOPLE COMMIT SUICIDE.
HUH?
IT IS?
WHAT, YOU DIDN'T KNOW THAT?
OKAY... I'M DONE, THEN.
I THINK I'VE HELPED ENOUGH PEOPLE ALREADY.

* BAG SAYS TOMATO CHIPS

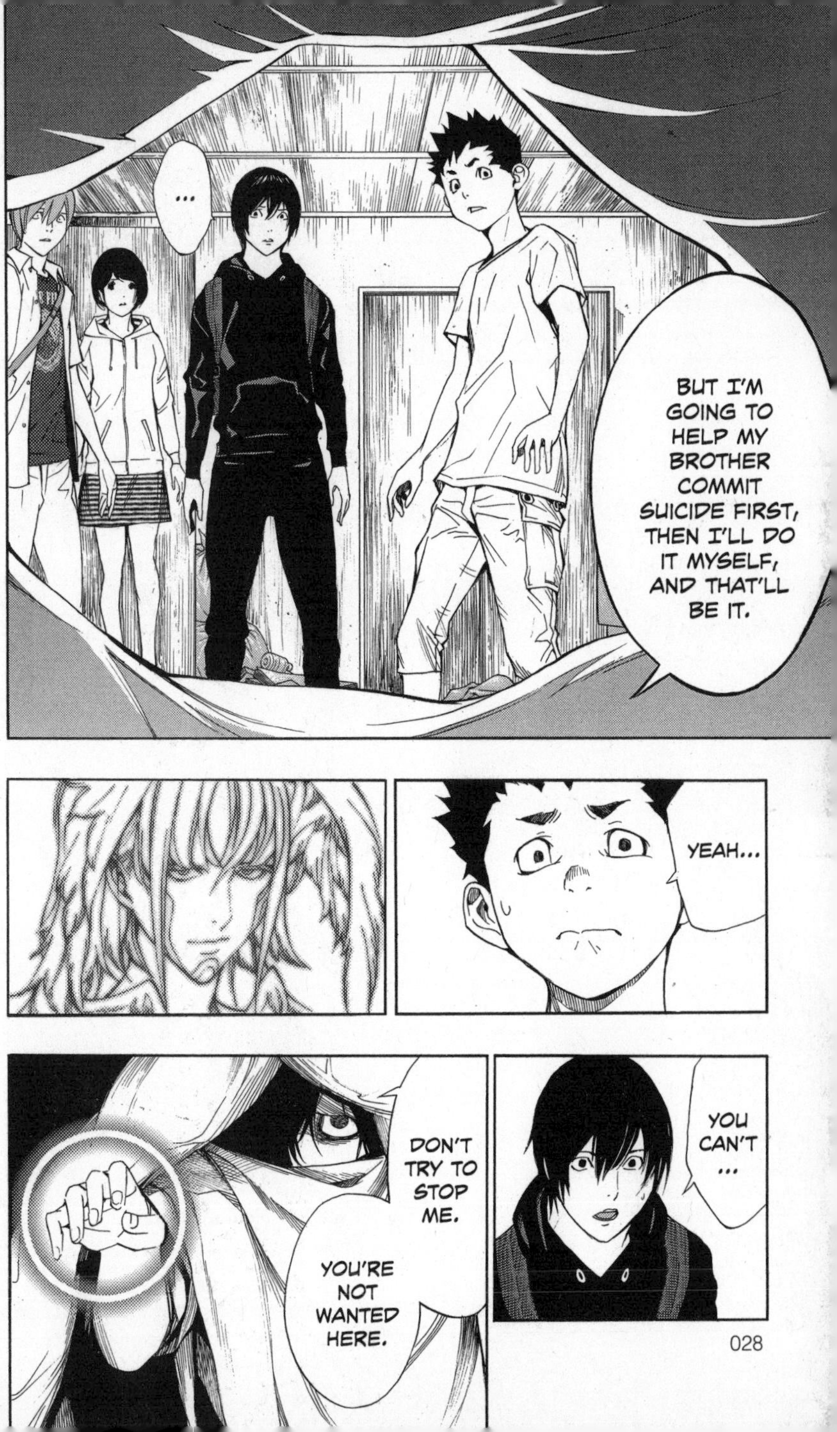
BUT I'M GOING TO HELP MY BROTHER COMMIT SUICIDE FIRST, THEN I'LL DO IT MYSELF, AND THAT'LL BE IT.
...
YEAH...
YOU CAN'T ...
DON'T TRY TO STOP ME.
YOU'RE NOT WANTED HERE.

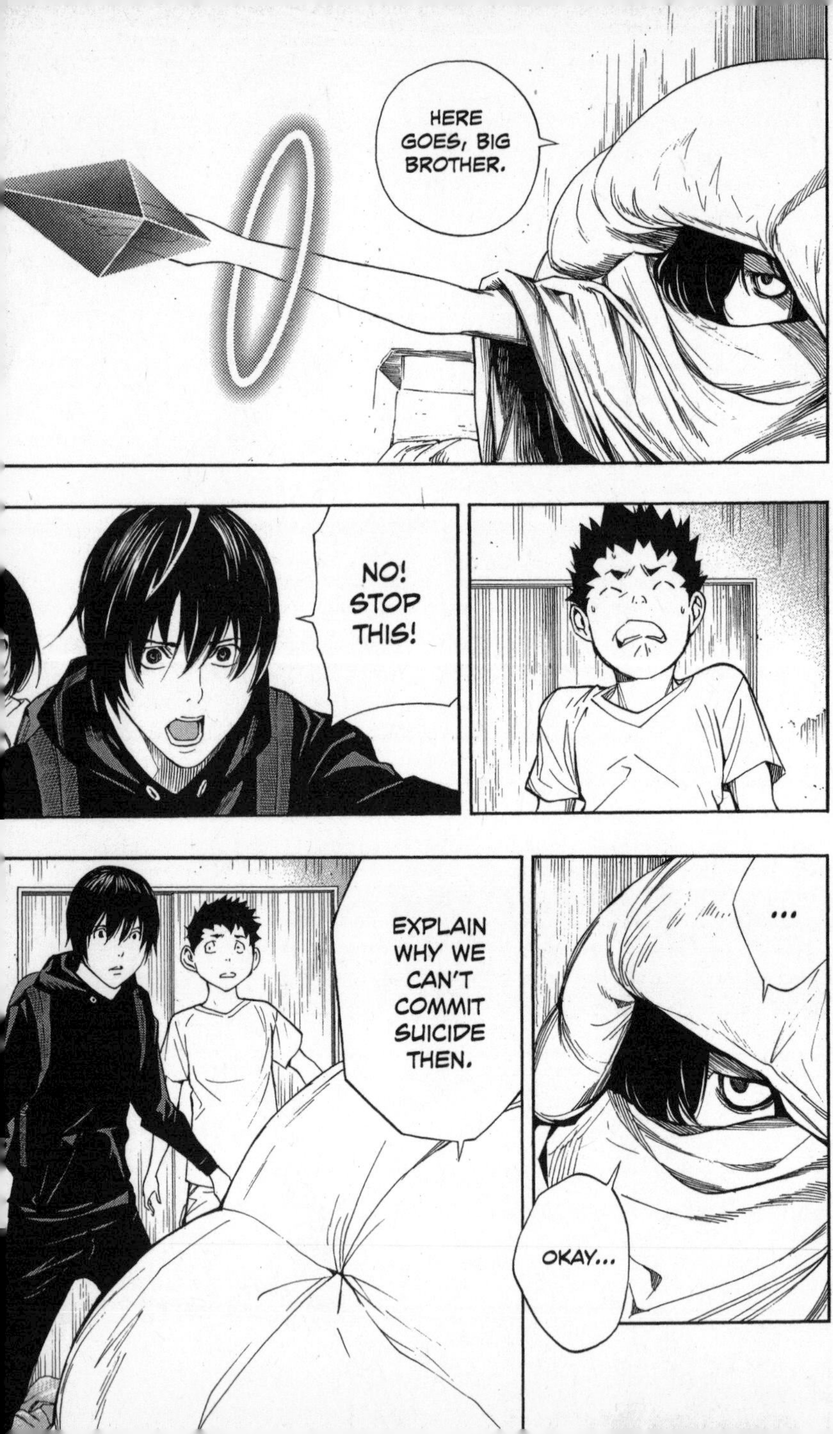
HERE GOES, BIG BROTHER.
NO! STOP THIS!
...
OKAY...
EXPLAIN WHY WE CAN'T COMMIT SUICIDE THEN.

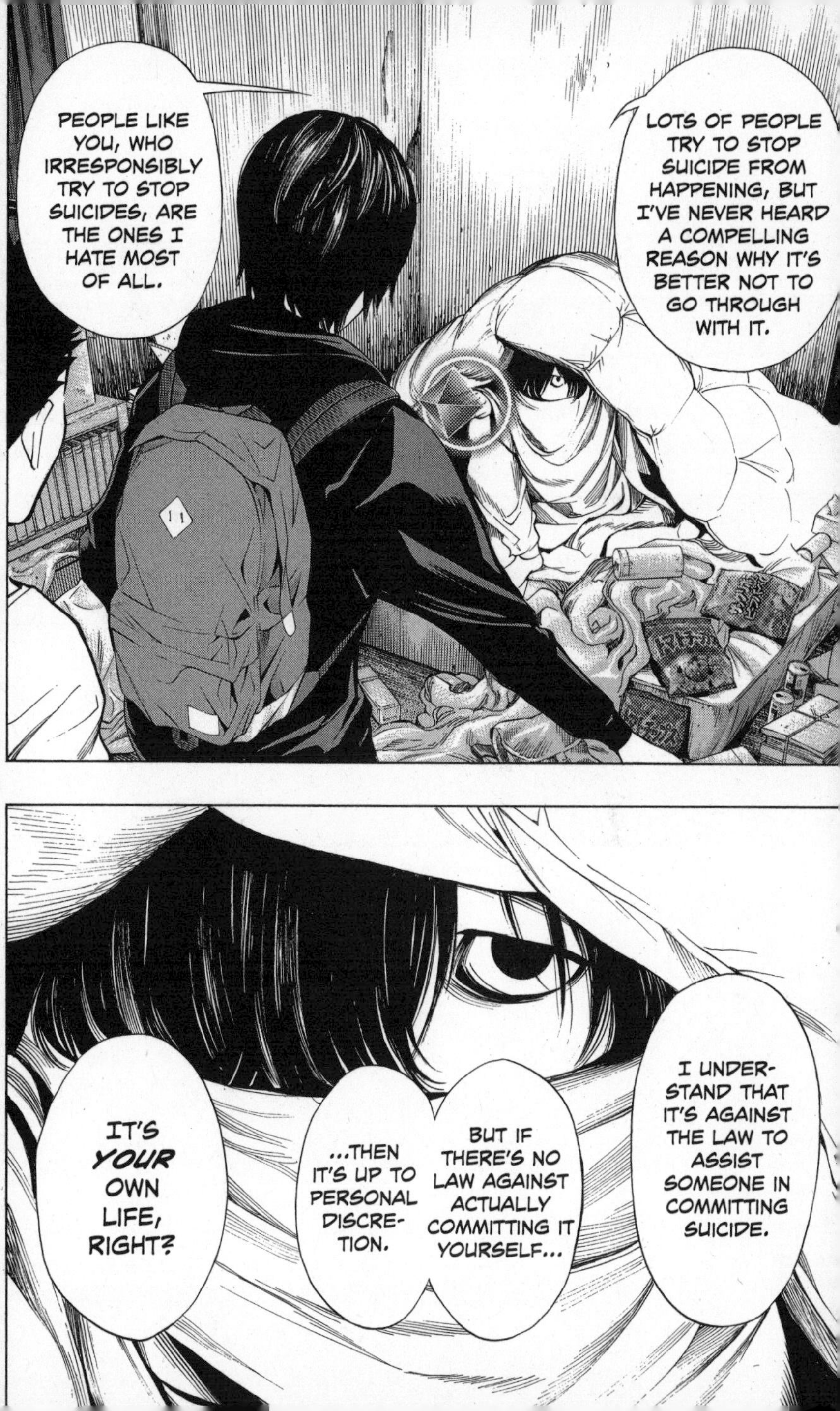
LOTS OF PEOPLE TRY TO STOP SUICIDE FROM HAPPENING, BUT I'VE NEVER HEARD A COMPELLING REASON WHY IT'S BETTER NOT TO GO THROUGH WITH IT.
PEOPLE LIKE YOU, WHO IRRESPONSIBLY TRY TO STOP SUICIDES, ARE THE ONES I HATE MOST OF ALL.
I UNDER-STAND THAT IT'S AGAINST THE LAW TO ASSIST SOMEONE IN COMMITTING SUICIDE.
BUT IF THERE'S NO LAW AGAINST ACTUALLY COMMITTING IT YOURSELF...
...THEN IT'S UP TO PERSONAL DISCRE-TION.
IT'S *YOUR* OWN LIFE, RIGHT?

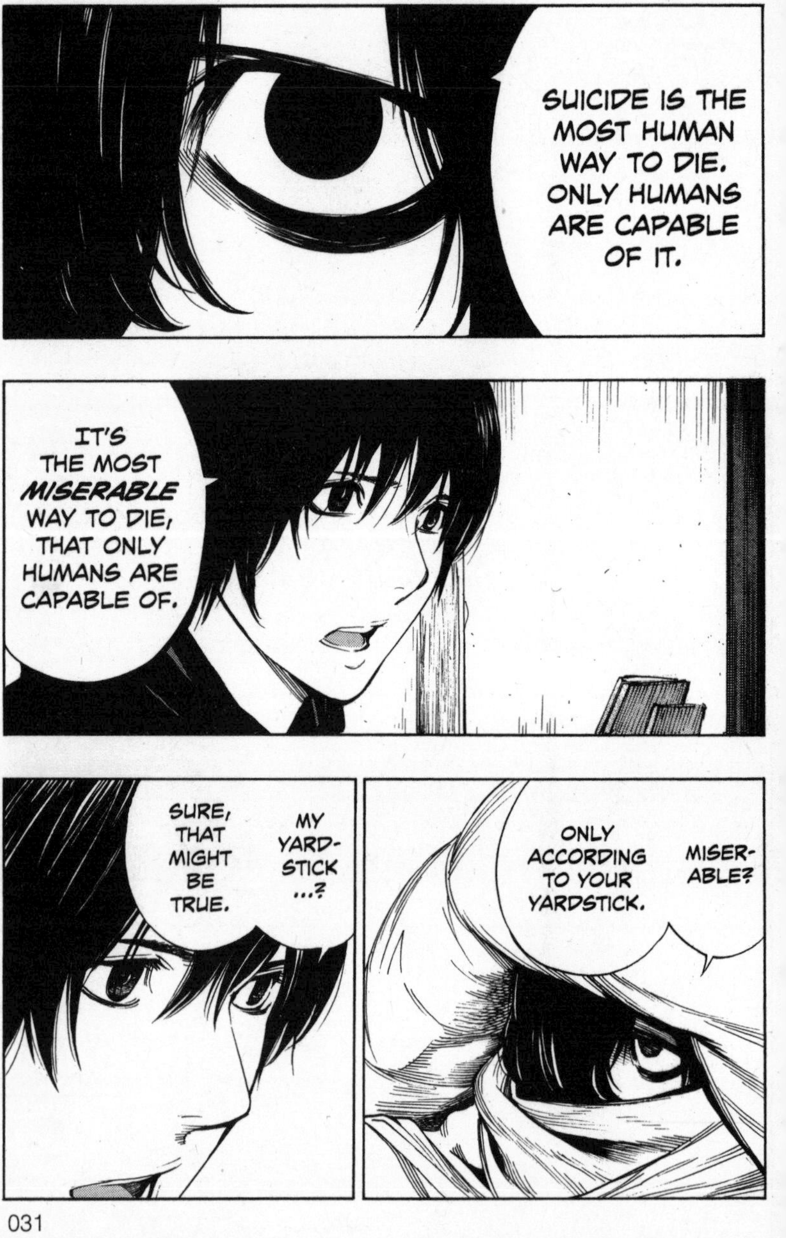
SUICIDE IS THE MOST HUMAN WAY TO DIE. ONLY HUMANS ARE CAPABLE OF IT.
IT'S THE MOST *MISERABLE* WAY TO DIE, THAT ONLY HUMANS ARE CAPABLE OF.
MISER-ABLE?
ONLY ACCORDING TO YOUR YARDSTICK.
MY YARD-STICK ...?
SURE, THAT MIGHT BE TRUE.

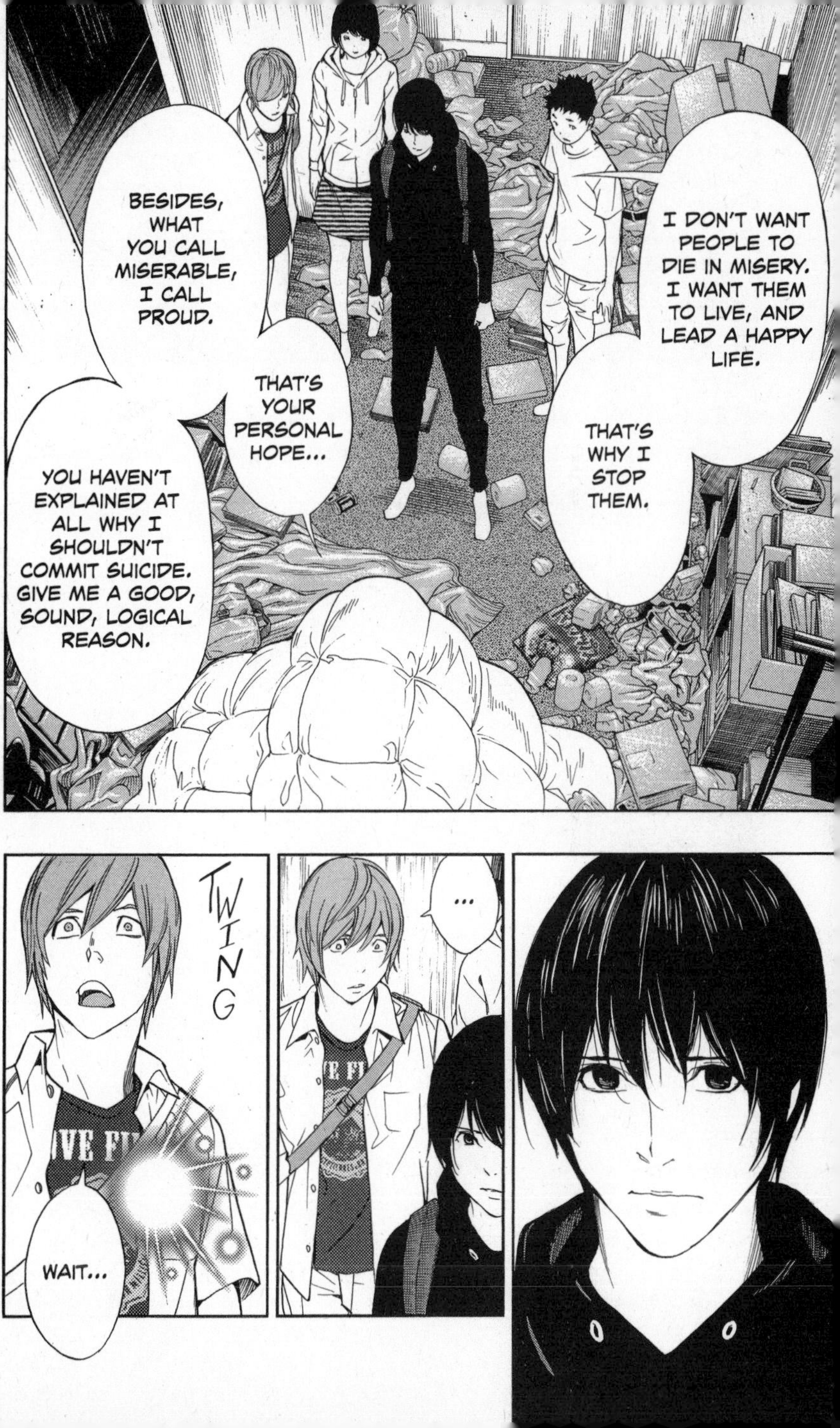
I DON'T WANT PEOPLE TO DIE IN MISERY. I WANT THEM TO LIVE, AND LEAD A HAPPY LIFE.
THAT'S WHY I STOP THEM.
THAT'S YOUR PERSONAL HOPE...
BESIDES, WHAT YOU CALL MISERABLE, I CALL PROUD.
YOU HAVEN'T EXPLAINED AT ALL WHY I SHOULDN'T COMMIT SUICIDE. GIVE ME A GOOD, SOUND, LOGICAL REASON.
...
TWING
WAIT...

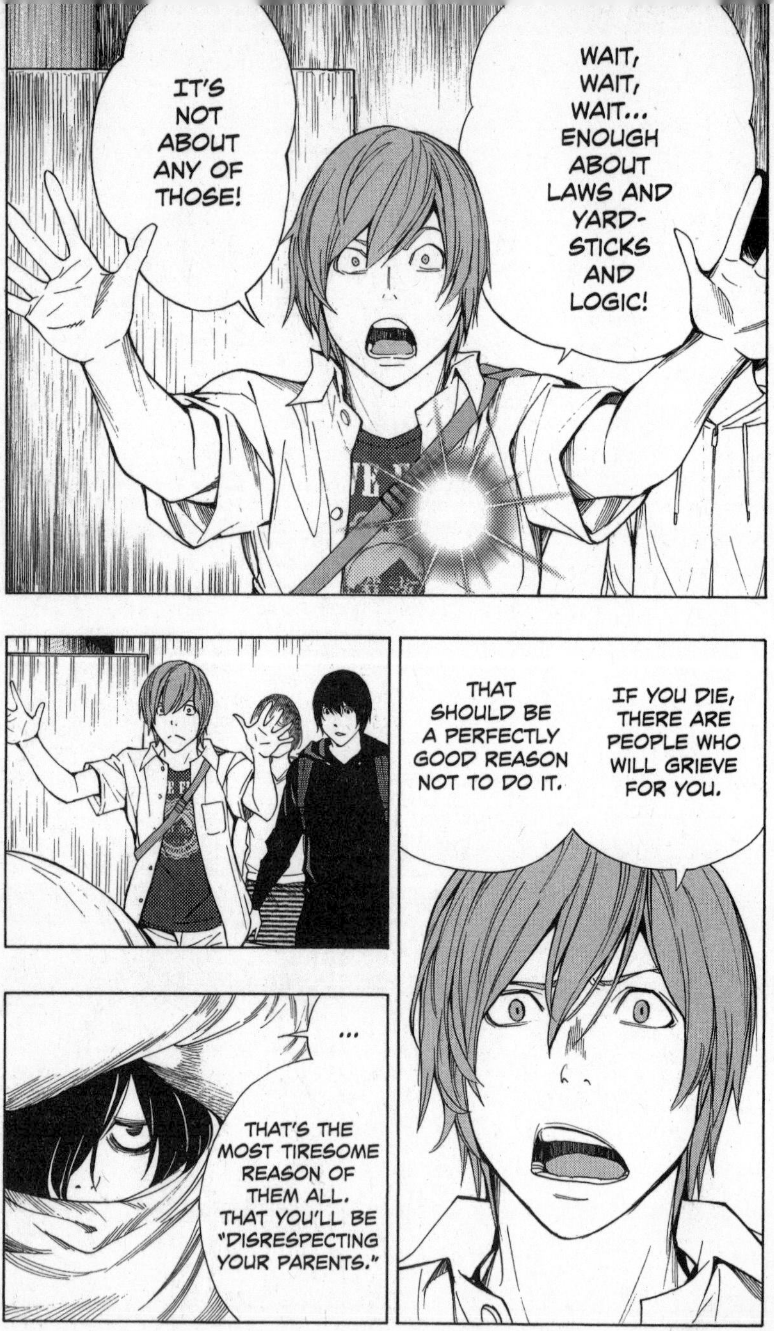
WAIT, WAIT, WAIT... ENOUGH ABOUT LAWS AND YARD-STICKS AND LOGIC!
IT'S NOT ABOUT ANY OF THOSE!
IF YOU DIE, THERE ARE PEOPLE WHO WILL GRIEVE FOR YOU.
THAT SHOULD BE A PERFECTLY GOOD REASON NOT TO DO IT.
...
THAT'S THE MOST TIRESOME REASON OF THEM ALL. THAT YOU'LL BE "DISRESPECTING YOUR PARENTS."

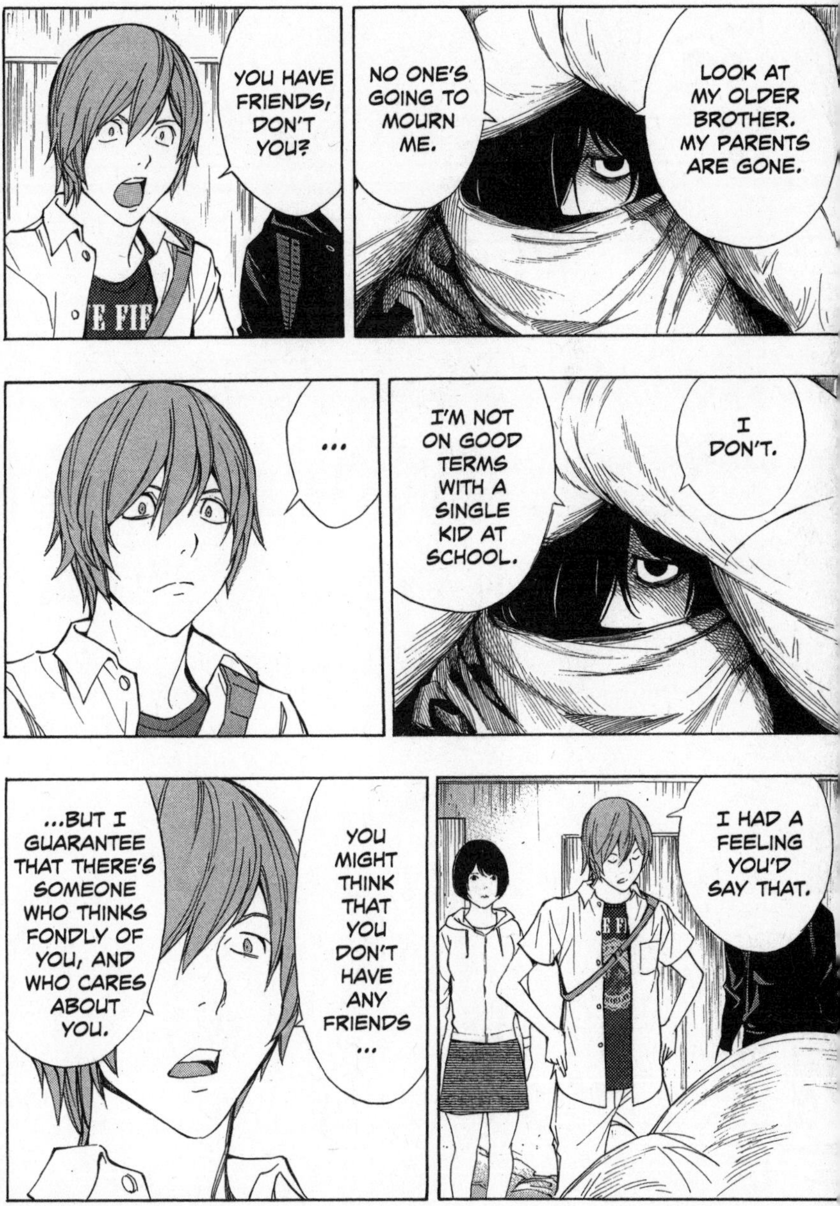
LOOK AT MY OLDER BROTHER. MY PARENTS ARE GONE.
NO ONE'S GOING TO MOURN ME.
YOU HAVE FRIENDS, DON'T YOU?
I DON'T.
I'M NOT ON GOOD TERMS WITH A SINGLE KID AT SCHOOL.
...
I HAD A FEELING YOU'D SAY THAT.
YOU MIGHT THINK THAT YOU DON'T HAVE ANY FRIENDS...
...BUT I GUARANTEE THAT THERE'S SOMEONE WHO THINKS FONDLY OF YOU, AND WHO CARES ABOUT YOU.

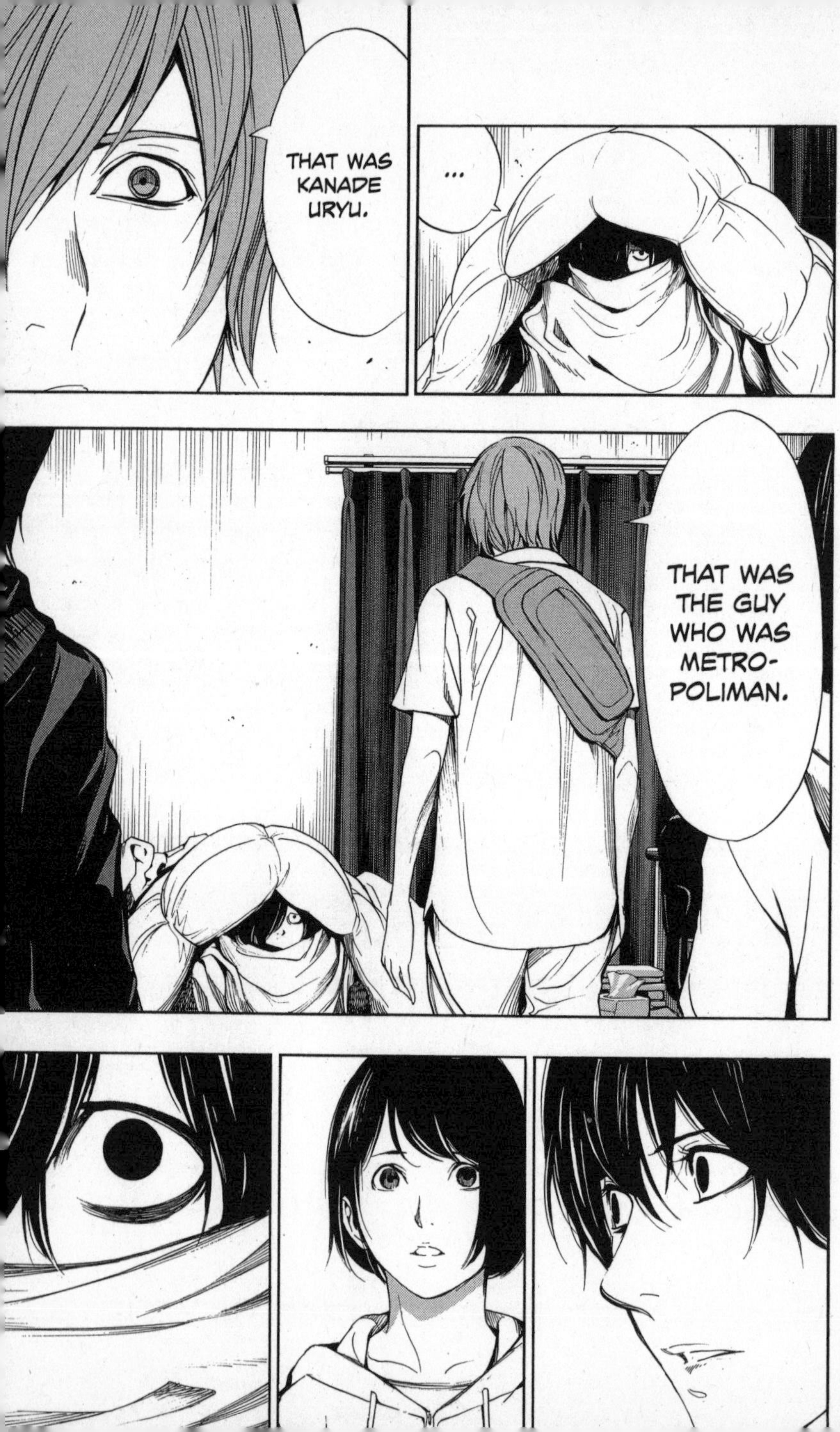
...
THAT WAS KANADE URYU.
THAT WAS THE GUY WHO WAS METRO-POLIMAN.

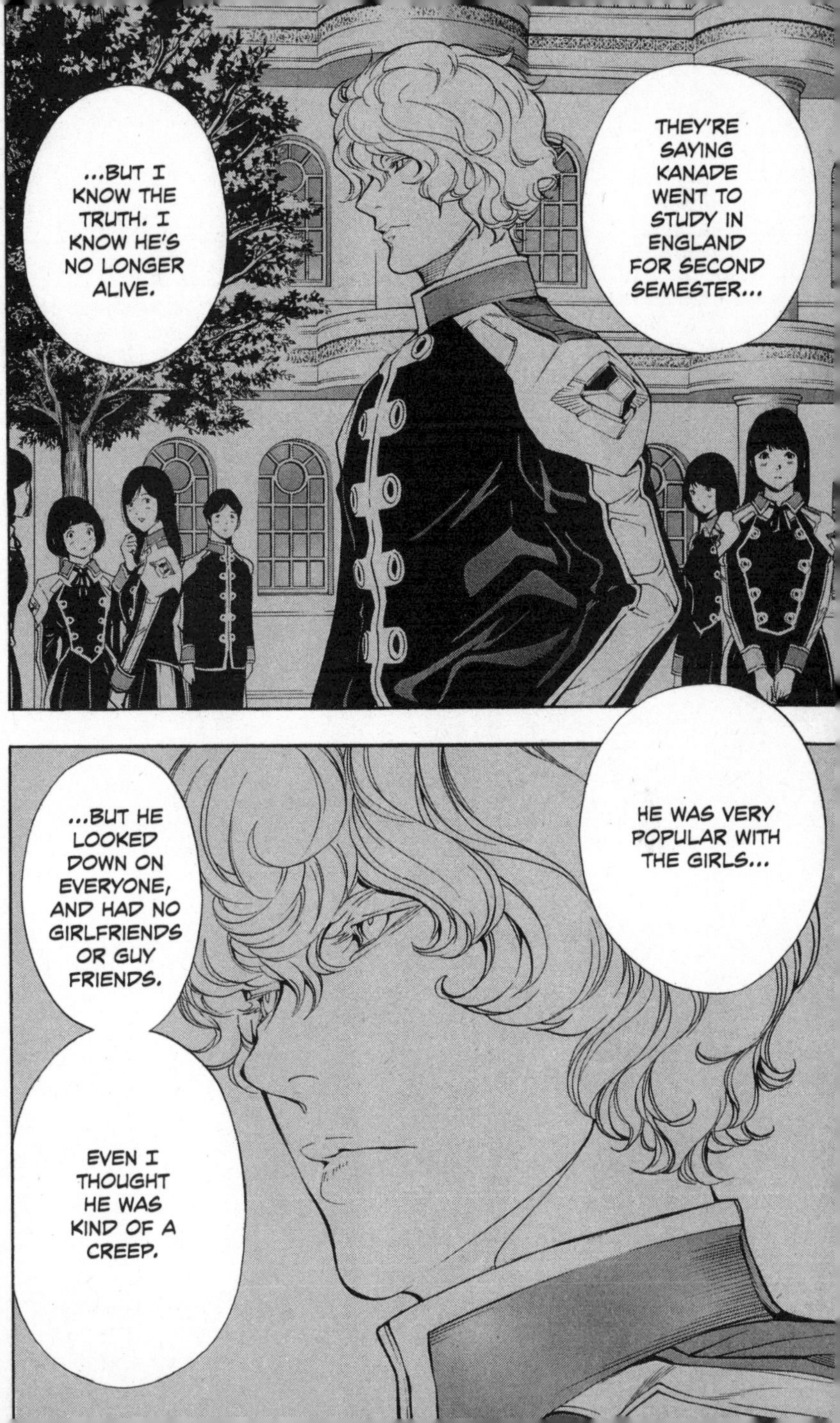
THEY'RE SAYING KANADE WENT TO STUDY IN ENGLAND FOR SECOND SEMESTER...
...BUT I KNOW THE TRUTH. I KNOW HE'S NO LONGER ALIVE.
HE WAS VERY POPULAR WITH THE GIRLS...
...BUT HE LOOKED DOWN ON EVERYONE, AND HAD NO GIRLFRIENDS OR GUY FRIENDS.
EVEN I THOUGHT HE WAS KIND OF A CREEP.

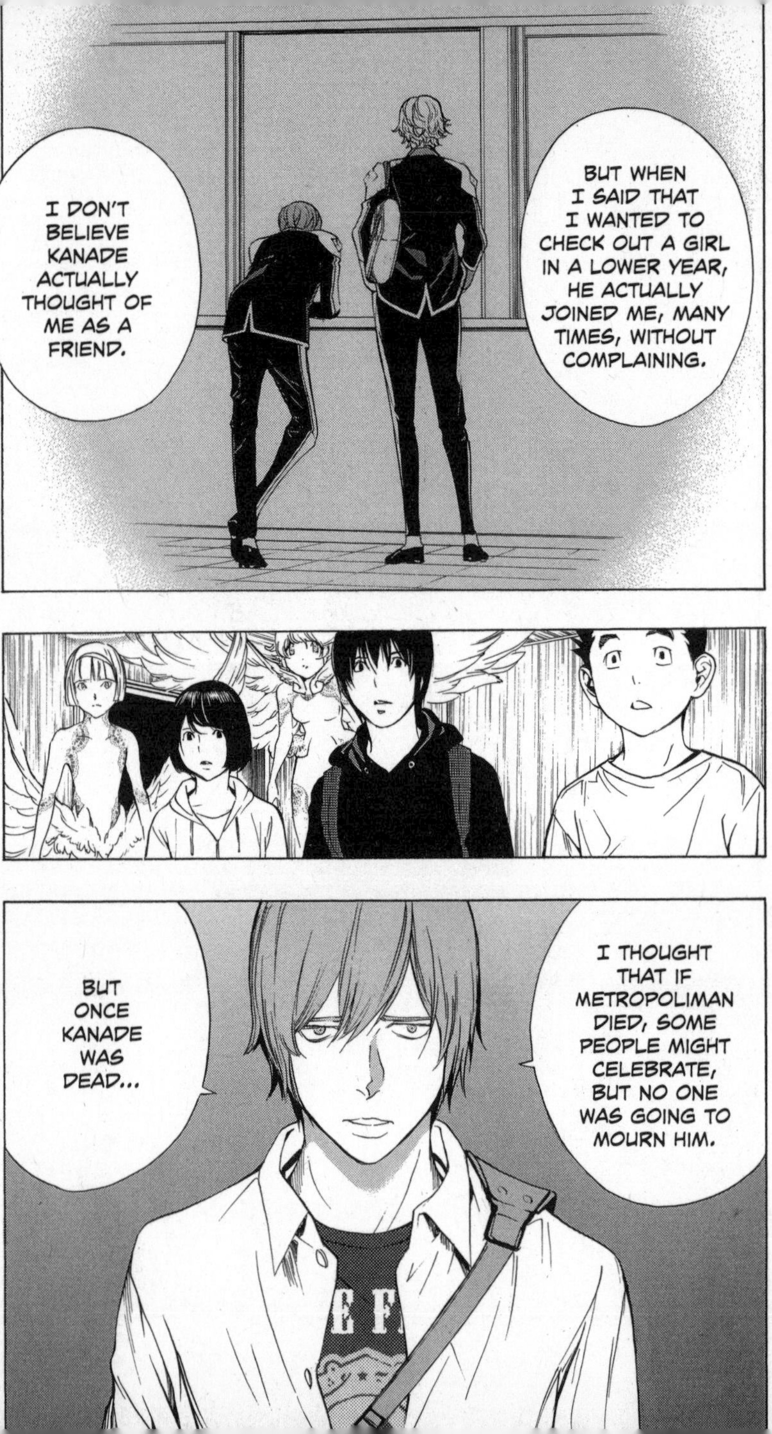
BUT WHEN I SAID THAT I WANTED TO CHECK OUT A GIRL IN A LOWER YEAR, HE ACTUALLY JOINED ME, MANY TIMES, WITHOUT COMPLAINING.
I DON'T BELIEVE KANADE ACTUALLY THOUGHT OF ME AS A FRIEND.
I THOUGHT THAT IF METROPOLIMAN DIED, SOME PEOPLE MIGHT CELEBRATE, BUT NO ONE WAS GOING TO MOURN HIM.
BUT ONCE KANADE WAS DEAD...

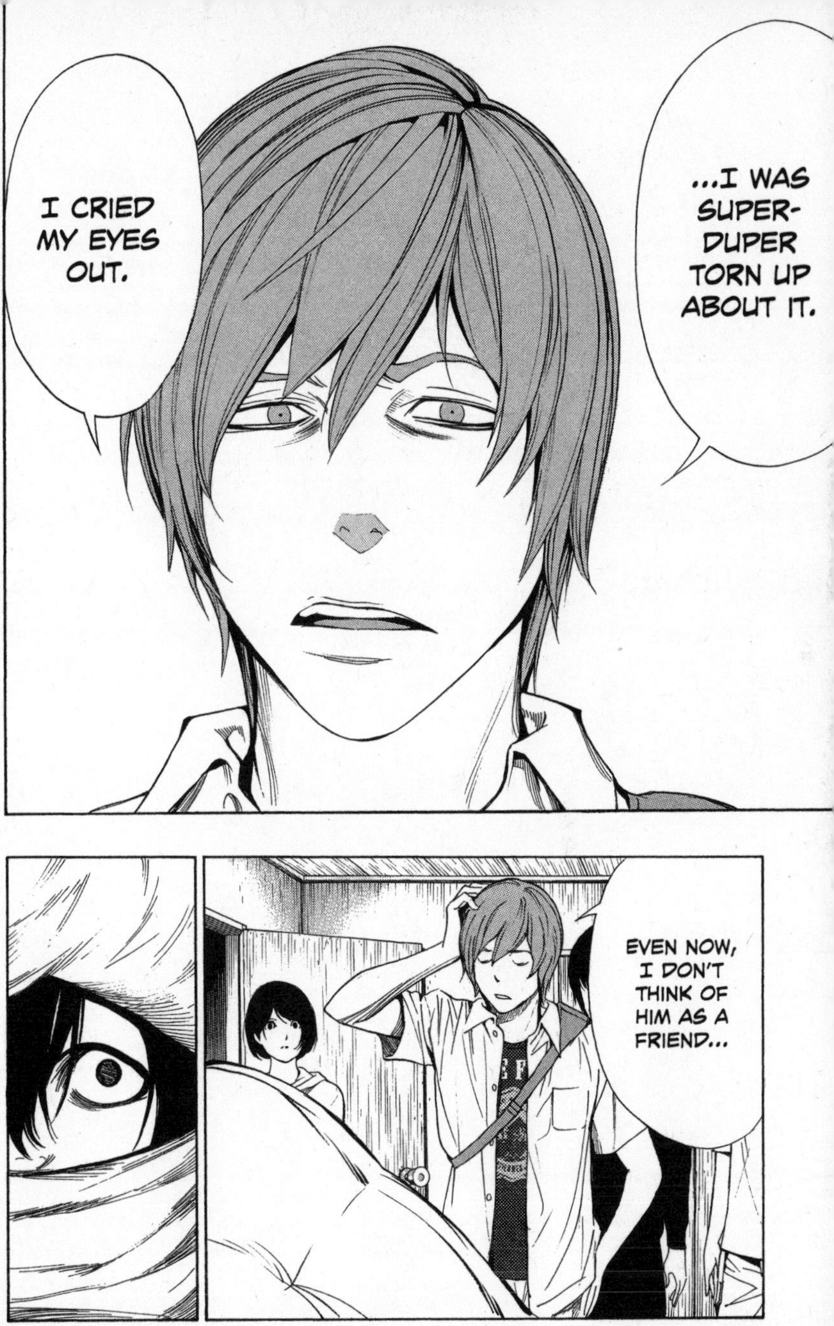
...I WAS SUPER-DUPER TORN UP ABOUT IT.
I CRIED MY EYES OUT.
EVEN NOW, I DON'T THINK OF HIM AS A FRIEND...

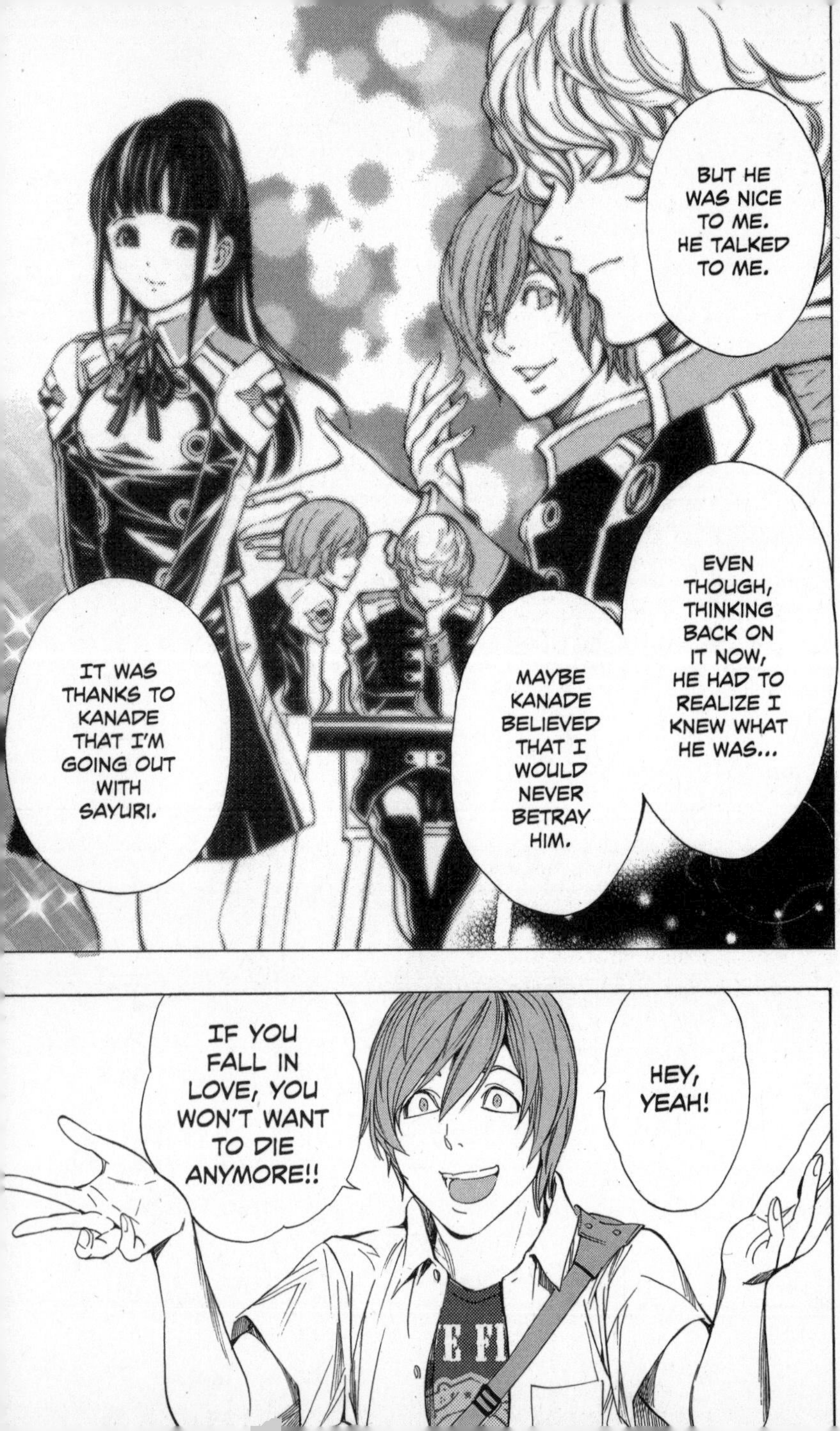
BUT HE WAS NICE TO ME. HE TALKED TO ME.
EVEN THOUGH, THINKING BACK ON IT NOW, HE HAD TO REALIZE I KNEW WHAT HE WAS...
MAYBE KANADE BELIEVED THAT I WOULD NEVER BETRAY HIM.
IT WAS THANKS TO KANADE THAT I'M GOING OUT WITH SAYURI.
HEY, YEAH!
IF YOU FALL IN LOVE, YOU WON'T WANT TO DIE ANYMORE!!

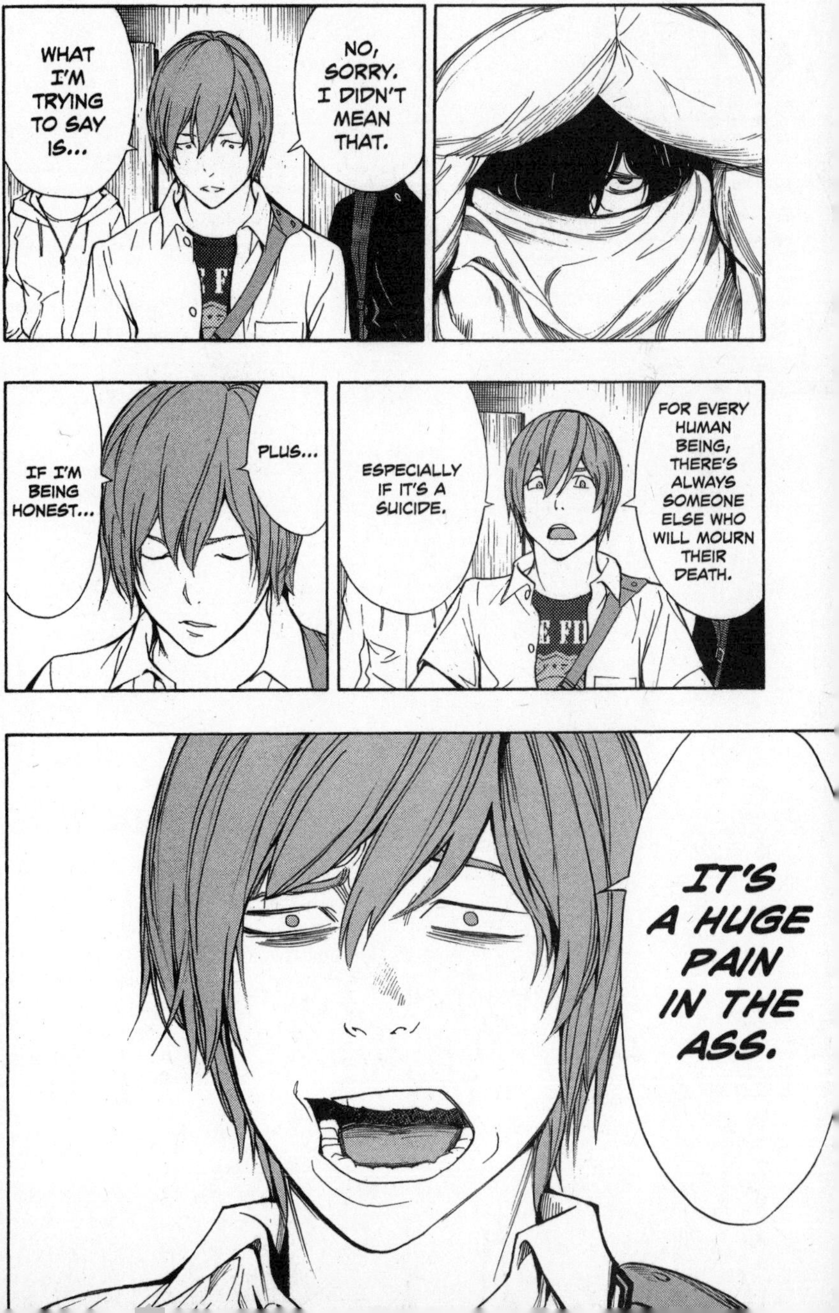
NO, SORRY. I DIDN'T MEAN THAT.
WHAT I'M TRYING TO SAY IS...
FOR EVERY HUMAN BEING, THERE'S ALWAYS SOMEONE ELSE WHO WILL MOURN THEIR DEATH.
ESPECIALLY IF IT'S A SUICIDE.
PLUS...
IF I'M BEING HONEST...
IT'S A HUGE PAIN IN THE ASS.

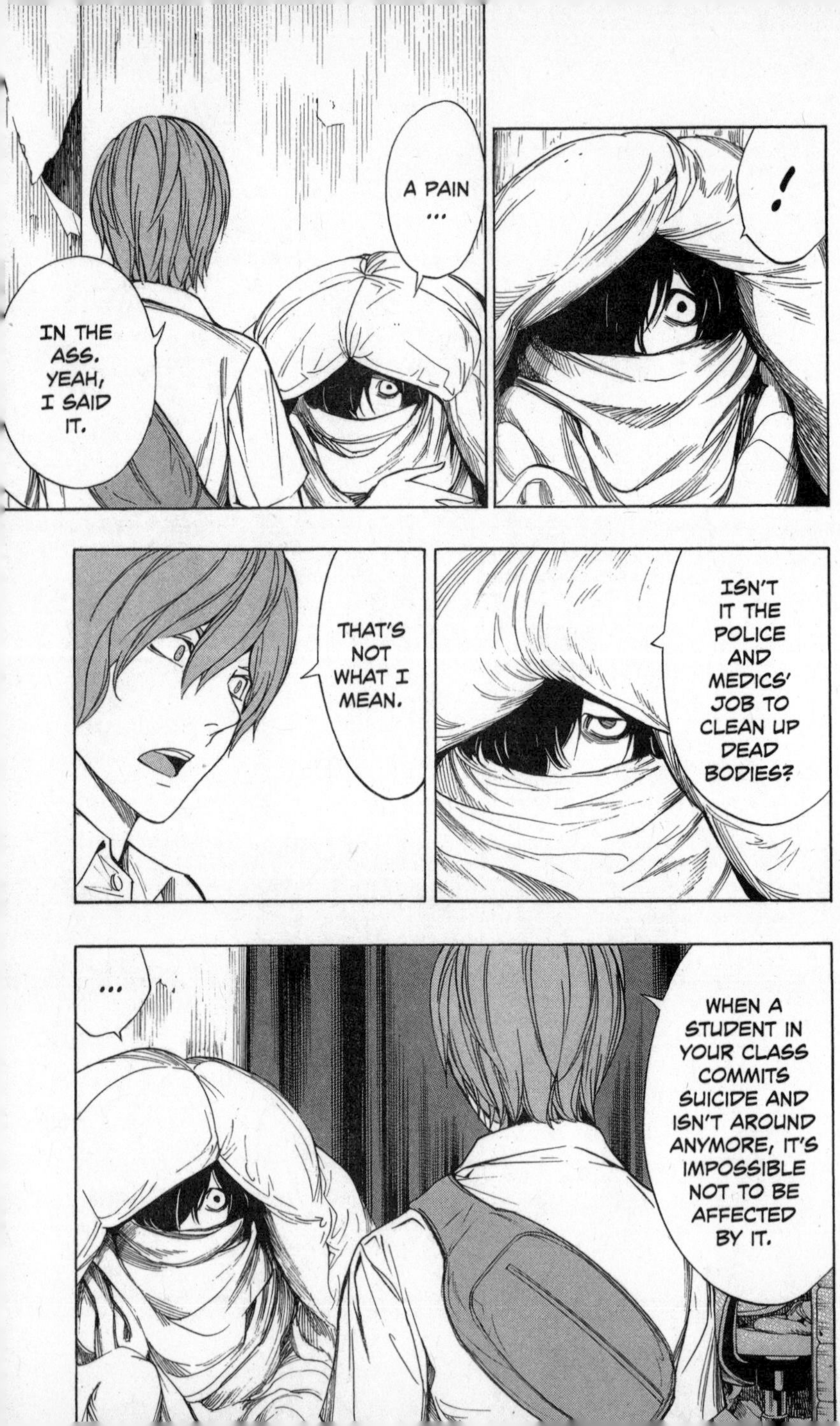
!
A PAIN ...
IN THE ASS. YEAH, I SAID IT.
ISN'T IT THE POLICE AND MEDICS' JOB TO CLEAN UP DEAD BODIES?
THAT'S NOT WHAT I MEAN.
WHEN A STUDENT IN YOUR CLASS COMMITS SUICIDE AND ISN'T AROUND ANYMORE, IT'S IMPOSSIBLE NOT TO BE AFFECTED BY IT.
...

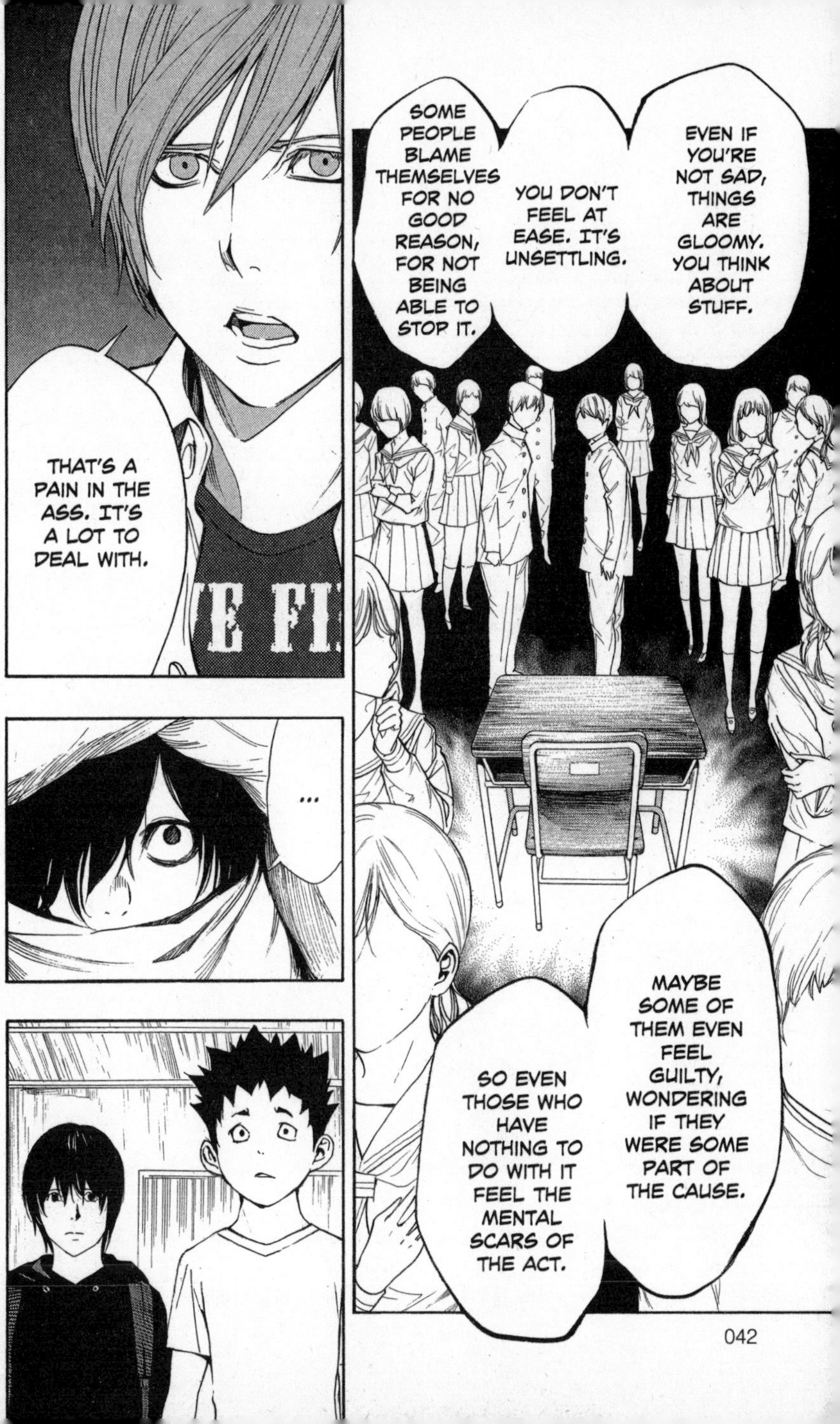
EVEN IF YOU'RE NOT SAD, THINGS ARE GLOOMY. YOU THINK ABOUT STUFF.
YOU DON'T FEEL AT EASE. IT'S UNSETTLING.
SOME PEOPLE BLAME THEMSELVES FOR NO GOOD REASON, FOR NOT BEING ABLE TO STOP IT.
MAYBE SOME OF THEM EVEN FEEL GUILTY, WONDERING IF THEY WERE SOME PART OF THE CAUSE.
SO EVEN THOSE WHO HAVE NOTHING TO DO WITH IT FEEL THE MENTAL SCARS OF THE ACT.
THAT'S A PAIN IN THE ASS. IT'S A LOT TO DEAL WITH.
...

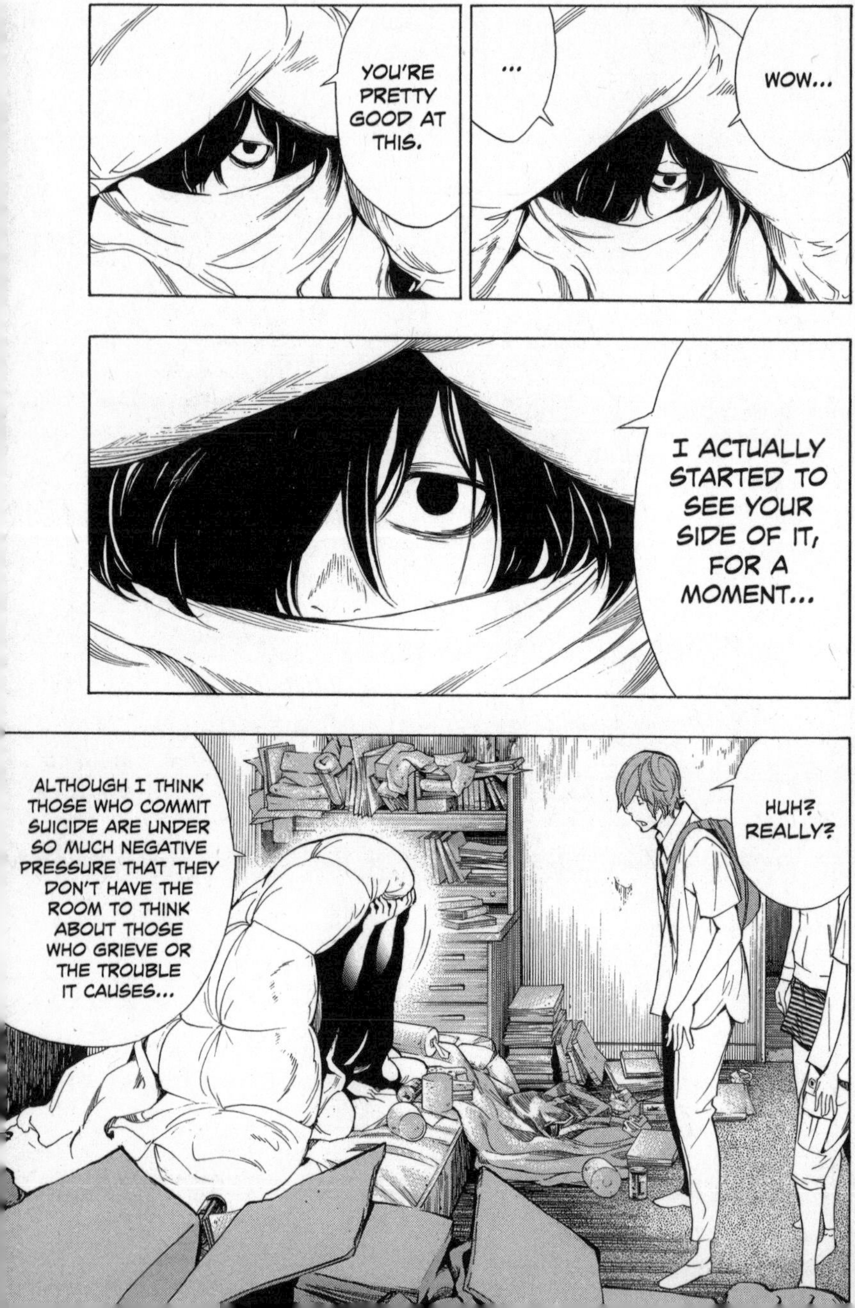
WOW...
...
YOU'RE PRETTY GOOD AT THIS.
I ACTUALLY STARTED TO SEE YOUR SIDE OF IT, FOR A MOMENT...
HUH? REALLY?
ALTHOUGH I THINK THOSE WHO COMMIT SUICIDE ARE UNDER SO MUCH NEGATIVE PRESSURE THAT THEY DON'T HAVE THE ROOM TO THINK ABOUT THOSE WHO GRIEVE OR THE TROUBLE IT CAUSES...

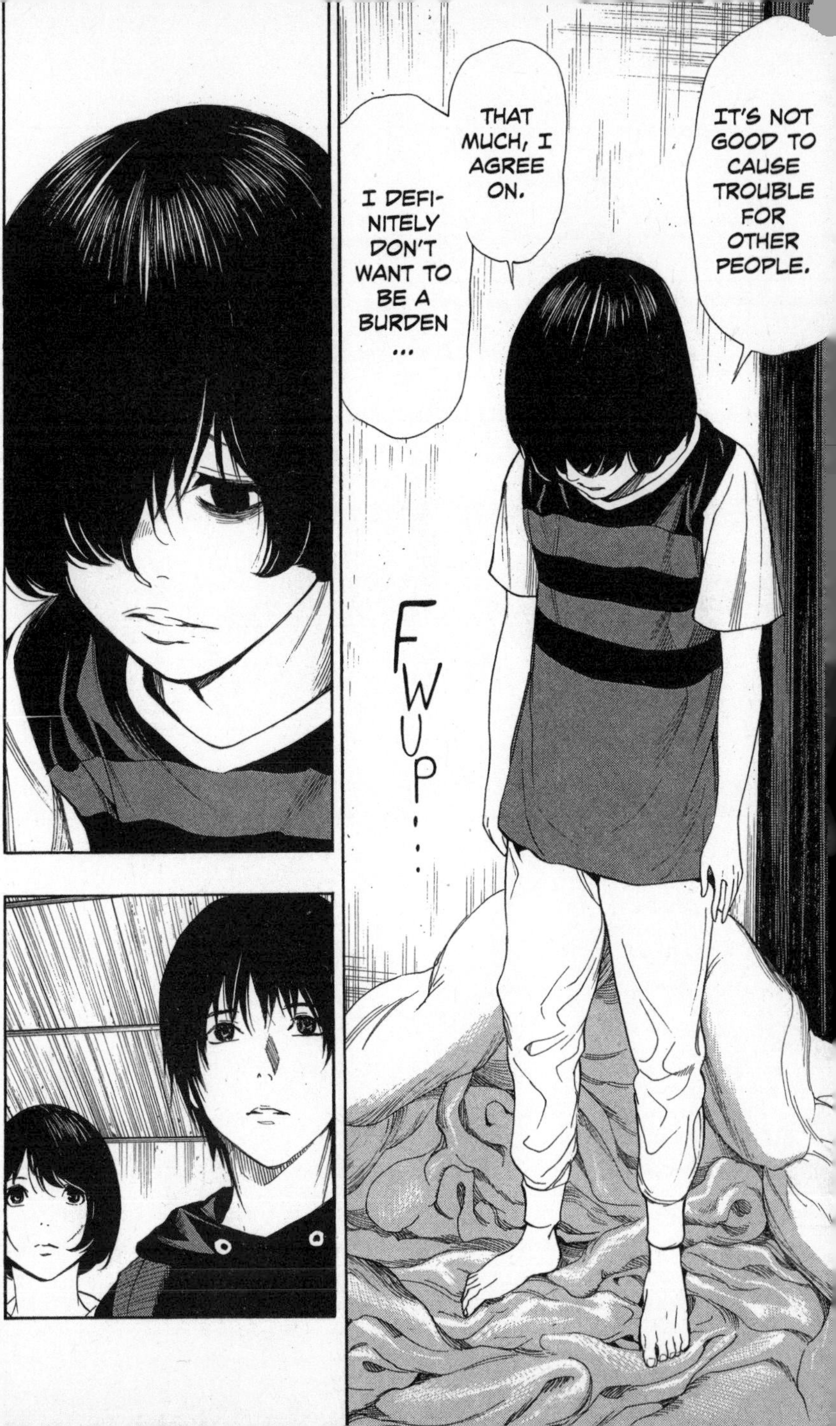
IT'S NOT GOOD TO CAUSE TROUBLE FOR OTHER PEOPLE.
THAT MUCH, I AGREE ON.
I DEFI-NITELY DON'T WANT TO BE A BURDEN...
FWUP...

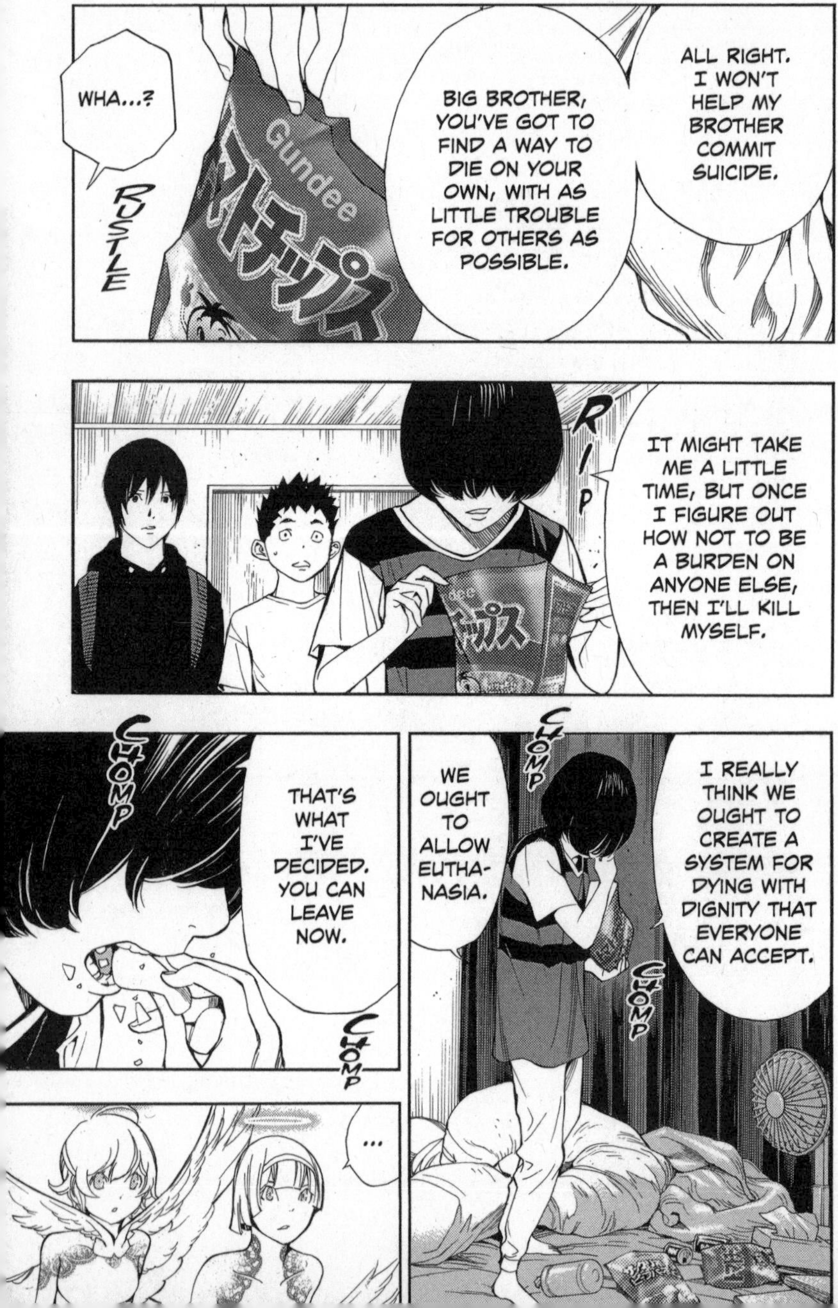
ALL RIGHT. I WON'T HELP MY BROTHER COMMIT SUICIDE.
BIG BROTHER, YOU'VE GOT TO FIND A WAY TO DIE ON YOUR OWN, WITH AS LITTLE TROUBLE FOR OTHERS AS POSSIBLE.
WHA...?
Gundee
RUSTLE
RIP
IT MIGHT TAKE ME A LITTLE TIME, BUT ONCE I FIGURE OUT HOW NOT TO BE A BURDEN ON ANYONE ELSE, THEN I'LL KILL MYSELF.
I REALLY THINK WE OUGHT TO CREATE A SYSTEM FOR DYING WITH DIGNITY THAT EVERYONE CAN ACCEPT.
CHOMP
WE OUGHT TO ALLOW EUTHANASIA.
CHOMP
THAT'S WHAT I'VE DECIDED. YOU CAN LEAVE NOW.
CHOMP
CHOMP
...

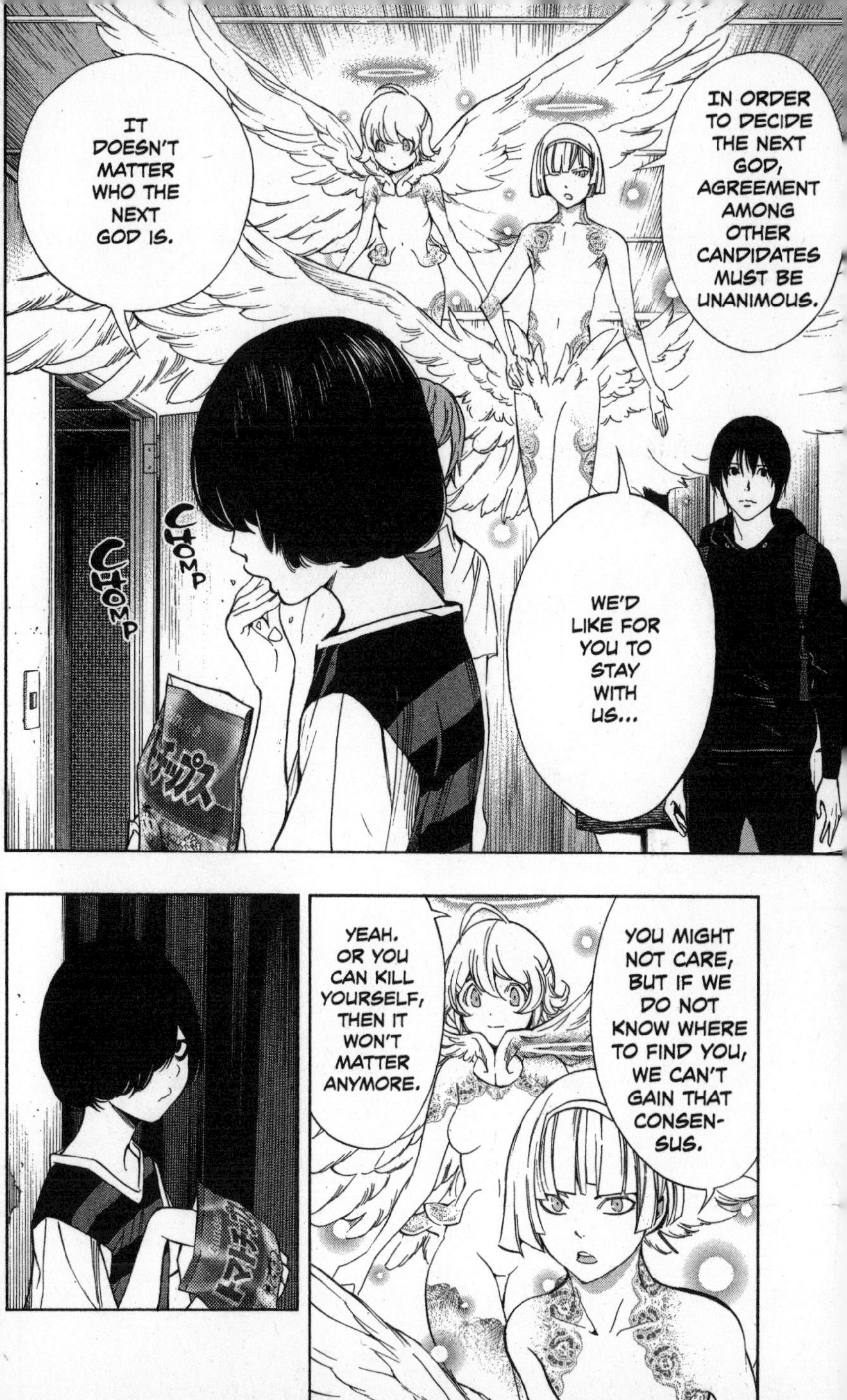
IN ORDER TO DECIDE THE NEXT GOD, AGREEMENT AMONG OTHER CANDIDATES MUST BE UNANIMOUS.
IT DOESN'T MATTER WHO THE NEXT GOD IS.
WE'D LIKE FOR YOU TO STAY WITH US...
CHOMP
CHOMP
YOU MIGHT NOT CARE, BUT IF WE DO NOT KNOW WHERE TO FIND YOU, WE CAN'T GAIN THAT CONSEN-SUS.
YEAH. OR YOU CAN KILL YOURSELF, THEN IT WON'T MATTER ANYMORE.

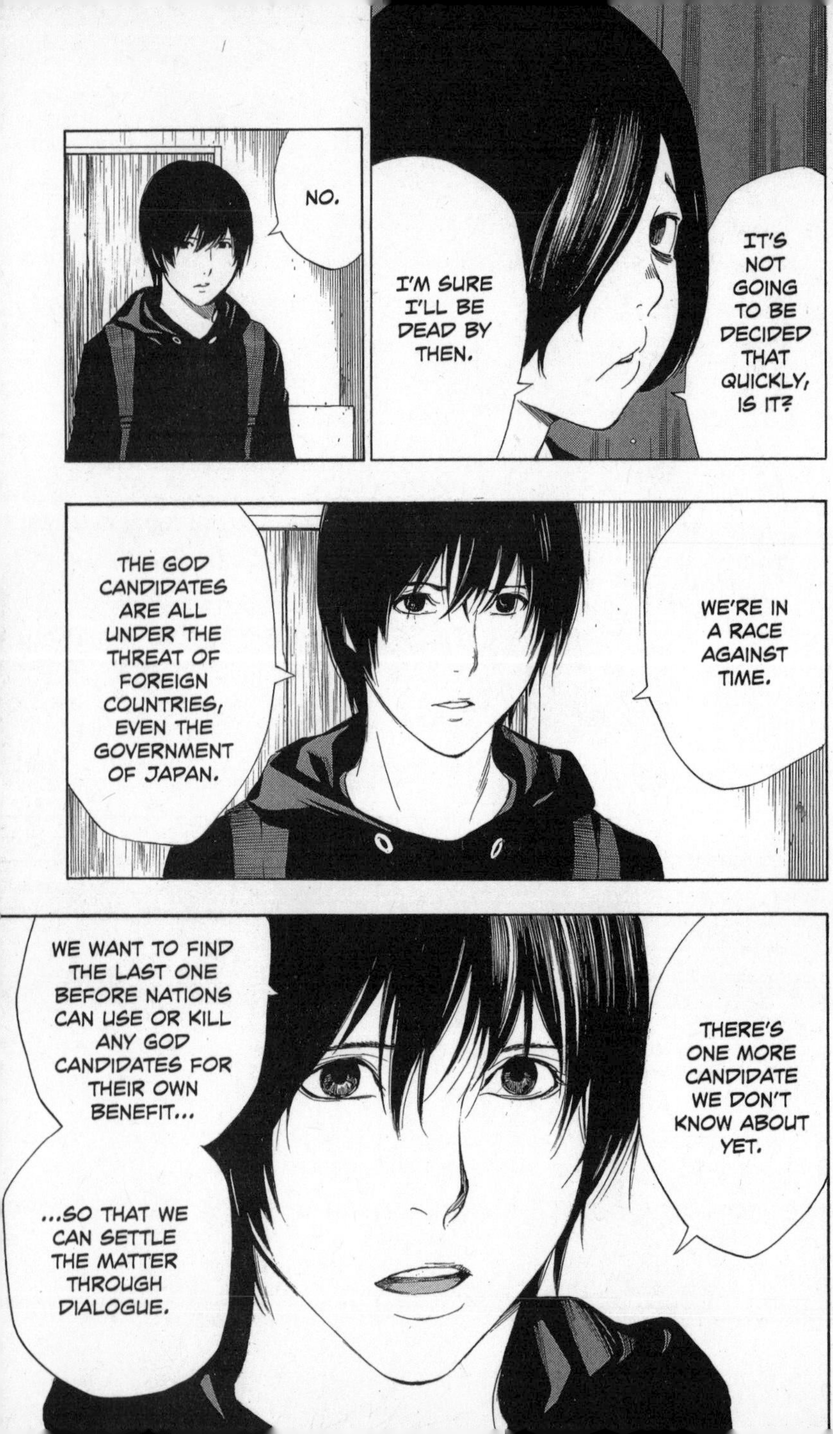
IT'S NOT GOING TO BE DECIDED THAT QUICKLY, IS IT?
I'M SURE I'LL BE DEAD BY THEN.
NO.
WE'RE IN A RACE AGAINST TIME.
THE GOD CANDIDATES ARE ALL UNDER THE THREAT OF FOREIGN COUNTRIES, EVEN THE GOVERNMENT OF JAPAN.
THERE'S ONE MORE CANDIDATE WE DON'T KNOW ABOUT YET.
WE WANT TO FIND THE LAST ONE BEFORE NATIONS CAN USE OR KILL ANY GOD CANDIDATES FOR THEIR OWN BENEFIT...
...SO THAT WE CAN SETTLE THE MATTER THROUGH DIALOGUE.

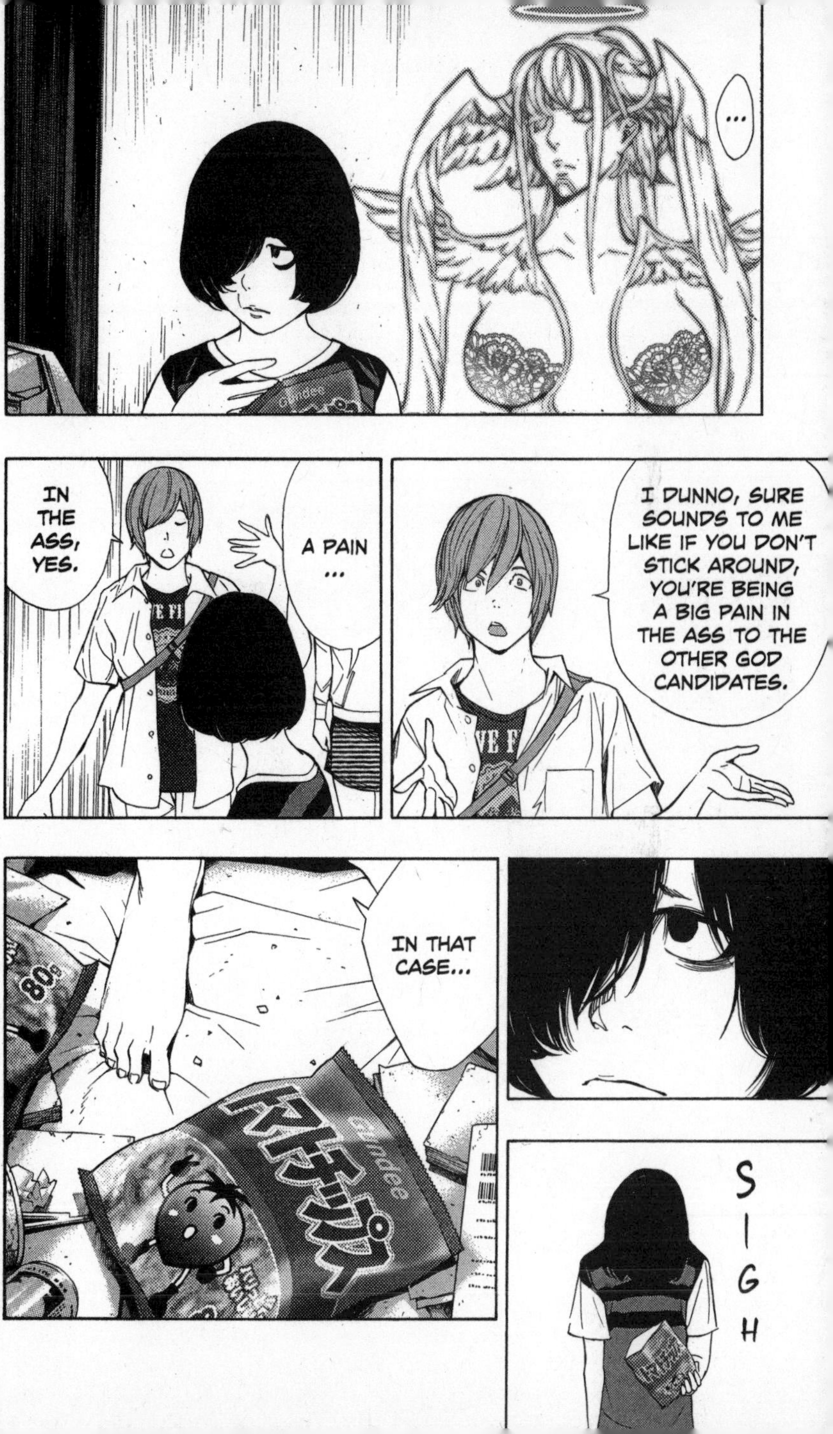
...
I DUNNO, SURE SOUNDS TO ME LIKE IF YOU DON'T STICK AROUND, YOU'RE BEING A BIG PAIN IN THE ASS TO THE OTHER GOD CANDIDATES.
A PAIN ...
IN THE ASS, YES.
SIGH
IN THAT CASE...

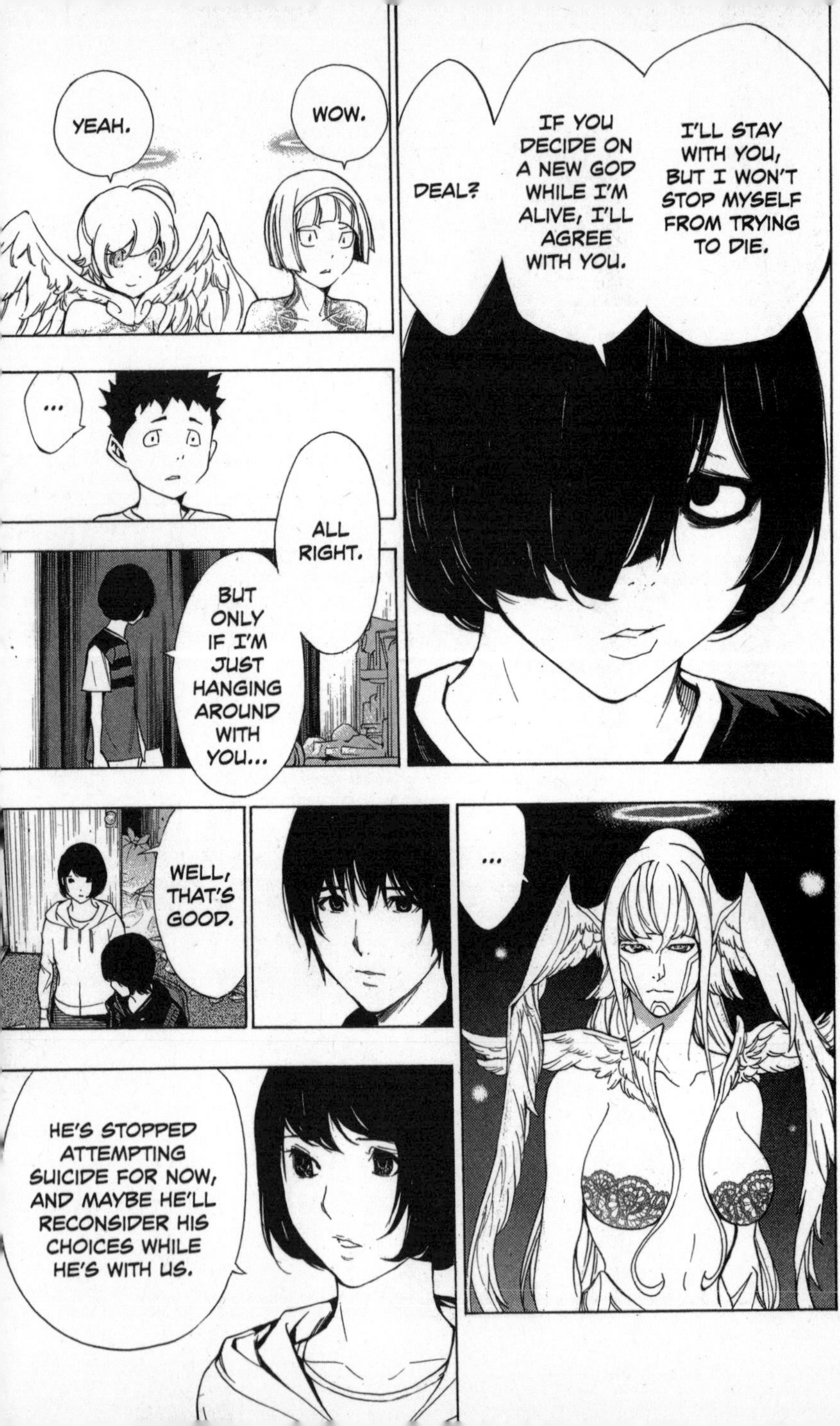
I'LL STAY WITH YOU, BUT I WON'T STOP MYSELF FROM TRYING TO DIE.
IF YOU DECIDE ON A NEW GOD WHILE I'M ALIVE, I'LL AGREE WITH YOU.
DEAL?
WOW.
YEAH.
...
ALL RIGHT.
BUT ONLY IF I'M JUST HANGING AROUND WITH YOU...
...
WELL, THAT'S GOOD.
HE'S STOPPED ATTEMPTING SUICIDE FOR NOW, AND MAYBE HE'LL RECONSIDER HIS CHOICES WHILE HE'S WITH US.

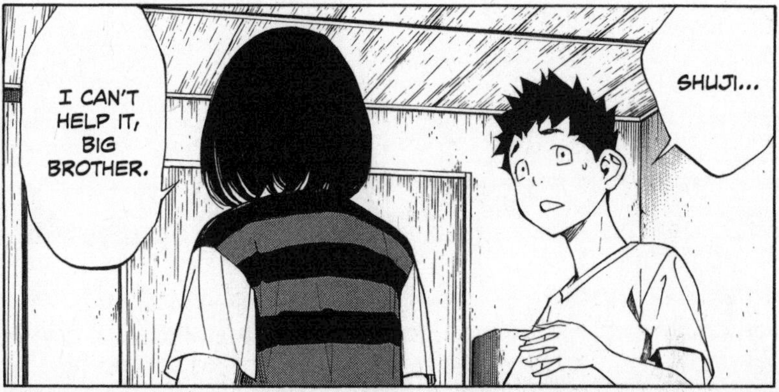
SHUJI...
I CAN'T HELP IT, BIG BROTHER.

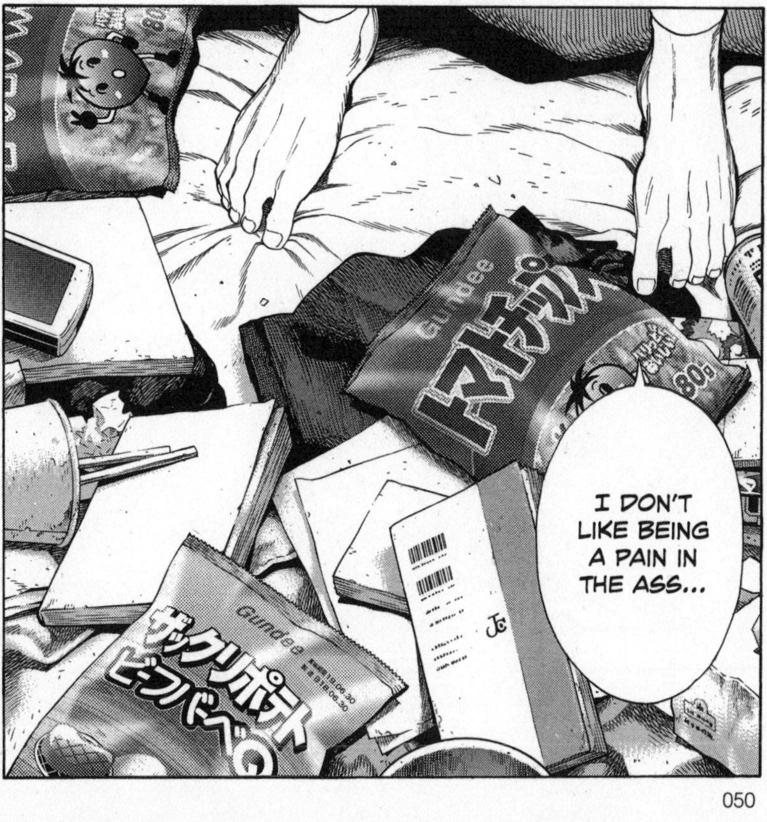
I DON'T LIKE BEING A PAIN IN THE ASS...

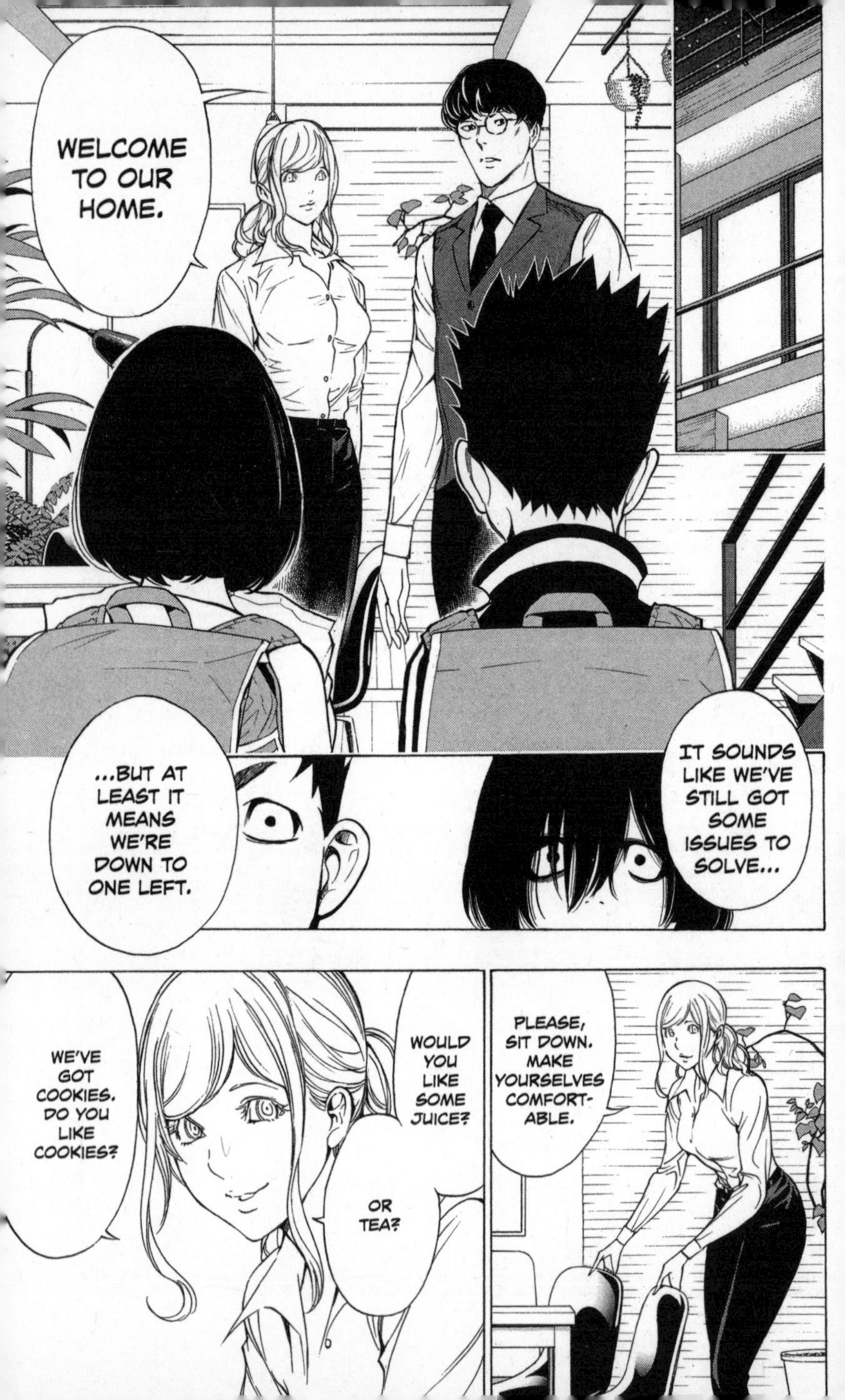
WELCOME TO OUR HOME.
IT SOUNDS LIKE WE'VE STILL GOT SOME ISSUES TO SOLVE...
...BUT AT LEAST IT MEANS WE'RE DOWN TO ONE LEFT.
PLEASE, SIT DOWN. MAKE YOURSELVES COMFORT-ABLE.
WOULD YOU LIKE SOME JUICE?
OR TEA?
WE'VE GOT COOKIES. DO YOU LIKE COOKIES?

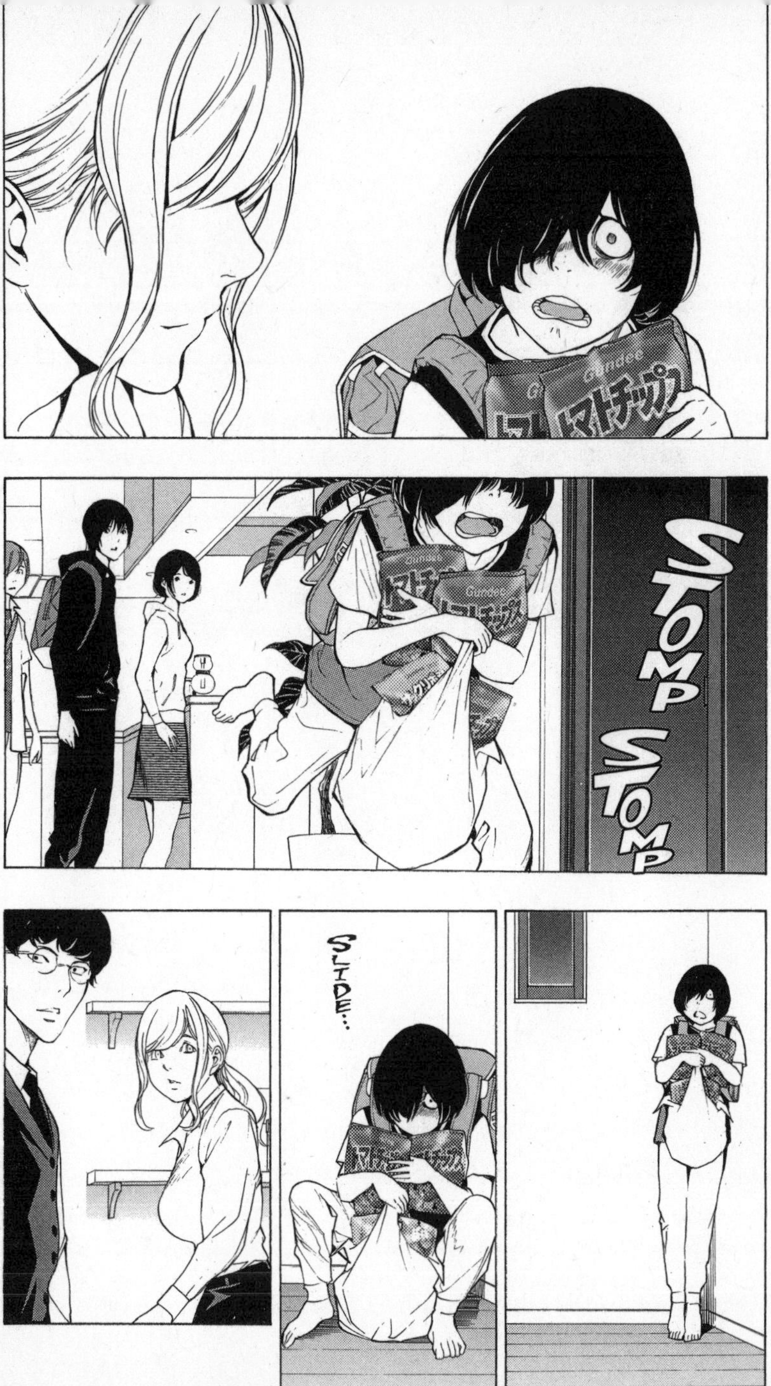
STOMP STOMP
SLIDE...

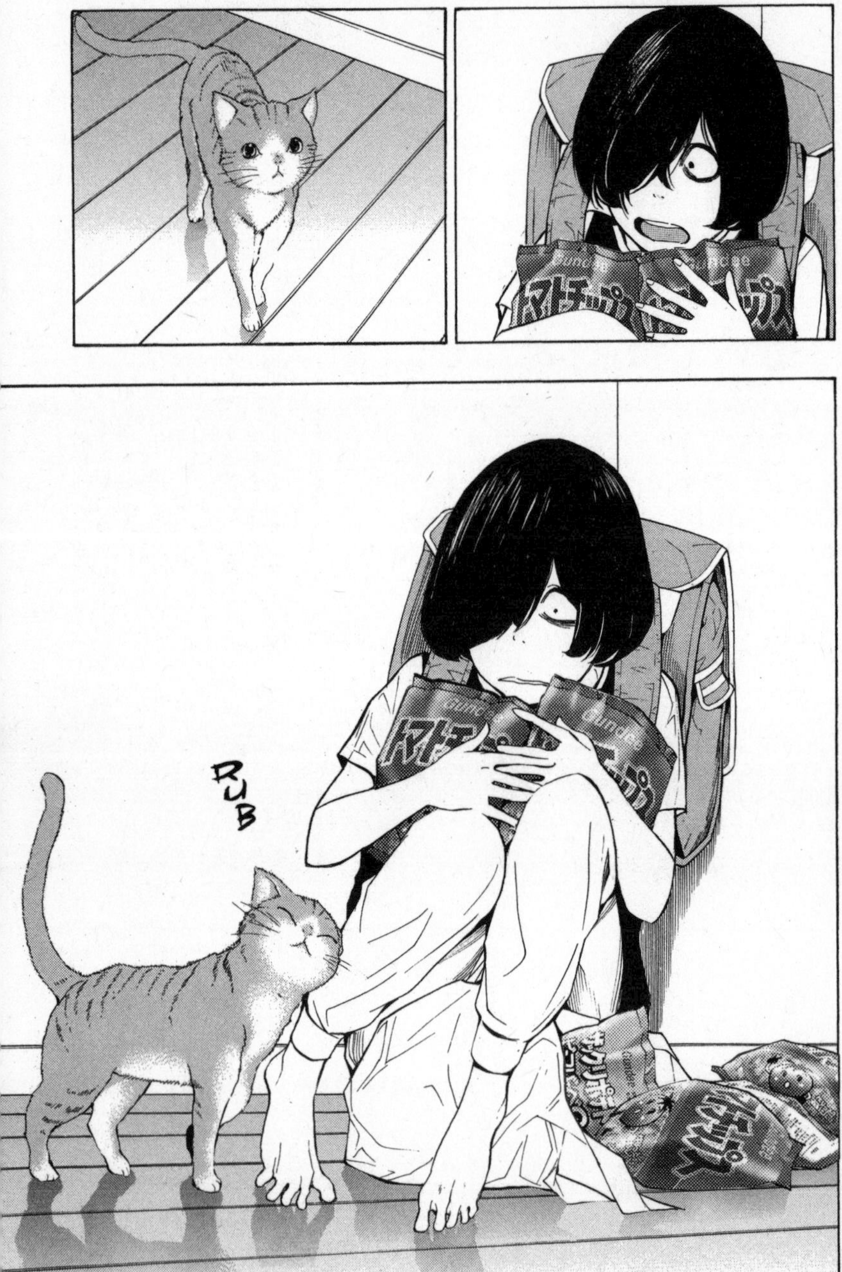
RUB

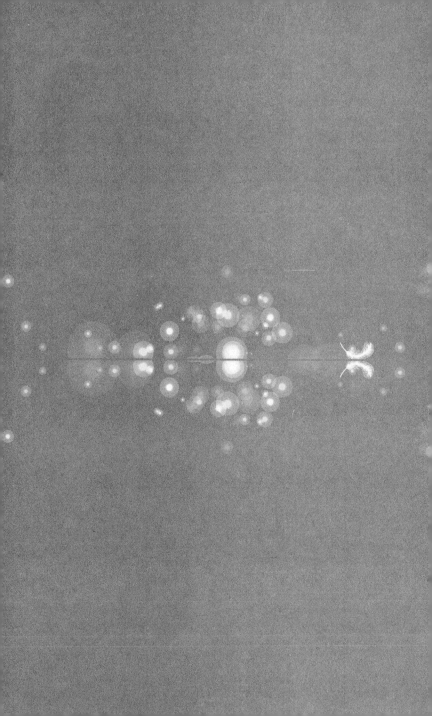

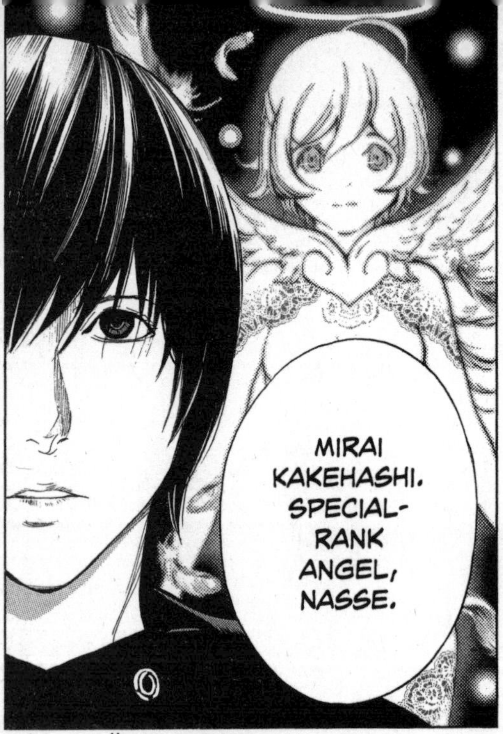
MIRAI KAKEHASHI. SPECIAL-RANK ANGEL, NASSE.

## #33 The Other Five

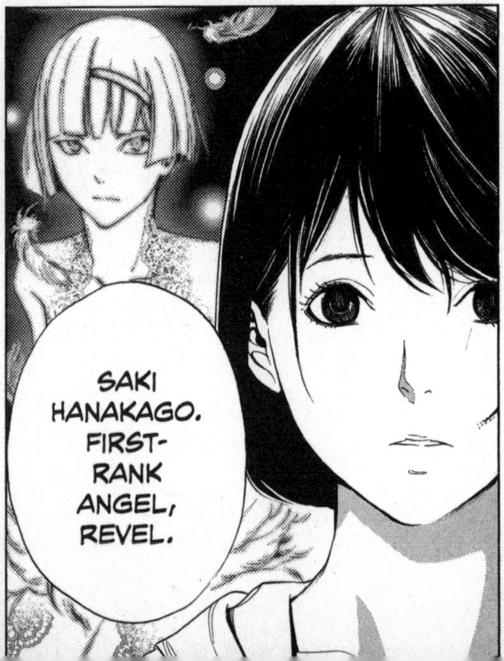
SAKI HANAKAGO. FIRST-RANK ANGEL, REVEL.

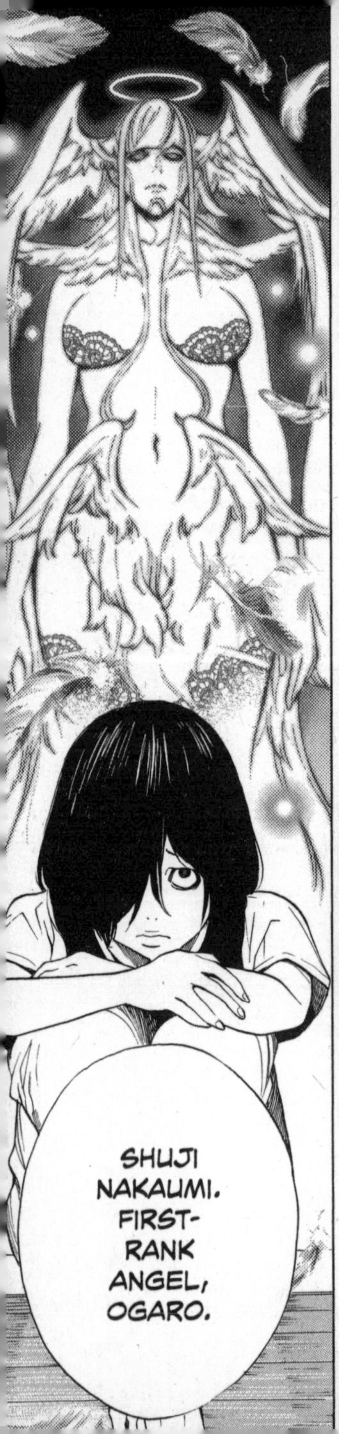
SHUJI NAKAUMI. FIRST-RANK ANGEL, OGARO.

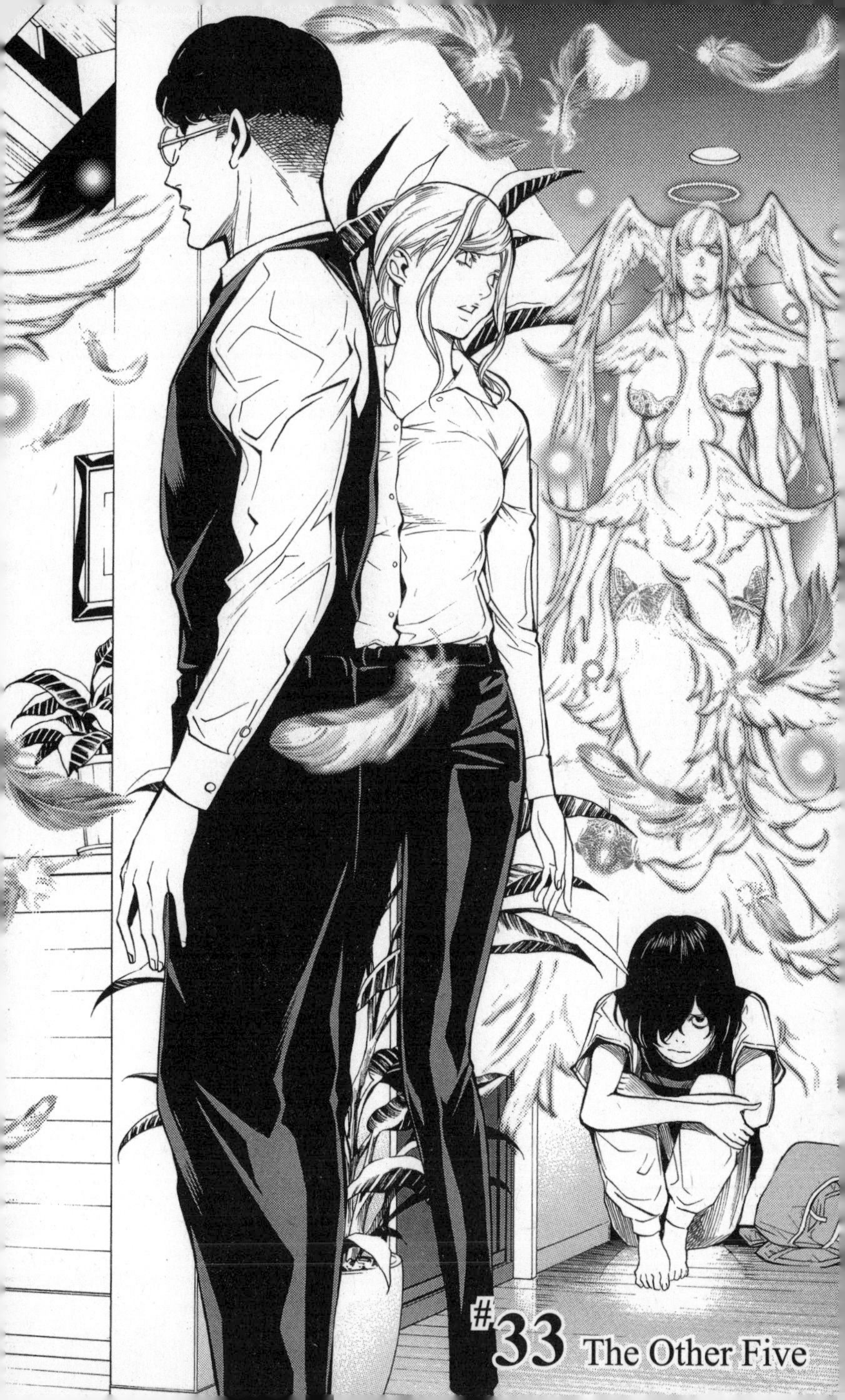
#33 The Other Five

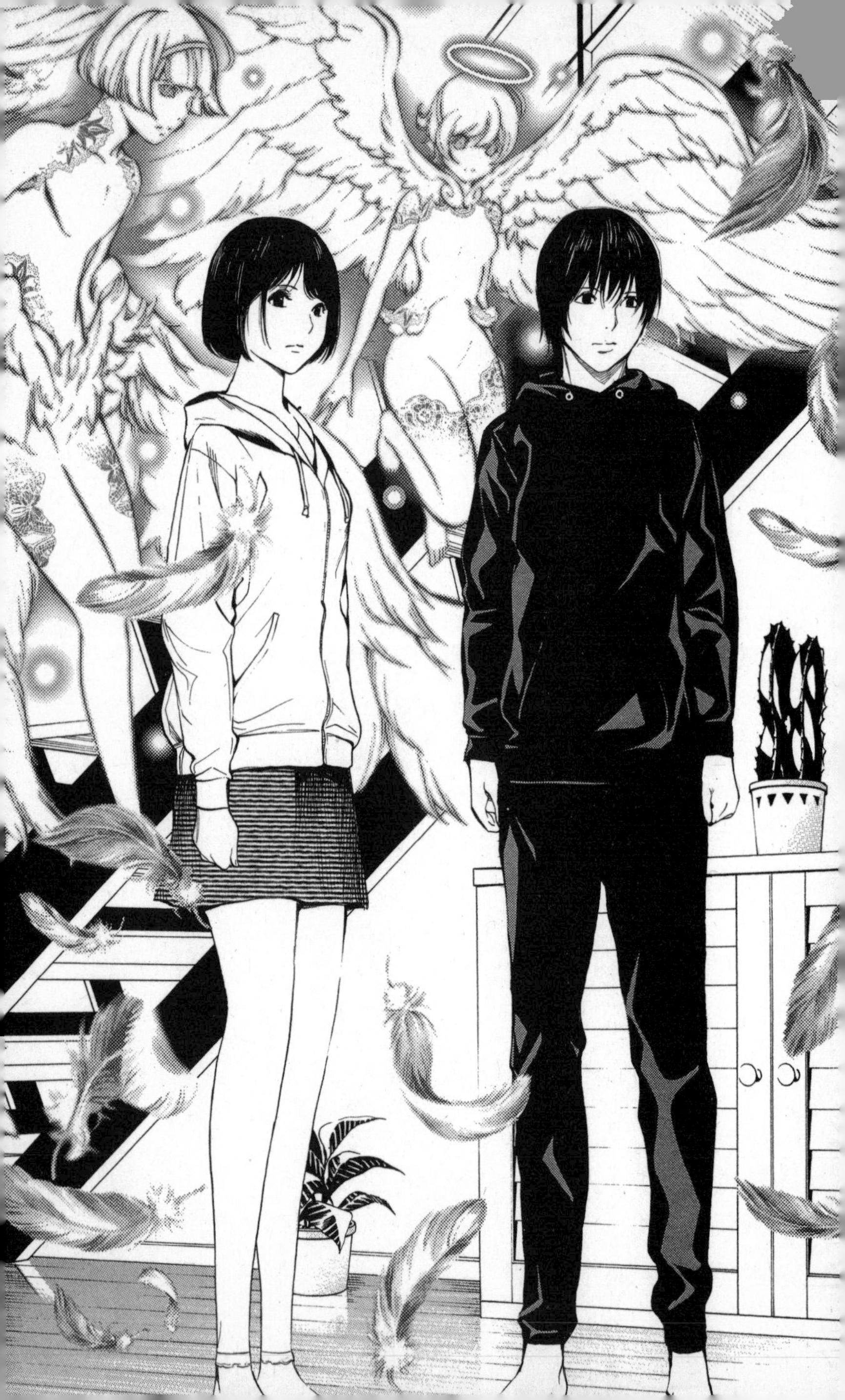

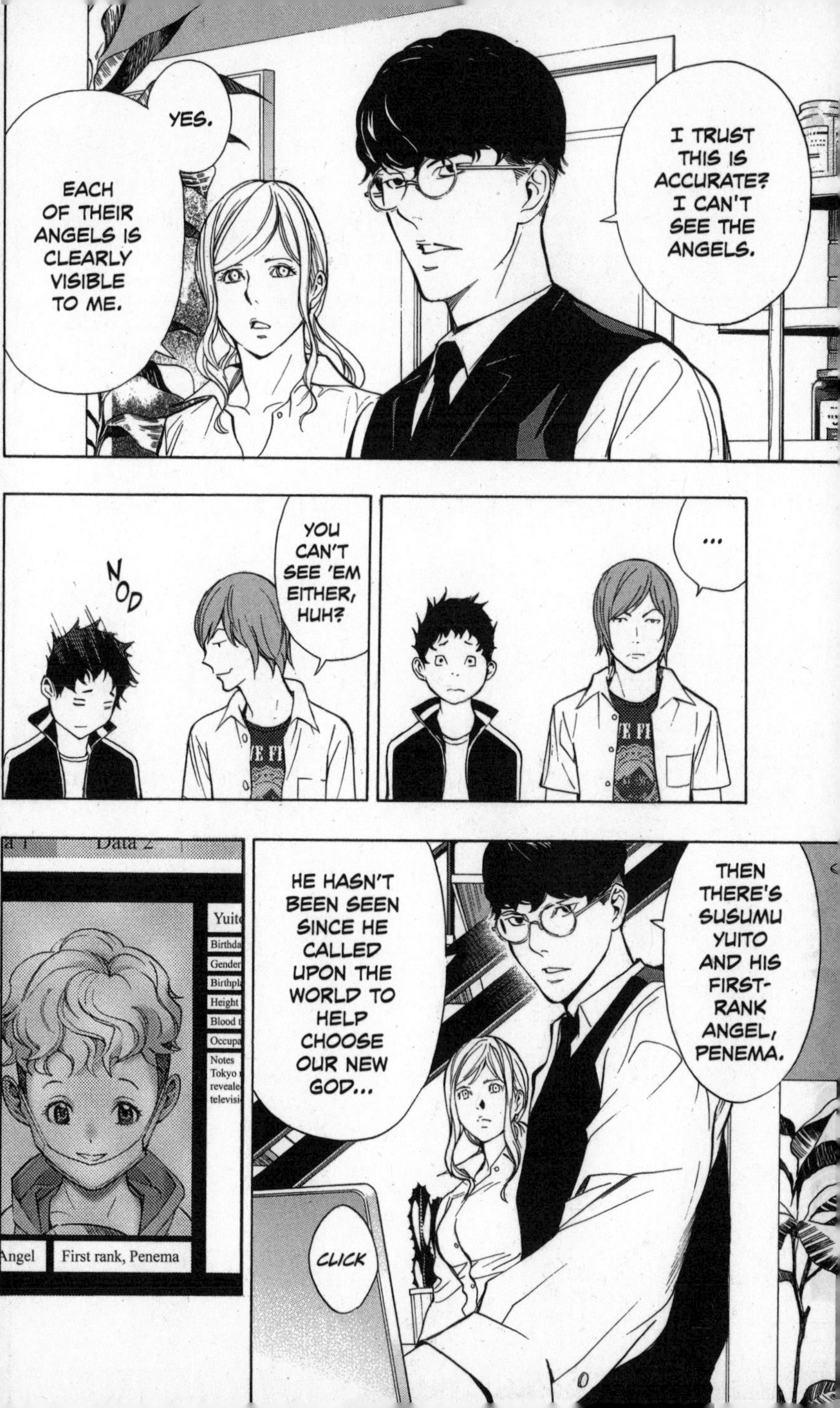
I TRUST THIS IS ACCURATE? I CAN'T SEE THE ANGELS.
YES.
EACH OF THEIR ANGELS IS CLEARLY VISIBLE TO ME.
...
YOU CAN'T SEE 'EM EITHER, HUH?
NOD
THEN THERE'S SUSUMU YUITO AND HIS FIRST-RANK ANGEL, PENEMA.
HE HASN'T BEEN SEEN SINCE HE CALLED UPON THE WORLD TO HELP CHOOSE OUR NEW GOD...
CLICK
Data 2
Notes
Angel
First rank, Penema

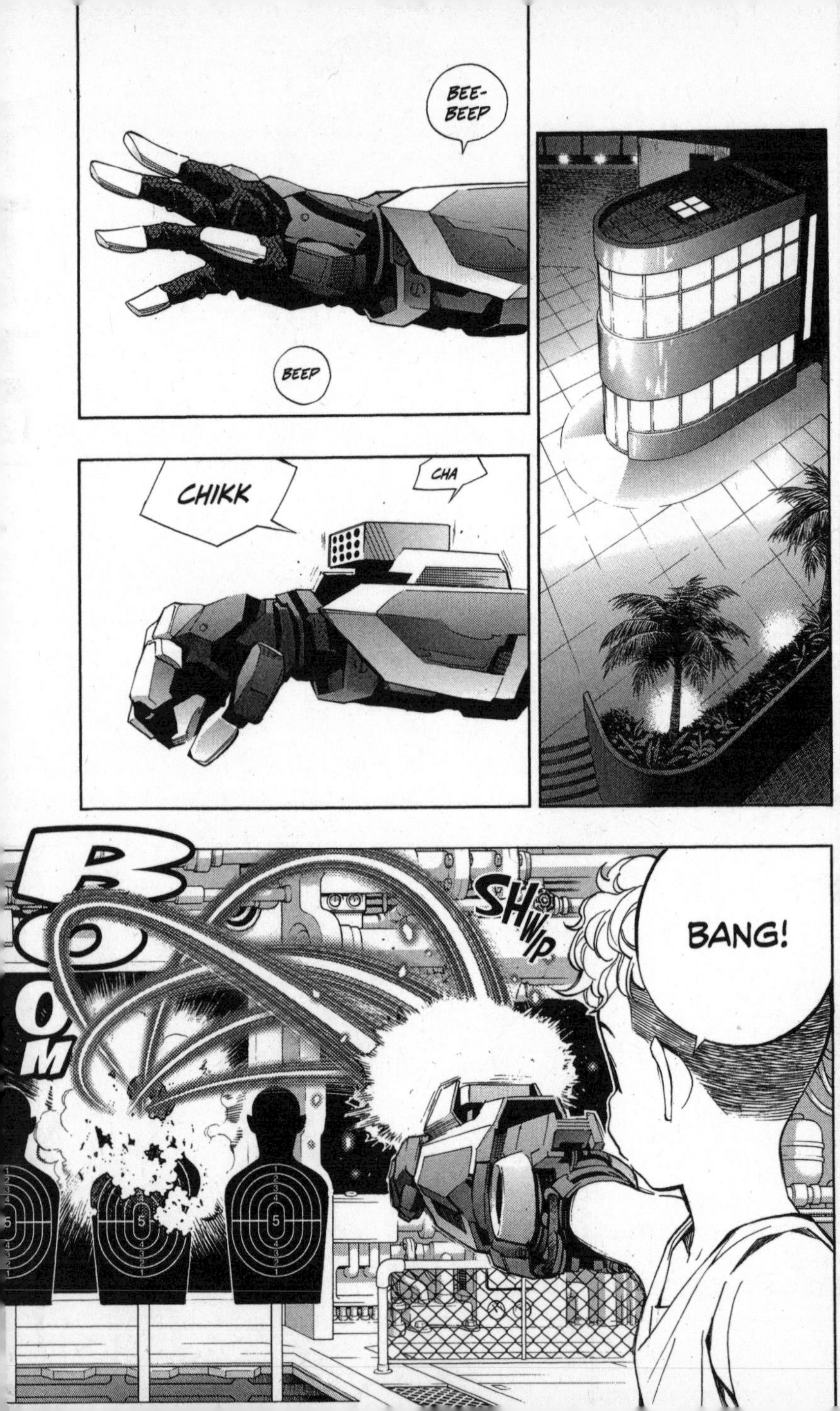
BEE-BEEP
BEEP
CHA
CHIKK
BANG!
SHWIP
BOOM

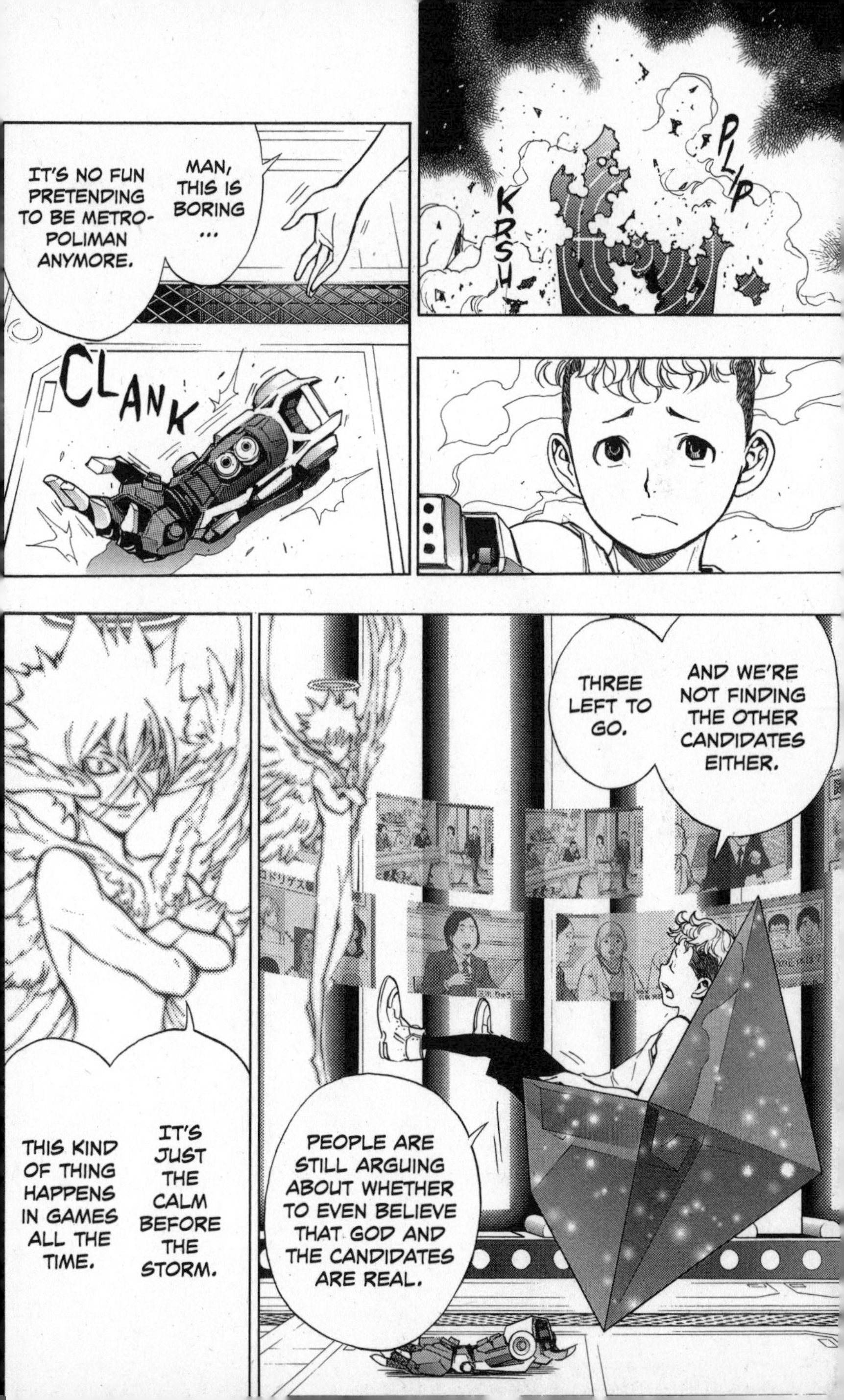
KRSH
PLIP
MAN, THIS IS BORING...
IT'S NO FUN PRETENDING TO BE METRO-POLIMAN ANYMORE.
CLANK
THREE LEFT TO GO.
AND WE'RE NOT FINDING THE OTHER CANDIDATES EITHER.
PEOPLE ARE STILL ARGUING ABOUT WHETHER TO EVEN BELIEVE THAT GOD AND THE CANDIDATES ARE REAL.
THIS KIND OF THING HAPPENS IN GAMES ALL THE TIME.
IT'S JUST THE CALM BEFORE THE STORM.

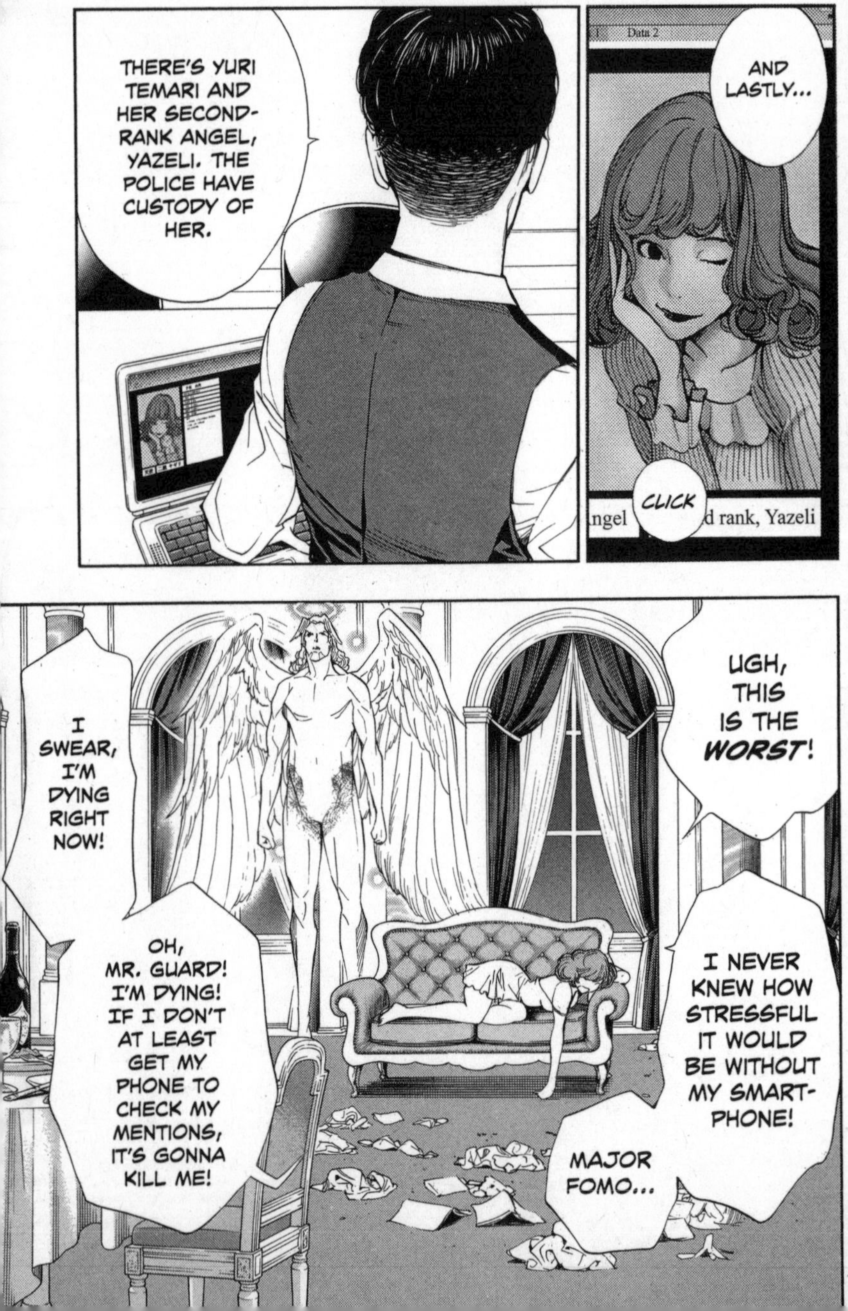
Data 2
AND LASTLY...
ngel
CLICK
d rank, Yazeli
THERE'S YURI TEMARI AND HER SECOND-RANK ANGEL, YAZELI. THE POLICE HAVE CUSTODY OF HER.
UGH, THIS IS THE *WORST*!
I SWEAR, I'M DYING RIGHT NOW!
I NEVER KNEW HOW STRESSFUL IT WOULD BE WITHOUT MY SMART-PHONE!
MAJOR FOMO...
OH, MR. GUARD! I'M DYING! IF I DON'T AT LEAST GET MY PHONE TO CHECK MY MENTIONS, IT'S GONNA KILL ME!

THAT'S RIGHT.

THAT LEAVES JUST ONE UNIDENTIFIED GOD CANDIDATE.

AND THEIR ANGEL WOULD BE MUNI, IF I UNDERSTAND CORRECTLY.

, Sus
2006
M
Japan
142.5
A
Sixth
Notes
Tokyo residen
revealed hims
television cam

Angel | First rank, Penema

Temari, Yu
Birthdate | 1995
Gender | F
Birthplace | Japan
Height | 168 c
Blood type | B+
Occupation | Unem
Notes
Worked for a r
After leaving t
Whereabouts o

Angel | Second rank, Yazeli

Birthdate
Gender
Birthplace
Height
Blood type
Occupation
Notes

NO IMAGE

Angel | Special rank, Muni

UMM...

WHAT IS IT?

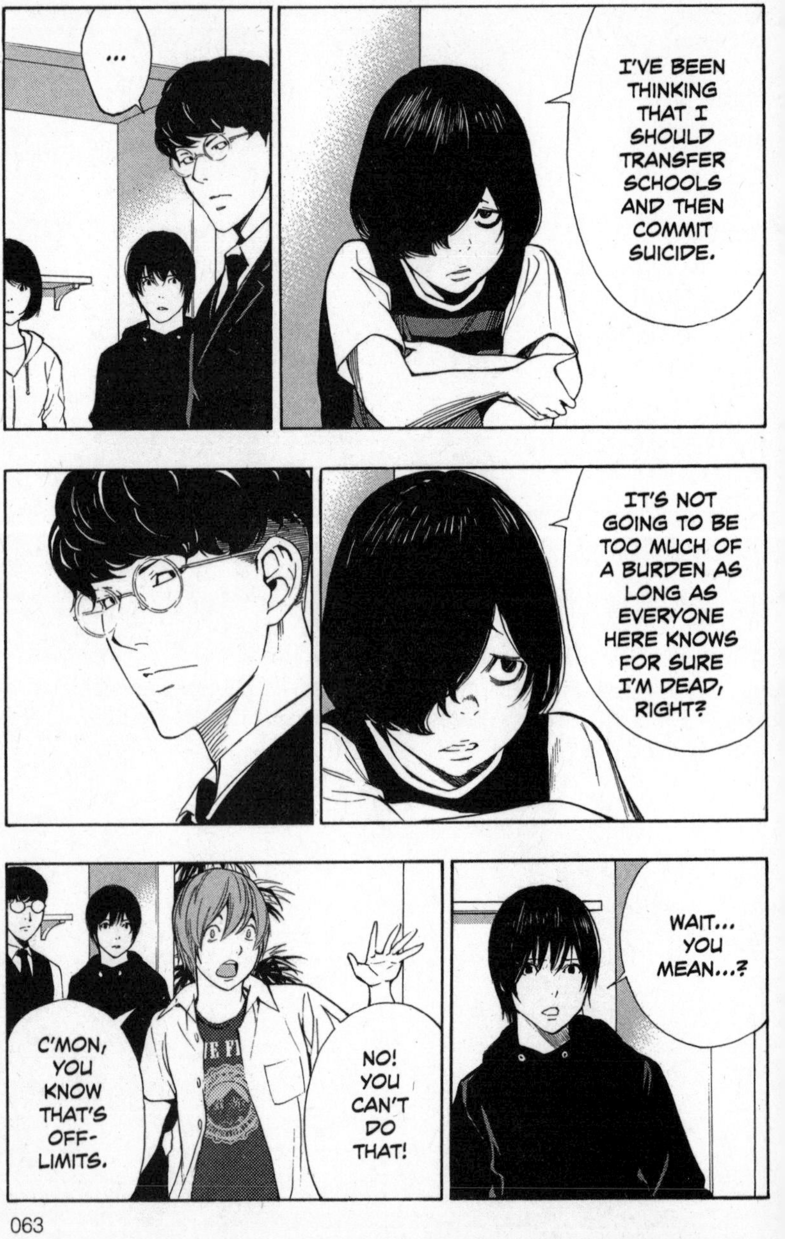
I'VE BEEN THINKING THAT I SHOULD TRANSFER SCHOOLS AND THEN COMMIT SUICIDE.
...
IT'S NOT GOING TO BE TOO MUCH OF A BURDEN AS LONG AS EVERYONE HERE KNOWS FOR SURE I'M DEAD, RIGHT?
WAIT... YOU MEAN...?
NO! YOU CAN'T DO THAT!
C'MON, YOU KNOW THAT'S OFF-LIMITS.

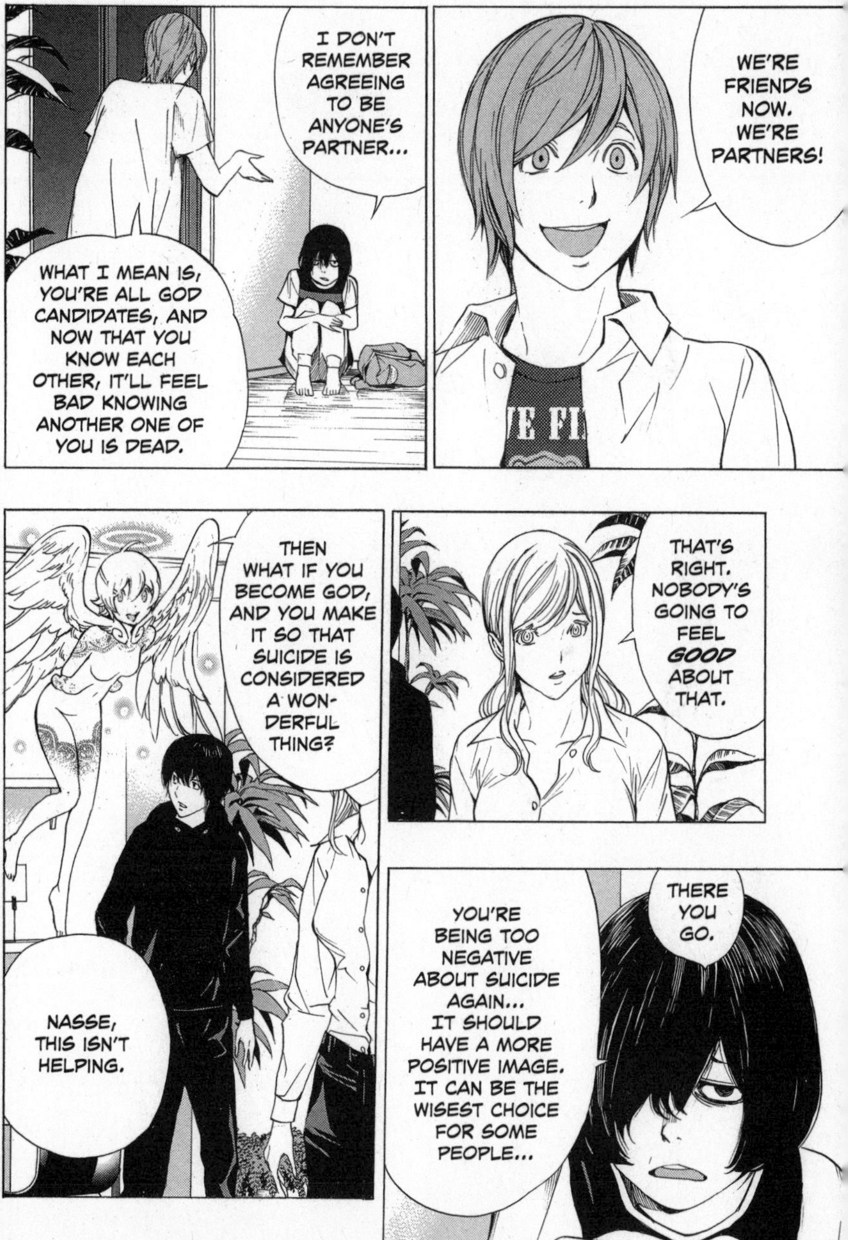
WE'RE FRIENDS NOW. WE'RE PARTNERS!
I DON'T REMEMBER AGREEING TO BE ANYONE'S PARTNER...
WHAT I MEAN IS, YOU'RE ALL GOD CANDIDATES, AND NOW THAT YOU KNOW EACH OTHER, IT'LL FEEL BAD KNOWING ANOTHER ONE OF YOU IS DEAD.
THAT'S RIGHT. NOBODY'S GOING TO FEEL *GOOD* ABOUT THAT.
THERE YOU GO.
YOU'RE BEING TOO NEGATIVE ABOUT SUICIDE AGAIN... IT SHOULD HAVE A MORE POSITIVE IMAGE. IT CAN BE THE WISEST CHOICE FOR SOME PEOPLE...
THEN WHAT IF YOU BECOME GOD, AND YOU MAKE IT SO THAT SUICIDE IS CONSIDERED A WONDERFUL THING?
NASSE, THIS ISN'T HELPING.

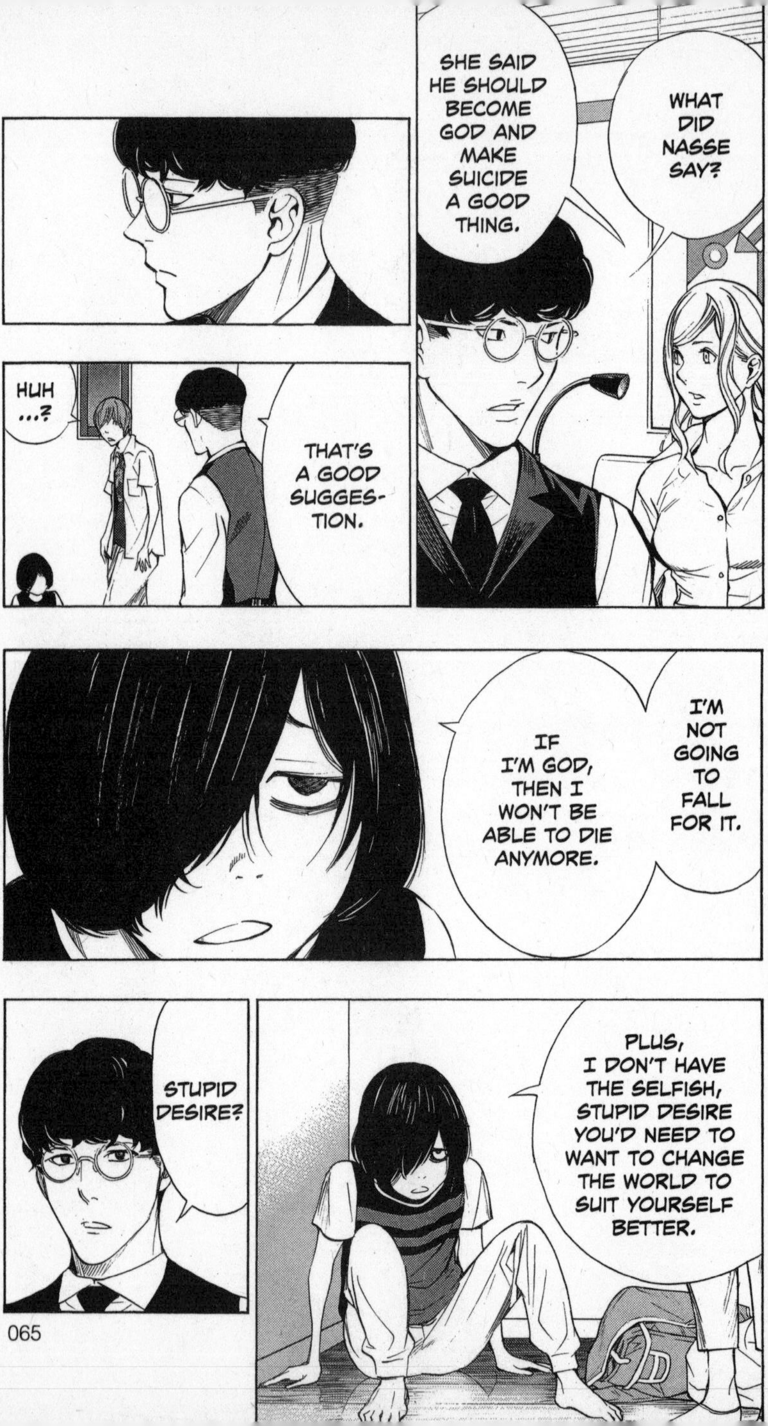
WHAT DID NASSE SAY?
SHE SAID HE SHOULD BECOME GOD AND MAKE SUICIDE A GOOD THING.
THAT'S A GOOD SUGGES-TION.
HUH ...?
I'M NOT GOING TO FALL FOR IT.
IF I'M GOD, THEN I WON'T BE ABLE TO DIE ANYMORE.
PLUS, I DON'T HAVE THE SELFISH, STUPID DESIRE YOU'D NEED TO WANT TO CHANGE THE WORLD TO SUIT YOURSELF BETTER.
STUPID DESIRE?

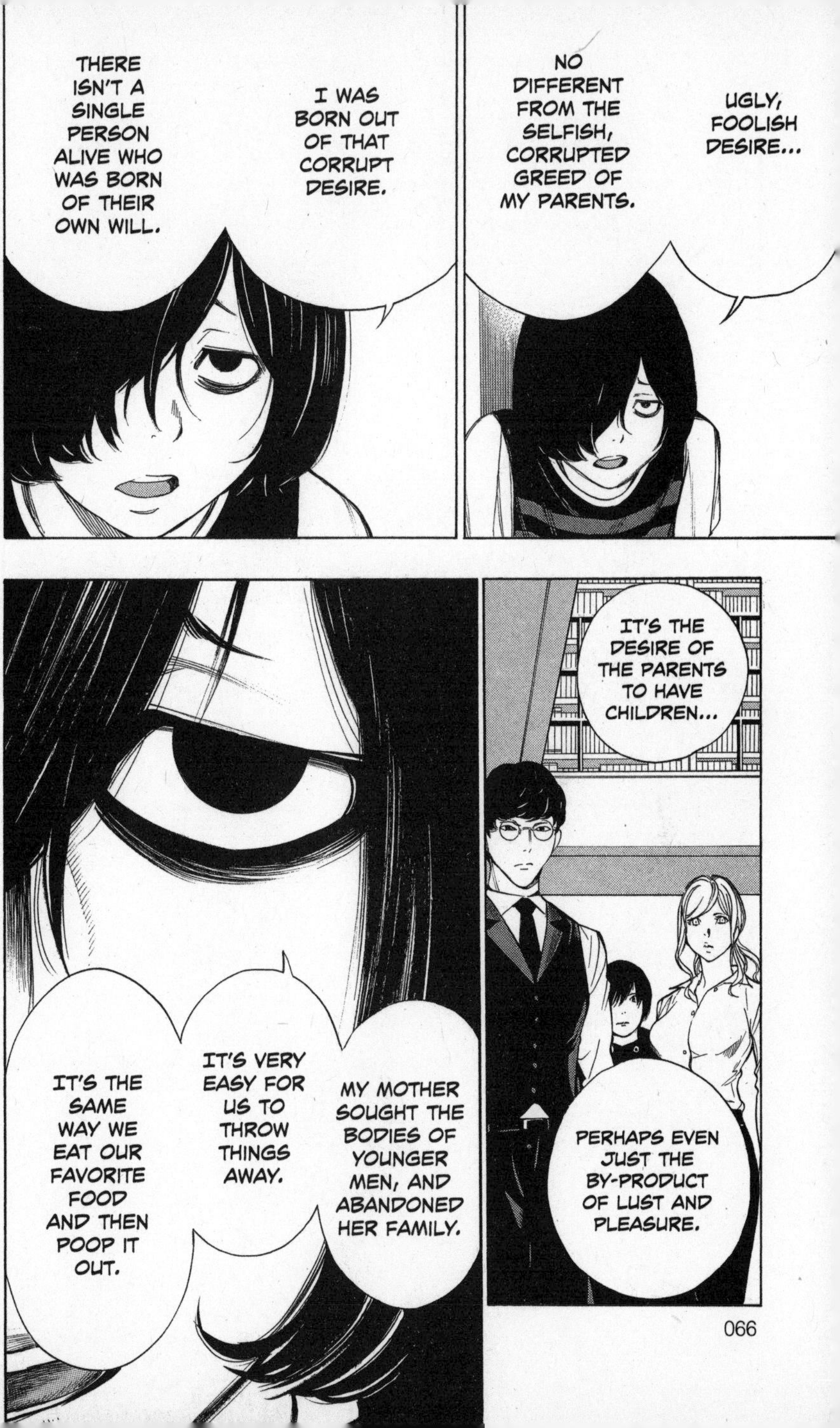
UGLY, FOOLISH DESIRE...
NO DIFFERENT FROM THE SELFISH, CORRUPTED GREED OF MY PARENTS.
I WAS BORN OUT OF THAT CORRUPT DESIRE.
THERE ISN'T A SINGLE PERSON ALIVE WHO WAS BORN OF THEIR OWN WILL.
IT'S THE DESIRE OF THE PARENTS TO HAVE CHILDREN...
PERHAPS EVEN JUST THE BY-PRODUCT OF LUST AND PLEASURE.
MY MOTHER SOUGHT THE BODIES OF YOUNGER MEN, AND ABANDONED HER FAMILY.
IT'S VERY EASY FOR US TO THROW THINGS AWAY.
IT'S THE SAME WAY WE EAT OUR FAVORITE FOOD AND THEN POOP IT OUT.

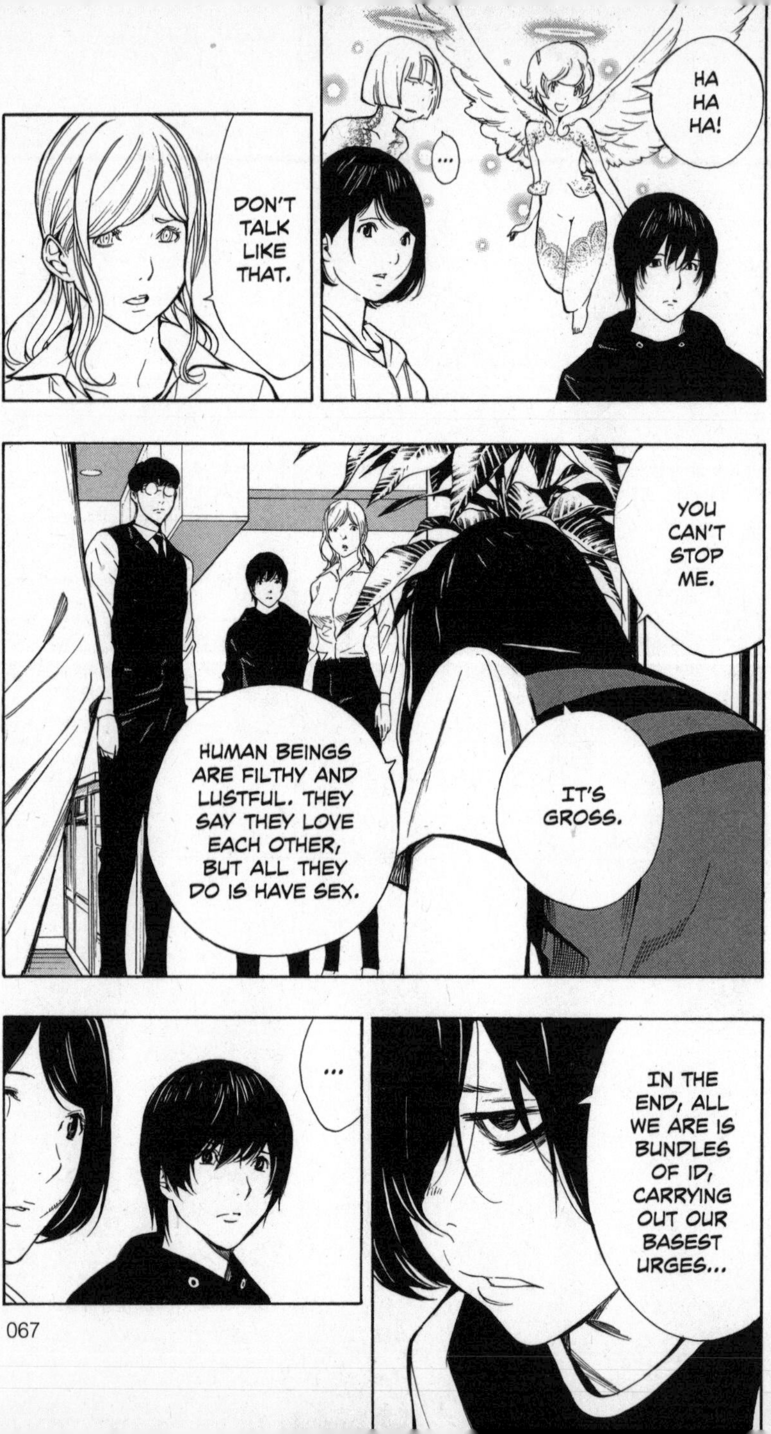
HA HA HA!
...
DON'T TALK LIKE THAT.
YOU CAN'T STOP ME.
IT'S GROSS.
HUMAN BEINGS ARE FILTHY AND LUSTFUL. THEY SAY THEY LOVE EACH OTHER, BUT ALL THEY DO IS HAVE SEX.
IN THE END, ALL WE ARE IS BUNDLES OF ID, CARRYING OUT OUR BASEST URGES...
...

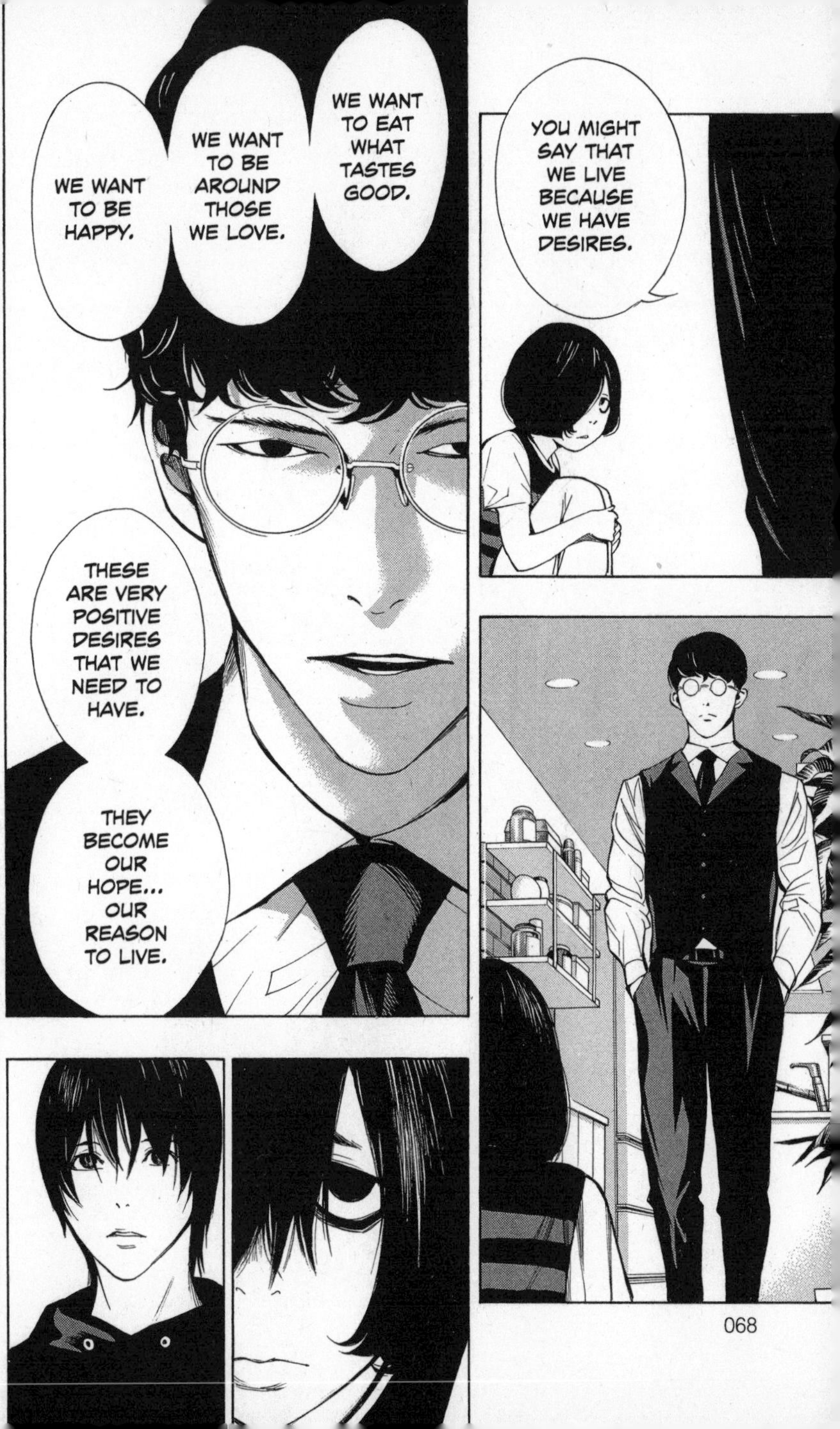
YOU MIGHT SAY THAT WE LIVE BECAUSE WE HAVE DESIRES.
WE WANT TO EAT WHAT TASTES GOOD.
WE WANT TO BE AROUND THOSE WE LOVE.
WE WANT TO BE HAPPY.
THESE ARE VERY POSITIVE DESIRES THAT WE NEED TO HAVE.
THEY BECOME OUR HOPE... OUR REASON TO LIVE.

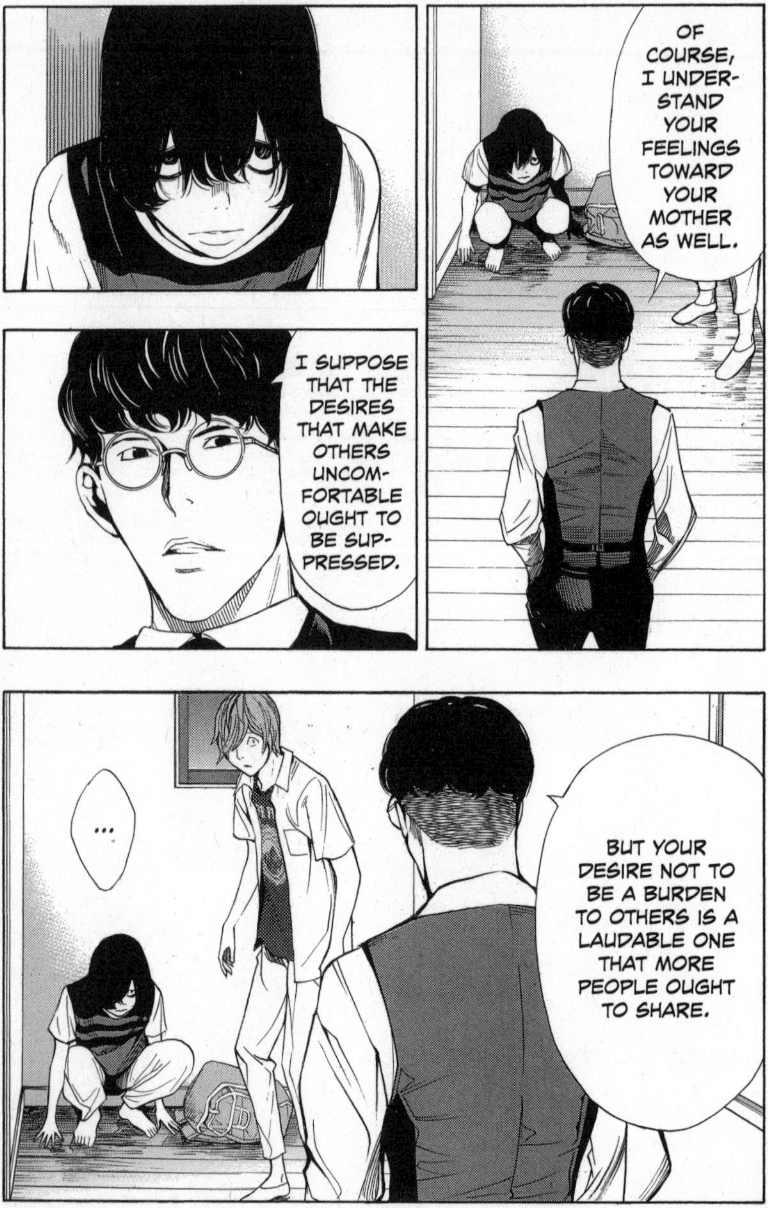
OF COURSE, I UNDERSTAND YOUR FEELINGS TOWARD YOUR MOTHER AS WELL.
I SUPPOSE THAT THE DESIRES THAT MAKE OTHERS UNCOMFORTABLE OUGHT TO BE SUPPRESSED.
BUT YOUR DESIRE NOT TO BE A BURDEN TO OTHERS IS A LAUDABLE ONE THAT MORE PEOPLE OUGHT TO SHARE.
...

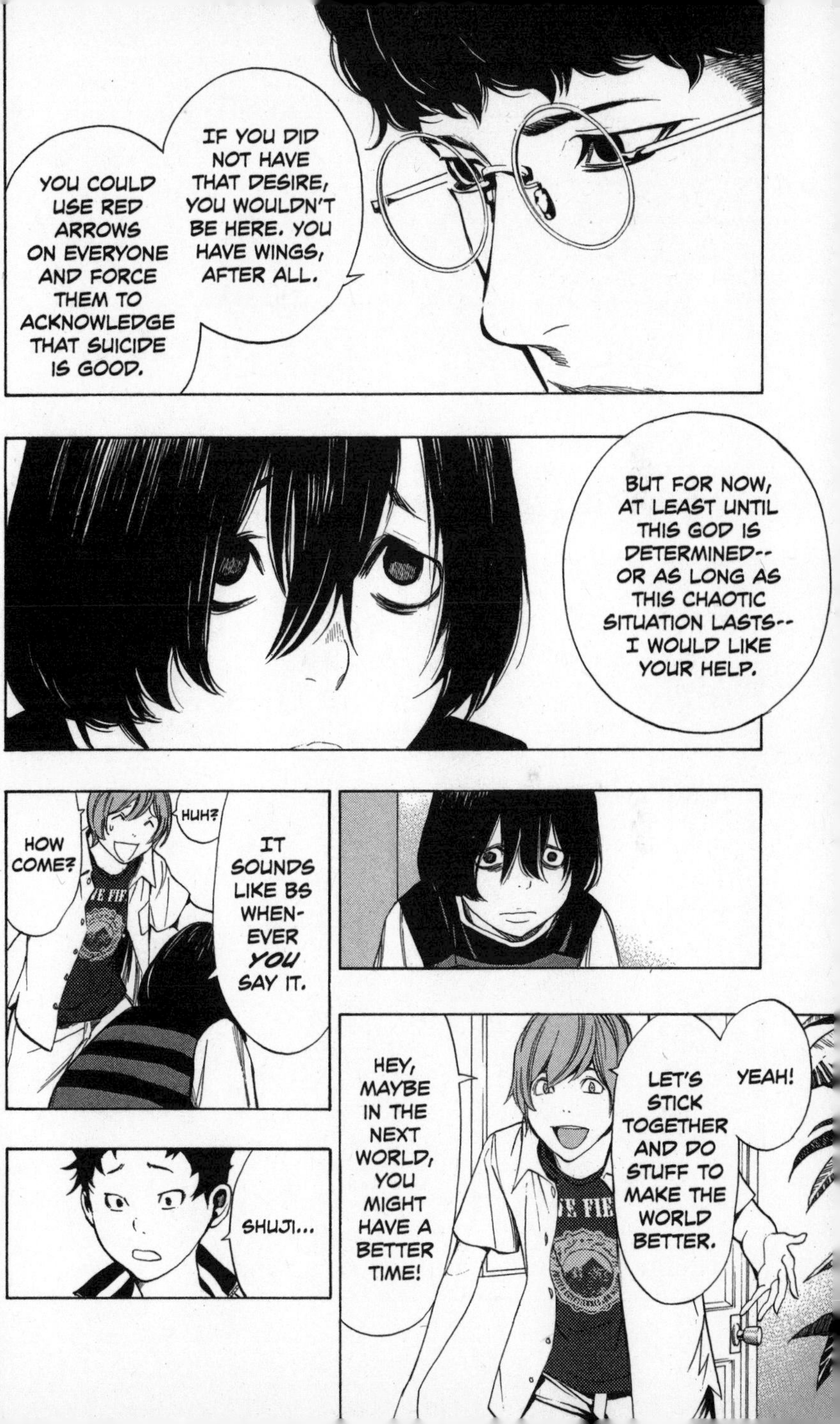
IF YOU DID NOT HAVE THAT DESIRE, YOU WOULDN'T BE HERE. YOU HAVE WINGS, AFTER ALL.
YOU COULD USE RED ARROWS ON EVERYONE AND FORCE THEM TO ACKNOWLEDGE THAT SUICIDE IS GOOD.
BUT FOR NOW, AT LEAST UNTIL THIS GOD IS DETERMINED-- OR AS LONG AS THIS CHAOTIC SITUATION LASTS-- I WOULD LIKE YOUR HELP.
IT SOUNDS LIKE BS WHENEVER *YOU* SAY IT.
HUH?
HOW COME?
YEAH!
LET'S STICK TOGETHER AND DO STUFF TO MAKE THE WORLD BETTER.
HEY, MAYBE IN THE NEXT WORLD, YOU MIGHT HAVE A BETTER TIME!
SHUJI...

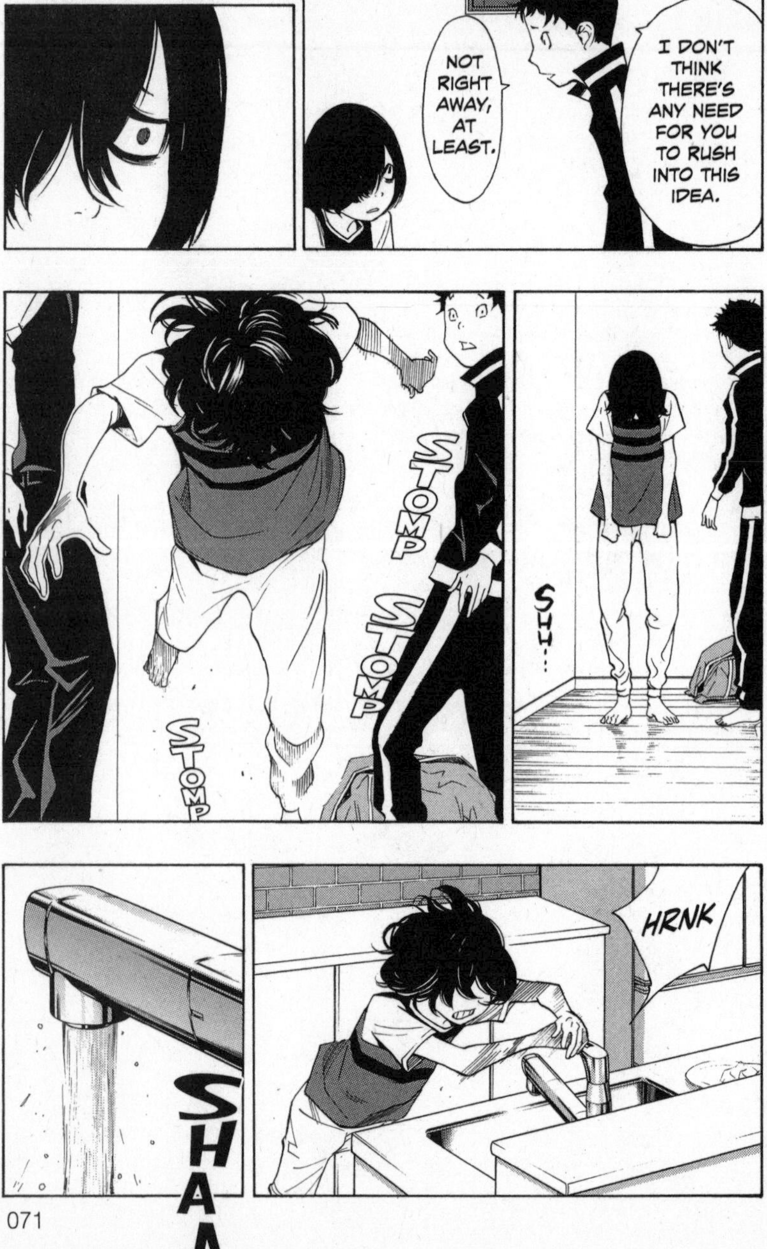
I DON'T THINK THERE'S ANY NEED FOR YOU TO RUSH INTO THIS IDEA.
NOT RIGHT AWAY, AT LEAST.
SHH...
STOMP
STOMP
STOMP
HRNK
SHAA

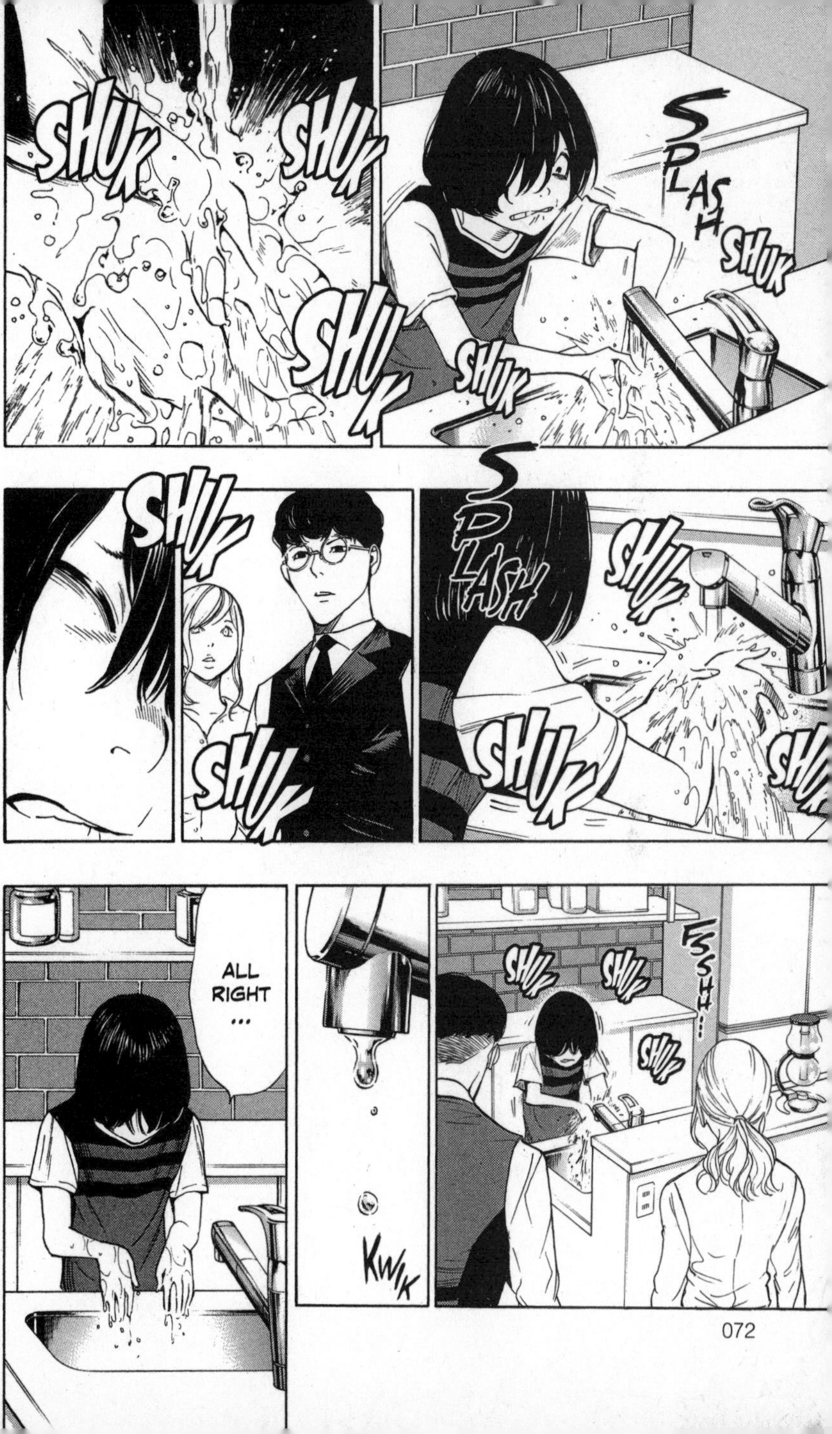
SPLASH
SHUK
SHUK
SHUK
SHUK
SHUK
SHUK
SPLASH
SHUK
SHUK
SHUK
SHUK
FSSHH...
SHUK
SHUK
SHUK
KWIK
ALL RIGHT ...

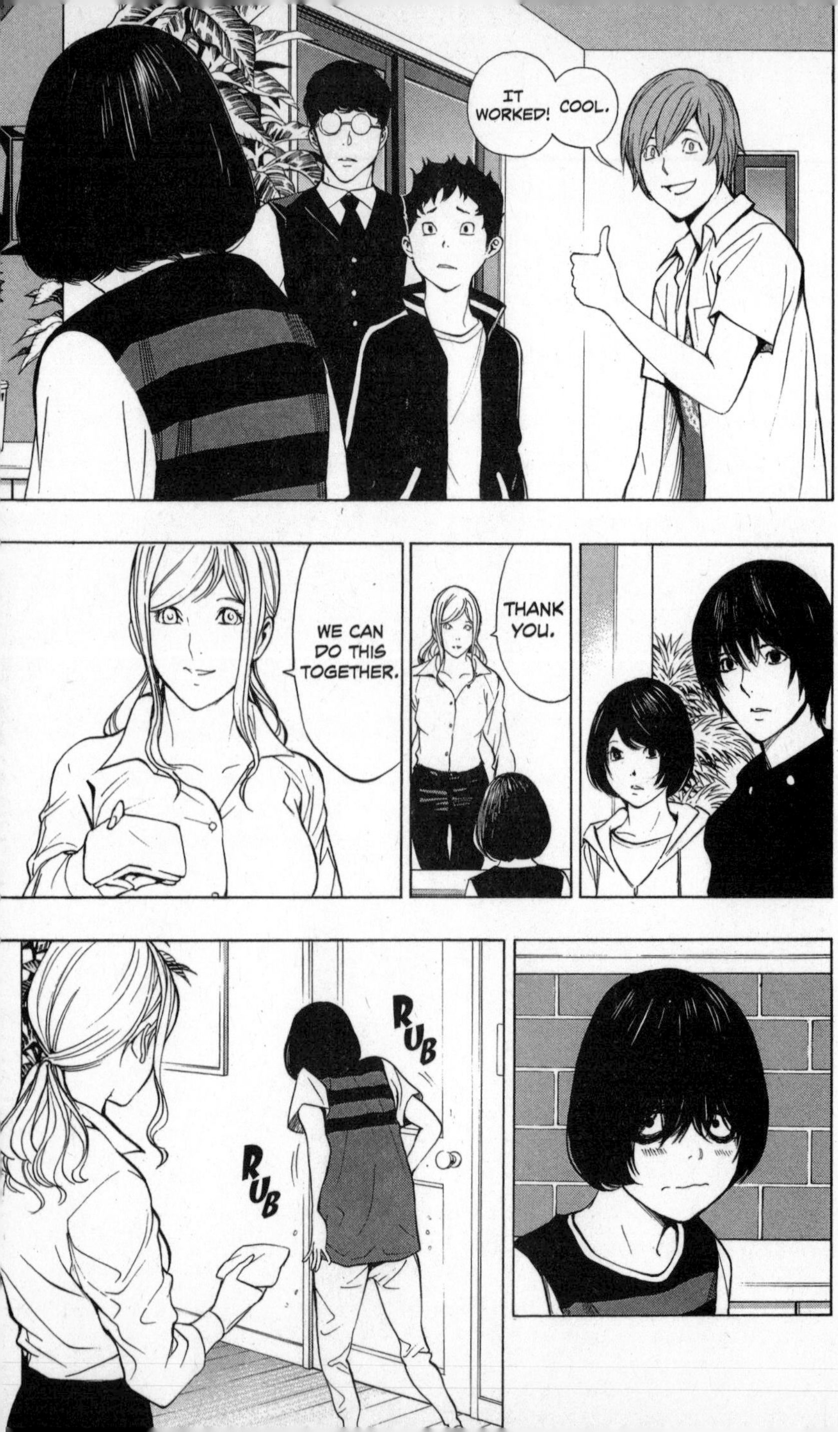
COOL.
IT WORKED!
THANK YOU.
WE CAN DO THIS TOGETHER.
RUB
RUB

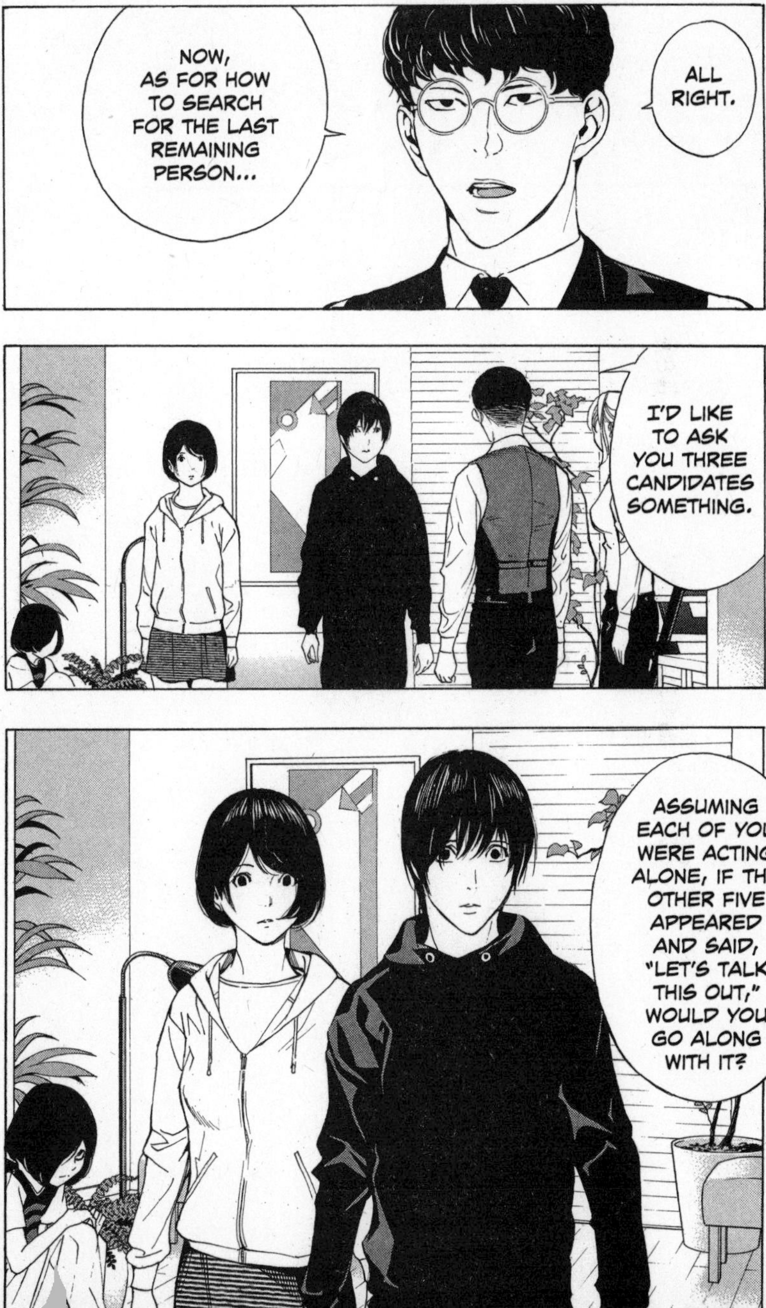
ALL RIGHT.
NOW, AS FOR HOW TO SEARCH FOR THE LAST REMAINING PERSON...
I'D LIKE TO ASK YOU THREE CANDIDATES SOMETHING.
ASSUMING EACH OF YOU WERE ACTING ALONE, IF THE OTHER FIVE APPEARED AND SAID, "LET'S TALK THIS OUT," WOULD YOU GO ALONG WITH IT?

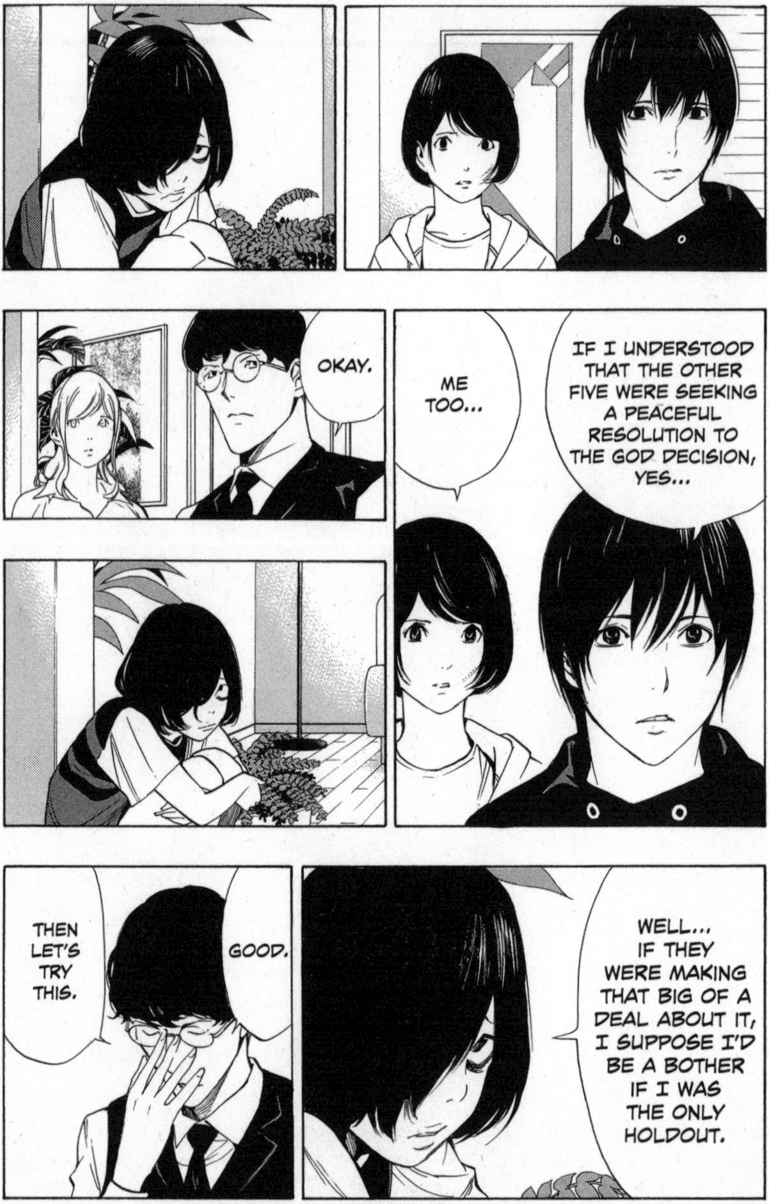
IF I UNDERSTOOD THAT THE OTHER FIVE WERE SEEKING A PEACEFUL RESOLUTION TO THE GOD DECISION, YES...
ME TOO...
OKAY.
WELL... IF THEY WERE MAKING THAT BIG OF A DEAL ABOUT IT, I SUPPOSE I'D BE A BOTHER IF I WAS THE ONLY HOLDOUT.
GOOD.
THEN LET'S TRY THIS.

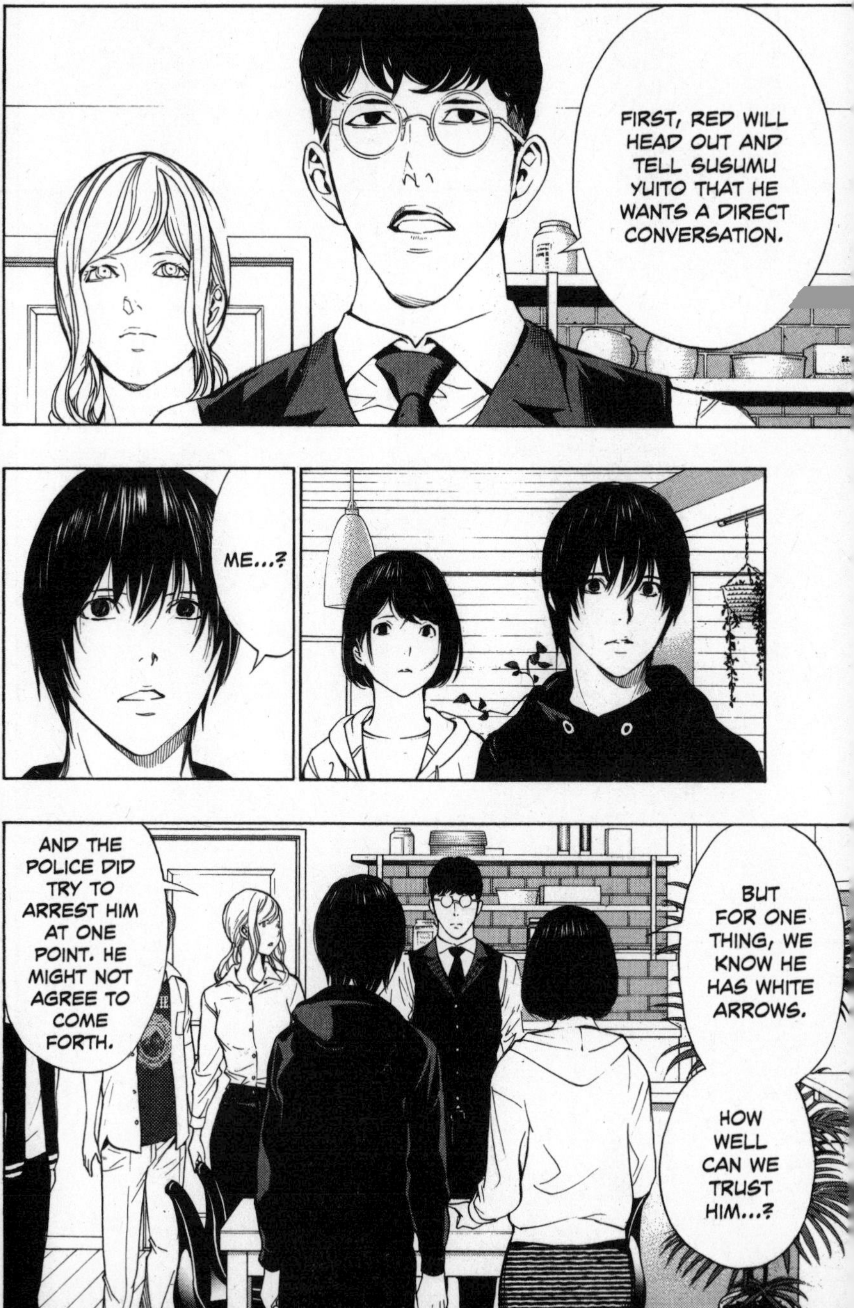
FIRST, RED WILL HEAD OUT AND TELL SUSUMU YUITO THAT HE WANTS A DIRECT CONVERSATION.
ME...?
BUT FOR ONE THING, WE KNOW HE HAS WHITE ARROWS.
HOW WELL CAN WE TRUST HIM...?
AND THE POLICE DID TRY TO ARREST HIM AT ONE POINT. HE MIGHT NOT AGREE TO COME FORTH.

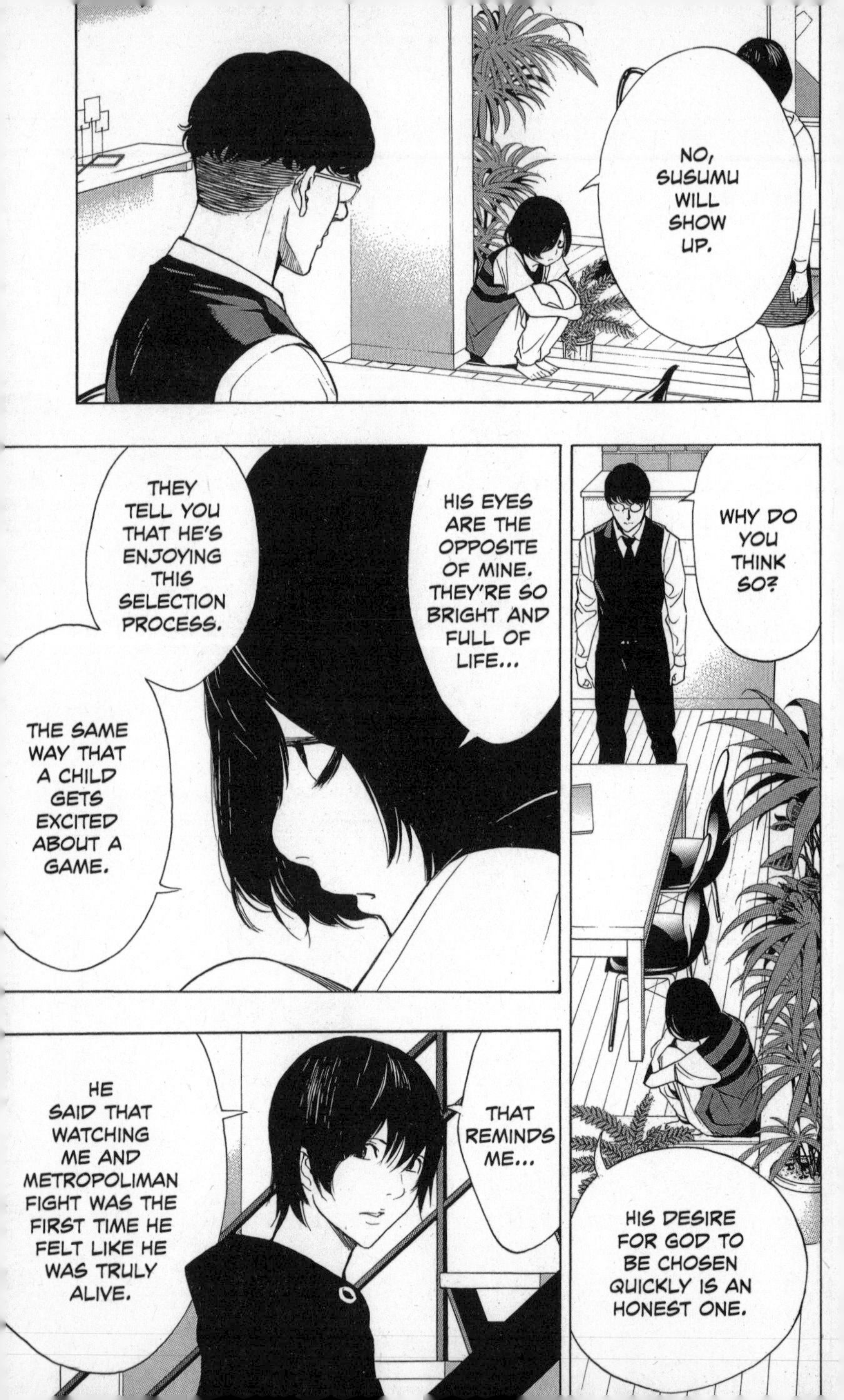
NO, SUSUMU WILL SHOW UP.
WHY DO YOU THINK SO?
HIS DESIRE FOR GOD TO BE CHOSEN QUICKLY IS AN HONEST ONE.
HIS EYES ARE THE OPPOSITE OF MINE. THEY'RE SO BRIGHT AND FULL OF LIFE...
THEY TELL YOU THAT HE'S ENJOYING THIS SELECTION PROCESS.
THE SAME WAY THAT A CHILD GETS EXCITED ABOUT A GAME.
THAT REMINDS ME...
HE SAID THAT WATCHING ME AND METROPOLIMAN FIGHT WAS THE FIRST TIME HE FELT LIKE HE WAS TRULY ALIVE.

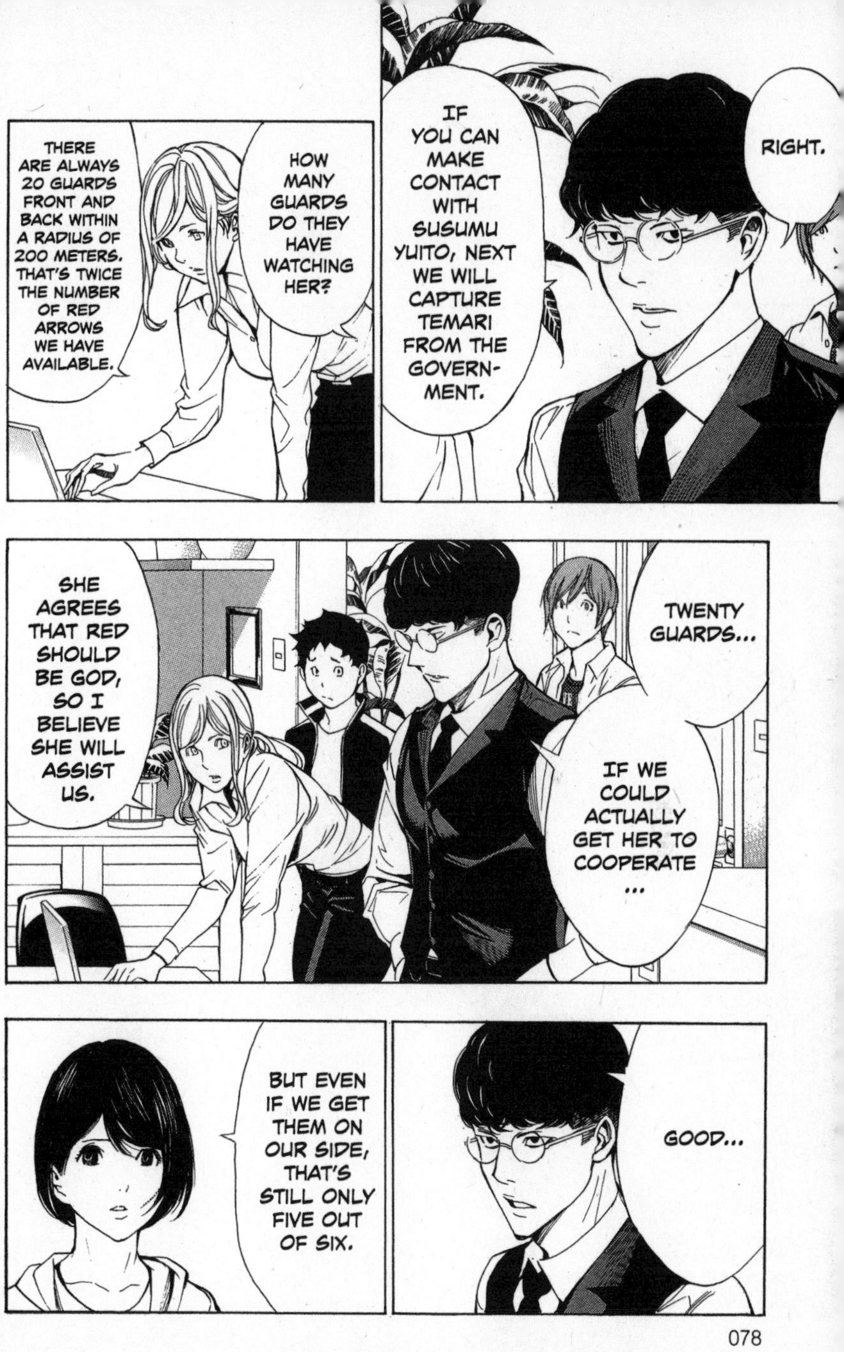
RIGHT.
IF YOU CAN MAKE CONTACT WITH SUSUMU YUITO, NEXT WE WILL CAPTURE TEMARI FROM THE GOVERN-MENT.
HOW MANY GUARDS DO THEY HAVE WATCHING HER?
THERE ARE ALWAYS 20 GUARDS FRONT AND BACK WITHIN A RADIUS OF 200 METERS. THAT'S TWICE THE NUMBER OF RED ARROWS WE HAVE AVAILABLE.
TWENTY GUARDS...
IF WE COULD ACTUALLY GET HER TO COOPERATE...
SHE AGREES THAT RED SHOULD BE GOD, SO I BELIEVE SHE WILL ASSIST US.
GOOD...
BUT EVEN IF WE GET THEM ON OUR SIDE, THAT'S STILL ONLY FIVE OUT OF SIX.

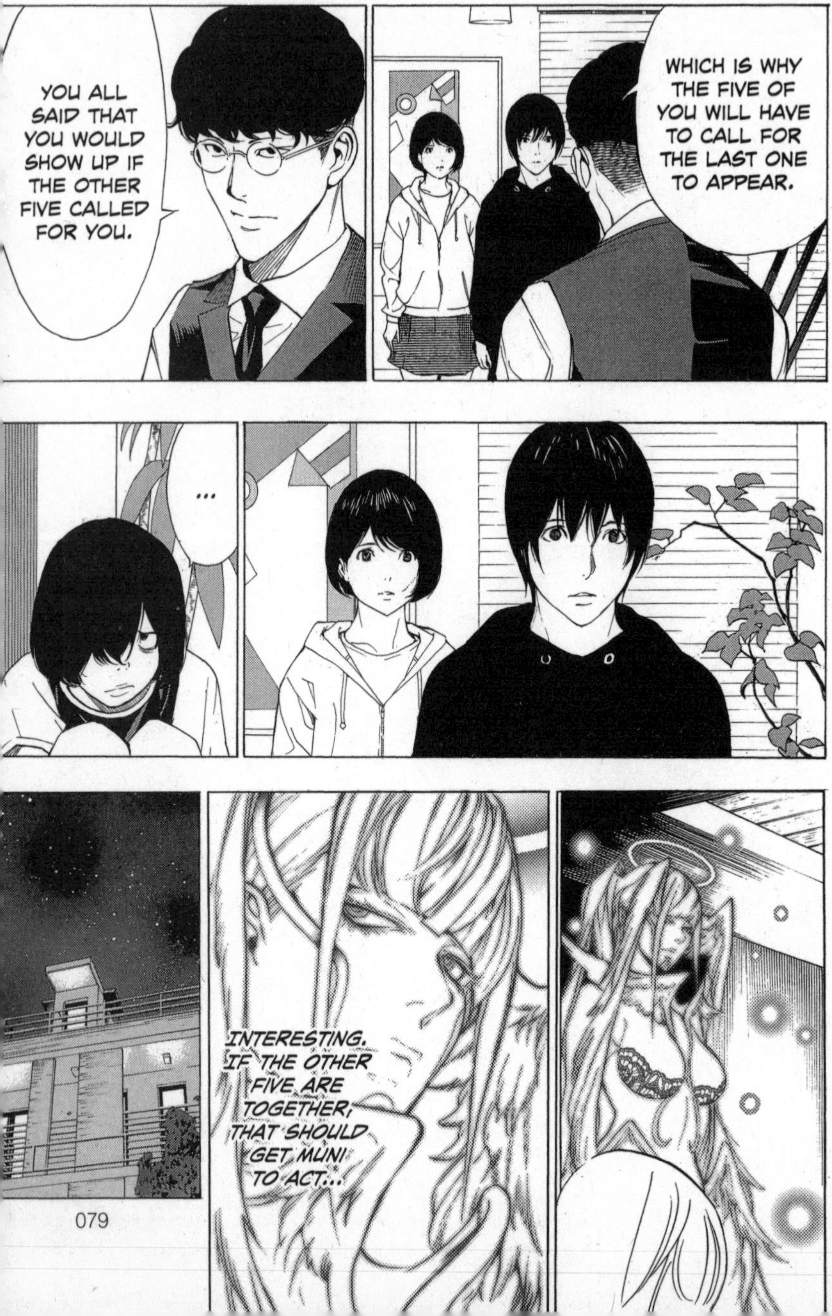
WHICH IS WHY THE FIVE OF YOU WILL HAVE TO CALL FOR THE LAST ONE TO APPEAR.
YOU ALL SAID THAT YOU WOULD SHOW UP IF THE OTHER FIVE CALLED FOR YOU.
...
INTERESTING. IF THE OTHER FIVE ARE TOGETHER, THAT SHOULD GET MUNI TO ACT...

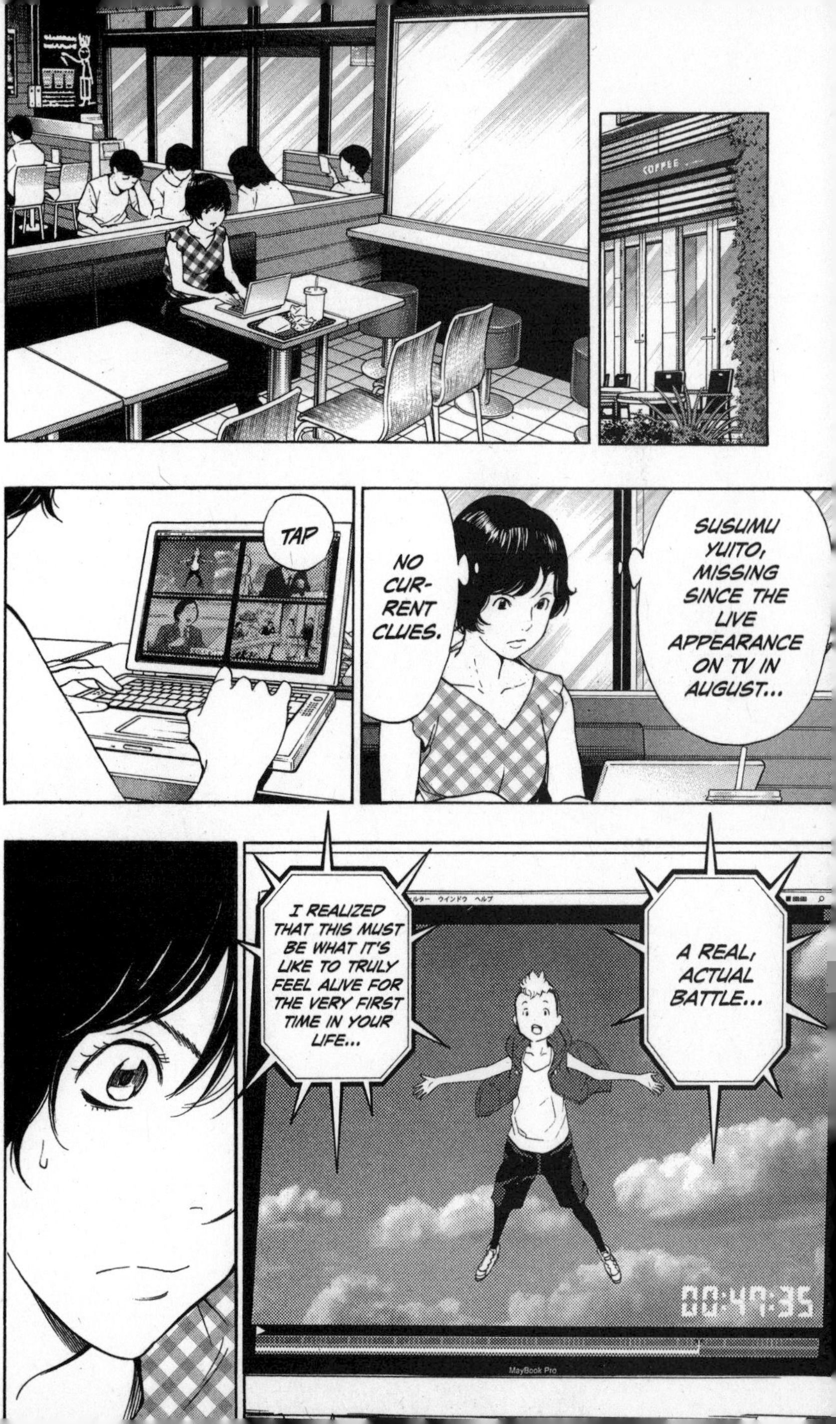
COFFEE
SUSUMU YUITO, MISSING SINCE THE LIVE APPEARANCE ON TV IN AUGUST...
NO CUR-RENT CLUES.
TAP
ルター ウインドウ ヘルプ
A REAL, ACTUAL BATTLE...
I REALIZED THAT THIS MUST BE WHAT IT'S LIKE TO TRULY FEEL ALIVE FOR THE VERY FIRST TIME IN YOUR LIFE...
00:47:35
MayBook Pro

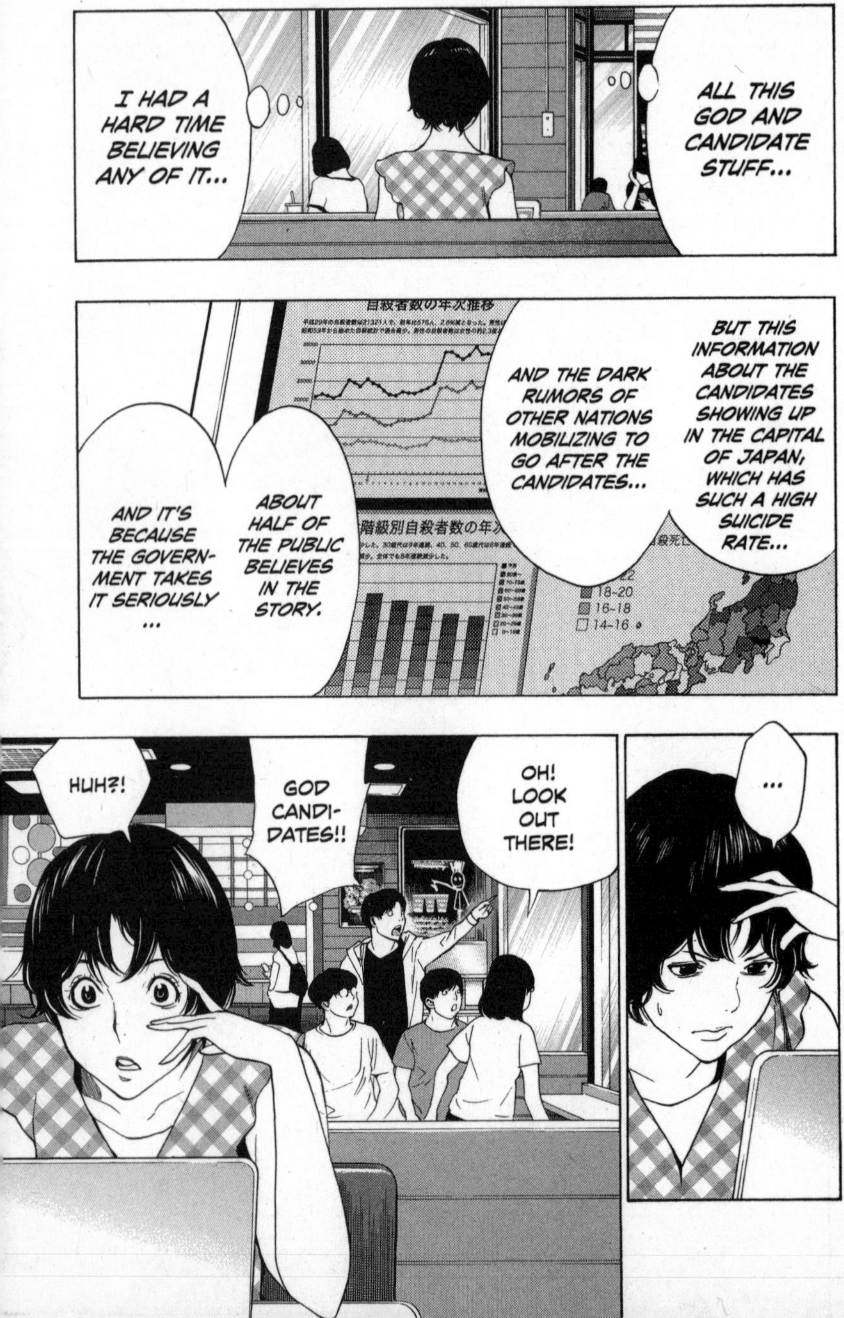
ALL THIS GOD AND CANDIDATE STUFF...
I HAD A HARD TIME BELIEVING ANY OF IT...
BUT THIS INFORMATION ABOUT THE CANDIDATES SHOWING UP IN THE CAPITAL OF JAPAN, WHICH HAS SUCH A HIGH SUICIDE RATE...
AND THE DARK RUMORS OF OTHER NATIONS MOBILIZING TO GO AFTER THE CANDIDATES...
自殺者数の年次推移
18~20
16~18
14~16
ABOUT HALF OF THE PUBLIC BELIEVES IN THE STORY.
AND IT'S BECAUSE THE GOVERN-MENT TAKES IT SERIOUSLY ...
...
OH! LOOK OUT THERE!
GOD CANDI-DATES!!
HUH?!

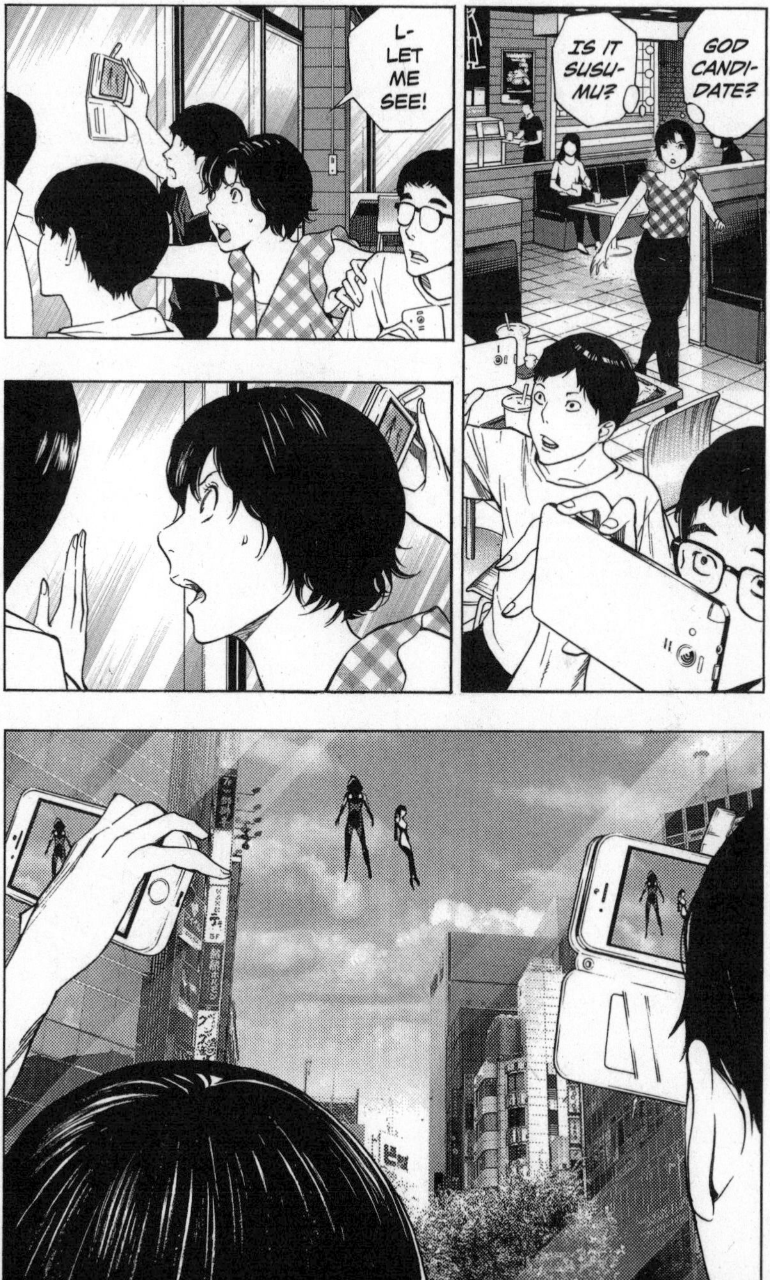
GOD CANDI-DATE?
IS IT SUSU-MU?
L-LET ME SEE!

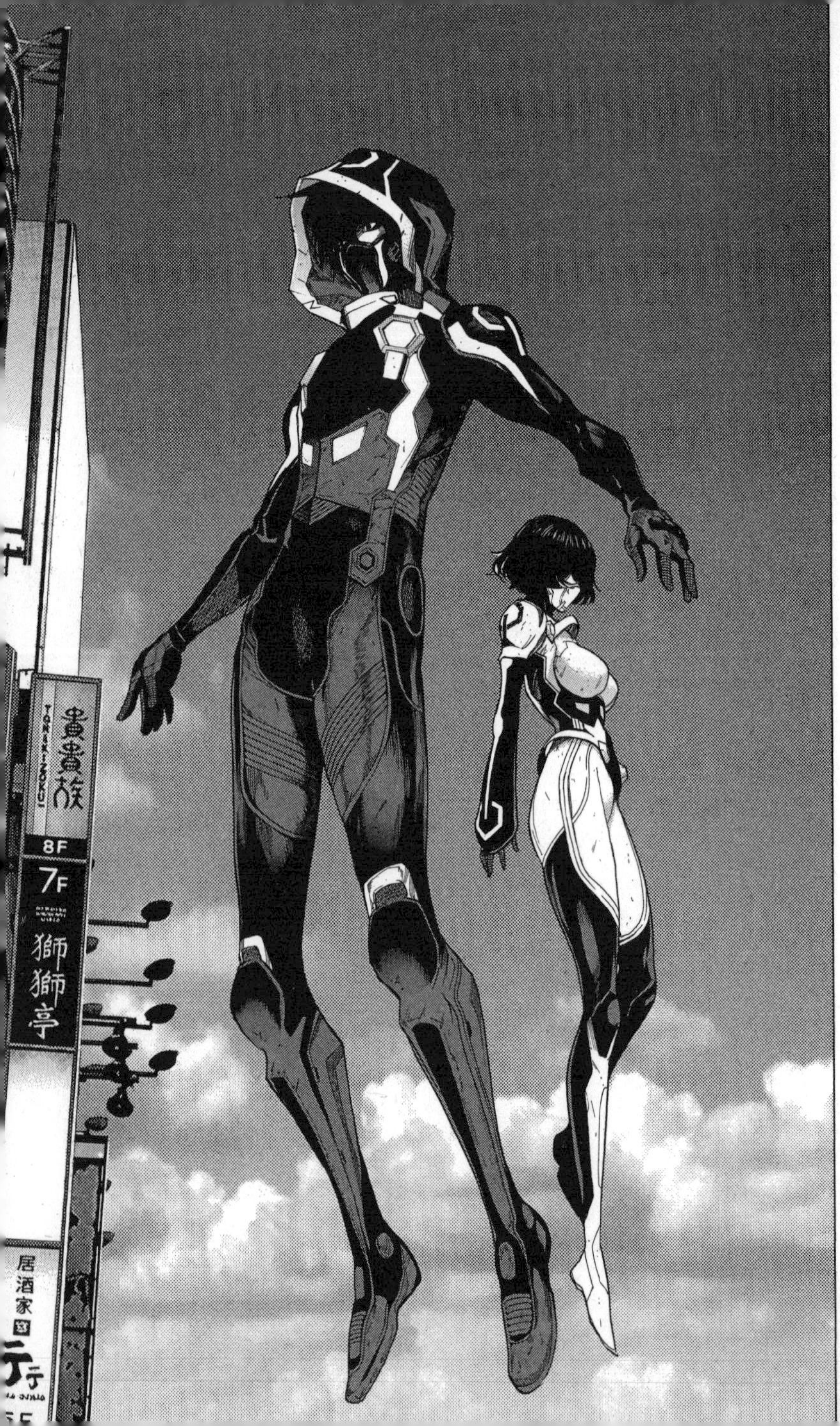

貴貴族
8F
7F
獅獅亭
居酒家

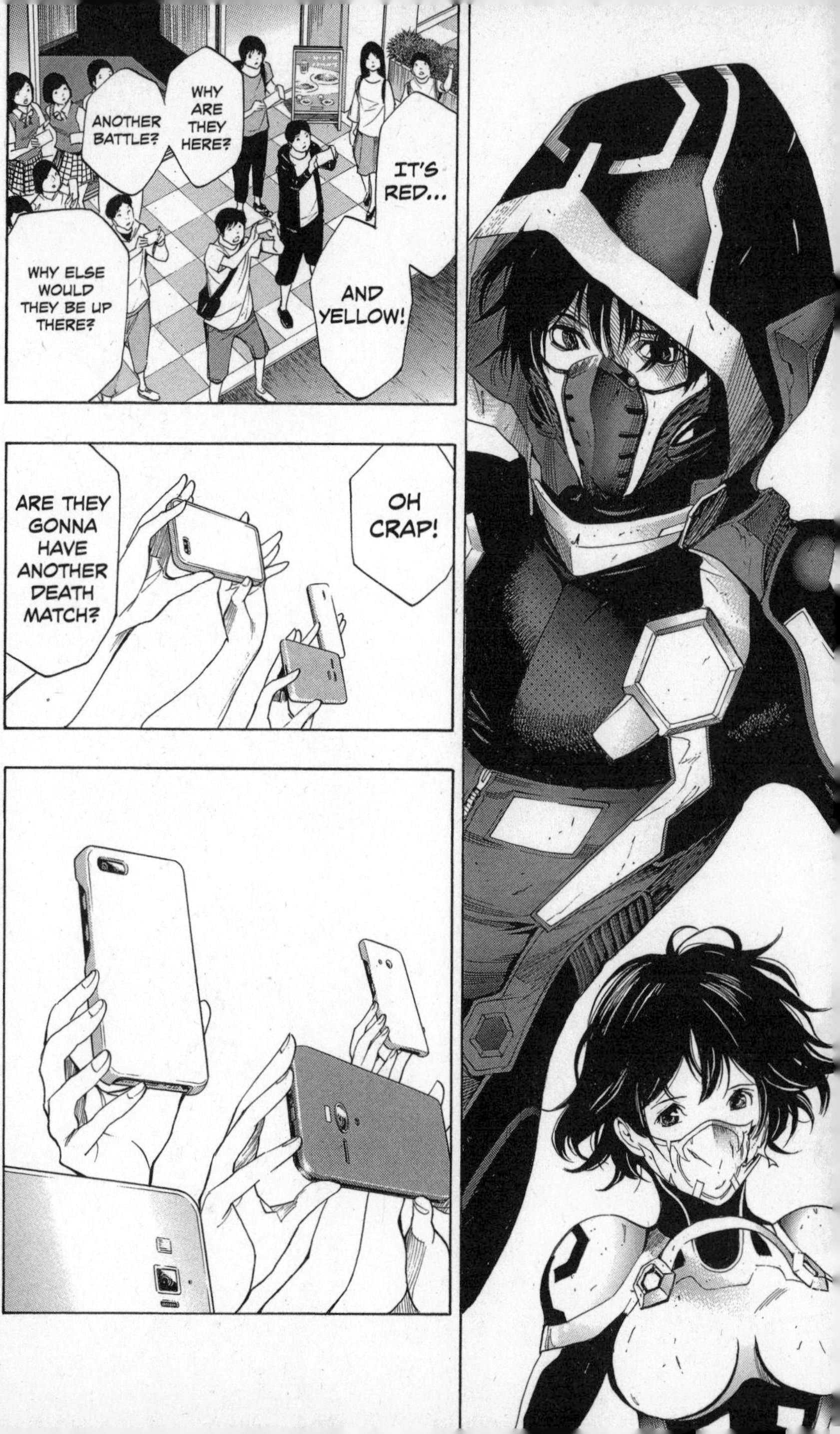
IT'S RED...
AND YELLOW!
WHY ARE THEY HERE?
ANOTHER BATTLE?
WHY ELSE WOULD THEY BE UP THERE?
OH CRAP!
ARE THEY GONNA HAVE ANOTHER DEATH MATCH?

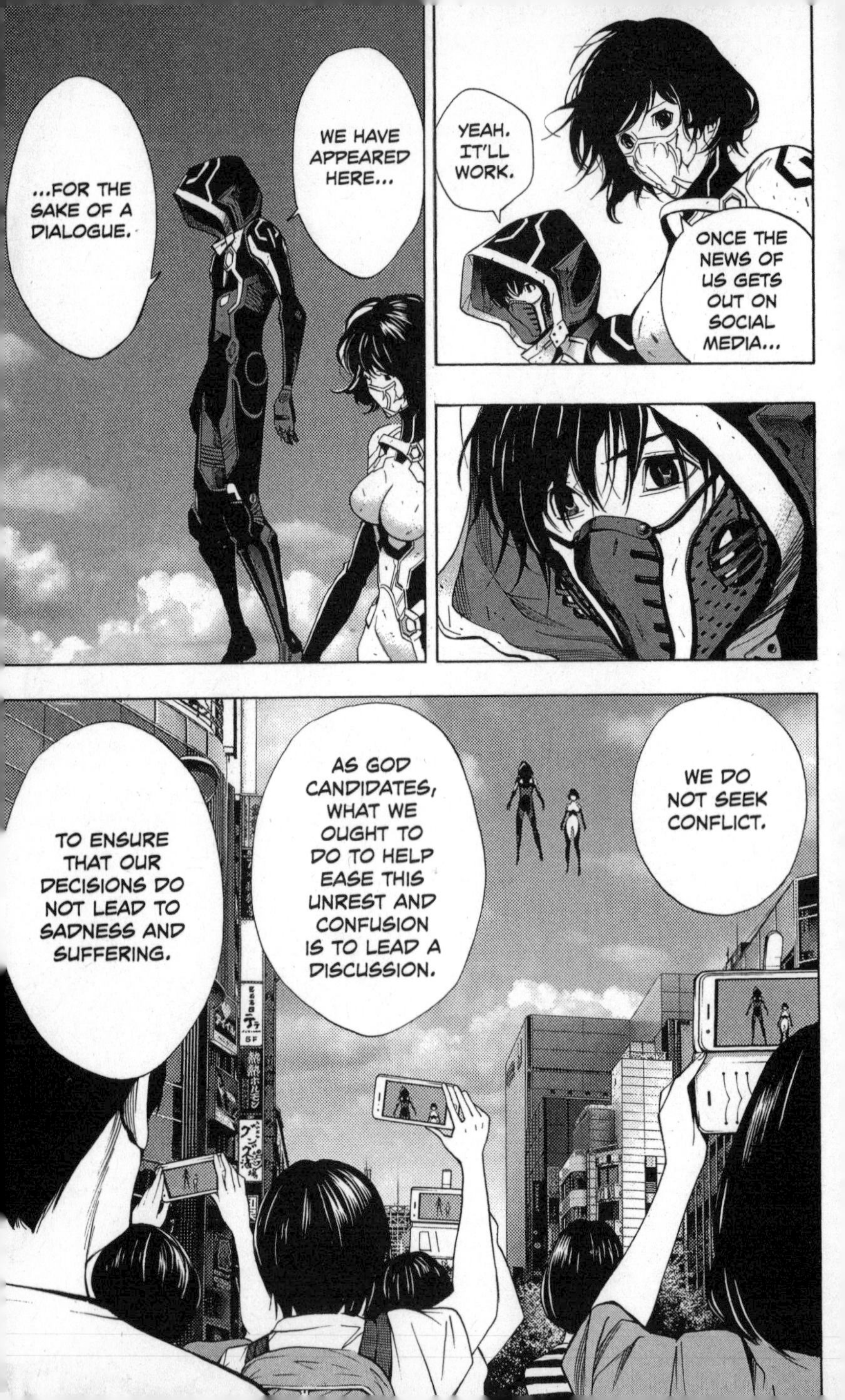
YEAH. IT'LL WORK.
ONCE THE NEWS OF US GETS OUT ON SOCIAL MEDIA...
WE HAVE APPEARED HERE...
...FOR THE SAKE OF A DIALOGUE.
WE DO NOT SEEK CONFLICT.
AS GOD CANDIDATES, WHAT WE OUGHT TO DO TO HELP EASE THIS UNREST AND CONFUSION IS TO LEAD A DISCUSSION.
TO ENSURE THAT OUR DECISIONS DO NOT LEAD TO SADNESS AND SUFFERING.

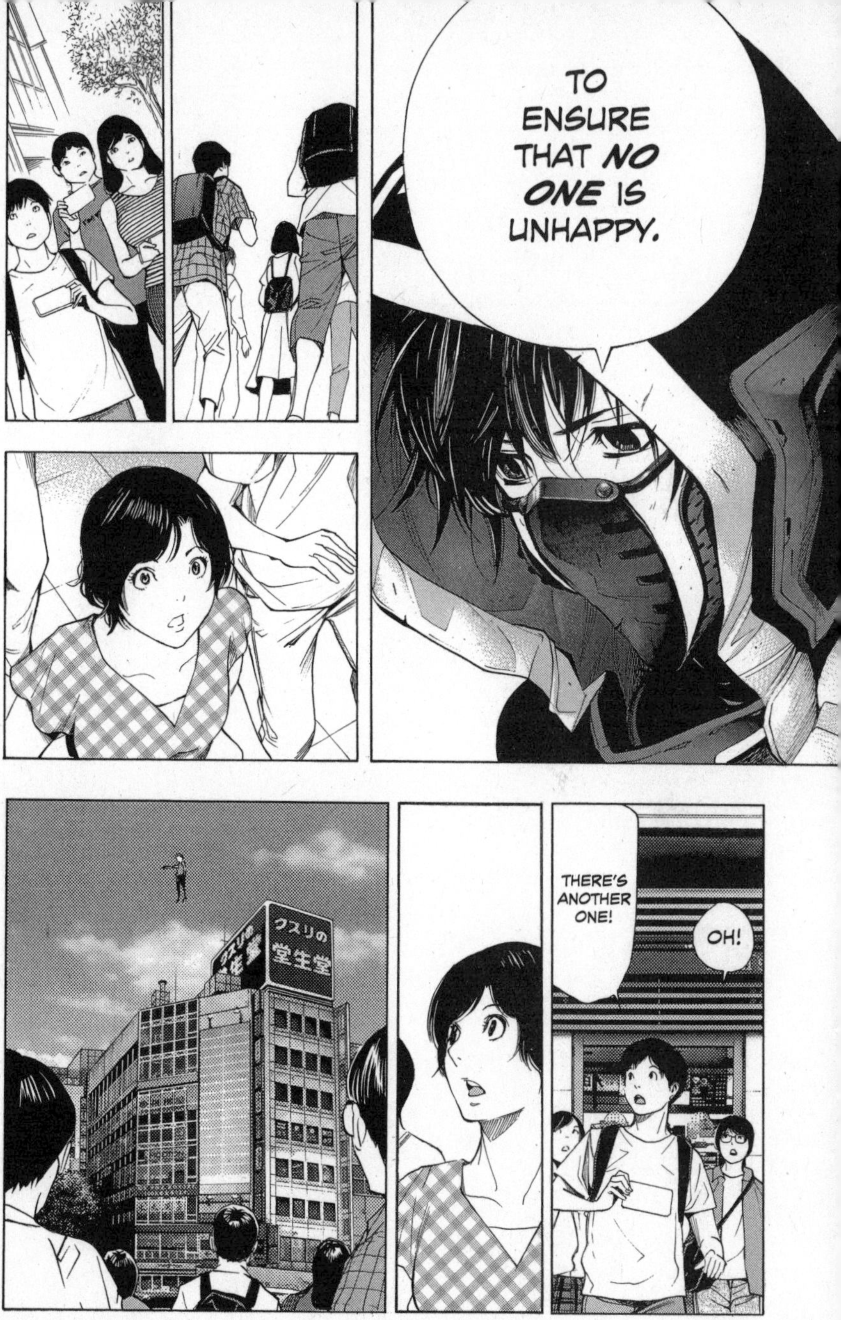
TO ENSURE THAT ***NO ONE*** IS UNHAPPY.
OH!
THERE'S ANOTHER ONE!
クスリの
堂生堂

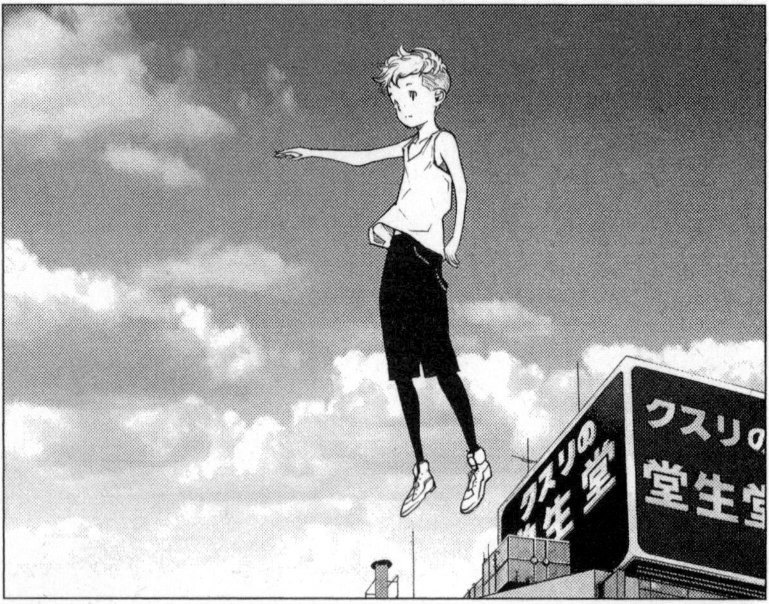
クスリの
堂生堂
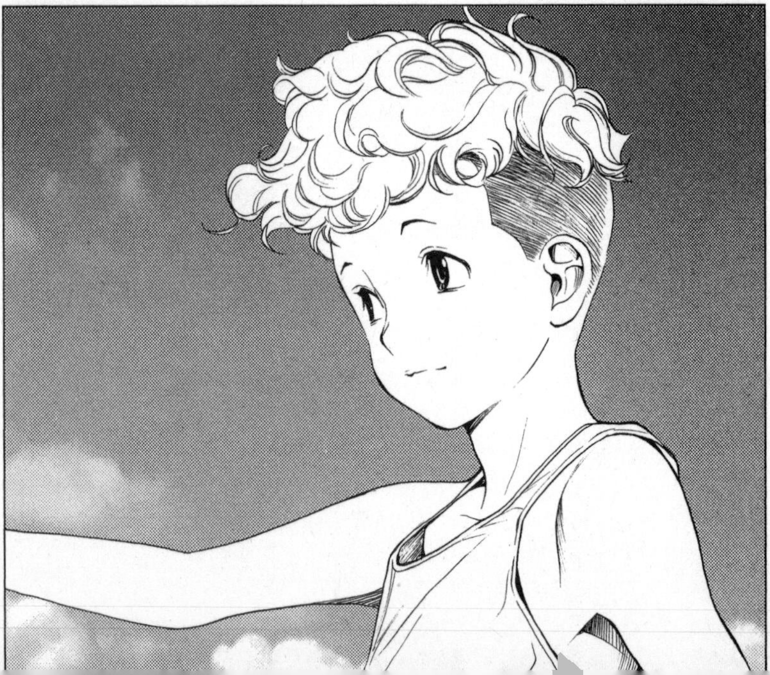

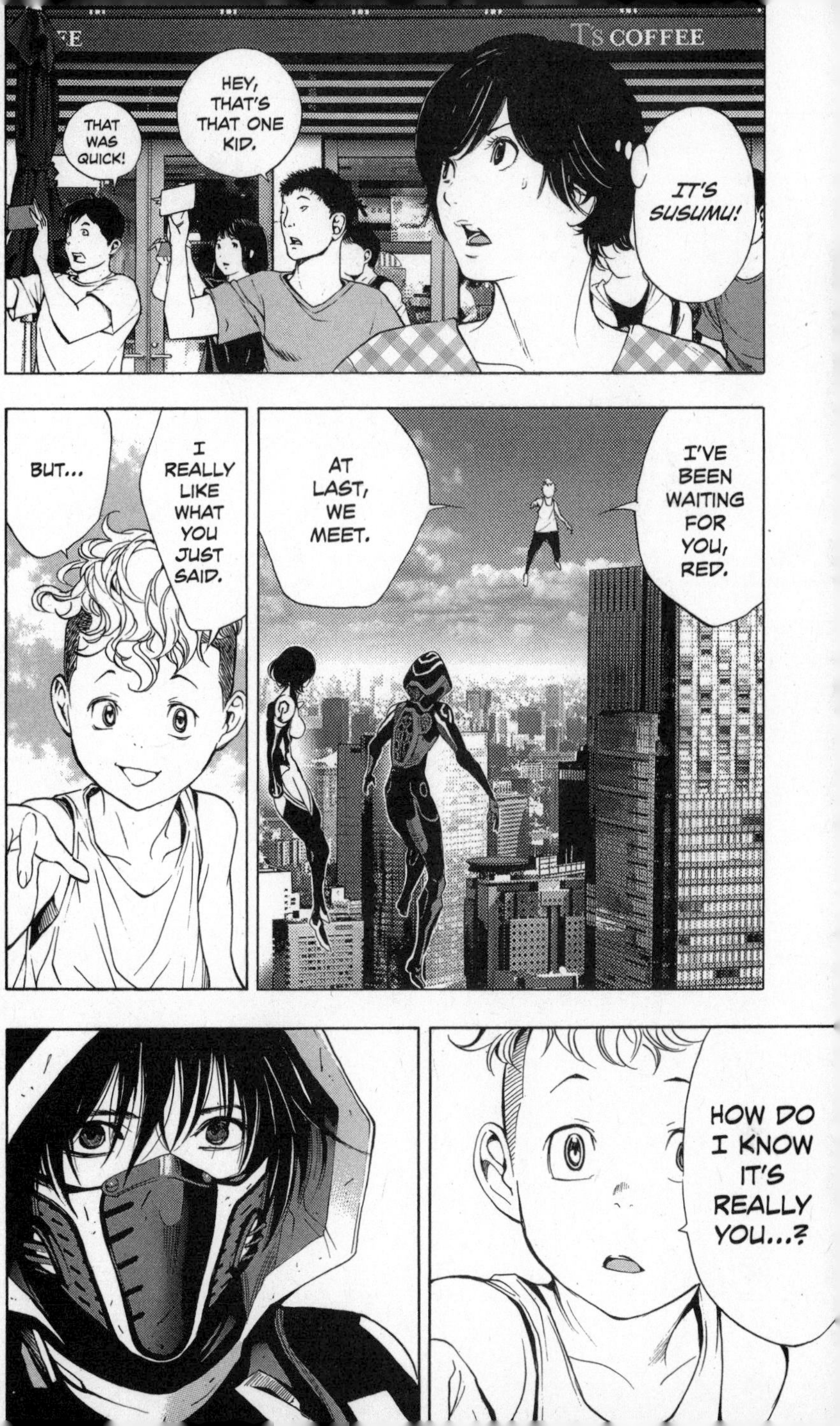
T'S COFFEE
IT'S SUSUMU!
HEY, THAT'S THAT ONE KID.
THAT WAS QUICK!
I'VE BEEN WAITING FOR YOU, RED.
AT LAST, WE MEET.
I REALLY LIKE WHAT YOU JUST SAID.
BUT...
HOW DO I KNOW IT'S REALLY YOU...?

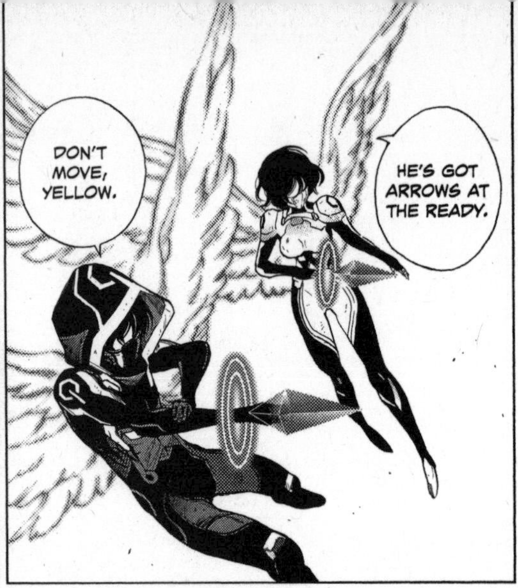
HE'S GOT ARROWS AT THE READY.
DON'T MOVE, YELLOW.
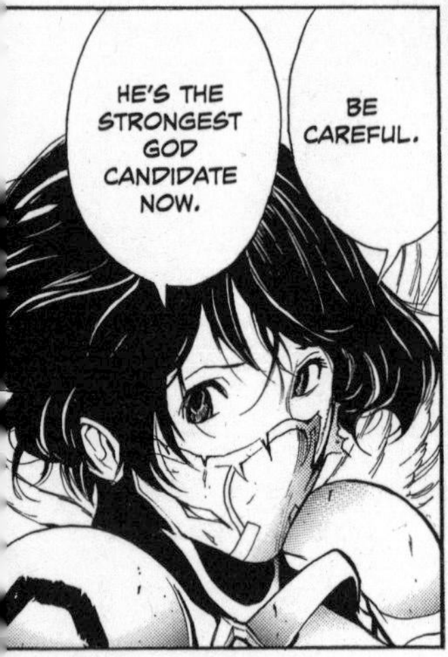
BE CAREFUL.
HE'S THE STRONGEST GOD CANDIDATE NOW.
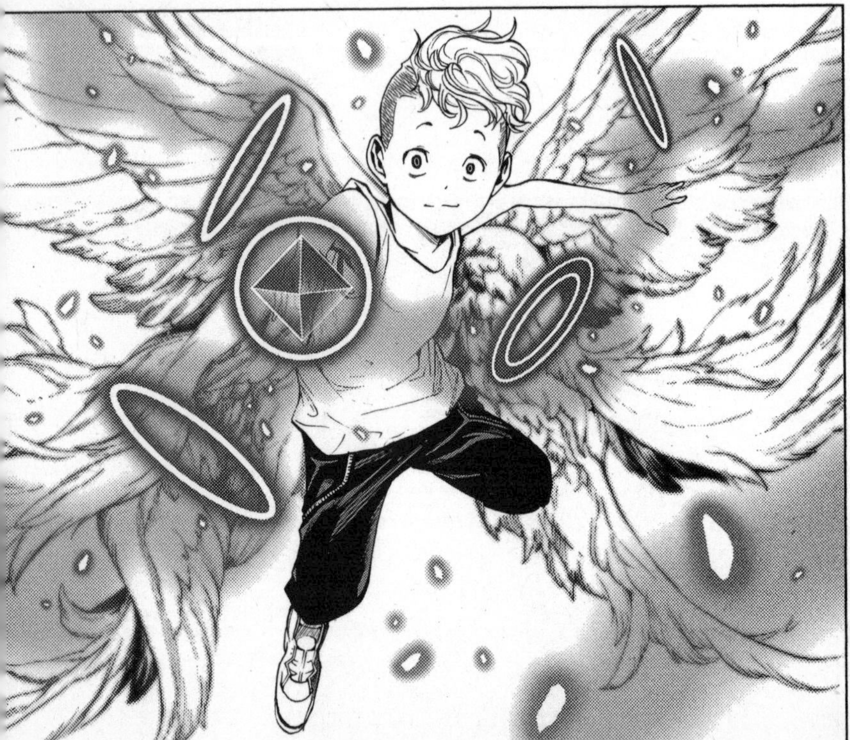

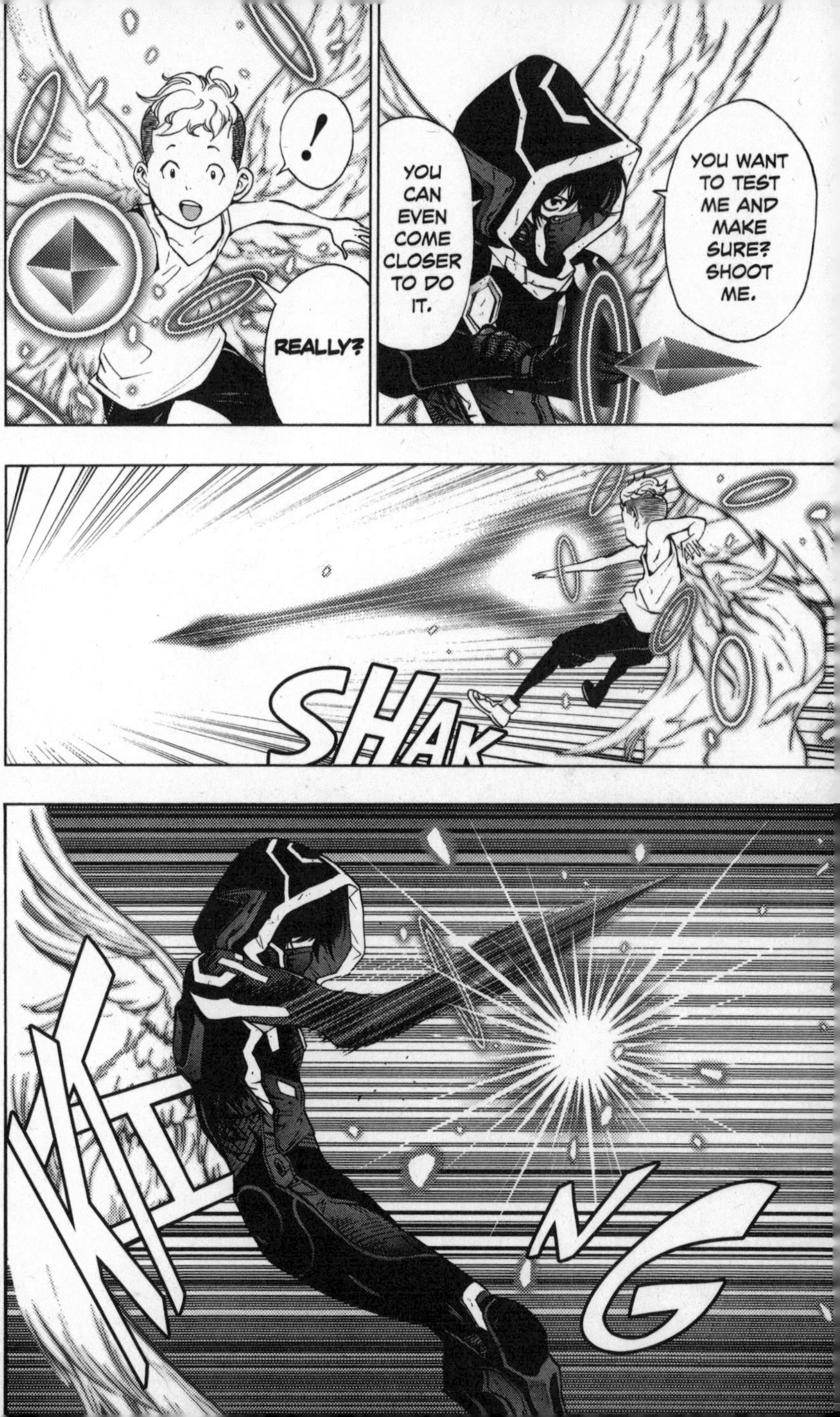
YOU WANT TO TEST ME AND MAKE SURE? SHOOT ME.
YOU CAN EVEN COME CLOSER TO DO IT.
!
REALLY?
SHAK
KING

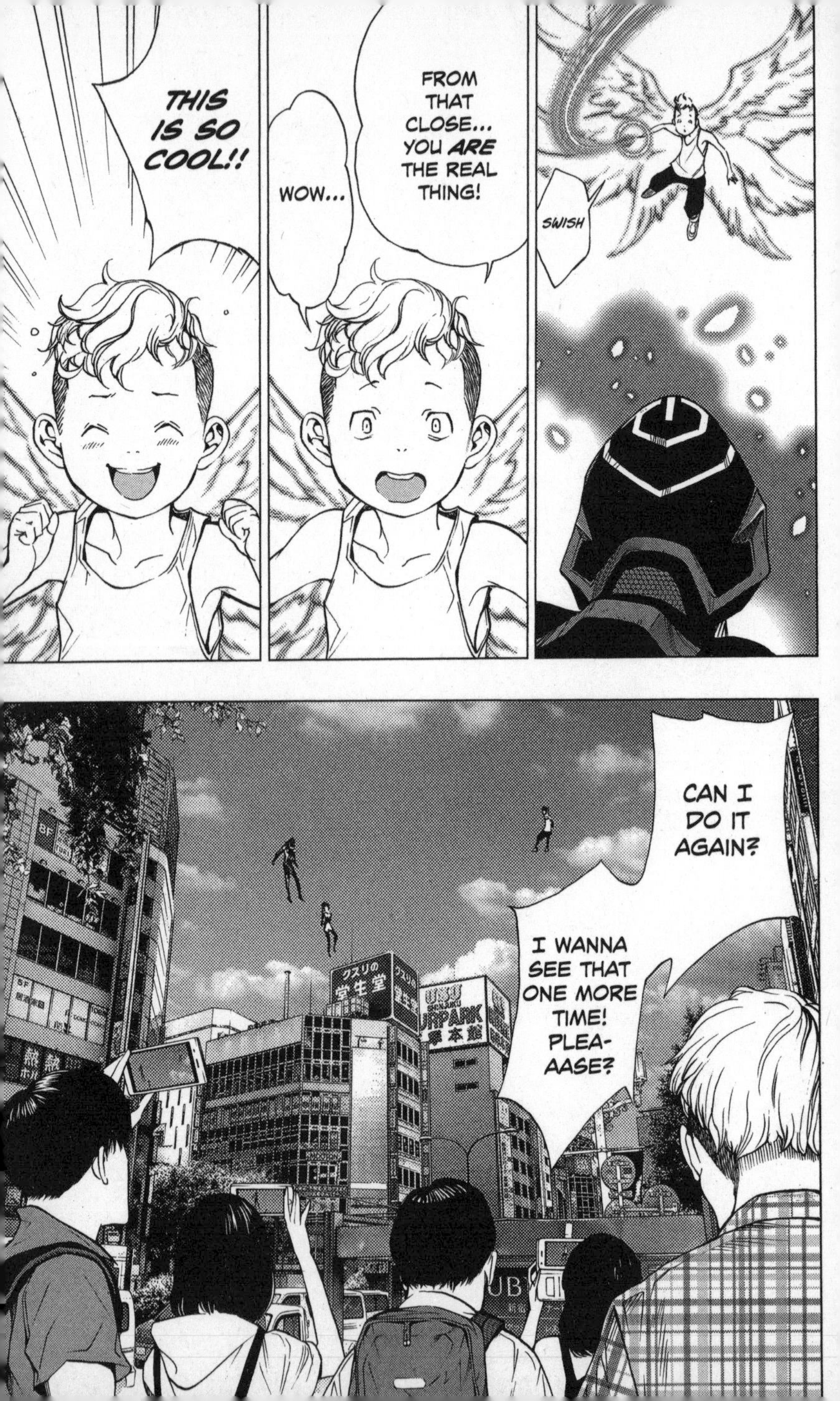
SWISH
FROM THAT CLOSE... YOU ARE THE REAL THING!
WOW...
THIS IS SO COOL!!
CAN I DO IT AGAIN?
I WANNA SEE THAT ONE MORE TIME! PLEA-AASE?

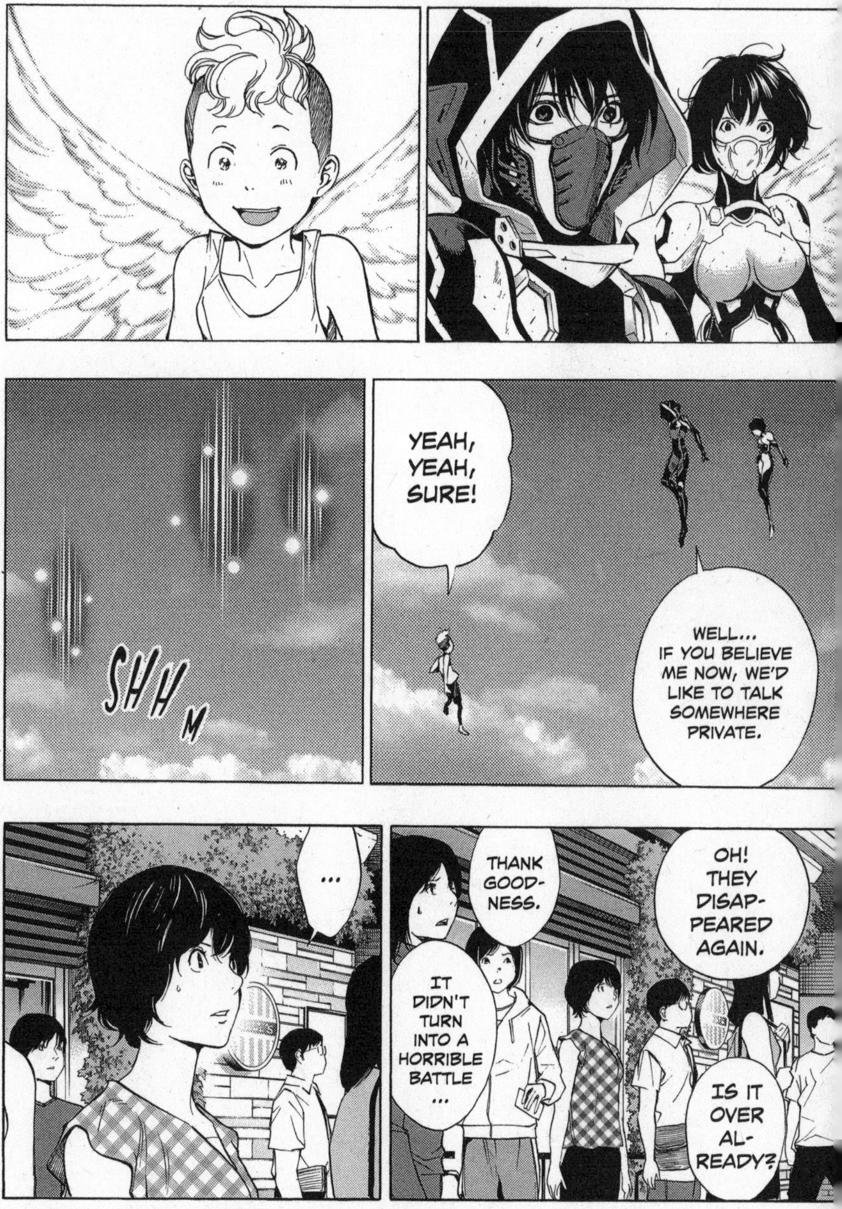
WELL... IF YOU BELIEVE ME NOW, WE'D LIKE TO TALK SOMEWHERE PRIVATE.
YEAH, YEAH, SURE!
SHHM
OH! THEY DISAP-PEARED AGAIN.
THANK GOOD-NESS.
IT DIDN'T TURN INTO A HORRIBLE BATTLE ...
IS IT OVER AL-READY?
...

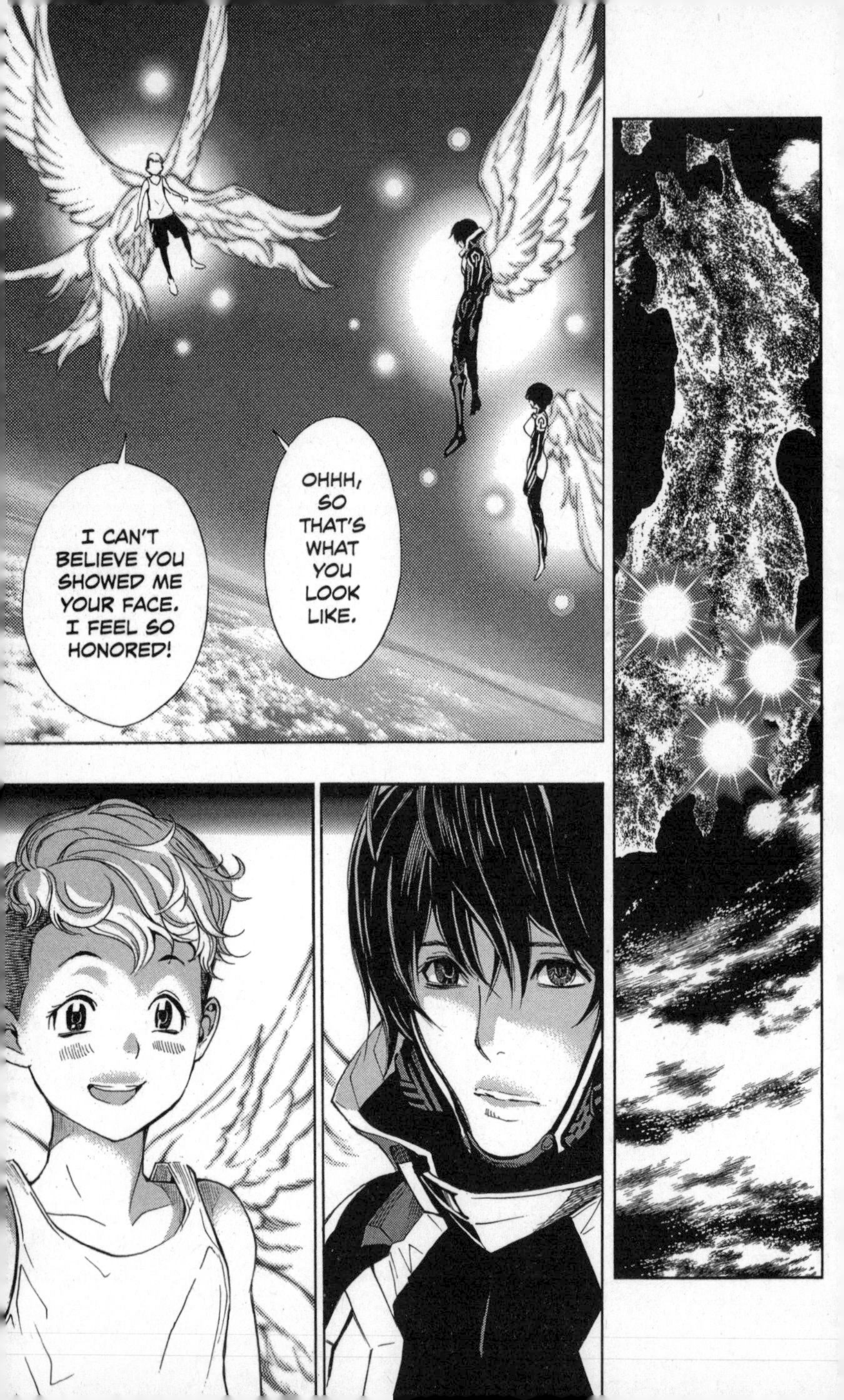
OHHH, SO THAT'S WHAT YOU LOOK LIKE.
I CAN'T BELIEVE YOU SHOWED ME YOUR FACE. I FEEL SO HONORED!

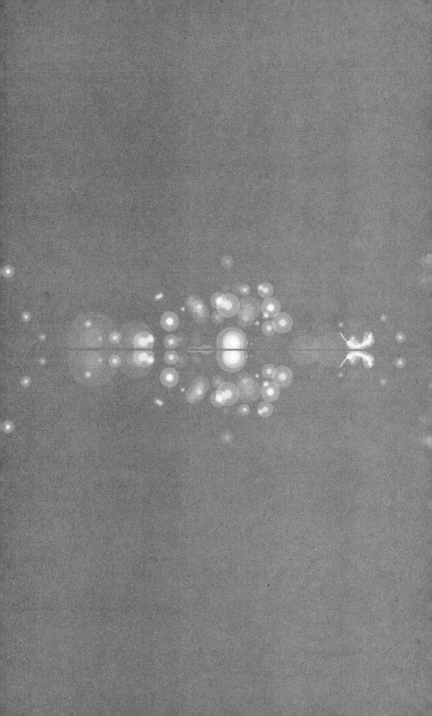

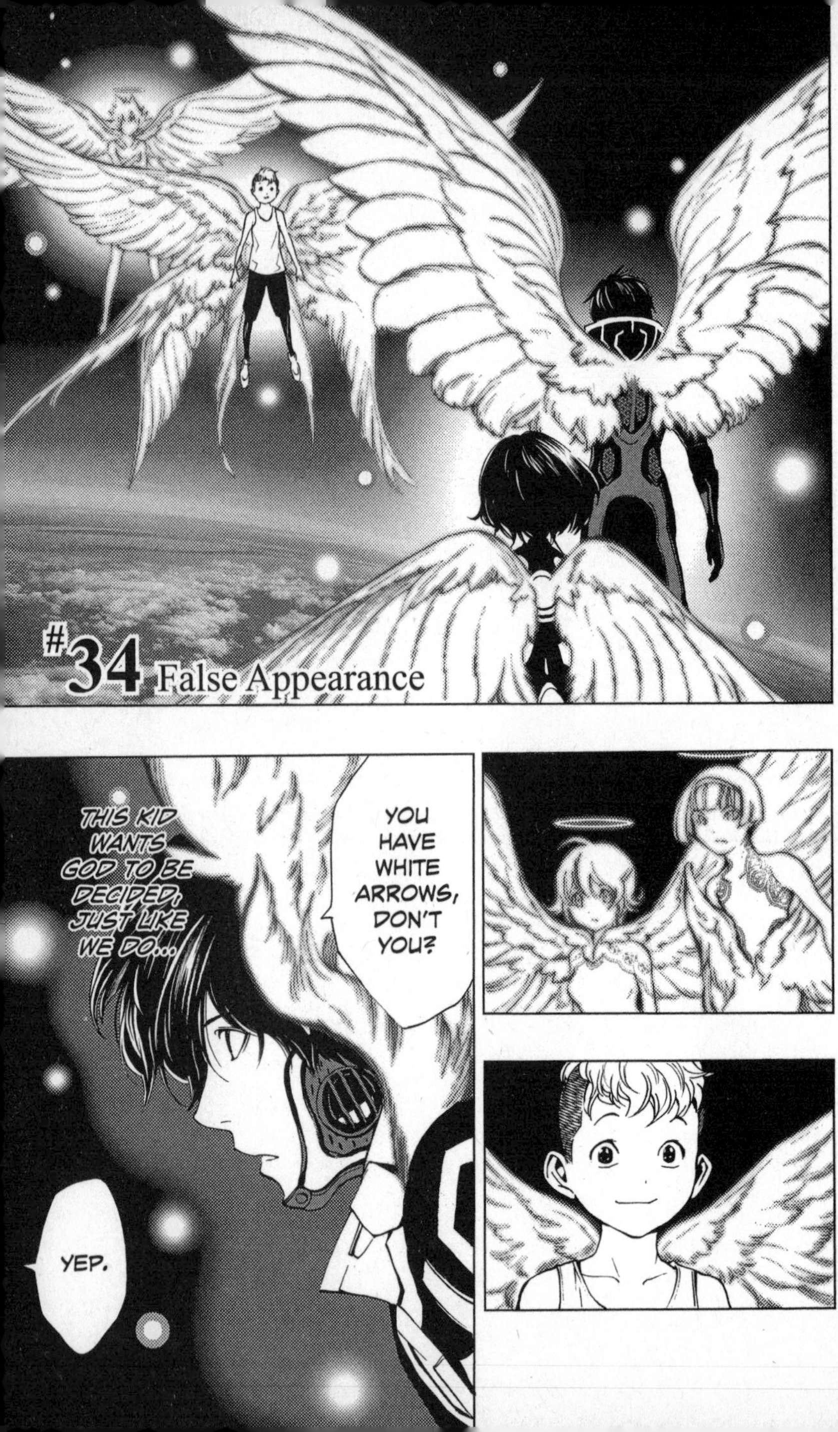
#34 False Appearance
YOU HAVE WHITE ARROWS, DON'T YOU?
THIS KID WANTS GOD TO BE DECIDED, JUST LIKE WE DO...
YEP.

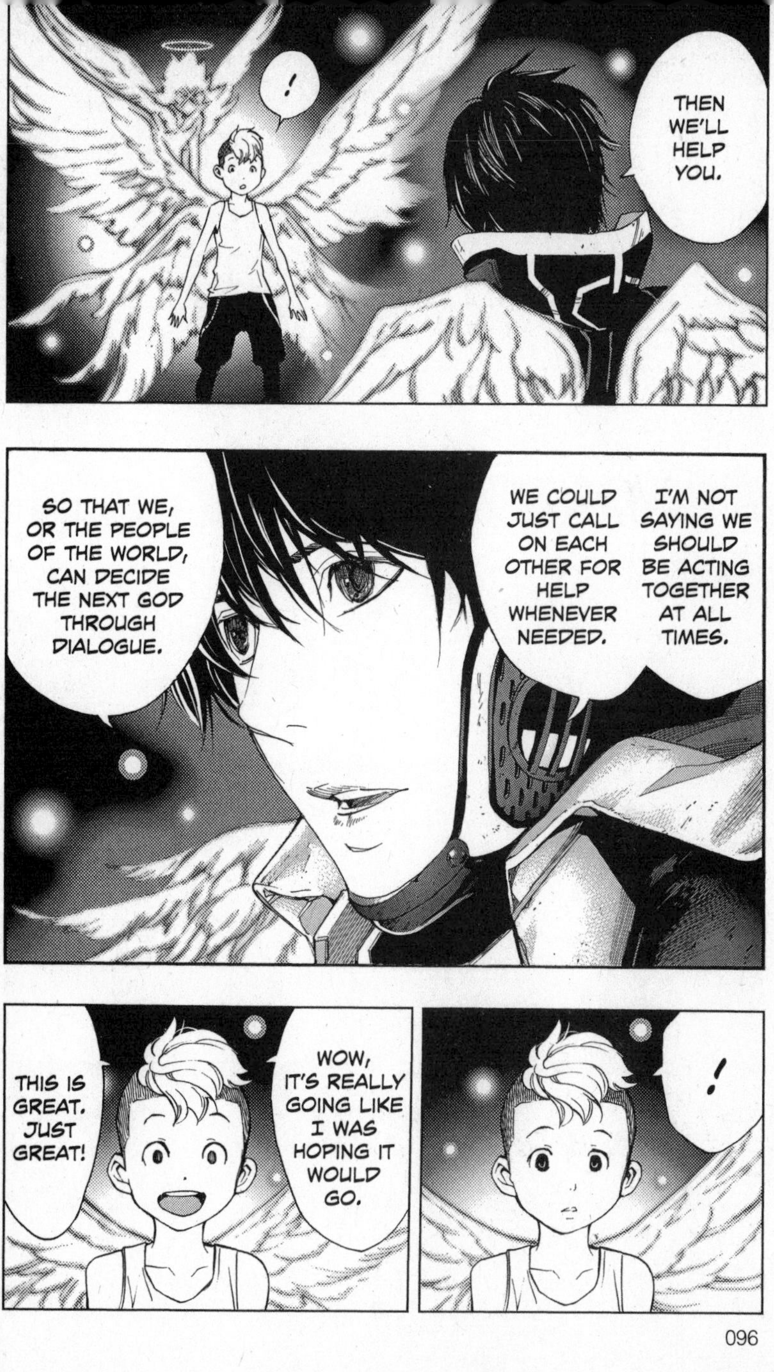
THEN WE'LL HELP YOU.
!
I'M NOT SAYING WE SHOULD BE ACTING TOGETHER AT ALL TIMES.
WE COULD JUST CALL ON EACH OTHER FOR HELP WHENEVER NEEDED.
SO THAT WE, OR THE PEOPLE OF THE WORLD, CAN DECIDE THE NEXT GOD THROUGH DIALOGUE.
!
WOW, IT'S REALLY GOING LIKE I WAS HOPING IT WOULD GO.
THIS IS GREAT. JUST GREAT!

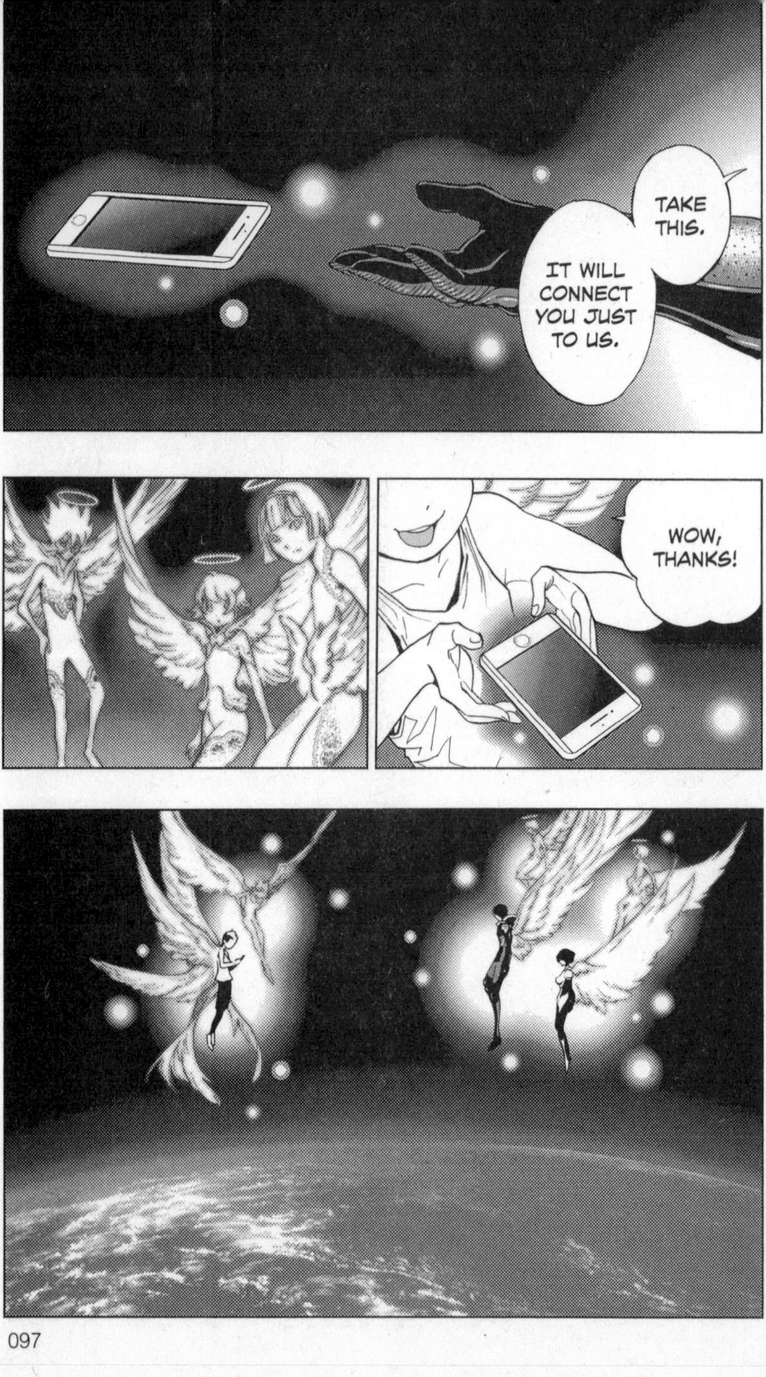
TAKE THIS.
IT WILL CONNECT YOU JUST TO US.
WOW, THANKS!

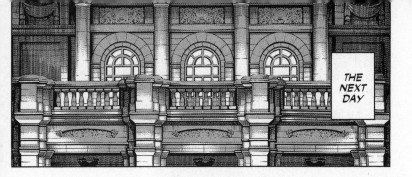

THE NEXT DAY

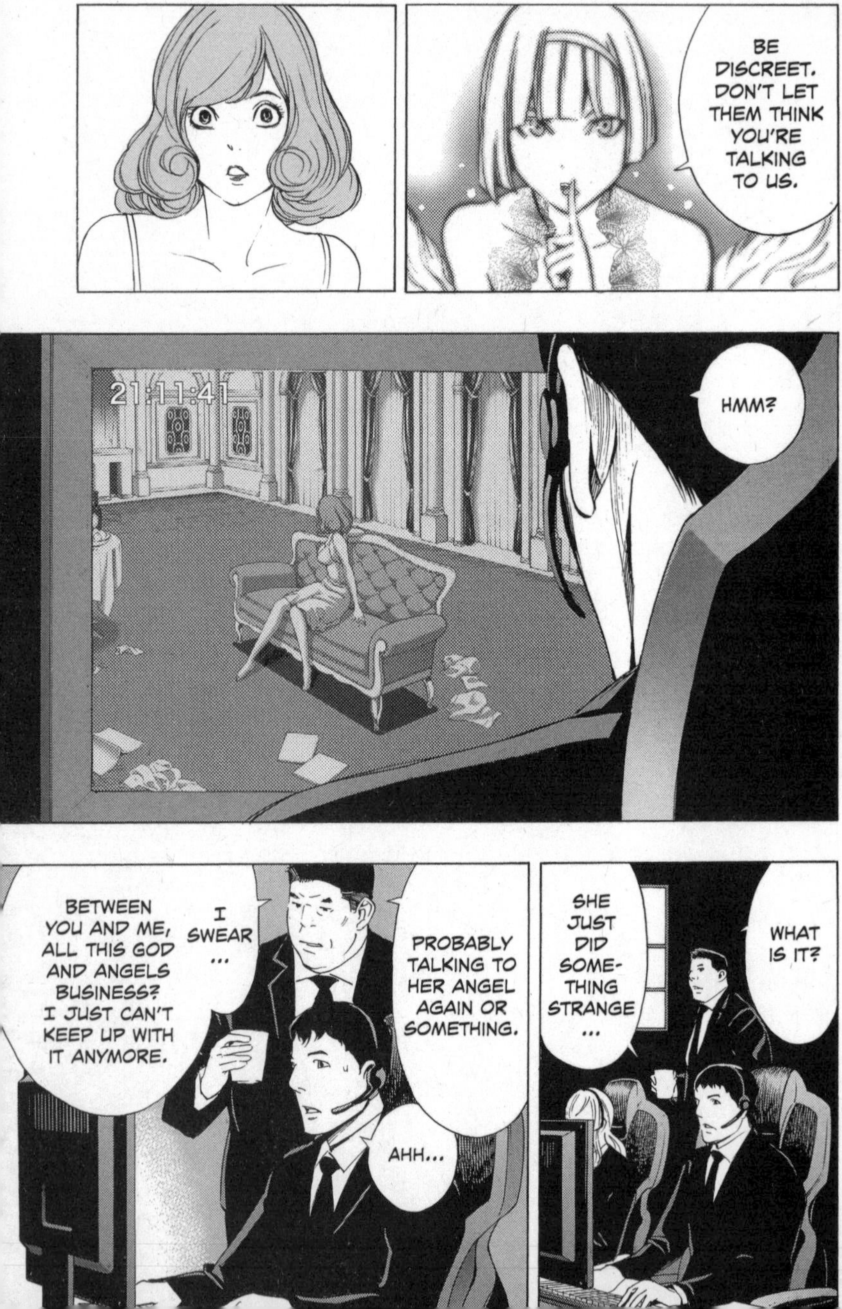
BE DISCREET. DON'T LET THEM THINK YOU'RE TALKING TO US.
21:11:41
HMM?
WHAT IS IT?
SHE JUST DID SOMETHING STRANGE...
PROBABLY TALKING TO HER ANGEL AGAIN OR SOMETHING.
AHH...
I SWEAR...
BETWEEN YOU AND ME, ALL THIS GOD AND ANGELS BUSINESS? I JUST CAN'T KEEP UP WITH IT ANYMORE.

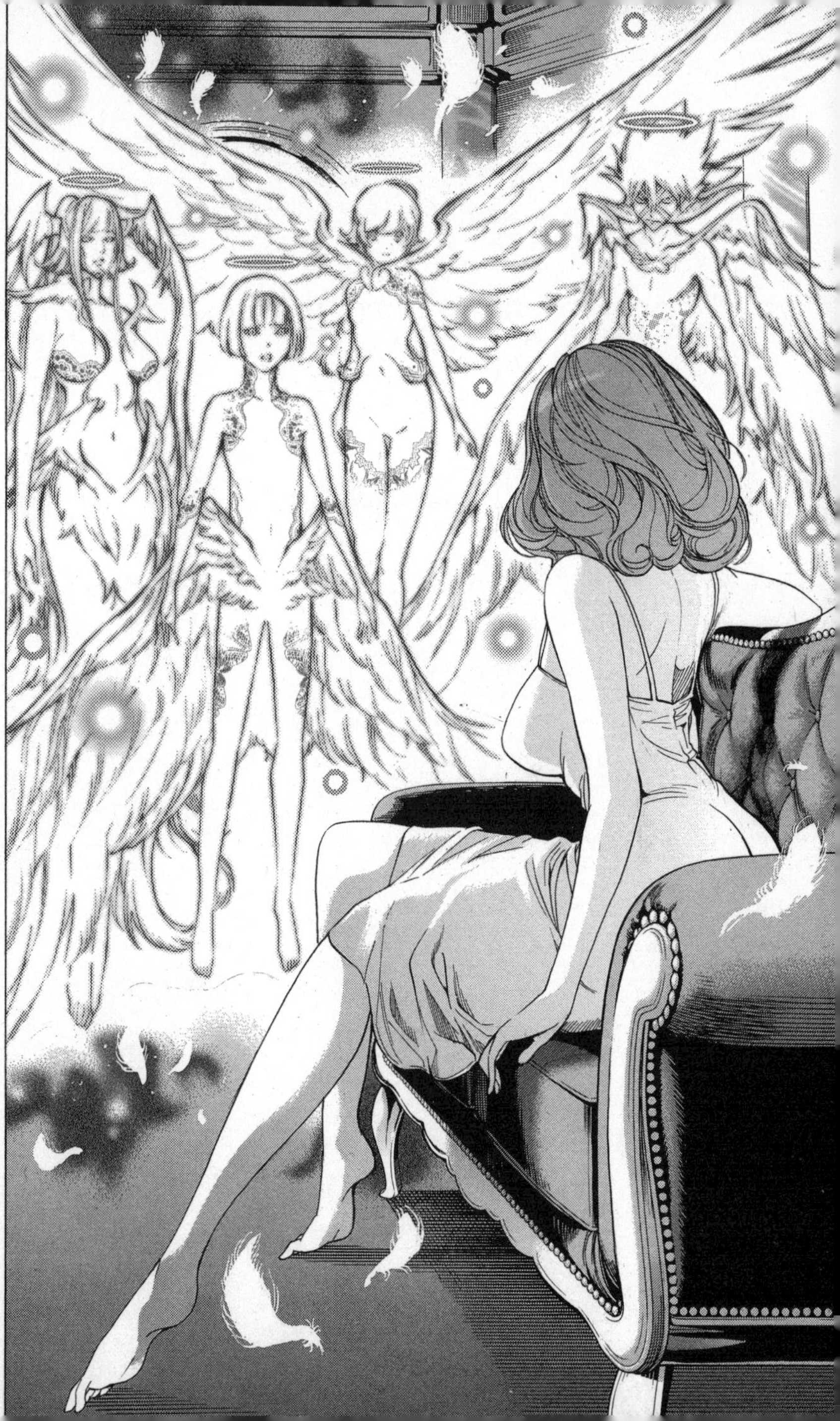

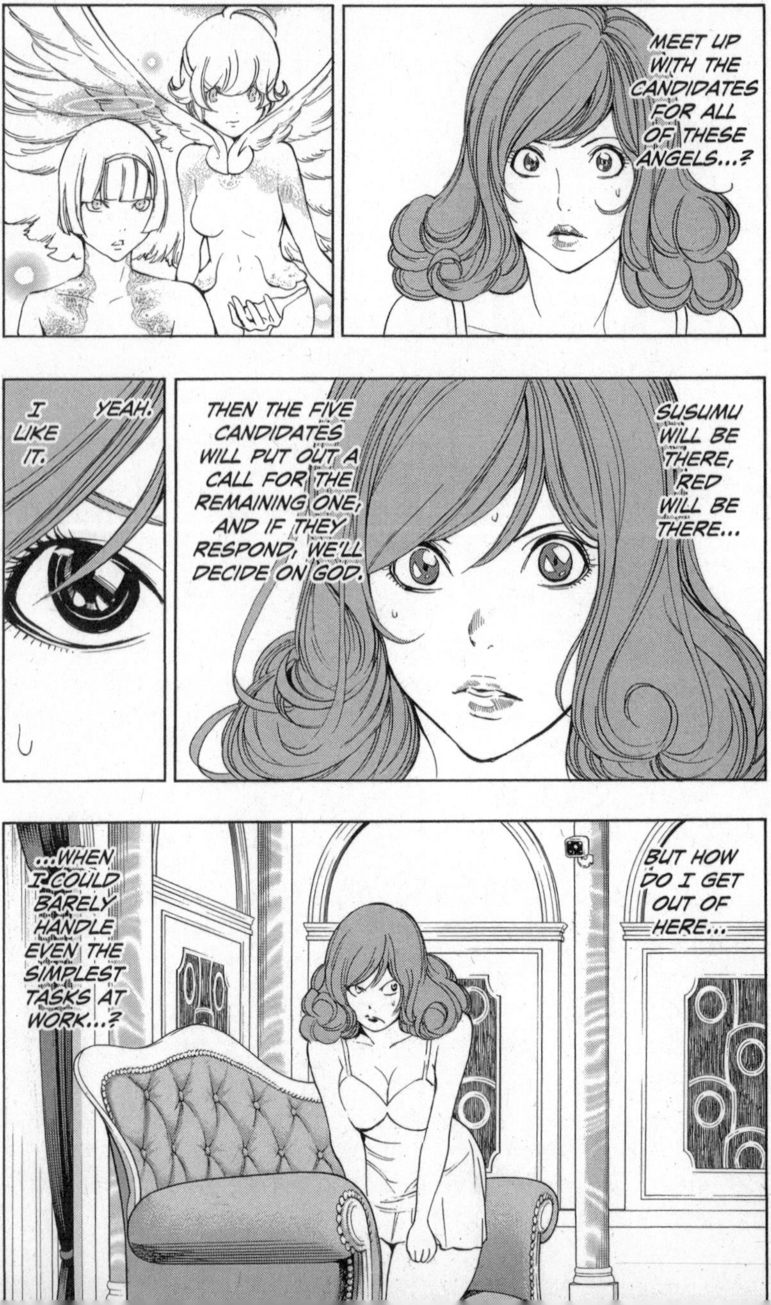
MEET UP WITH THE CANDIDATES FOR ALL OF THESE ANGELS...?
SUSUMU WILL BE THERE, RED WILL BE THERE...
THEN THE FIVE CANDIDATES WILL PUT OUT A CALL FOR THE REMAINING ONE, AND IF THEY RESPOND, WE'LL DECIDE ON GOD.
YEAH.
I LIKE IT.
BUT HOW DO I GET OUT OF HERE...
...WHEN I COULD BARELY HANDLE EVEN THE SIMPLEST TASKS AT WORK...?

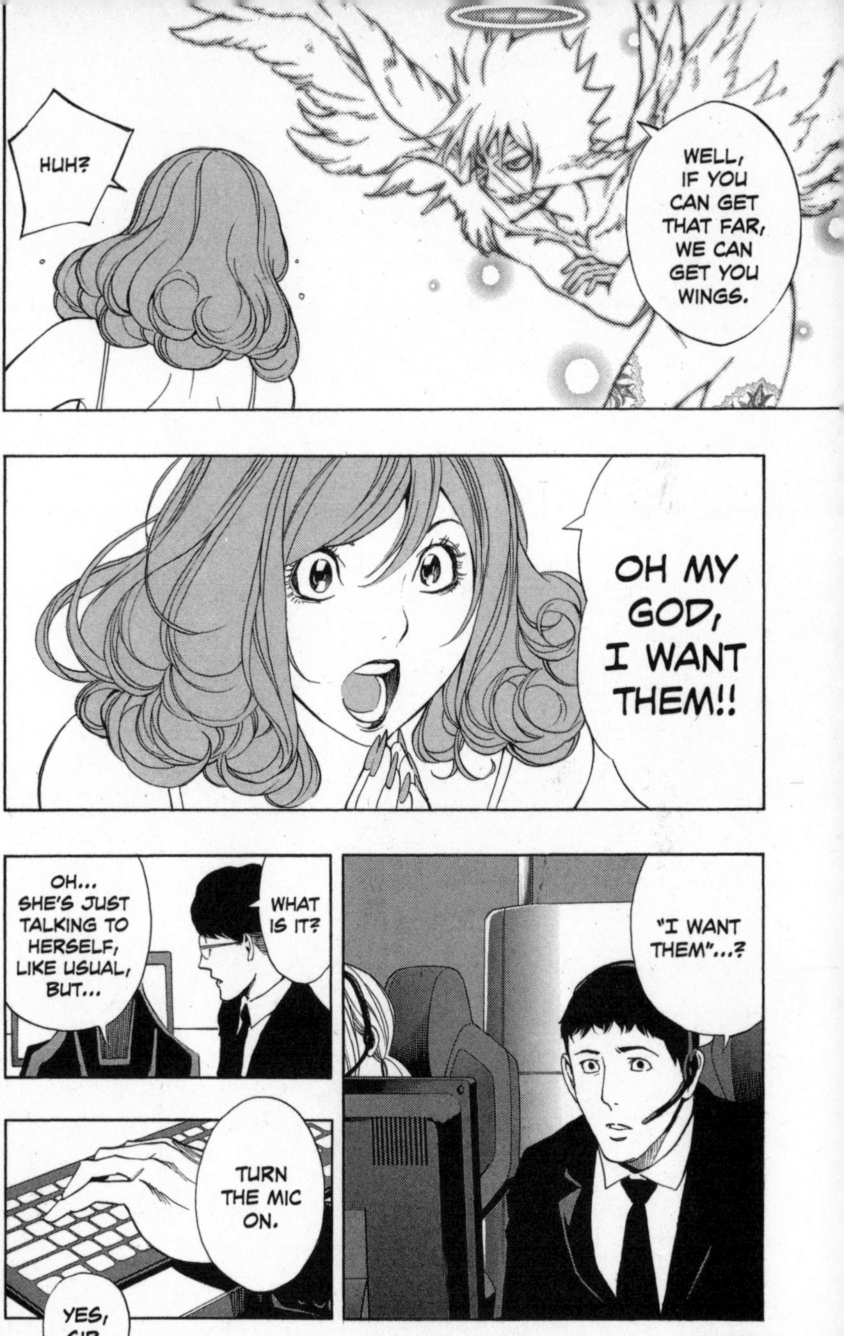
WELL, IF YOU CAN GET THAT FAR, WE CAN GET YOU WINGS.
HUH?
OH MY GOD, I WANT THEM!!
"I WANT THEM"...?
WHAT IS IT?
OH... SHE'S JUST TALKING TO HERSELF, LIKE USUAL, BUT...
TURN THE MIC ON.
YES, SIR.

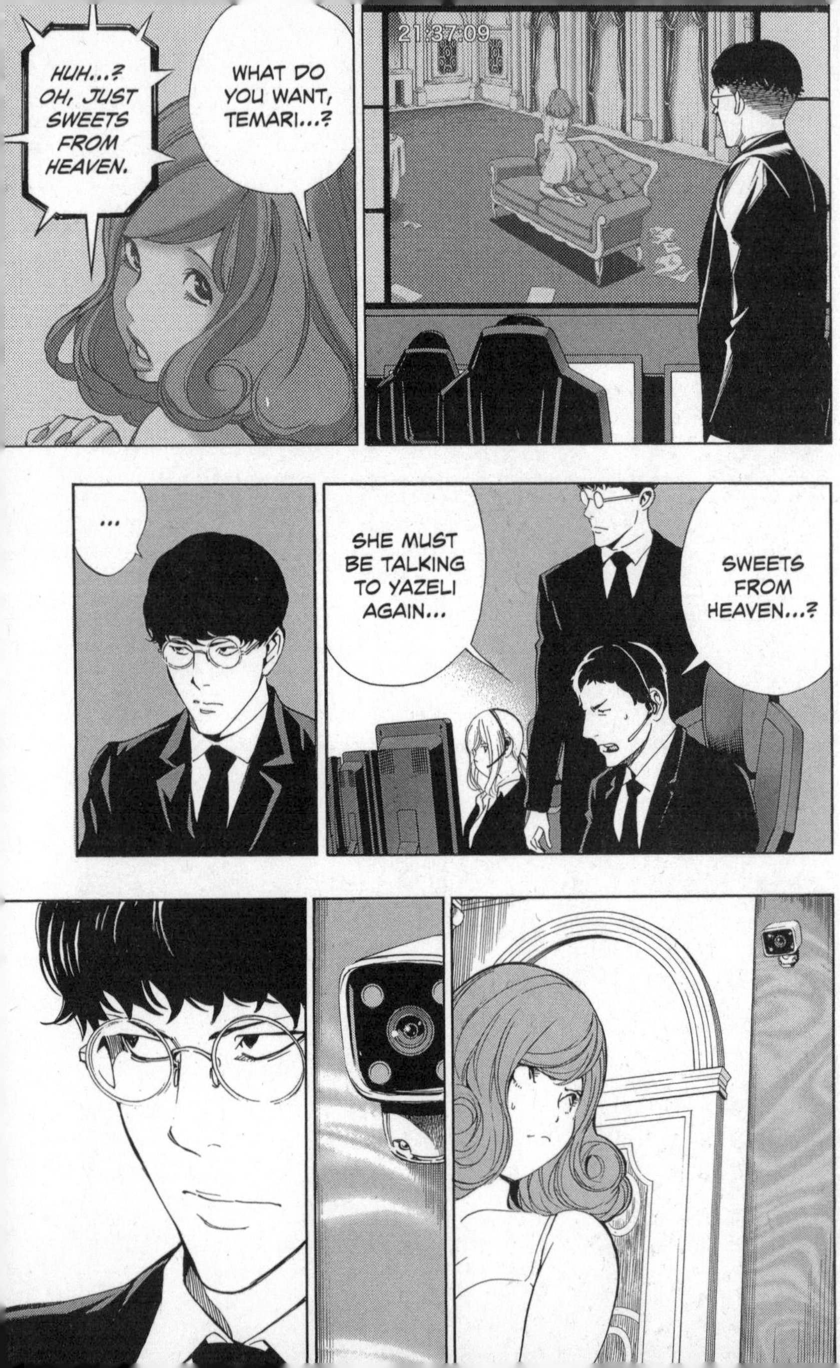
21:37:09
WHAT DO YOU WANT, TEMARI...?
HUH...? OH, JUST SWEETS FROM HEAVEN.
SWEETS FROM HEAVEN...?
SHE MUST BE TALKING TO YAZELI AGAIN...
...

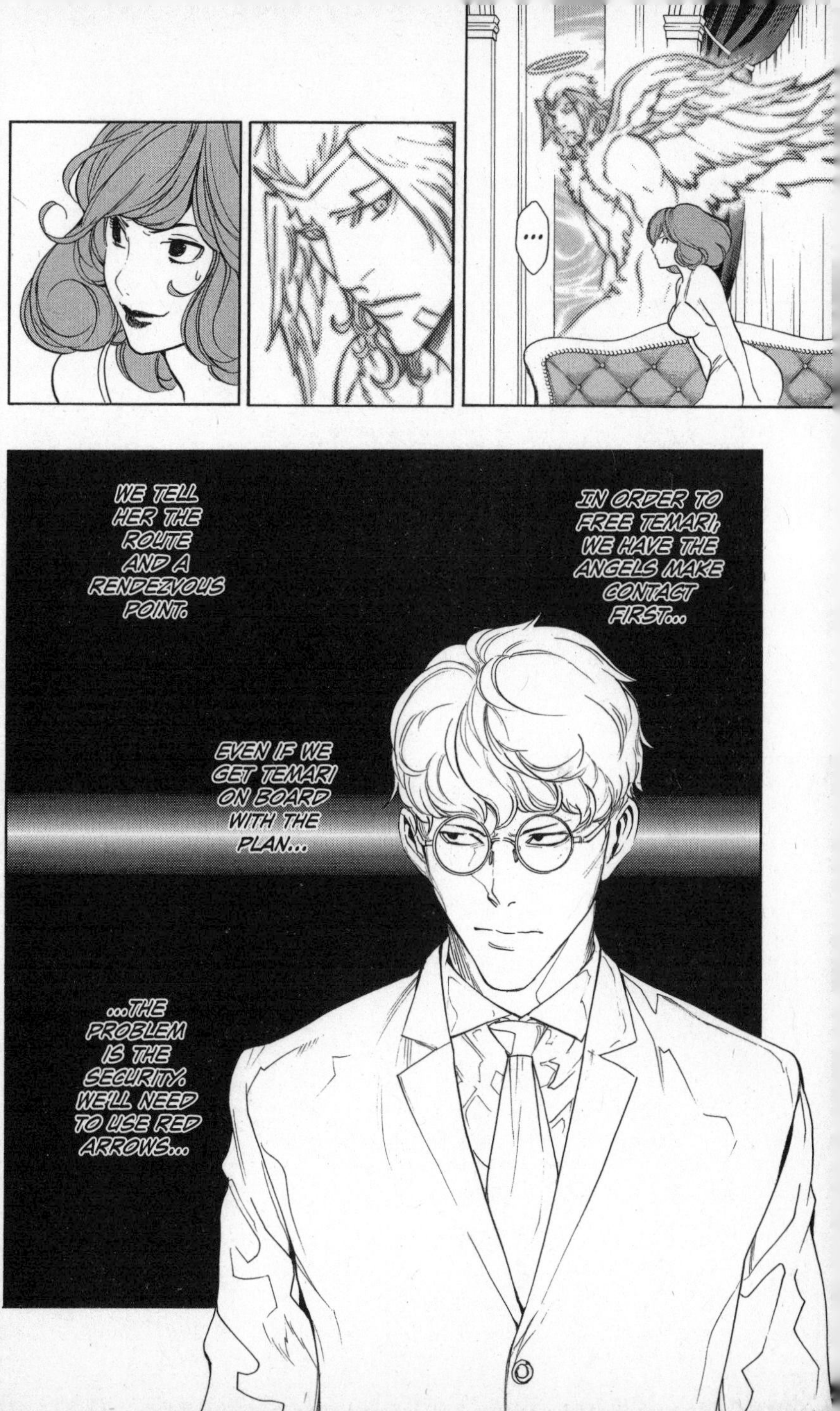
...
IN ORDER TO FREE TEMARI, WE HAVE THE ANGELS MAKE CONTACT FIRST...
WE TELL HER THE ROUTE AND A RENDEZVOUS POINT.
EVEN IF WE GET TEMARI ON BOARD WITH THE PLAN...
...THE PROBLEM IS THE SECURITY. WE'LL NEED TO USE RED ARROWS...

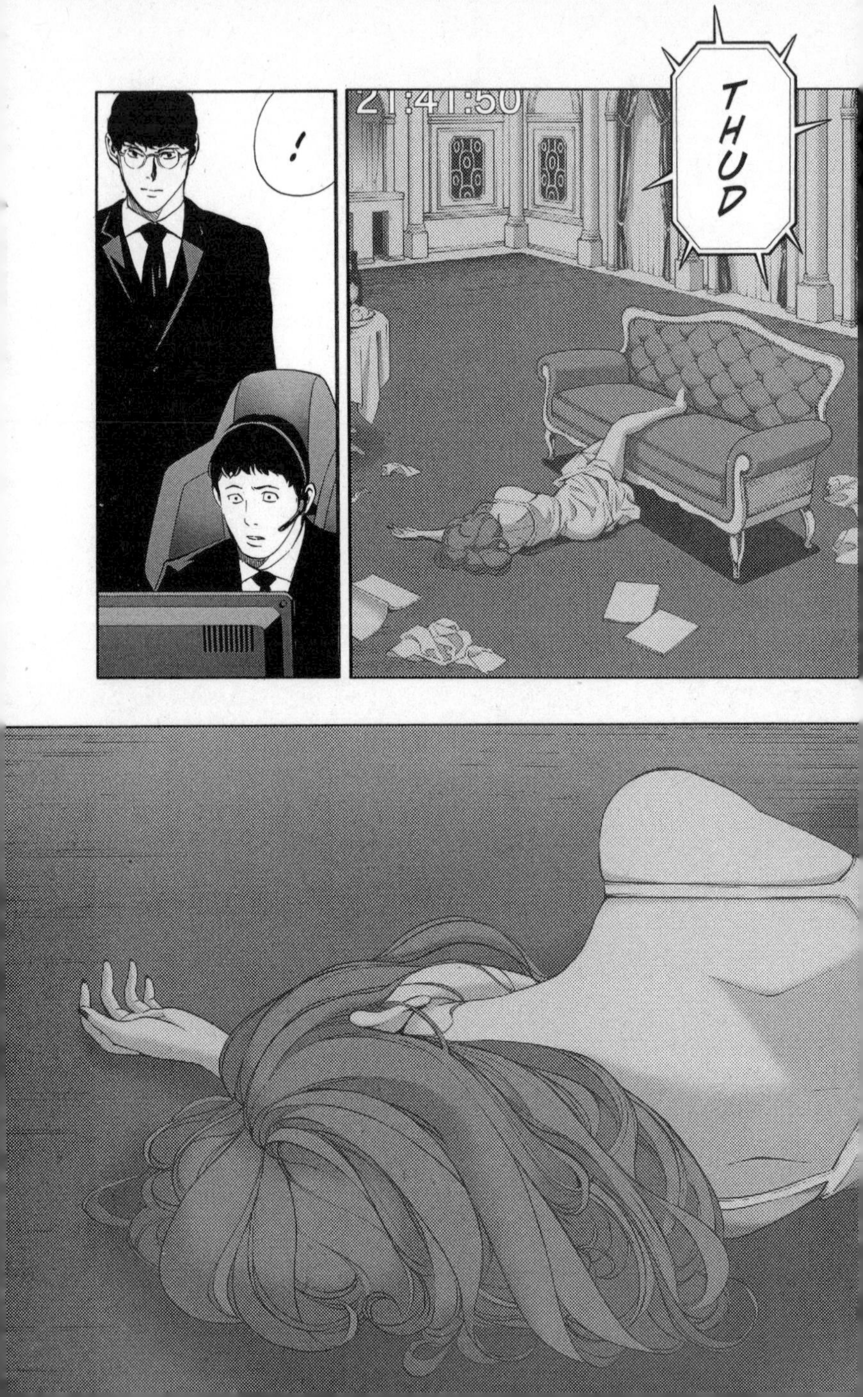
21:41:50
THUD
!

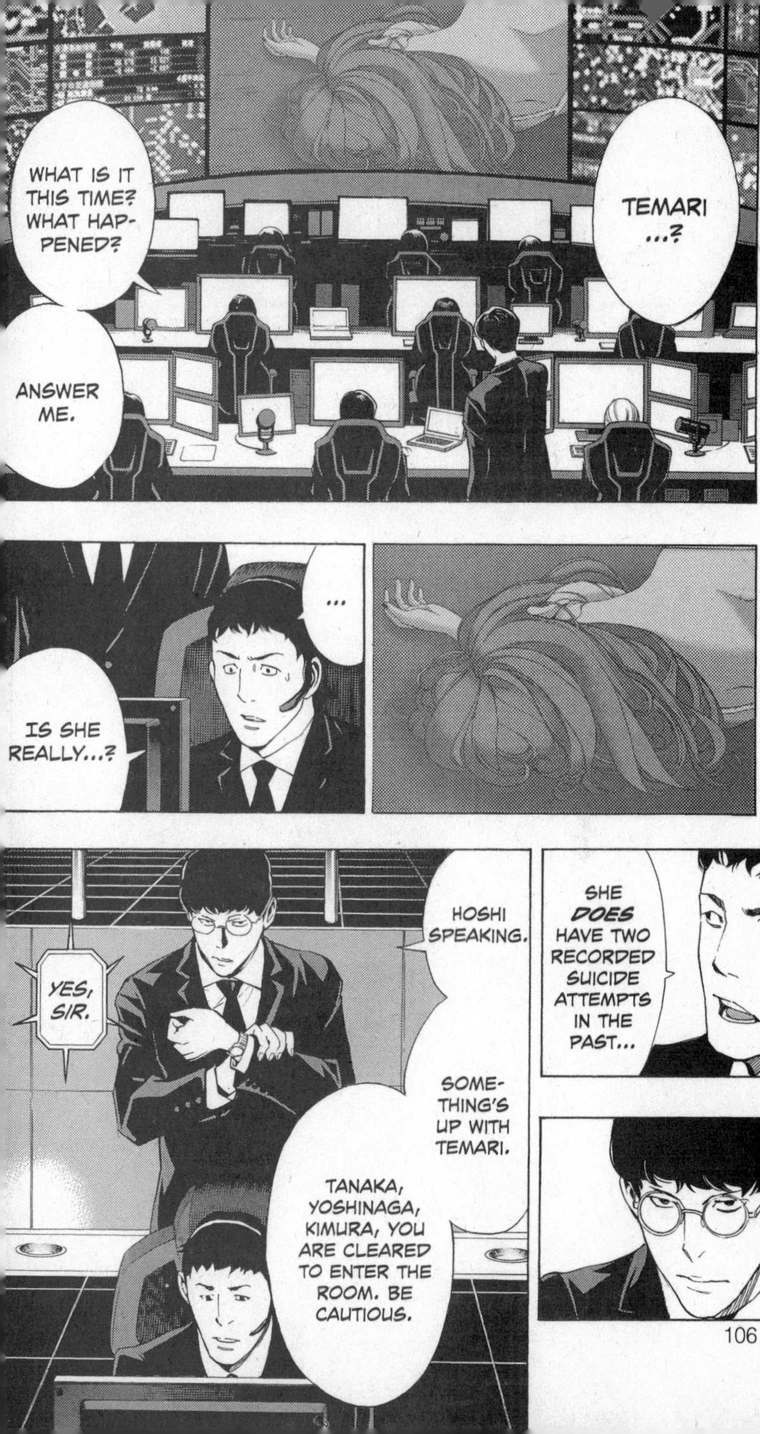
TEMARI ...?
WHAT IS IT THIS TIME? WHAT HAPPENED?
ANSWER ME.
...
IS SHE REALLY...?
SHE *DOES* HAVE TWO RECORDED SUICIDE ATTEMPTS IN THE PAST...
HOSHI SPEAKING.
YES, SIR.
SOMETHING'S UP WITH TEMARI.
TANAKA, YOSHINAGA, KIMURA, YOU ARE CLEARED TO ENTER THE ROOM. BE CAUTIOUS.

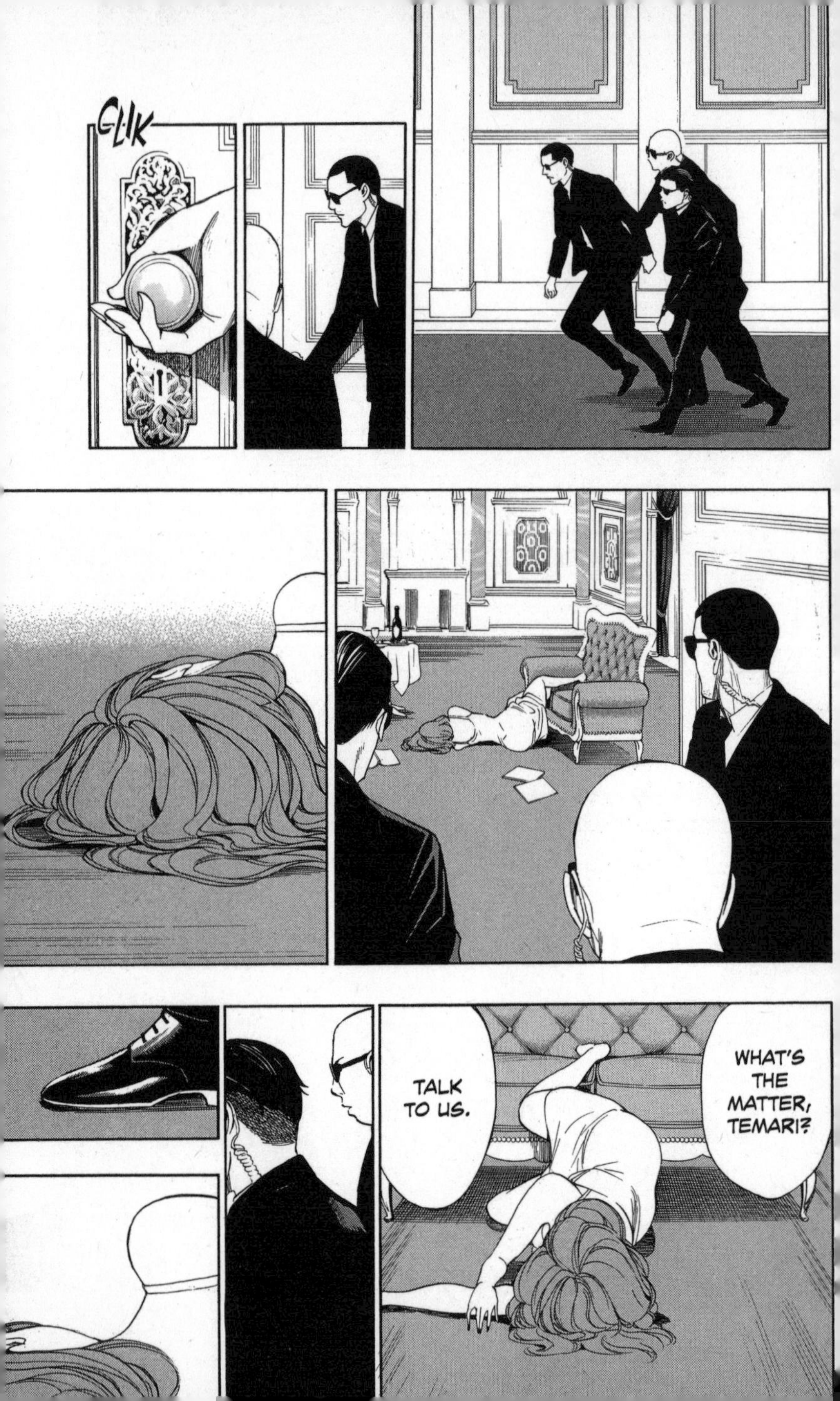
CLIK
WHAT'S THE MATTER, TEMARI?
TALK TO US.

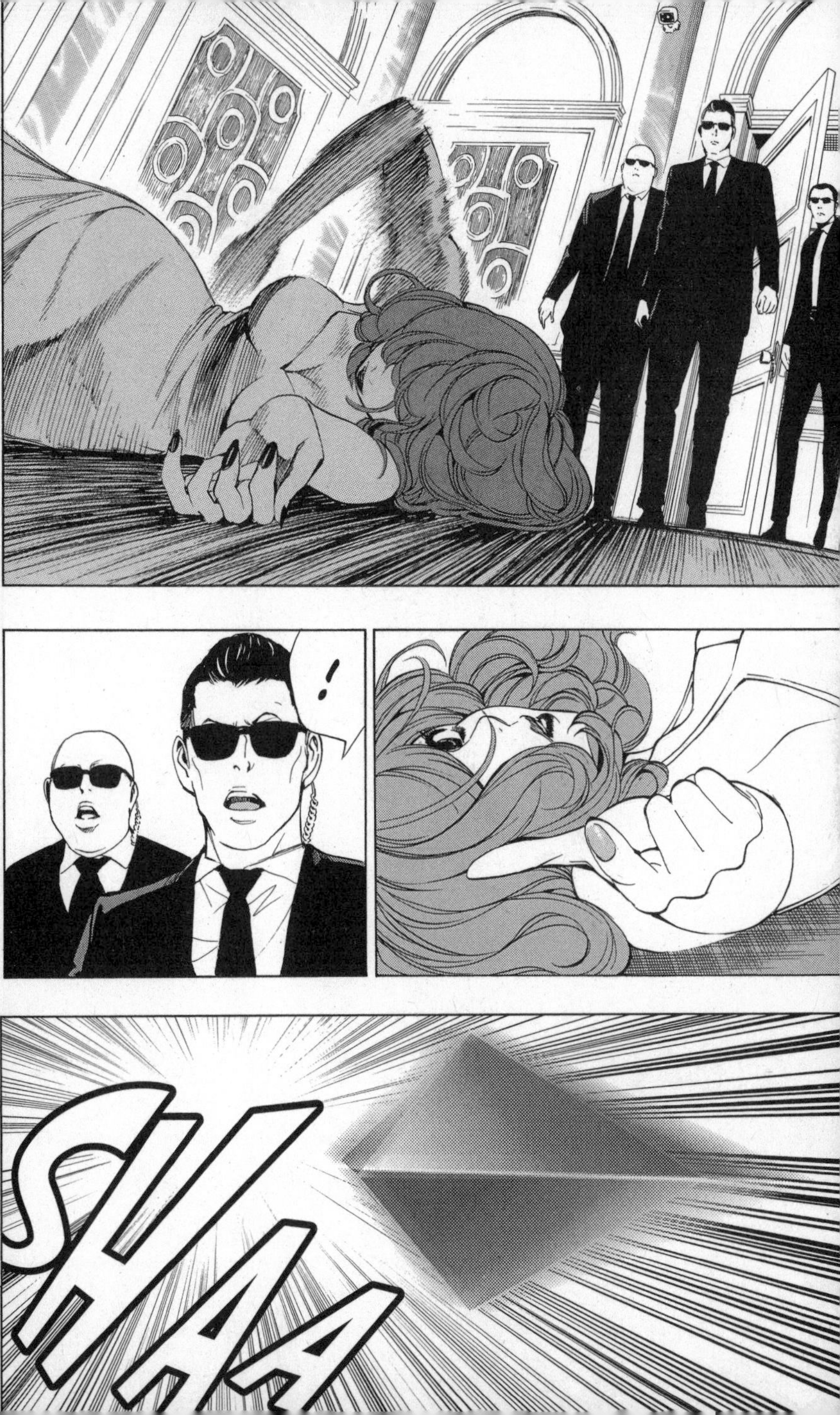
!
SHAA

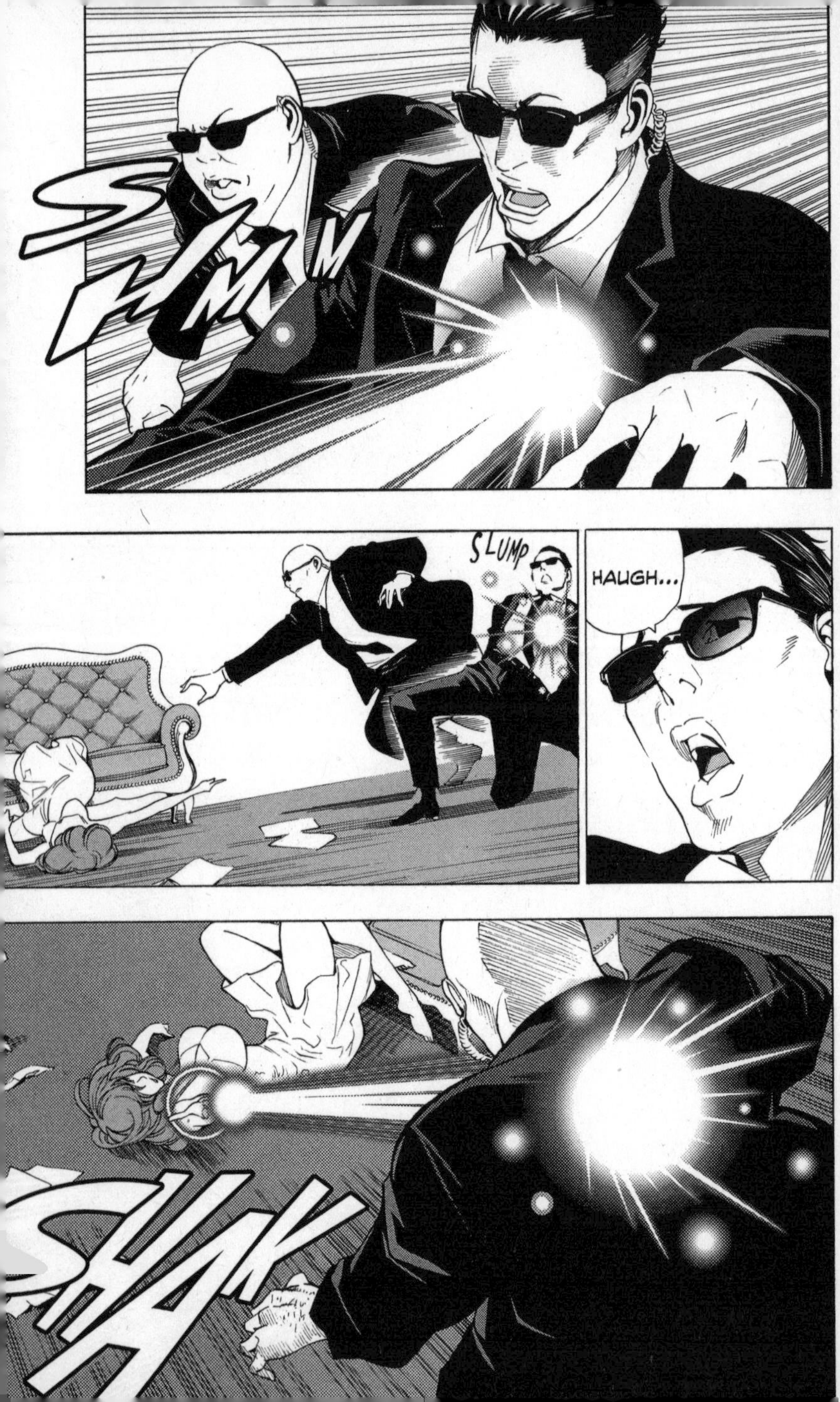
SHMM
HAUGH...
SLUMP
SHAK

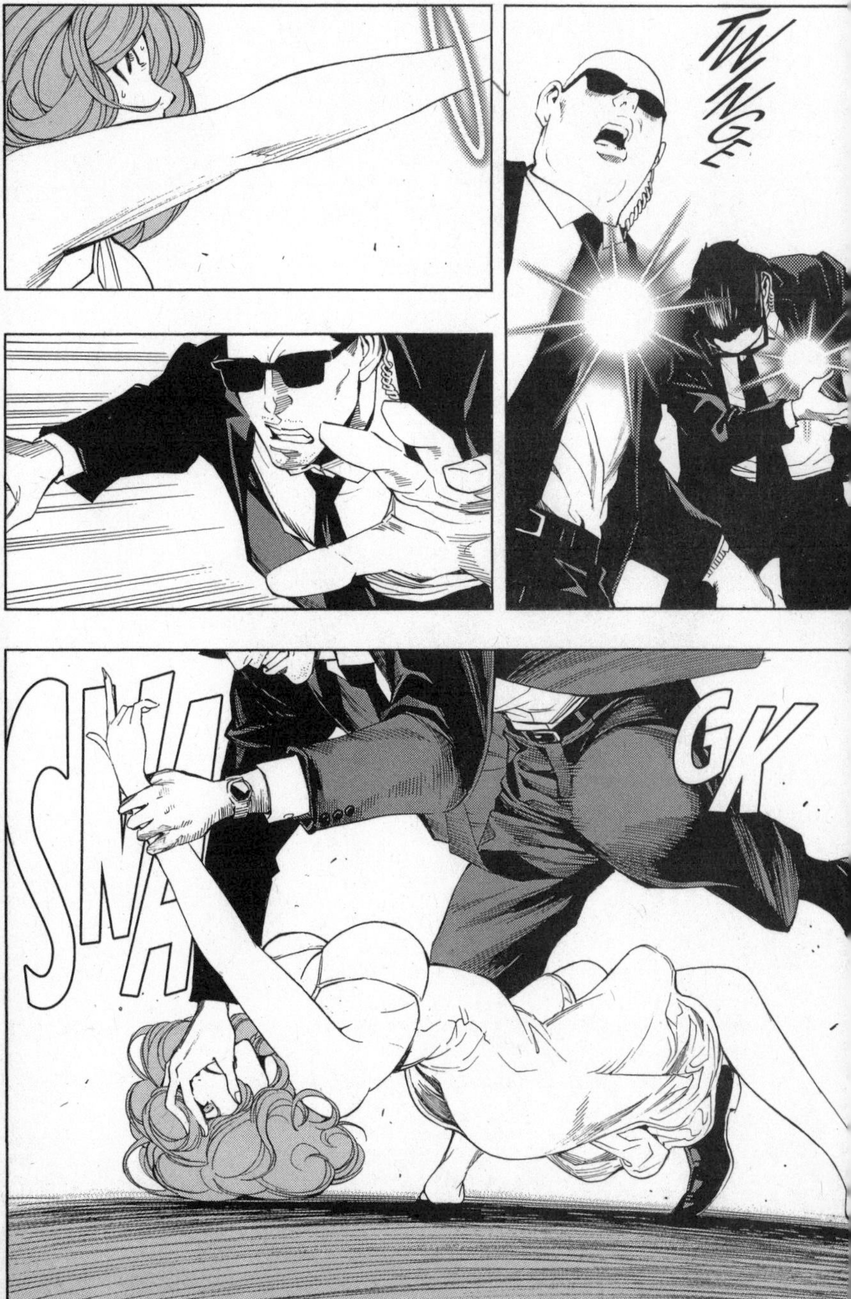
TWINGE
GK
SMA

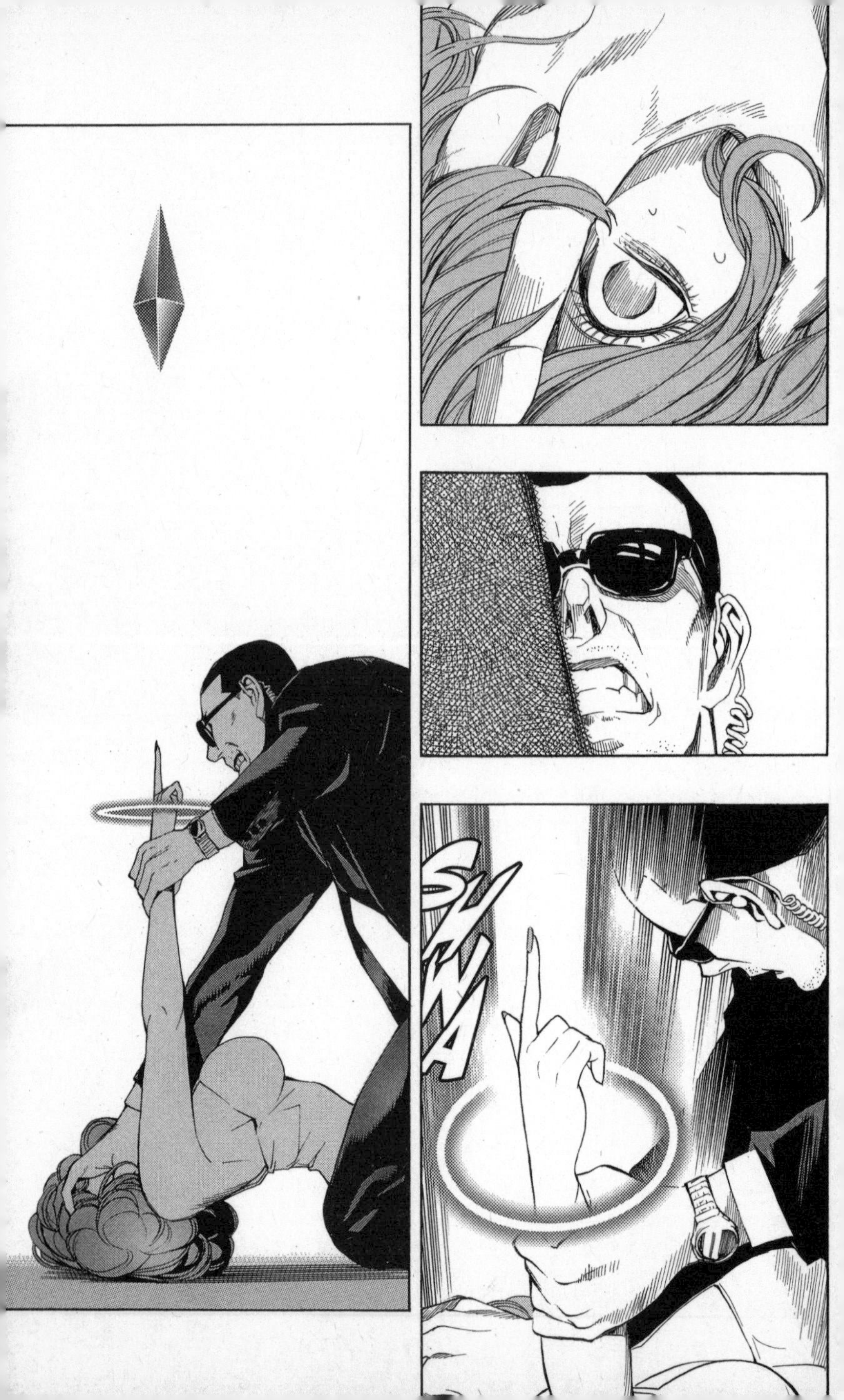
SHWA

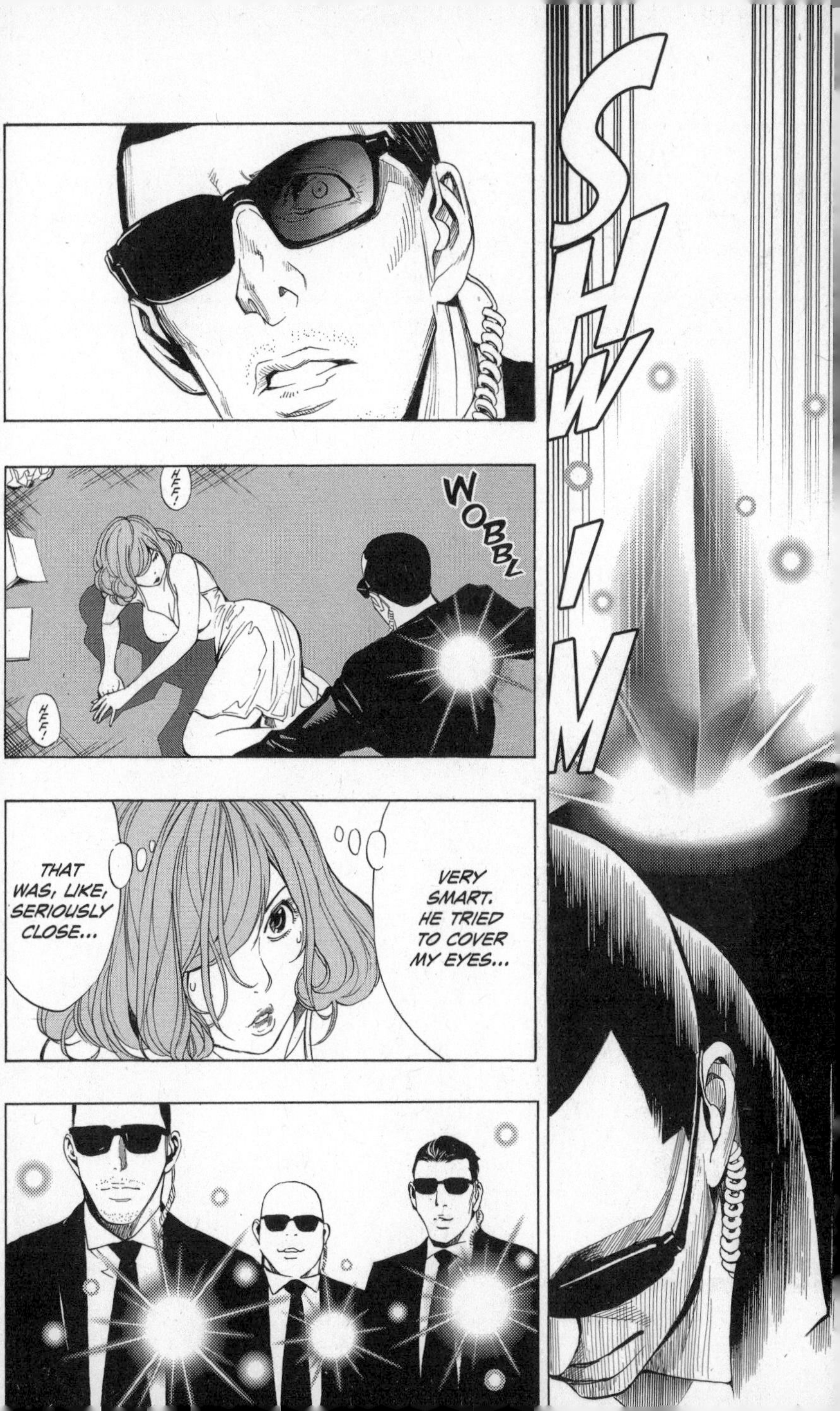
SHWIM
WOBBL
HEF!
HEF!
VERY SMART. HE TRIED TO COVER MY EYES...
THAT WAS, LIKE, SERIOUSLY CLOSE...

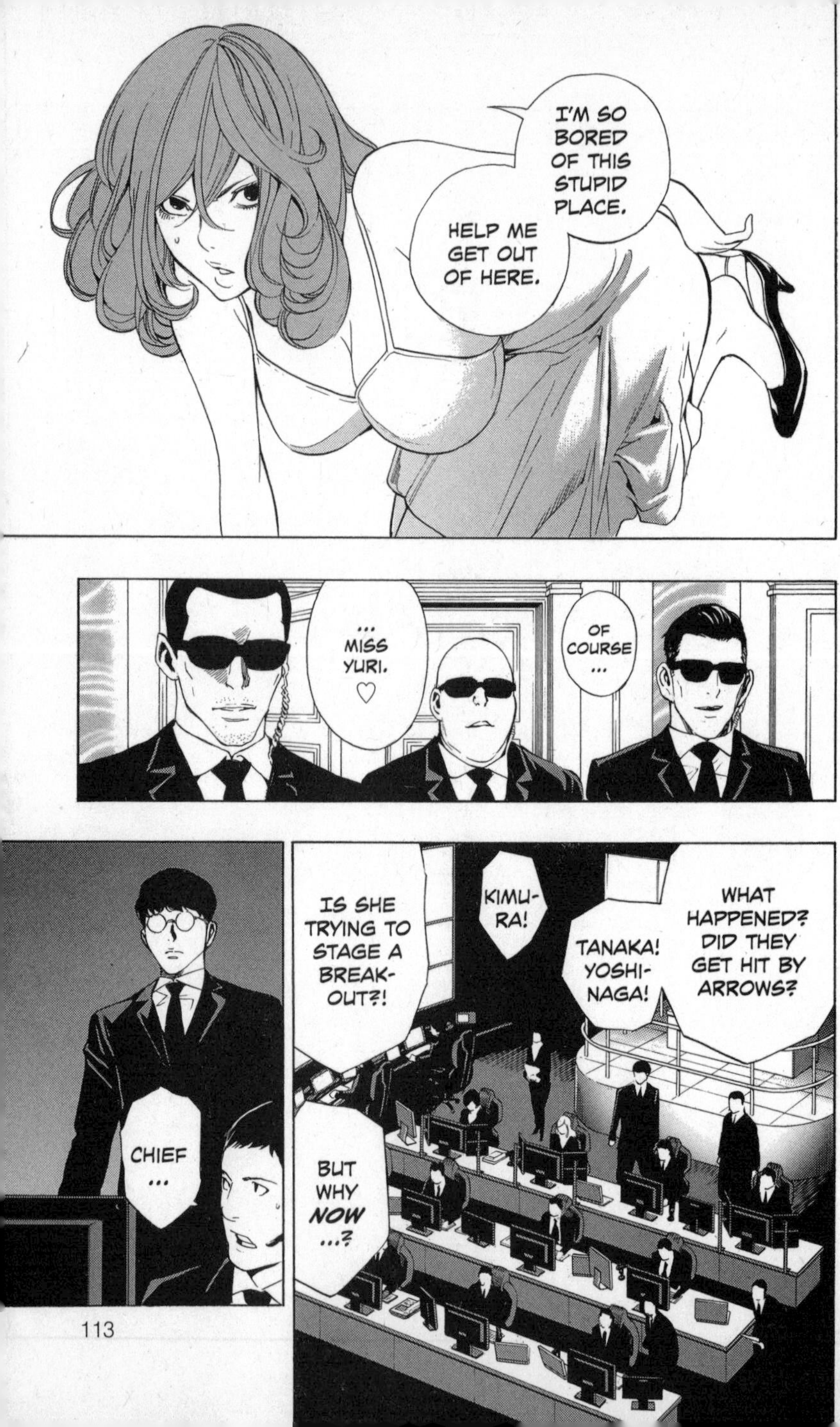
I'M SO BORED OF THIS STUPID PLACE.
HELP ME GET OUT OF HERE.
OF COURSE ...
... MISS YURI. ♡
WHAT HAPPENED? DID THEY GET HIT BY ARROWS?
TANAKA! YOSHI-NAGA!
KIMU-RA!
IS SHE TRYING TO STAGE A BREAK-OUT?!
BUT WHY *NOW* ...?
CHIEF ...

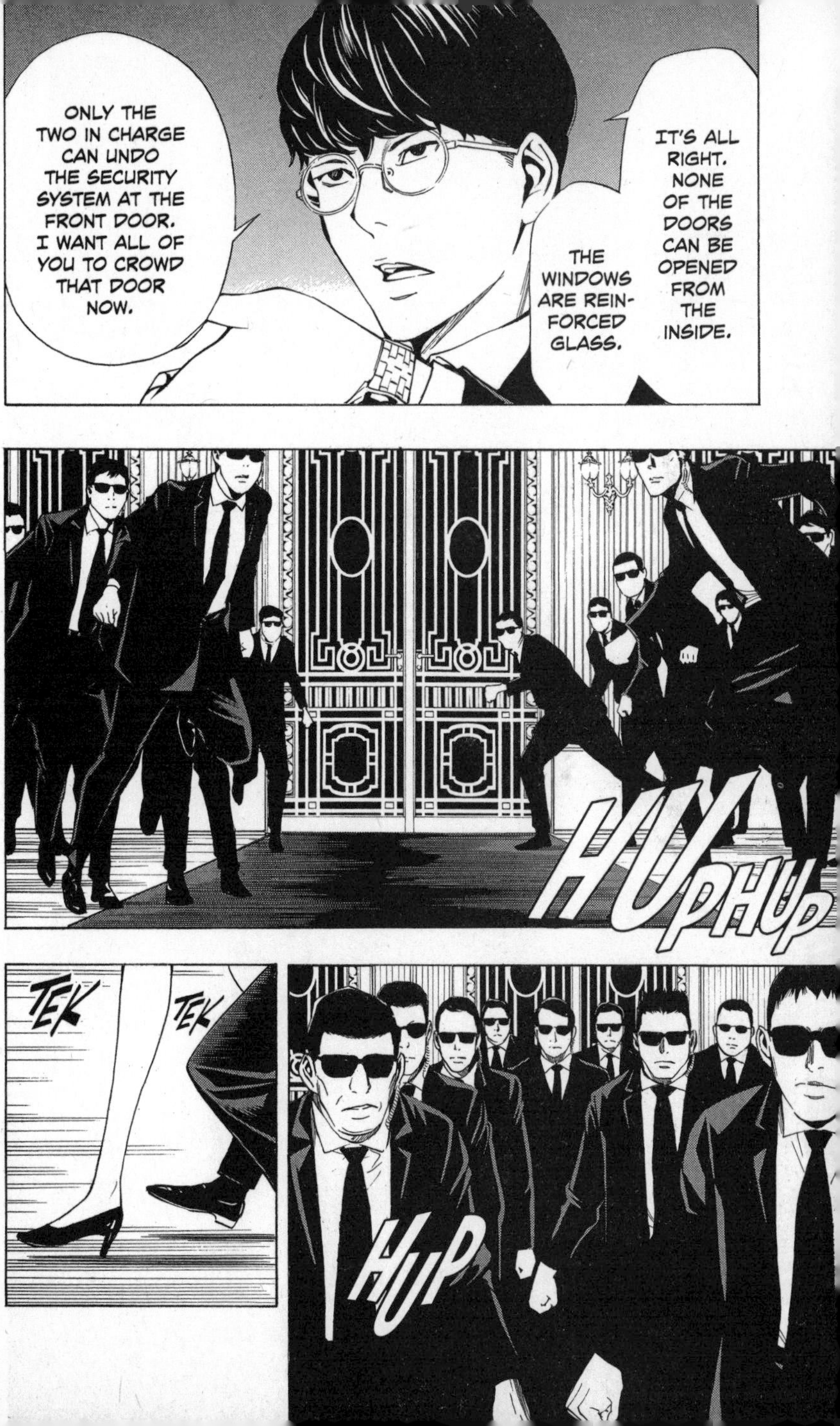
IT'S ALL RIGHT. NONE OF THE DOORS CAN BE OPENED FROM THE INSIDE.
THE WINDOWS ARE REIN-FORCED GLASS.
ONLY THE TWO IN CHARGE CAN UNDO THE SECURITY SYSTEM AT THE FRONT DOOR. I WANT ALL OF YOU TO CROWD THAT DOOR NOW.
HUP HUP
HUP
TEK
TEK

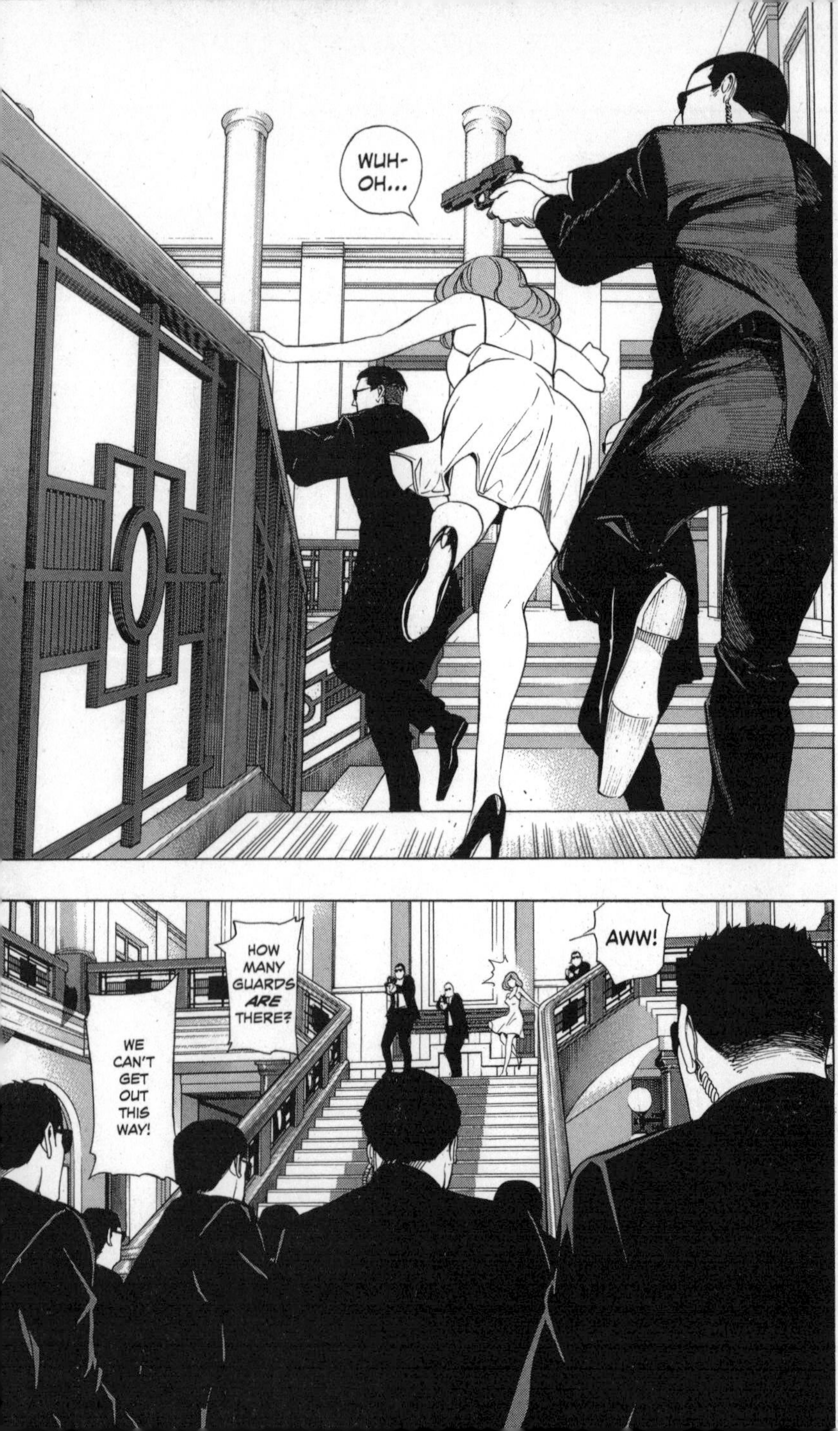
WUH-OH...
AWW!
HOW MANY GUARDS *ARE* THERE?
WE CAN'T GET OUT THIS WAY!

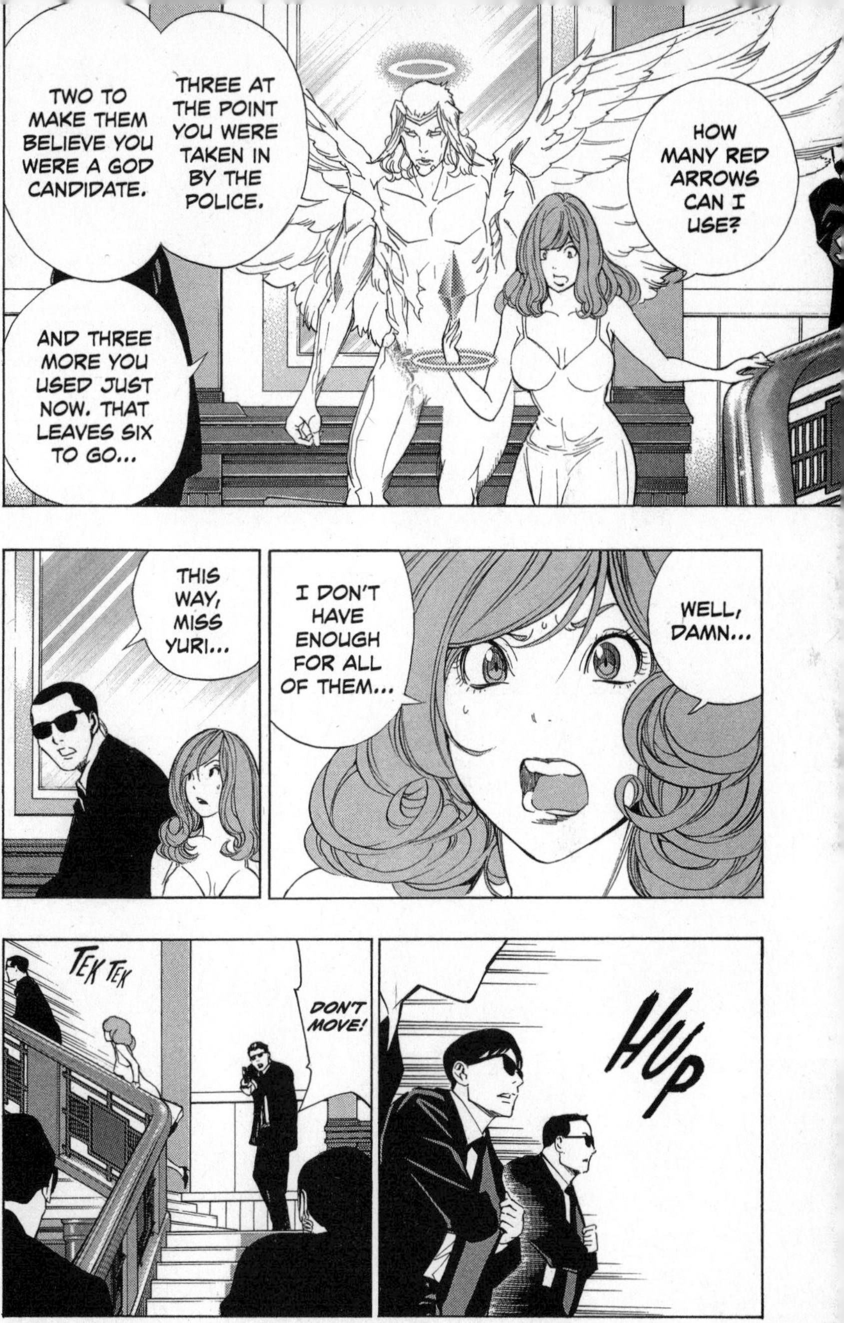

HOW MANY RED ARROWS CAN I USE?
THREE AT THE POINT YOU WERE TAKEN IN BY THE POLICE.
TWO TO MAKE THEM BELIEVE YOU WERE A GOD CANDIDATE.
AND THREE MORE YOU USED JUST NOW. THAT LEAVES SIX TO GO...
WELL, DAMN...
I DON'T HAVE ENOUGH FOR ALL OF THEM...
THIS WAY, MISS YURI...
HUP
DON'T MOVE!
TEK TEK

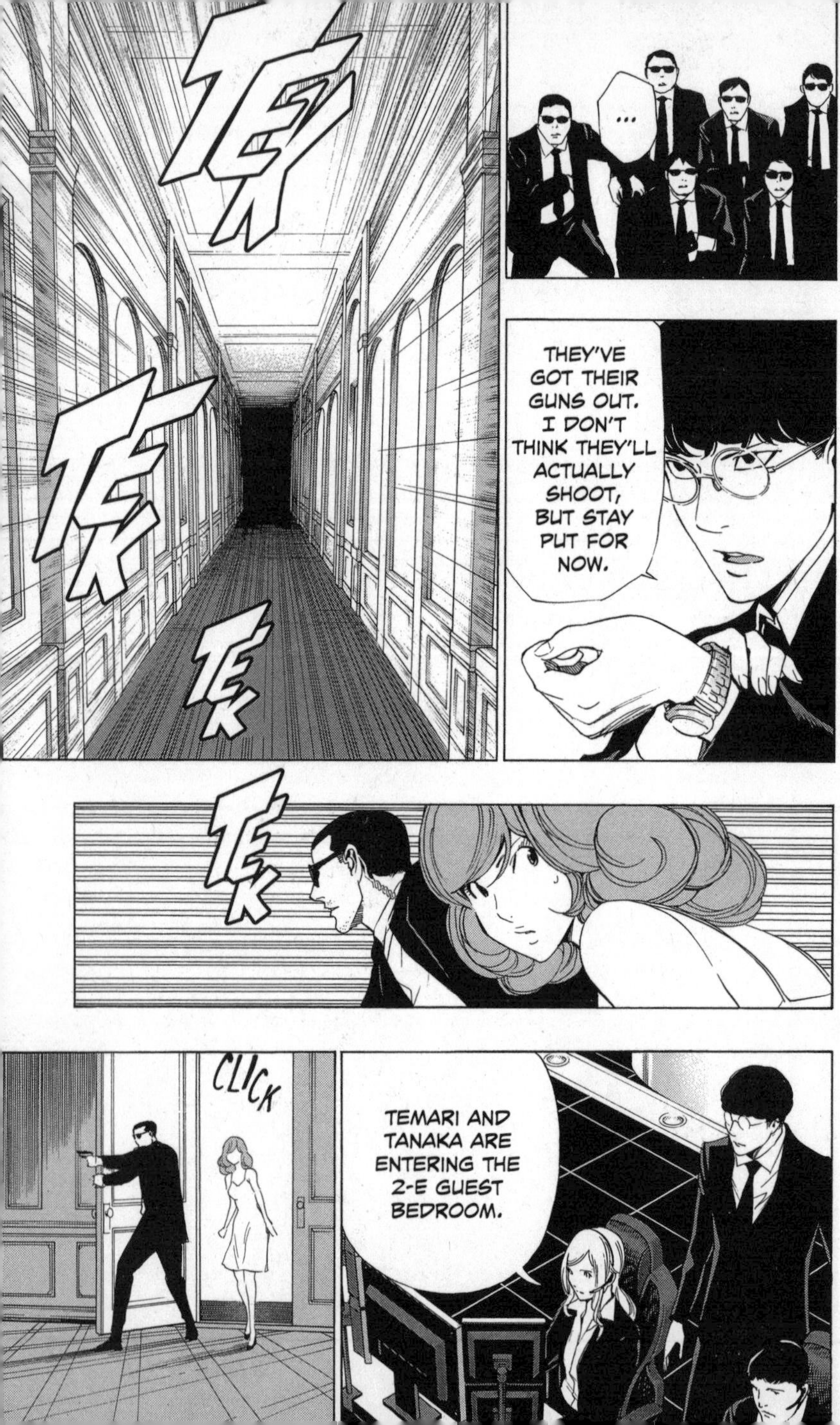
...
TEK
TEK
TEK
THEY'VE GOT THEIR GUNS OUT. I DON'T THINK THEY'LL ACTUALLY SHOOT, BUT STAY PUT FOR NOW.
TEK
TEMARI AND TANAKA ARE ENTERING THE 2-E GUEST BEDROOM.
CLICK

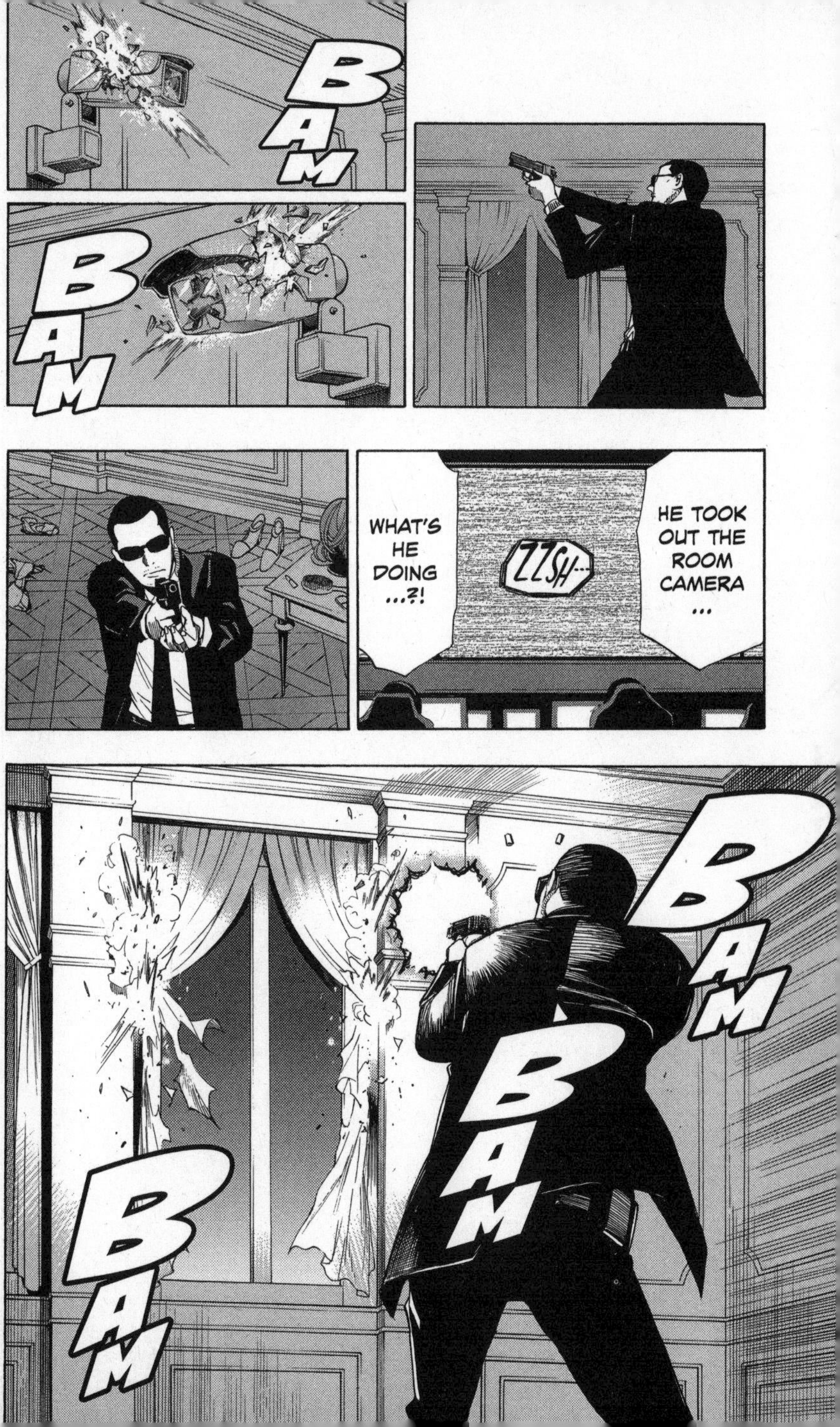
BAM
BAM
HE TOOK OUT THE ROOM CAMERA ...
ZZSH...
WHAT'S HE DOING ...?!
BAM
BAM
BAM

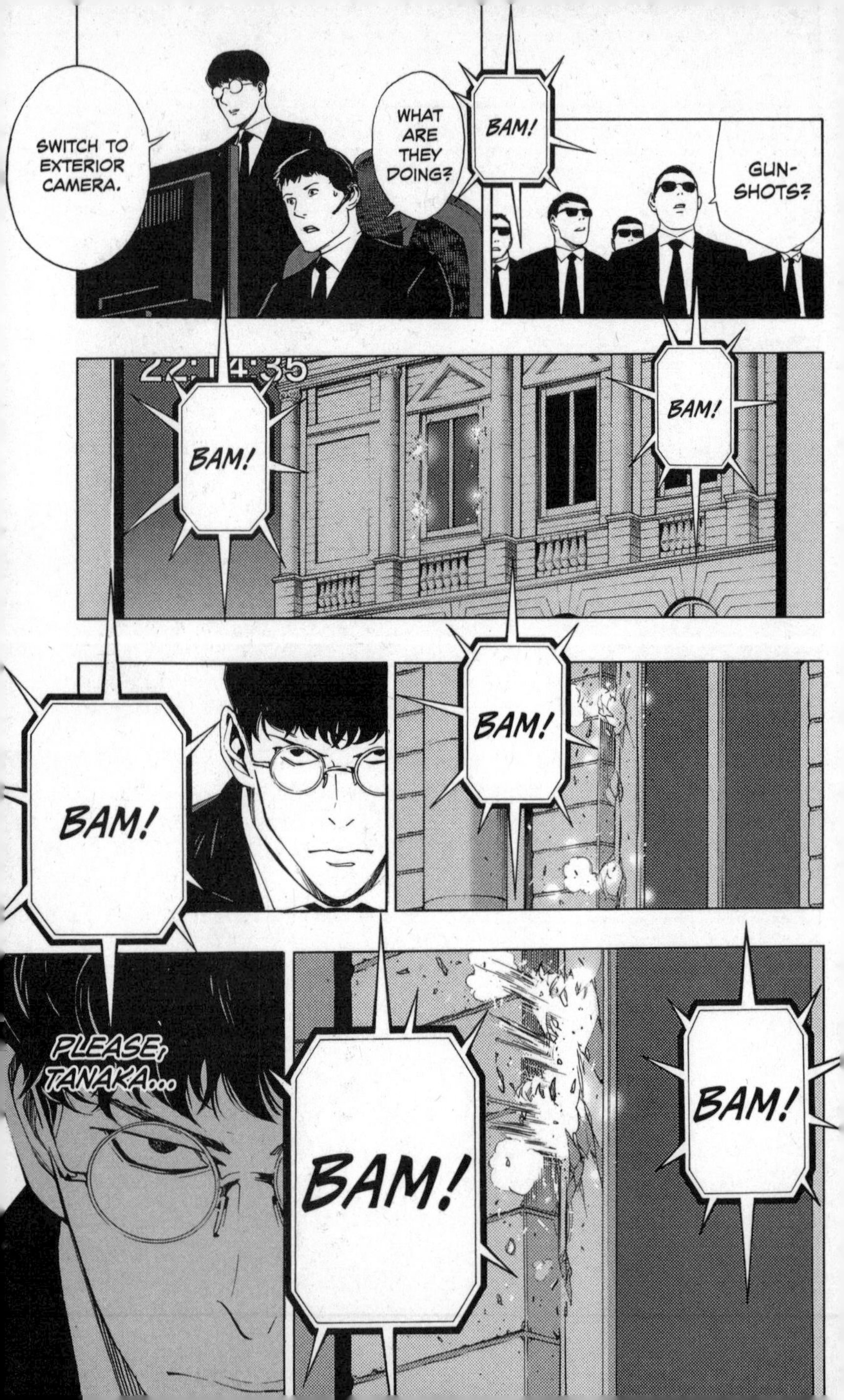
GUN-SHOTS?
BAM!
WHAT ARE THEY DOING?
SWITCH TO EXTERIOR CAMERA.
BAM!
22:14:35
BAM!
BAM!
BAM!
BAM!
BAM!
PLEASE, TANAKA...

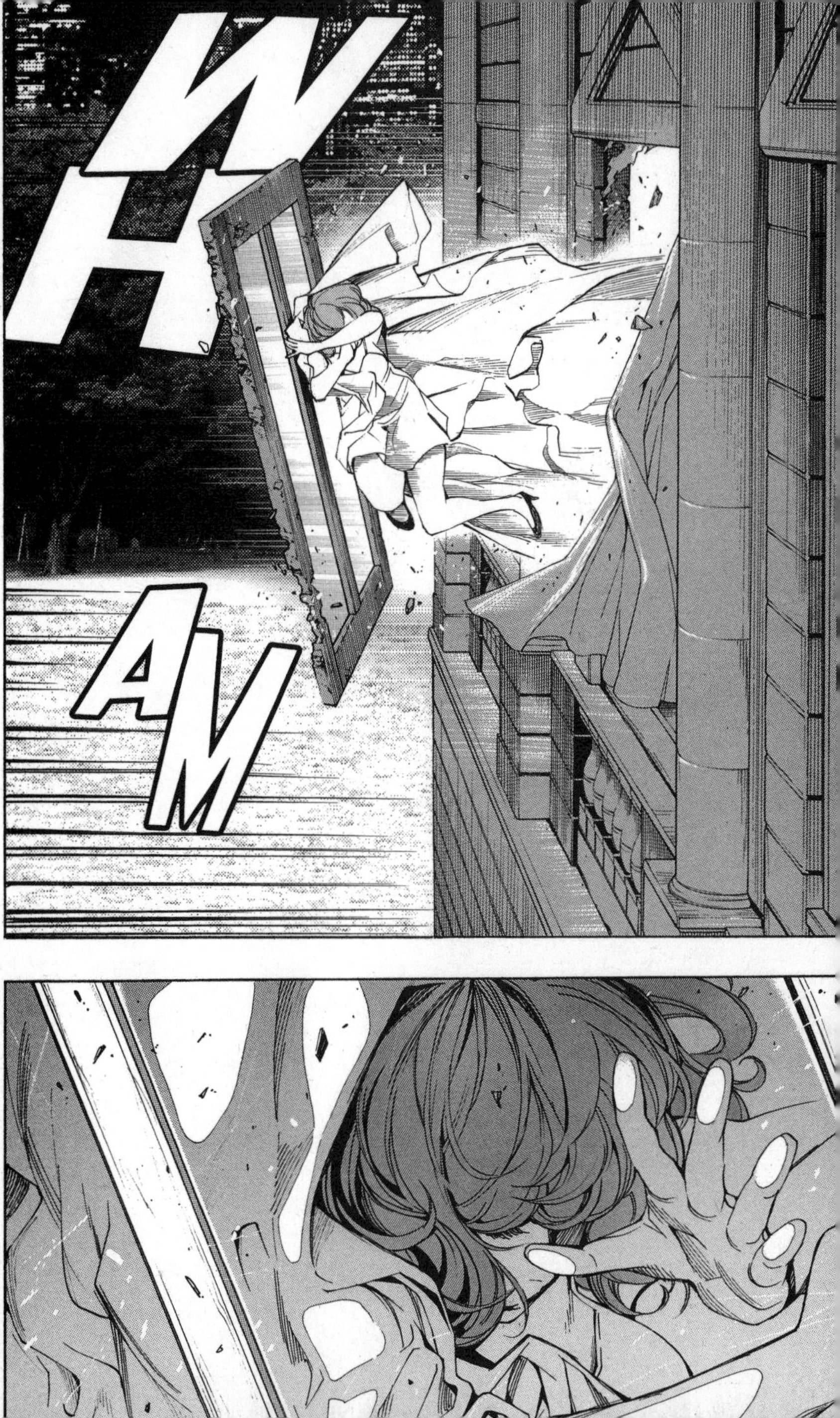
WHAM

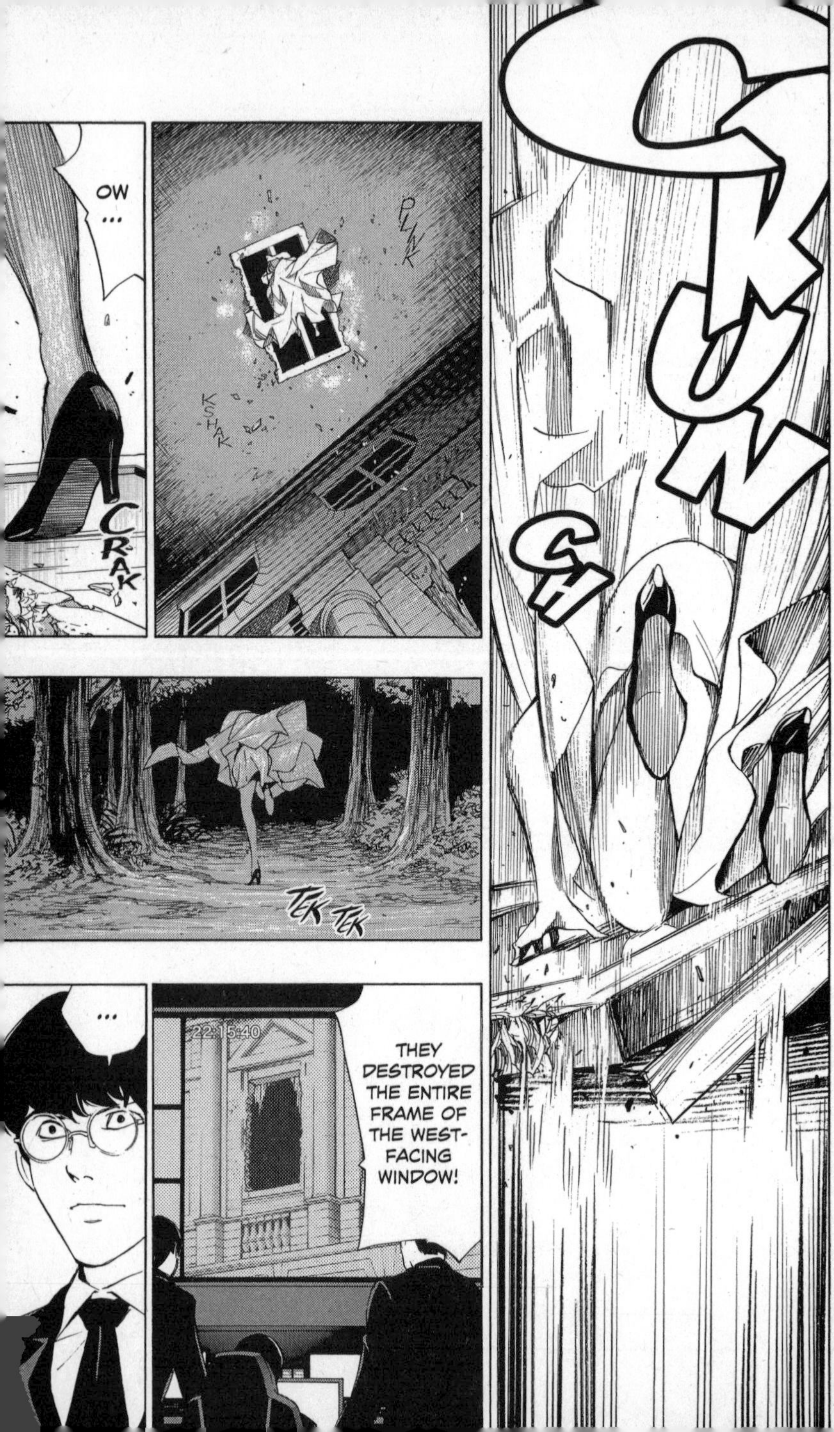
CKUNCH
PLINK
KSHAK
OW ...
CRAK
TEK TEK
22:15:40
THEY DESTROYED THE ENTIRE FRAME OF THE WEST-FACING WINDOW!
...

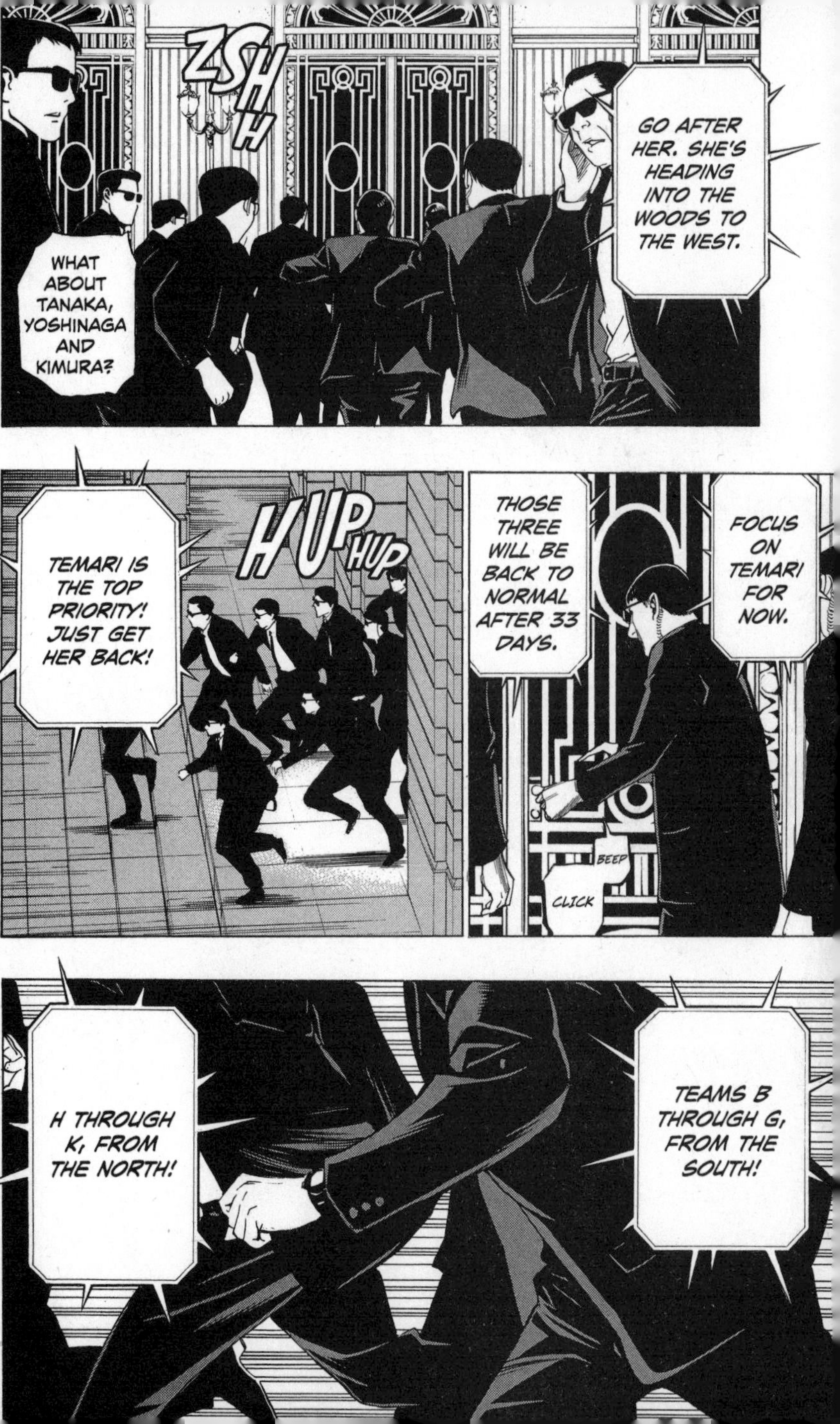
GO AFTER HER. SHE'S HEADING INTO THE WOODS TO THE WEST.
ZSHH
WHAT ABOUT TANAKA, YOSHINAGA AND KIMURA?
THOSE THREE WILL BE BACK TO NORMAL AFTER 33 DAYS.
FOCUS ON TEMARI FOR NOW.
BEEP
CLICK
HUP HUP HUP
TEMARI IS THE TOP PRIORITY! JUST GET HER BACK!
TEAMS B THROUGH G, FROM THE SOUTH!
H THROUGH K, FROM THE NORTH!

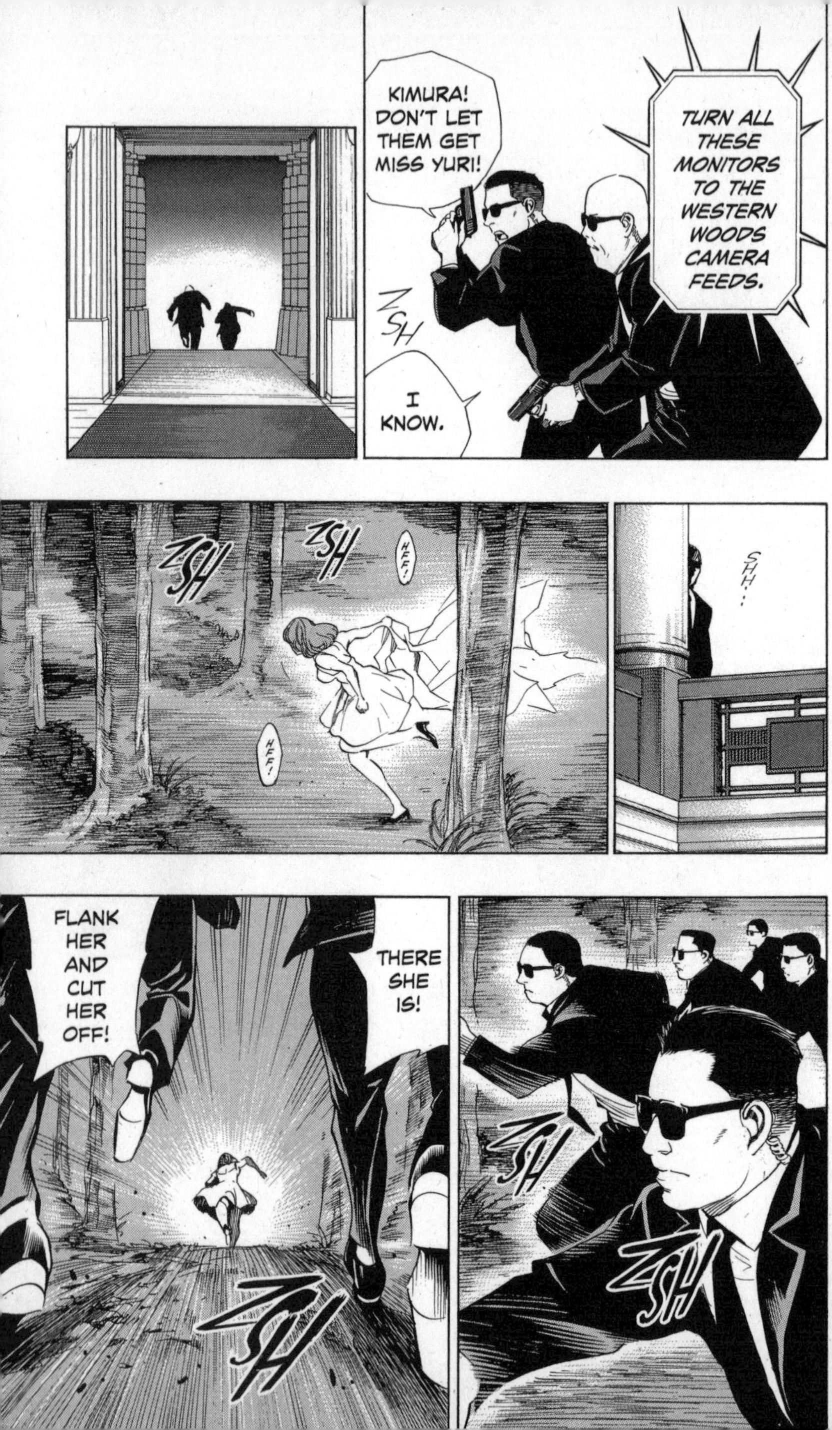
TURN ALL THESE MONITORS TO THE WESTERN WOODS CAMERA FEEDS.
KIMURA! DON'T LET THEM GET MISS YURI!
ZSH
I KNOW.
SHH...
ZSH
HFF!
ZSH
HFF!
ZSH
ZSH
THERE SHE IS!
FLANK HER AND CUT HER OFF!
ZSH

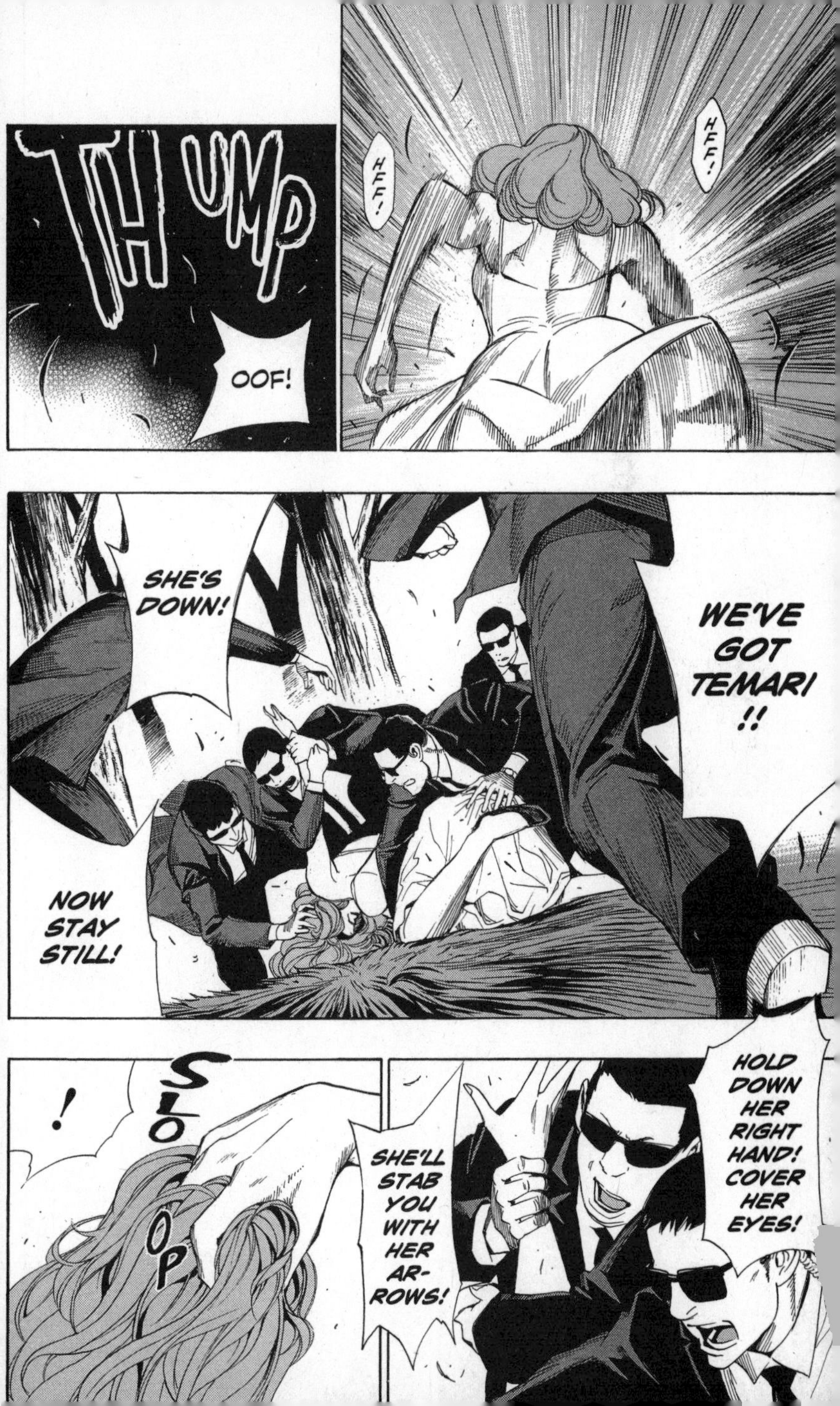
HFF!
HFF!
THUMP
OOF!
WE'VE GOT TEMARI !!
SHE'S DOWN!
NOW STAY STILL!
HOLD DOWN HER RIGHT HAND! COVER HER EYES!
SHE'LL STAB YOU WITH HER AR-ROWS!
!
SLOOP

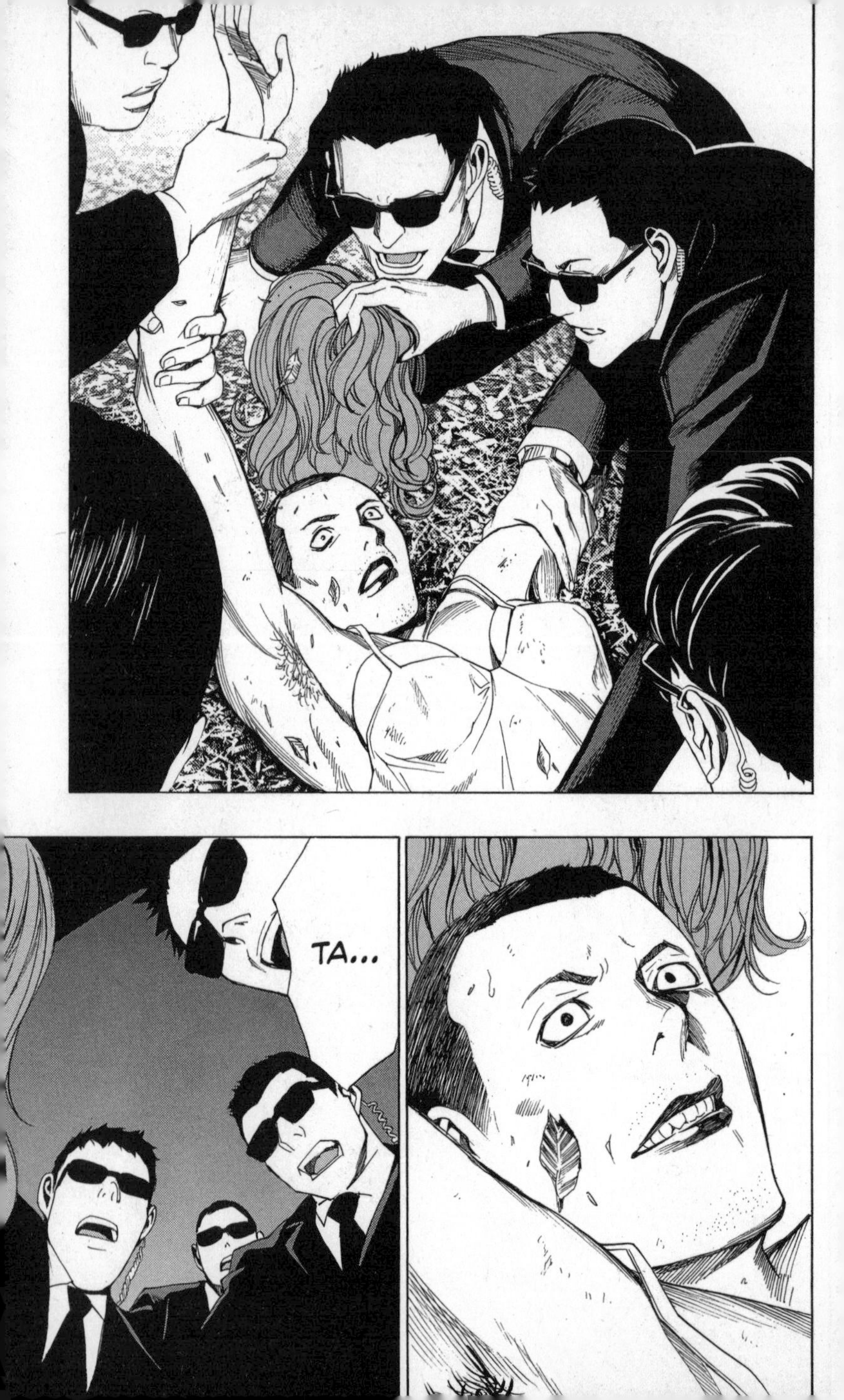
TA...

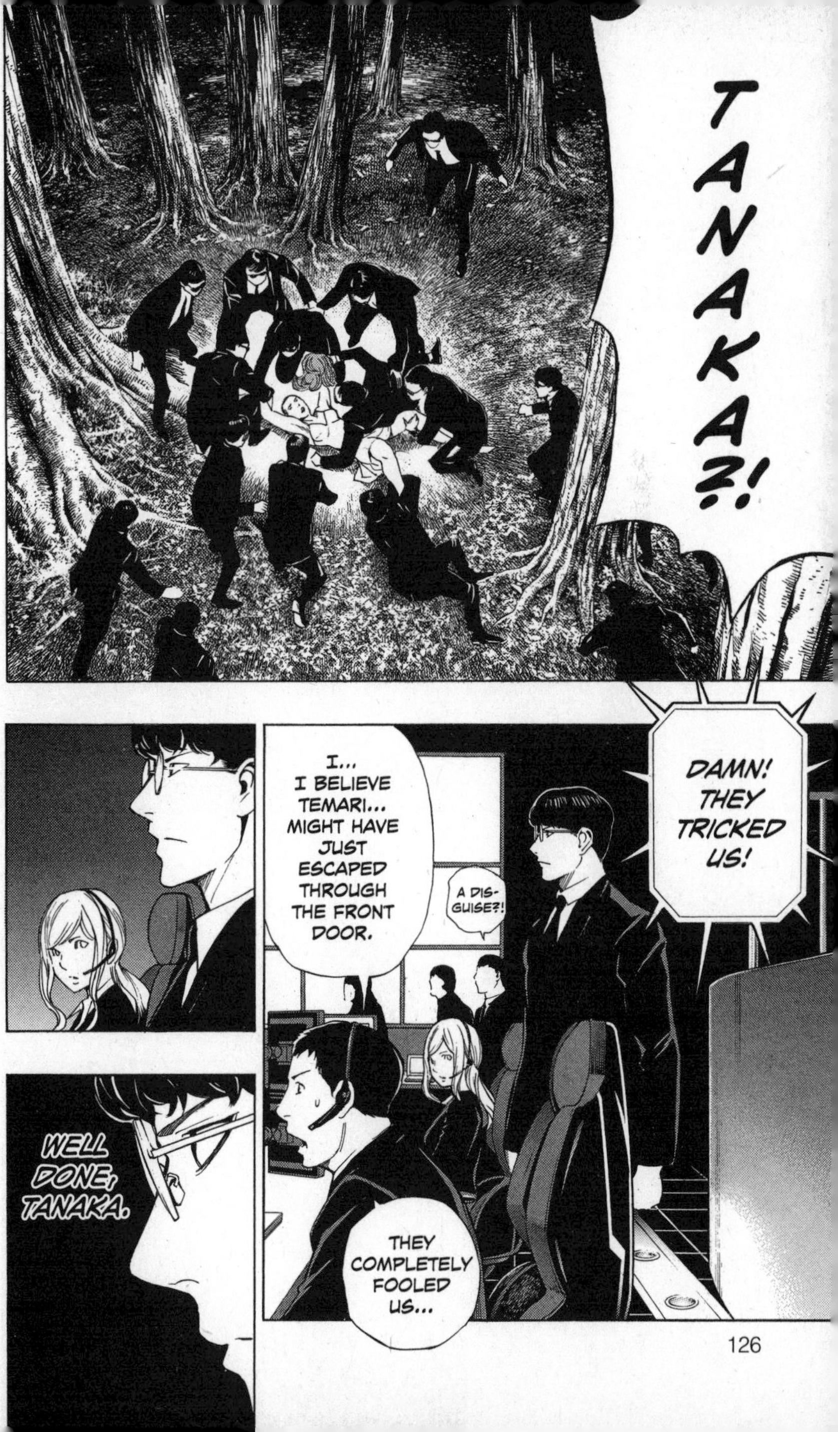
TANAKA?!
DAMN! THEY TRICKED US!
A DIS-GUISE?!
I... I BELIEVE TEMARI... MIGHT HAVE JUST ESCAPED THROUGH THE FRONT DOOR.
THEY COMPLETELY FOOLED US...
WELL DONE, TANAKA.

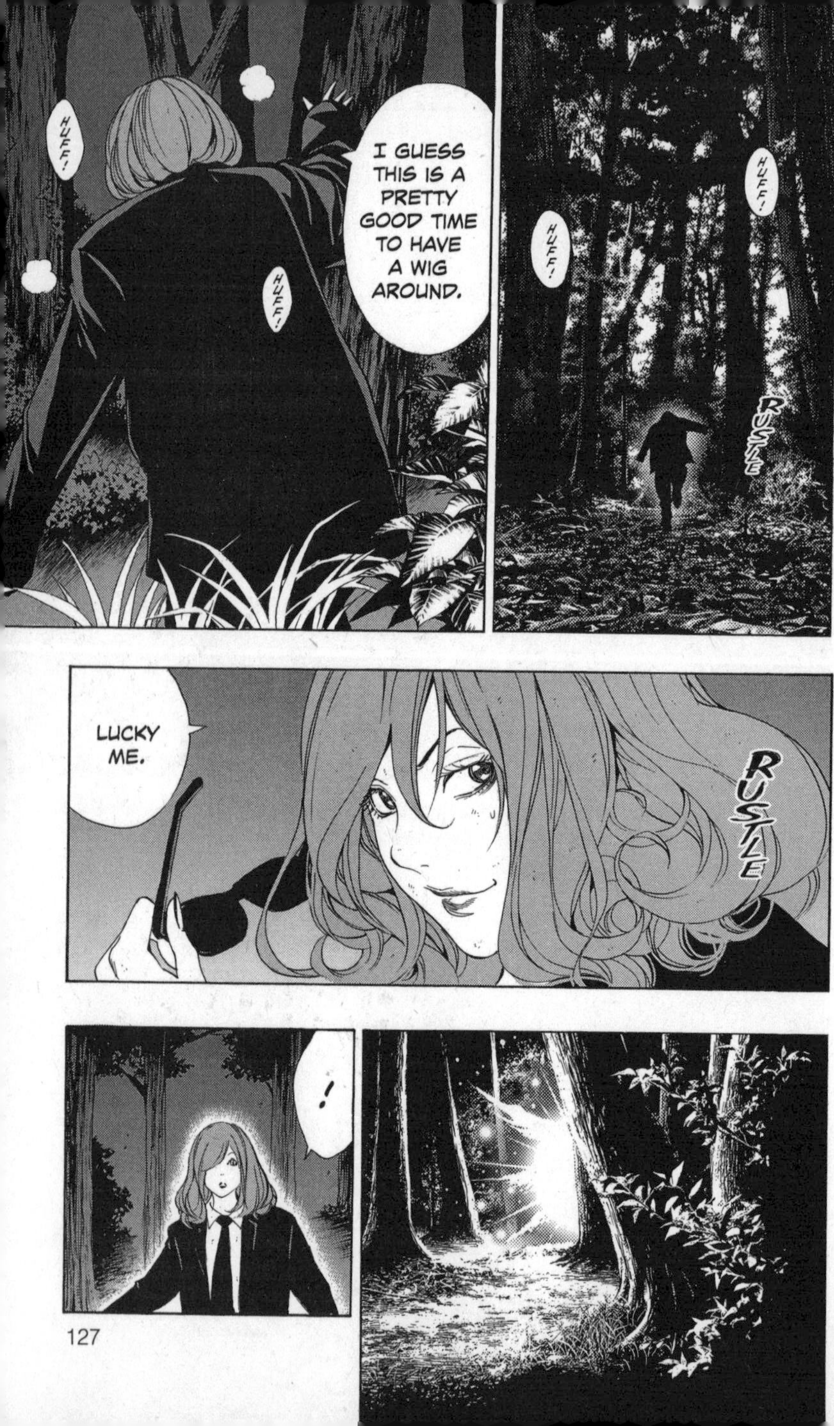
HUFF!
HUFF!
RUSTLE
I GUESS THIS IS A PRETTY GOOD TIME TO HAVE A WIG AROUND.
HUFF!
HUFF!
RUSTLE
LUCKY ME.
!

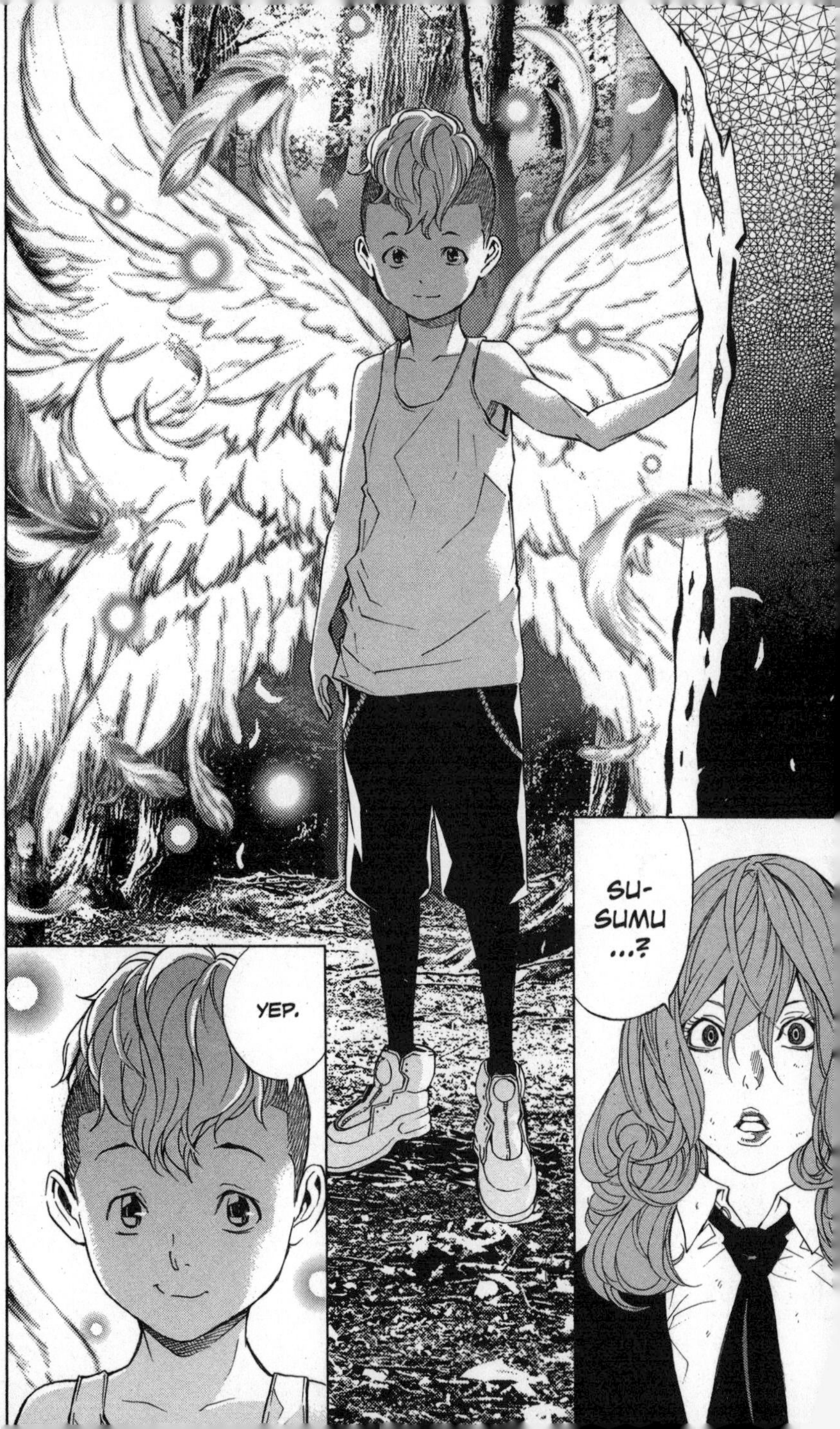
SU-SUMU ...?
YEP.

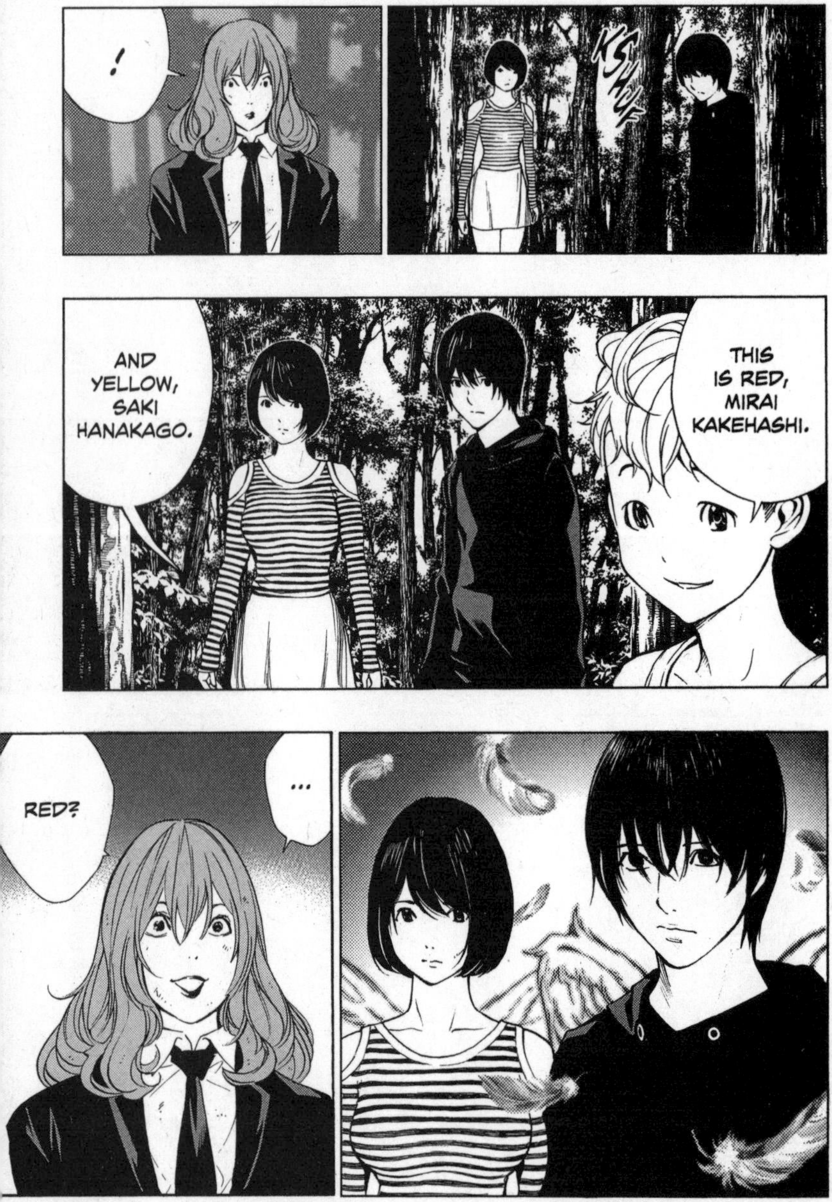
KSHUF
!
THIS IS RED, MIRAI KAKEHASHI.
AND YELLOW, SAKI HANAKAGO.
...
RED?

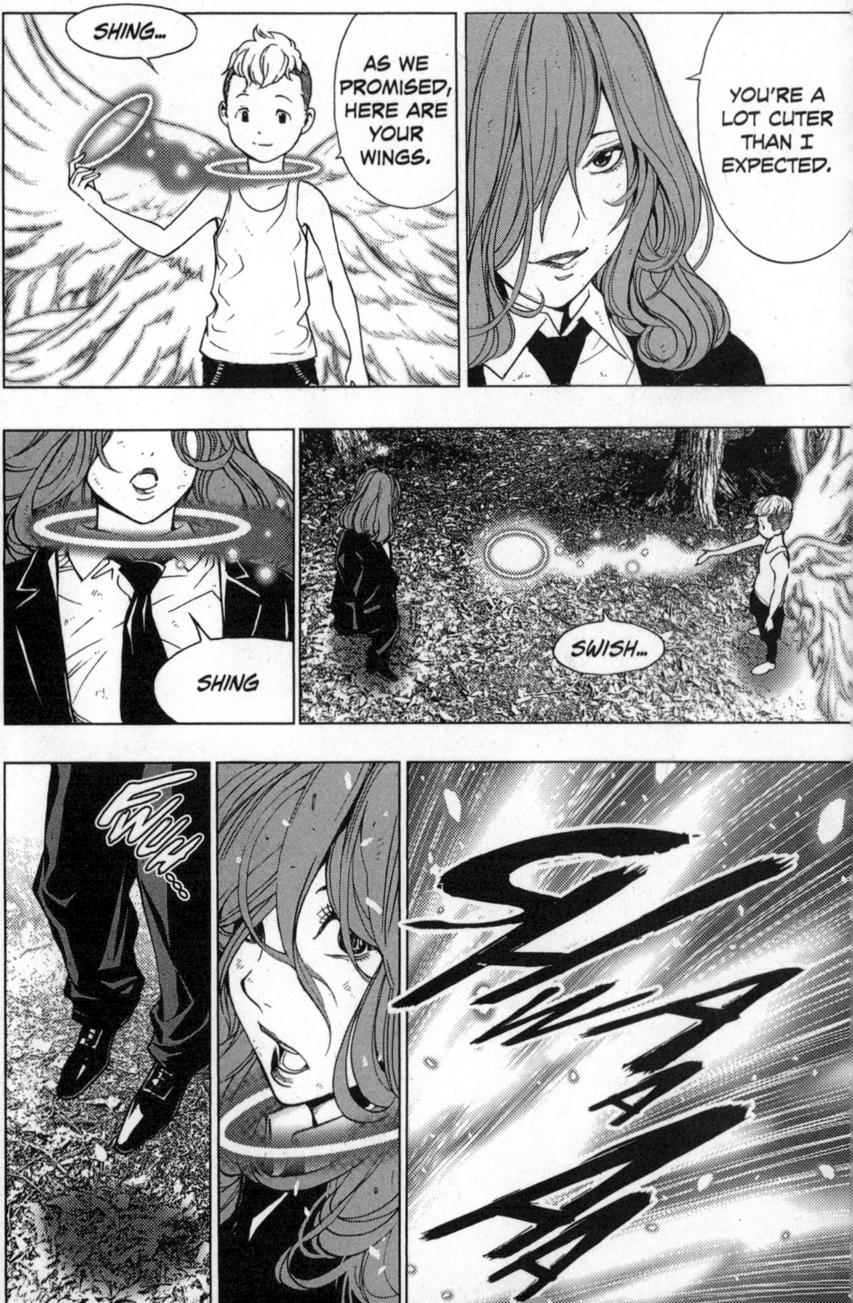
YOU'RE A LOT CUTER THAN I EXPECTED.
AS WE PROMISED, HERE ARE YOUR WINGS.
SHING...
SWISH...
SHING
SHAAAAA
FWUH...

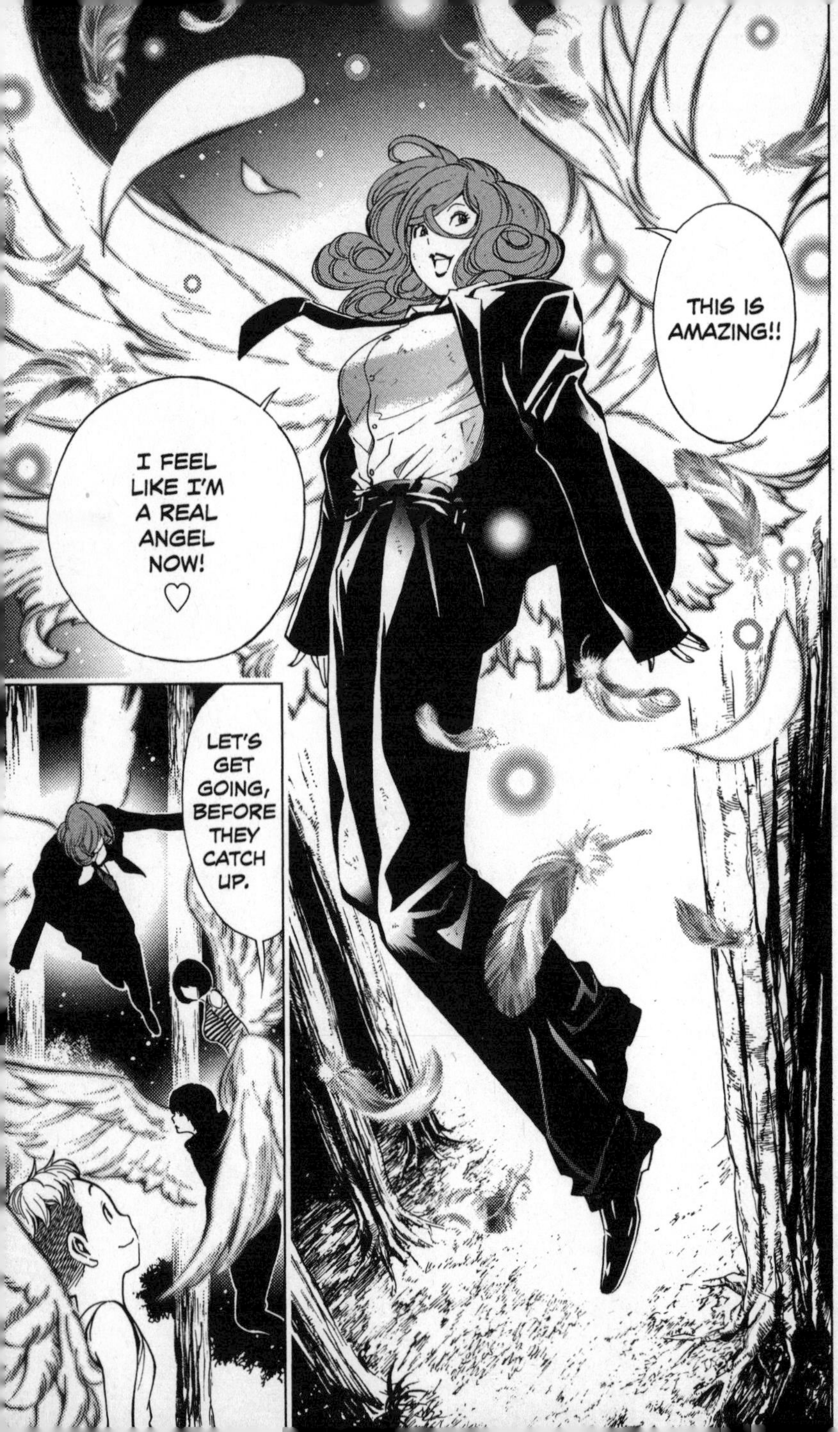
THIS IS AMAZING!!
I FEEL LIKE I'M A REAL ANGEL NOW! ♡
LET'S GET GOING, BEFORE THEY CATCH UP.

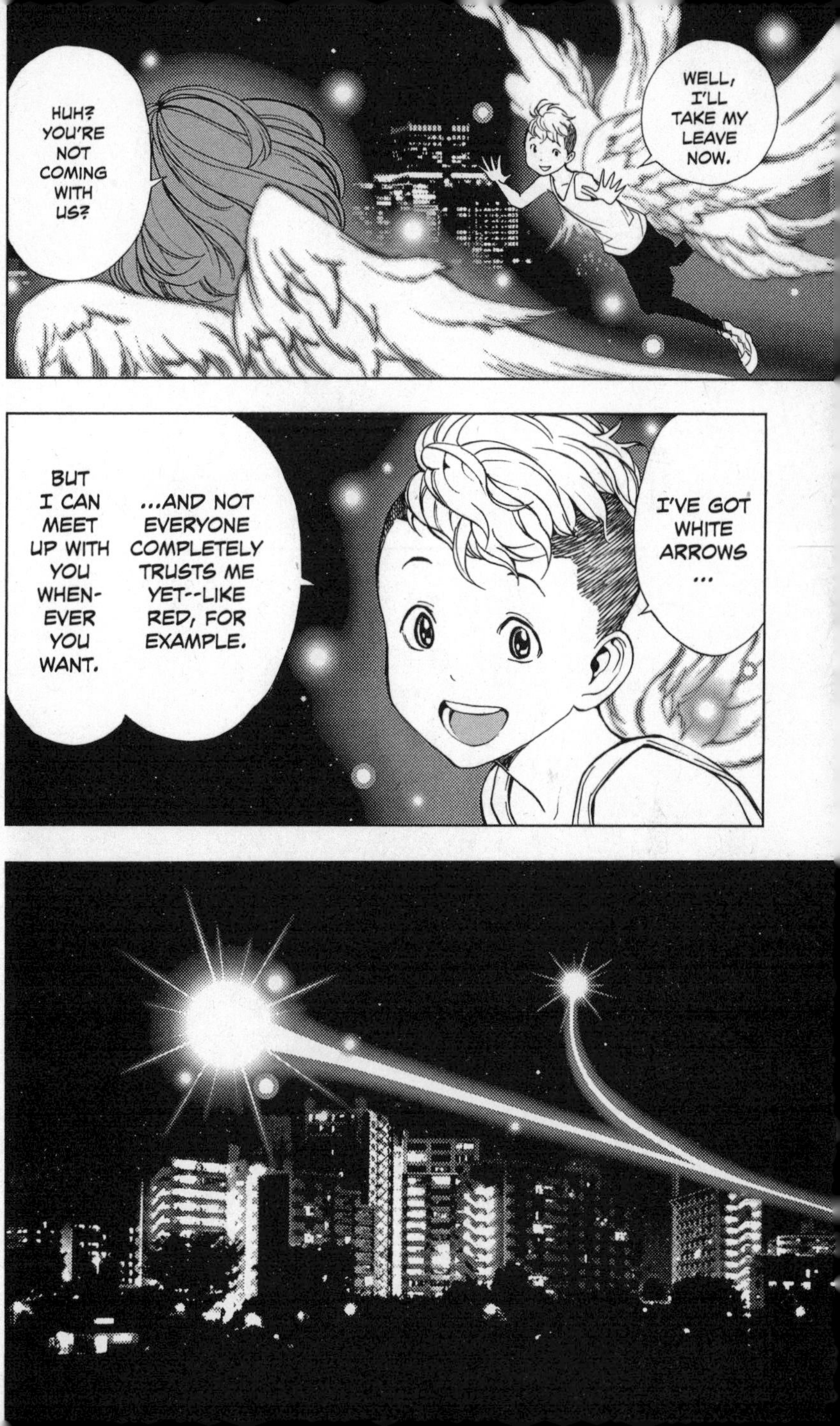
WELL, I'LL TAKE MY LEAVE NOW.
HUH? YOU'RE NOT COMING WITH US?
I'VE GOT WHITE ARROWS...
...AND NOT EVERYONE COMPLETELY TRUSTS ME YET--LIKE RED, FOR EXAMPLE.
BUT I CAN MEET UP WITH YOU WHEN-EVER YOU WANT.

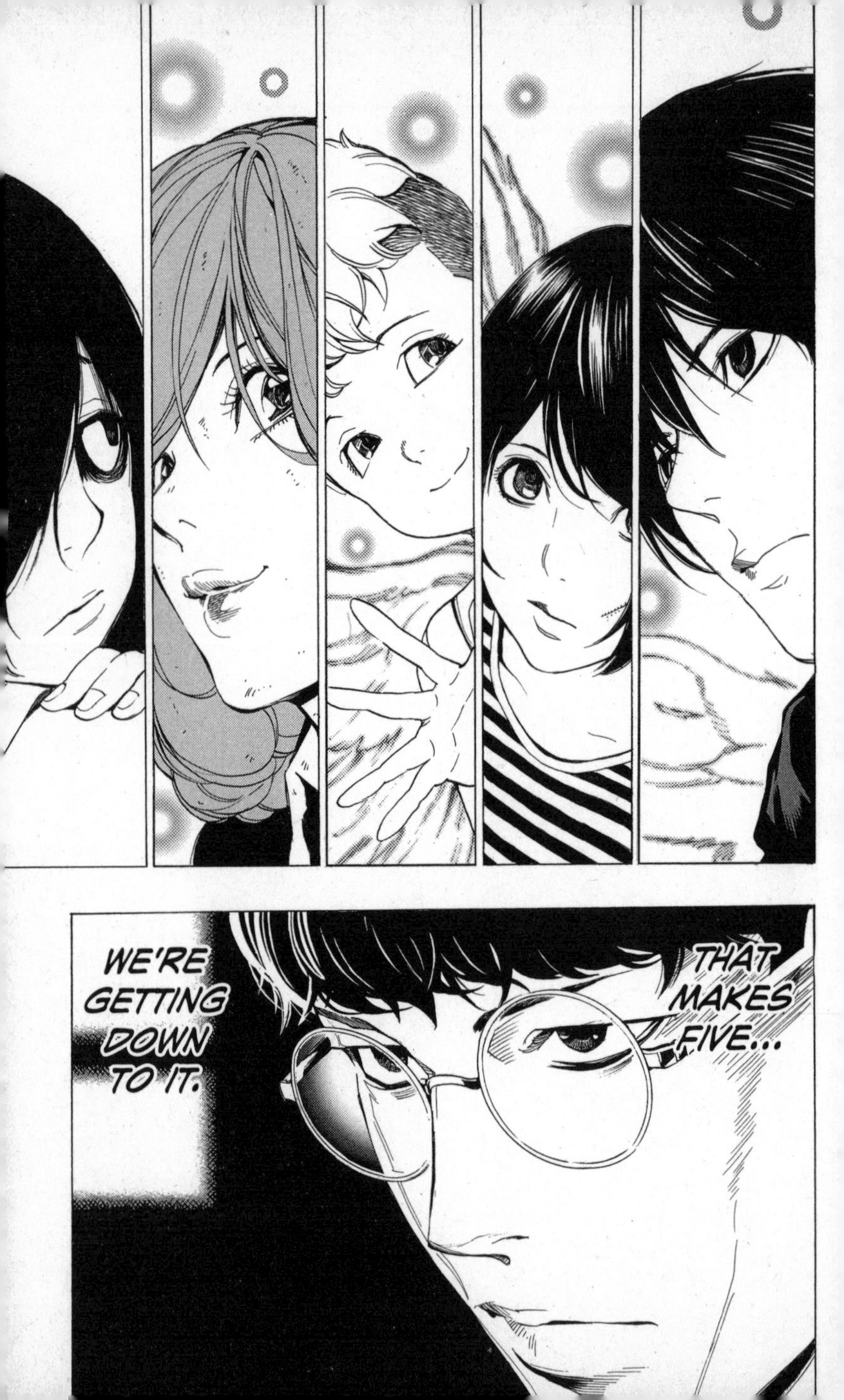
THAT MAKES FIVE...
WE'RE GETTING DOWN TO IT.

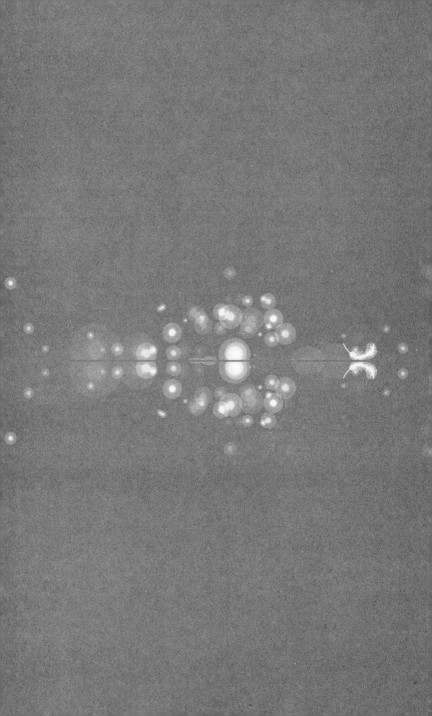

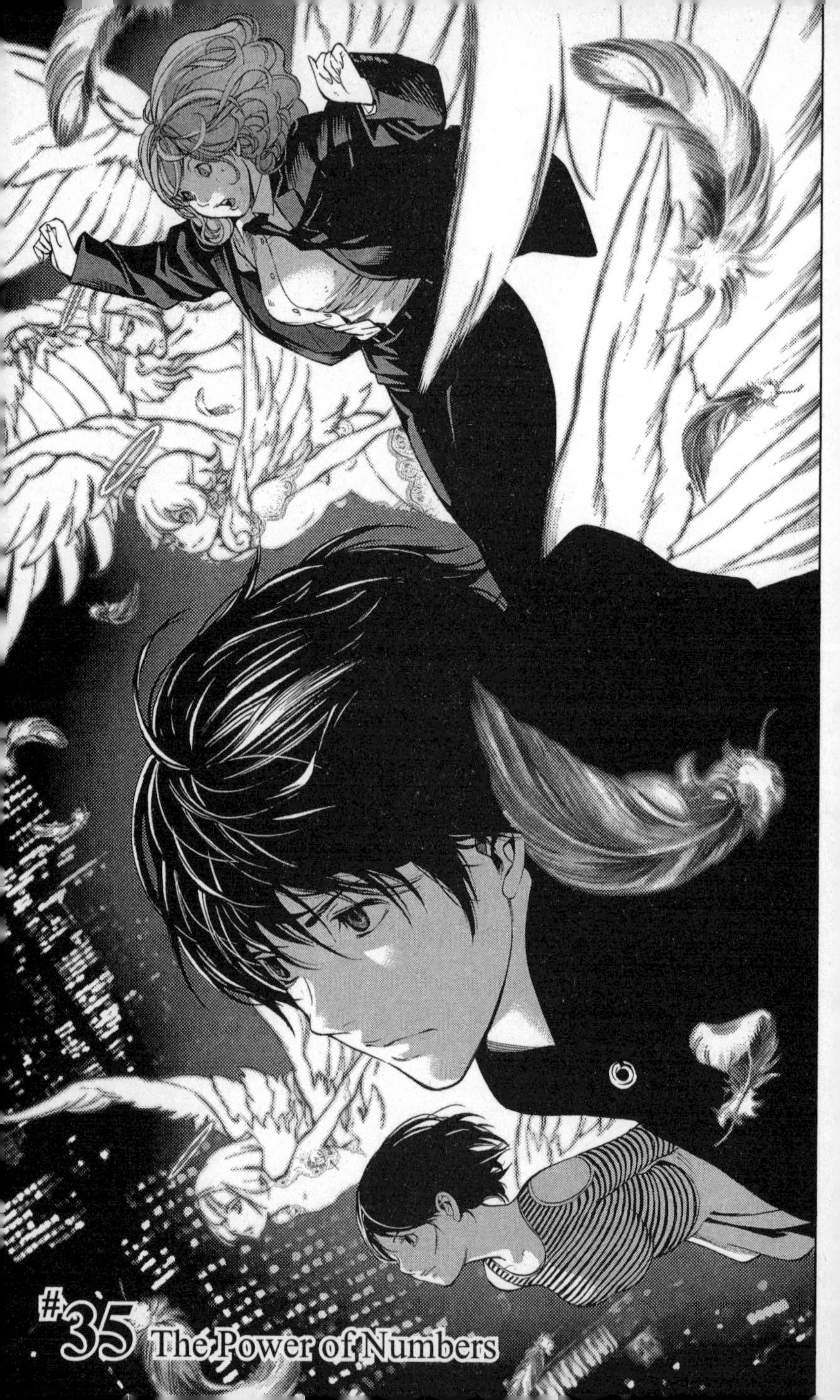

#35 The Power of Numbers

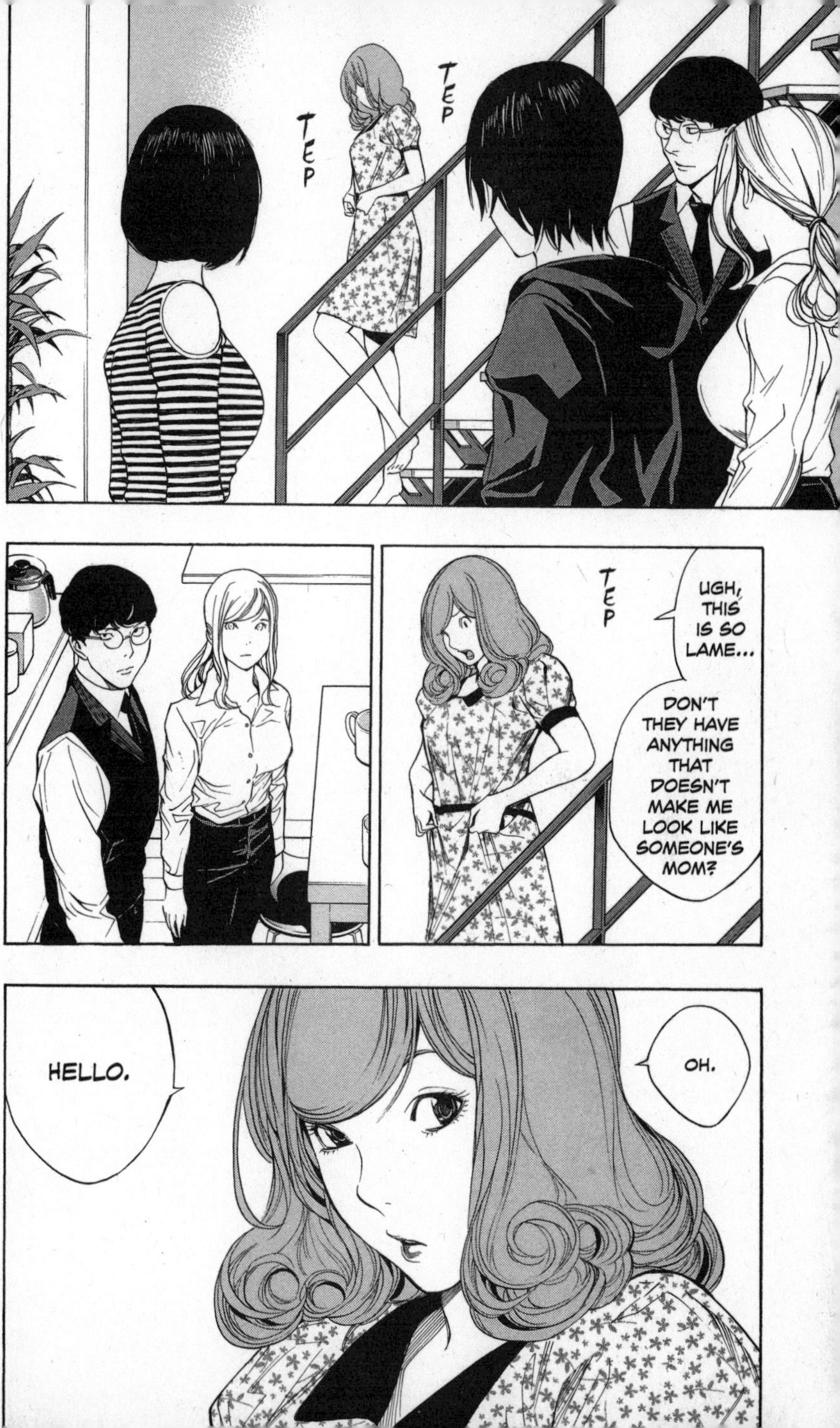
TEP
TEP
TEP
UGH, THIS IS SO LAME...
DON'T THEY HAVE ANYTHING THAT DOESN'T MAKE ME LOOK LIKE SOMEONE'S MOM?
OH.
HELLO.

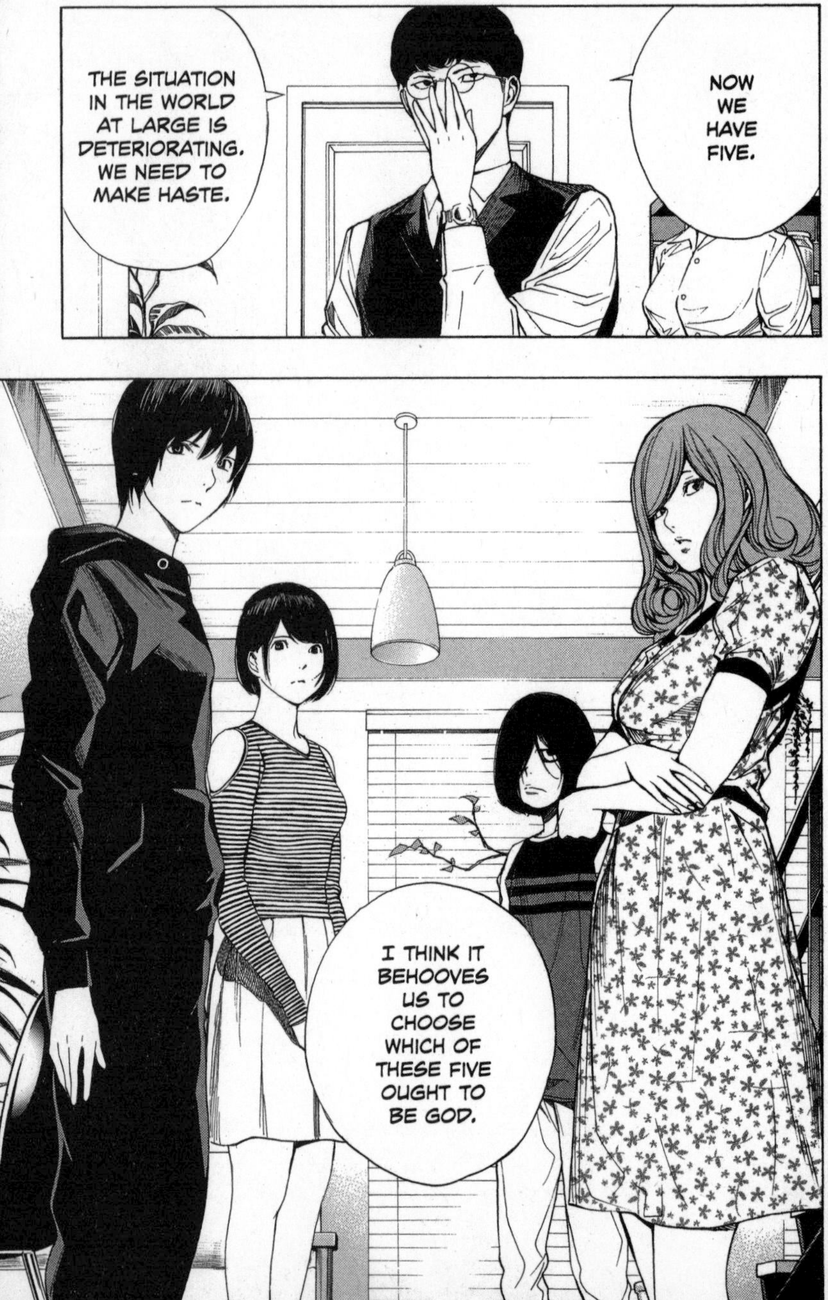
NOW WE HAVE FIVE.
THE SITUATION IN THE WORLD AT LARGE IS DETERIORATING. WE NEED TO MAKE HASTE.
I THINK IT BEHOOVES US TO CHOOSE WHICH OF THESE FIVE OUGHT TO BE GOD.

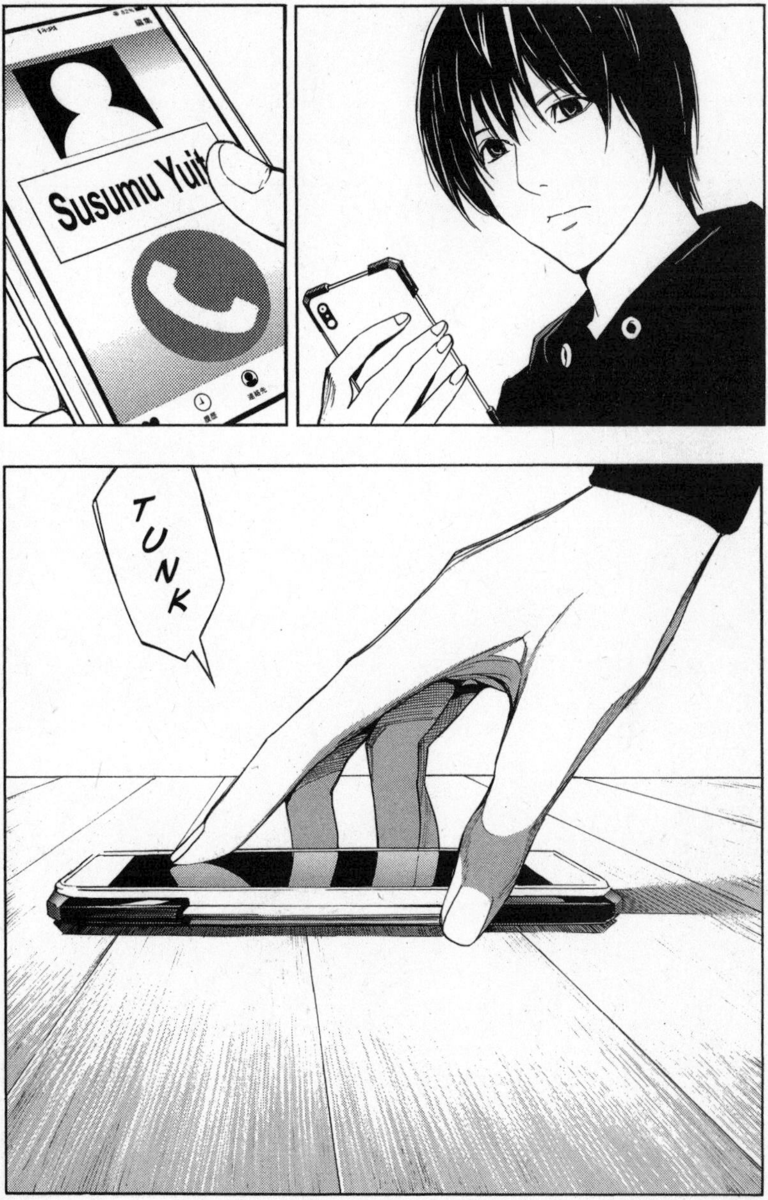
Susumu Yuit
TUNK

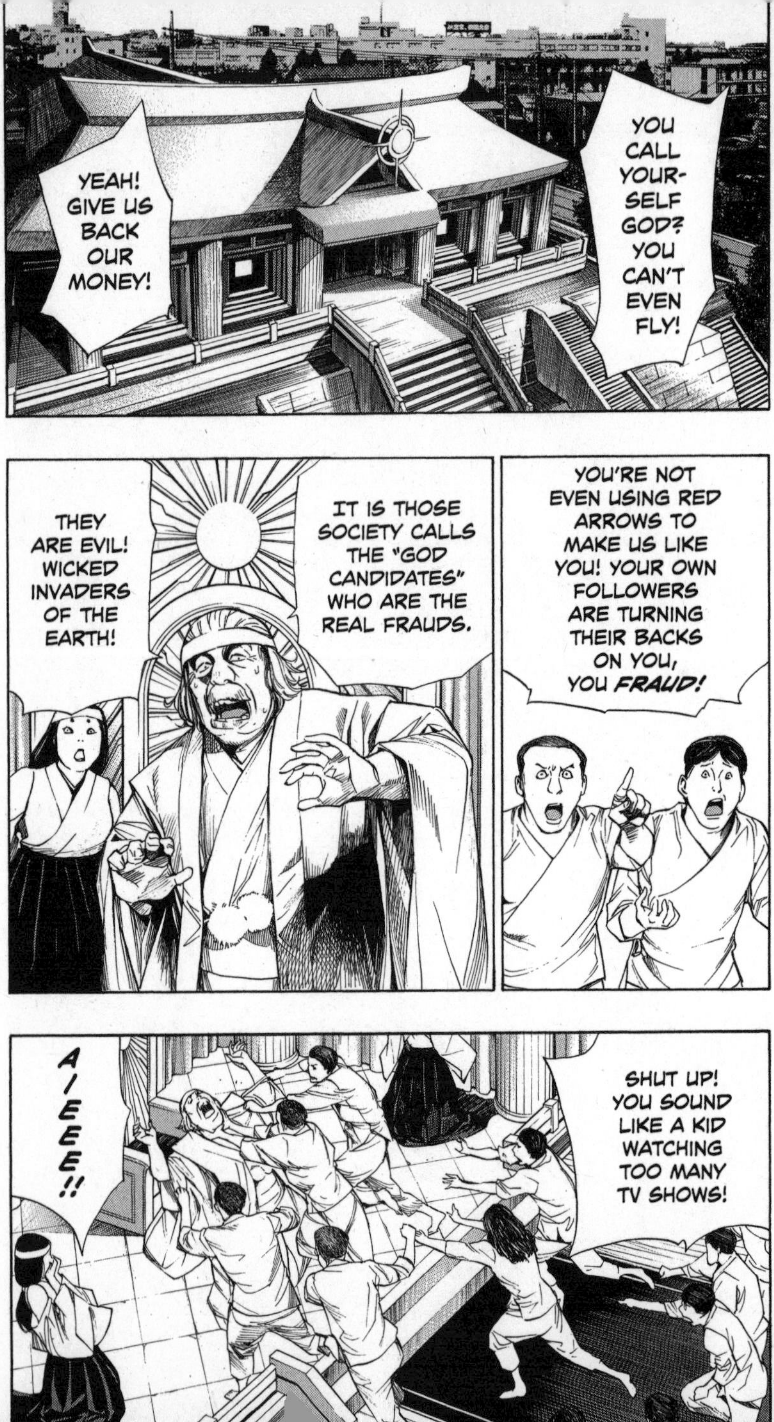
YOU CALL YOUR-SELF GOD? YOU CAN'T EVEN FLY!
YEAH! GIVE US BACK OUR MONEY!
YOU'RE NOT EVEN USING RED ARROWS TO MAKE US LIKE YOU! YOUR OWN FOLLOWERS ARE TURNING THEIR BACKS ON YOU, YOU *FRAUD!*
IT IS THOSE SOCIETY CALLS THE "GOD CANDIDATES" WHO ARE THE REAL FRAUDS.
THEY ARE EVIL! WICKED INVADERS OF THE EARTH!
SHUT UP! YOU SOUND LIKE A KID WATCHING TOO MANY TV SHOWS!
AIEEEE!!

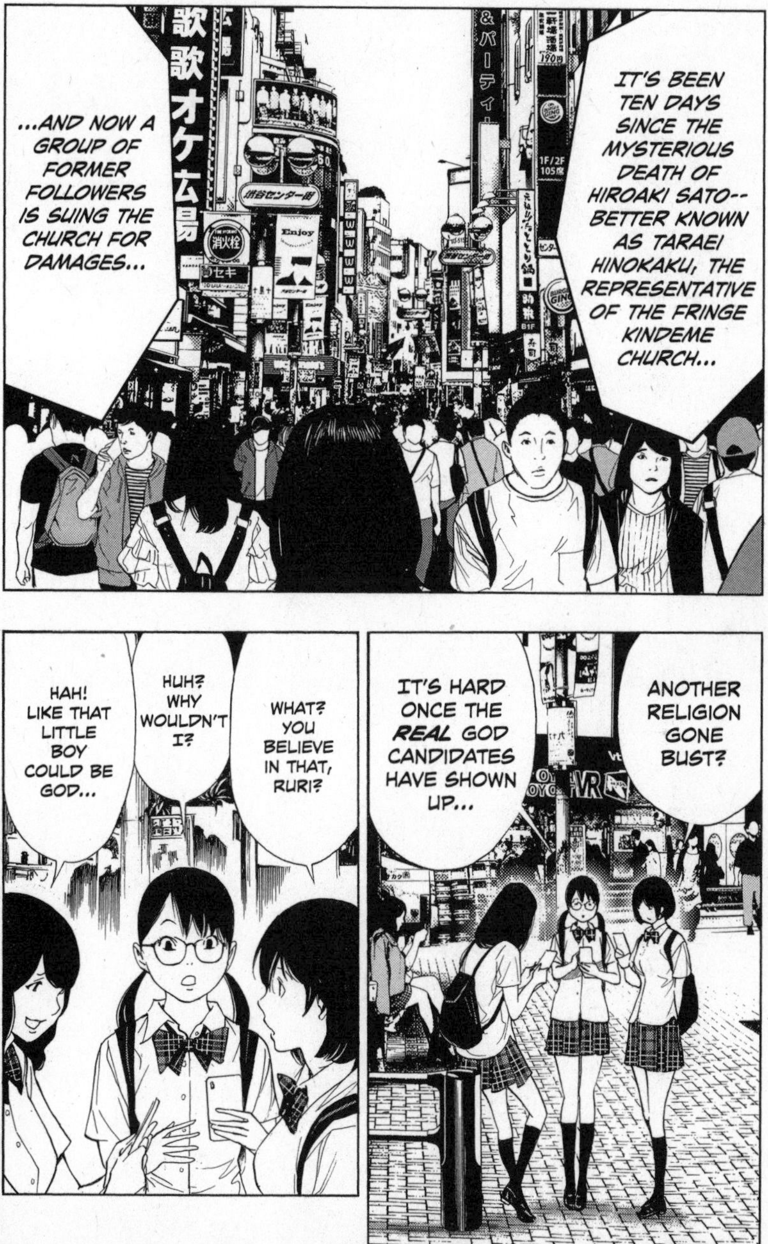
IT'S BEEN TEN DAYS SINCE THE MYSTERIOUS DEATH OF HIROAKI SATO--BETTER KNOWN AS TARAEI HINOKAKU, THE REPRESENTATIVE OF THE FRINGE KINDEME CHURCH...
...AND NOW A GROUP OF FORMER FOLLOWERS IS SUING THE CHURCH FOR DAMAGES...
ANOTHER RELIGION GONE BUST?
IT'S HARD ONCE THE *REAL* GOD CANDIDATES HAVE SHOWN UP...
WHAT? YOU BELIEVE IN THAT, RURI?
HUH? WHY WOULDN'T I?
HAH! LIKE THAT LITTLE BOY COULD BE GOD...

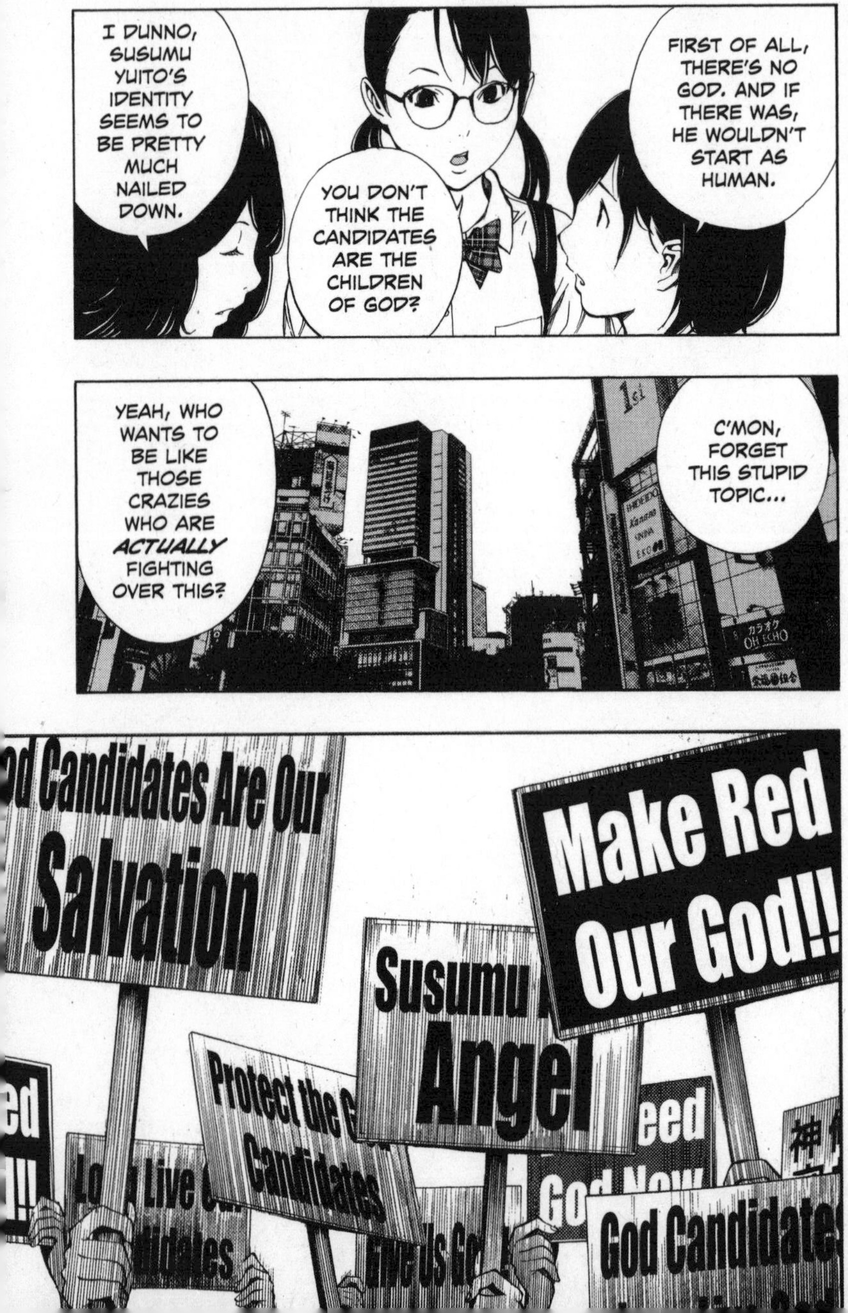
FIRST OF ALL, THERE'S NO GOD. AND IF THERE WAS, HE WOULDN'T START AS HUMAN.
I DUNNO, SUSUMU YUITO'S IDENTITY SEEMS TO BE PRETTY MUCH NAILED DOWN.
YOU DON'T THINK THE CANDIDATES ARE THE CHILDREN OF GOD?
C'MON, FORGET THIS STUPID TOPIC...
YEAH, WHO WANTS TO BE LIKE THOSE CRAZIES WHO ARE *ACTUALLY* FIGHTING OVER THIS?
Make Red Our God!!
Angel
Salvation

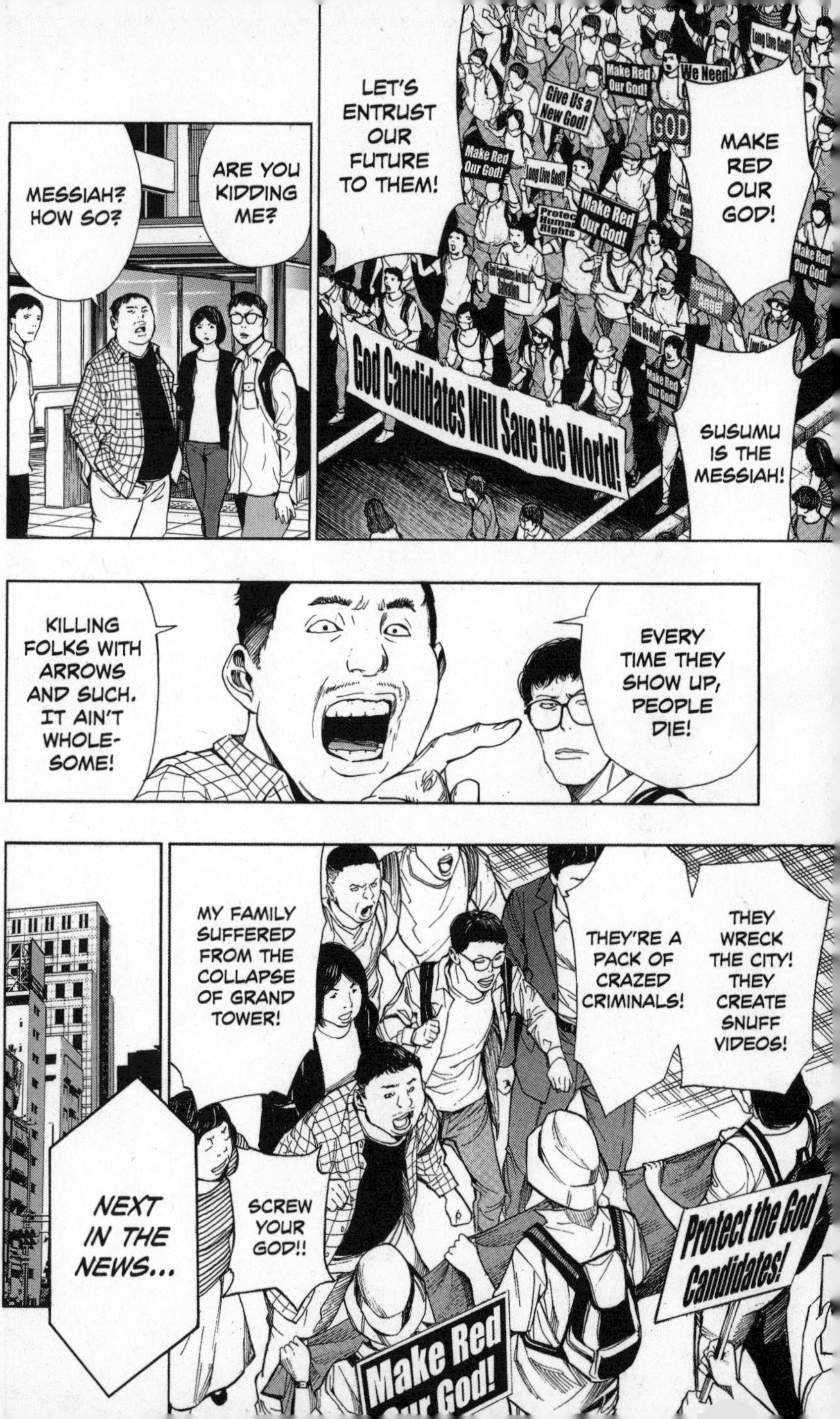
Long Live God!
We Need
Make Red Our God!
MAKE RED OUR GOD!
LET'S ENTRUST OUR FUTURE TO THEM!
Give Us a New God!
GOD
Make Red Our God!
Long Live God!
Make Red Our God!
Protect Human Rights
Make Red Our God!
Give Us God!
Make Red Our God!
God Candidates Will Save the World!
SUSUMU IS THE MESSIAH!
MESSIAH? HOW SO?
ARE YOU KIDDING ME?
EVERY TIME THEY SHOW UP, PEOPLE DIE!
KILLING FOLKS WITH ARROWS AND SUCH. IT AIN'T WHOLE-SOME!
THEY WRECK THE CITY! THEY CREATE SNUFF VIDEOS!
THEY'RE A PACK OF CRAZED CRIMINALS!
MY FAMILY SUFFERED FROM THE COLLAPSE OF GRAND TOWER!
Protect the God Candidates!
SCREW YOUR GOD!!
Make Red
NEXT IN THE NEWS...

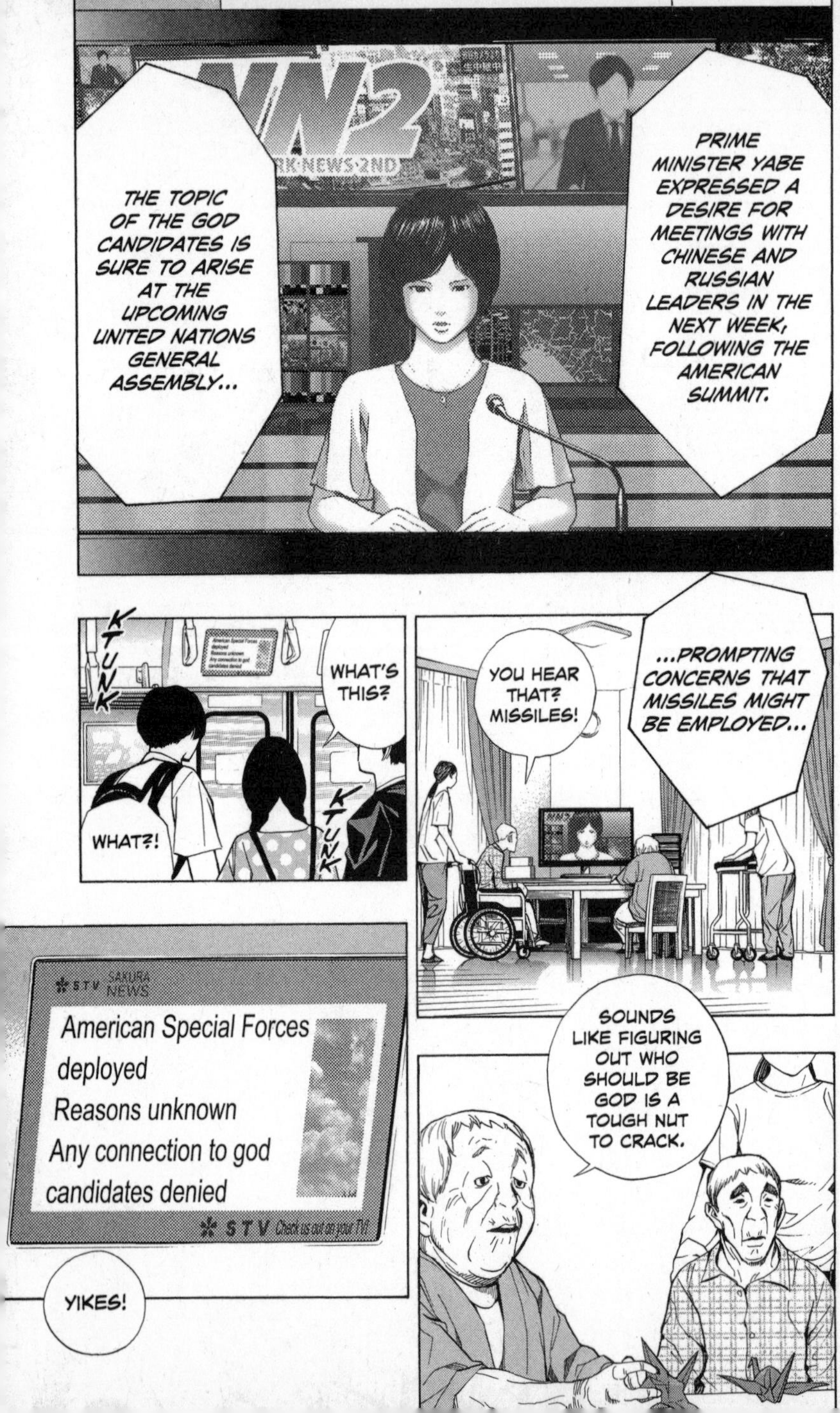
PRIME MINISTER YABE EXPRESSED A DESIRE FOR MEETINGS WITH CHINESE AND RUSSIAN LEADERS IN THE NEXT WEEK, FOLLOWING THE AMERICAN SUMMIT.
THE TOPIC OF THE GOD CANDIDATES IS SURE TO ARISE AT THE UPCOMING UNITED NATIONS GENERAL ASSEMBLY...
...PROMPTING CONCERNS THAT MISSILES MIGHT BE EMPLOYED...
YOU HEAR THAT? MISSILES!
WHAT'S THIS?
KTUNK
WHAT?!
KTUNK
SOUNDS LIKE FIGURING OUT WHO SHOULD BE GOD IS A TOUGH NUT TO CRACK.
STV SAKURA NEWS
American Special Forces deployed
Reasons unknown
Any connection to god candidates denied
STV Check us out on your TV!
YIKES!

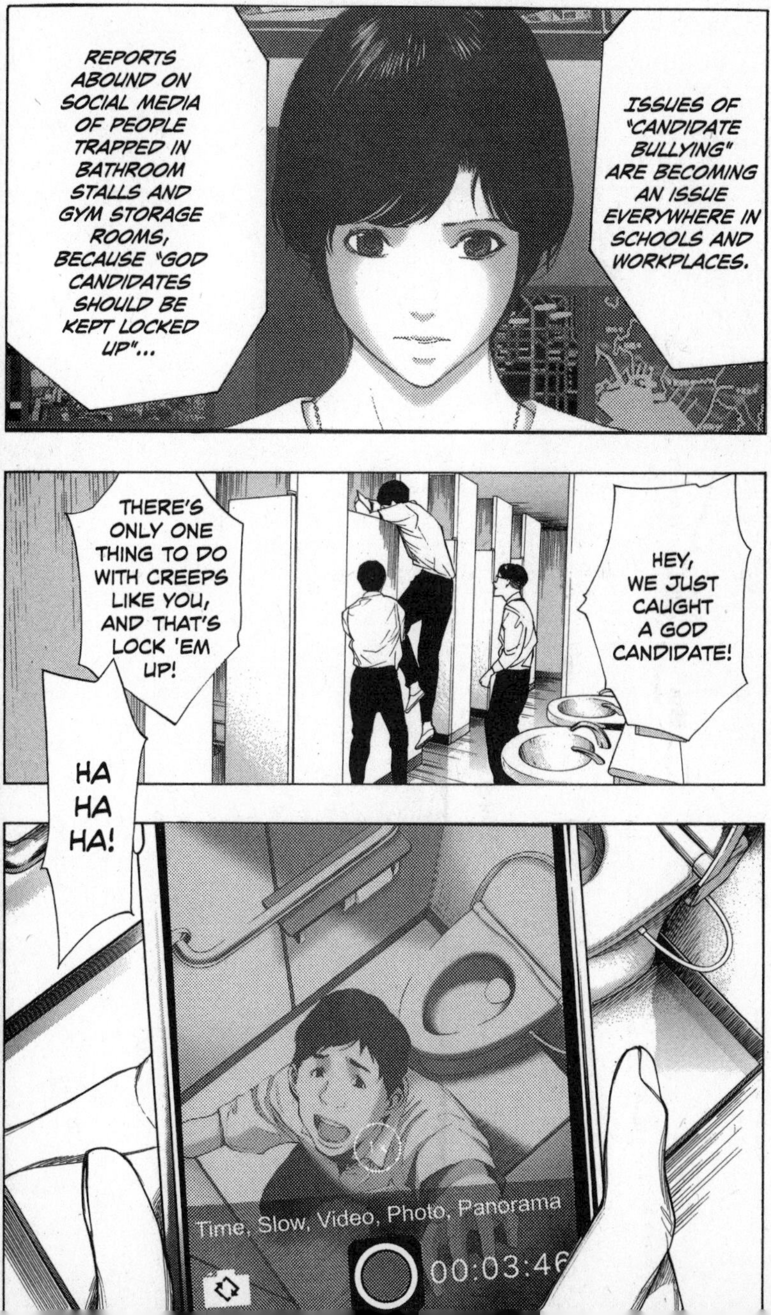
ISSUES OF "CANDIDATE BULLYING" ARE BECOMING AN ISSUE EVERYWHERE IN SCHOOLS AND WORKPLACES.
REPORTS ABOUND ON SOCIAL MEDIA OF PEOPLE TRAPPED IN BATHROOM STALLS AND GYM STORAGE ROOMS, BECAUSE "GOD CANDIDATES SHOULD BE KEPT LOCKED UP"...
HEY, WE JUST CAUGHT A GOD CANDIDATE!
THERE'S ONLY ONE THING TO DO WITH CREEPS LIKE YOU, AND THAT'S LOCK 'EM UP!
HA HA HA!
Time, Slow, Video, Photo, Panorama
00:03:46

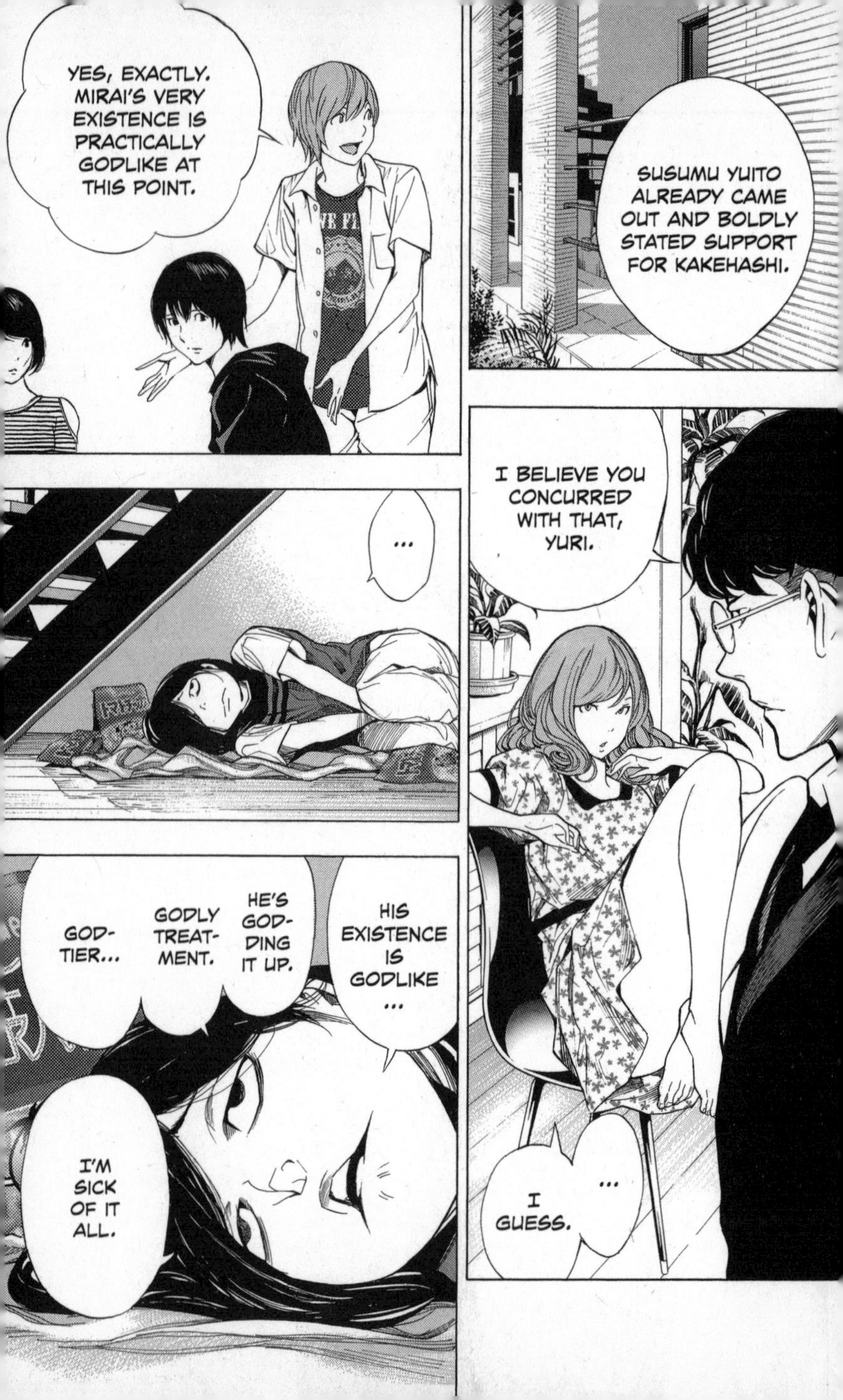
SUSUMU YUITO ALREADY CAME OUT AND BOLDLY STATED SUPPORT FOR KAKEHASHI.
YES, EXACTLY. MIRAI'S VERY EXISTENCE IS PRACTICALLY GODLIKE AT THIS POINT.
I BELIEVE YOU CONCURRED WITH THAT, YURI.
... I GUESS.
...
HIS EXISTENCE IS GODLIKE ...
HE'S GOD-DING IT UP.
GODLY TREAT-MENT.
GOD-TIER...
I'M SICK OF IT ALL.

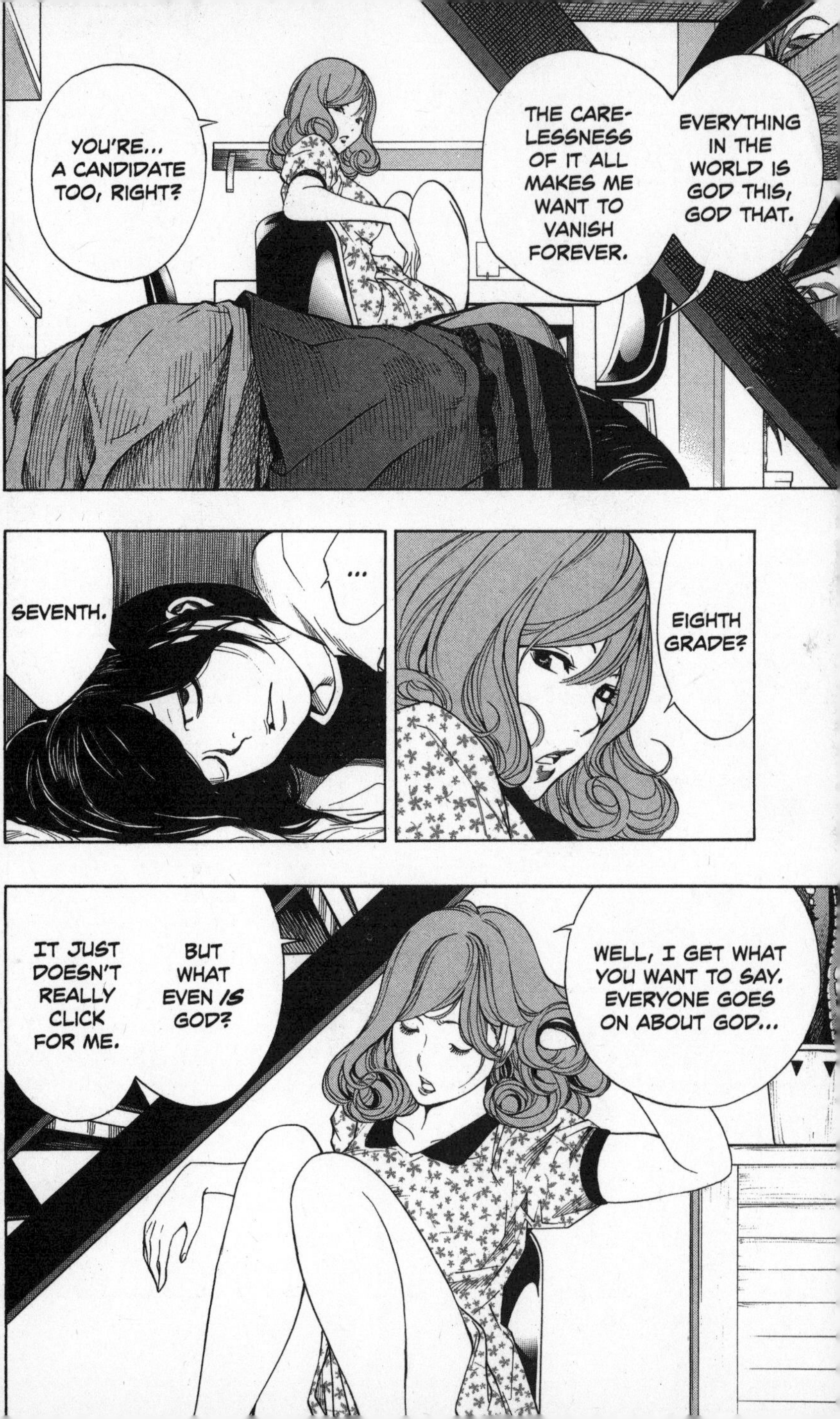
EVERYTHING IN THE WORLD IS GOD THIS, GOD THAT.
THE CARELESSNESS OF IT ALL MAKES ME WANT TO VANISH FOREVER.
YOU'RE... A CANDIDATE TOO, RIGHT?
EIGHTH GRADE?
...
SEVENTH.
WELL, I GET WHAT YOU WANT TO SAY. EVERYONE GOES ON ABOUT GOD...
BUT WHAT EVEN *IS* GOD?
IT JUST DOESN'T REALLY CLICK FOR ME.

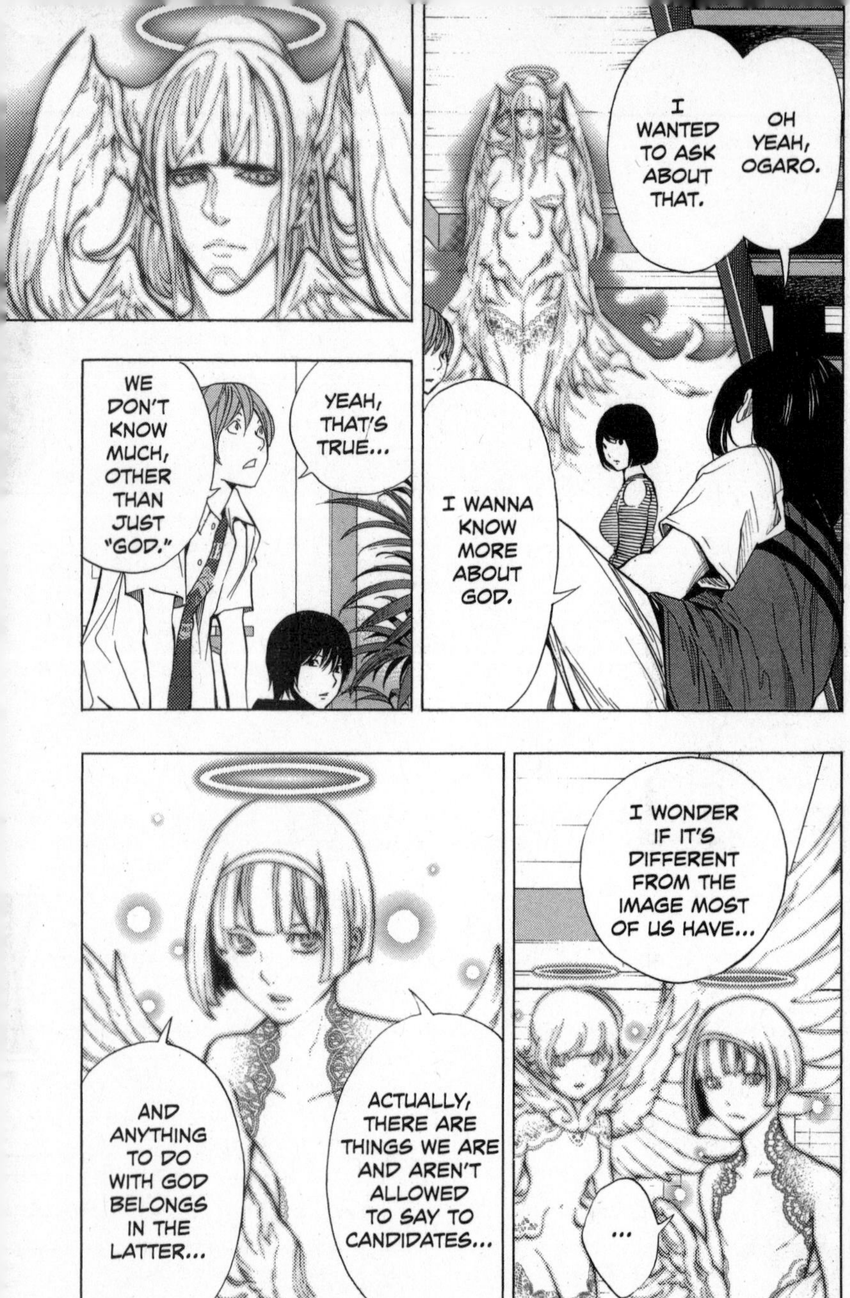
OH YEAH, OGARO.
I WANTED TO ASK ABOUT THAT.
I WANNA KNOW MORE ABOUT GOD.
YEAH, THAT'S TRUE...
WE DON'T KNOW MUCH, OTHER THAN JUST "GOD."
I WONDER IF IT'S DIFFERENT FROM THE IMAGE MOST OF US HAVE...
...
ACTUALLY, THERE ARE THINGS WE ARE AND AREN'T ALLOWED TO SAY TO CANDIDATES...
AND ANYTHING TO DO WITH GOD BELONGS IN THE LATTER...

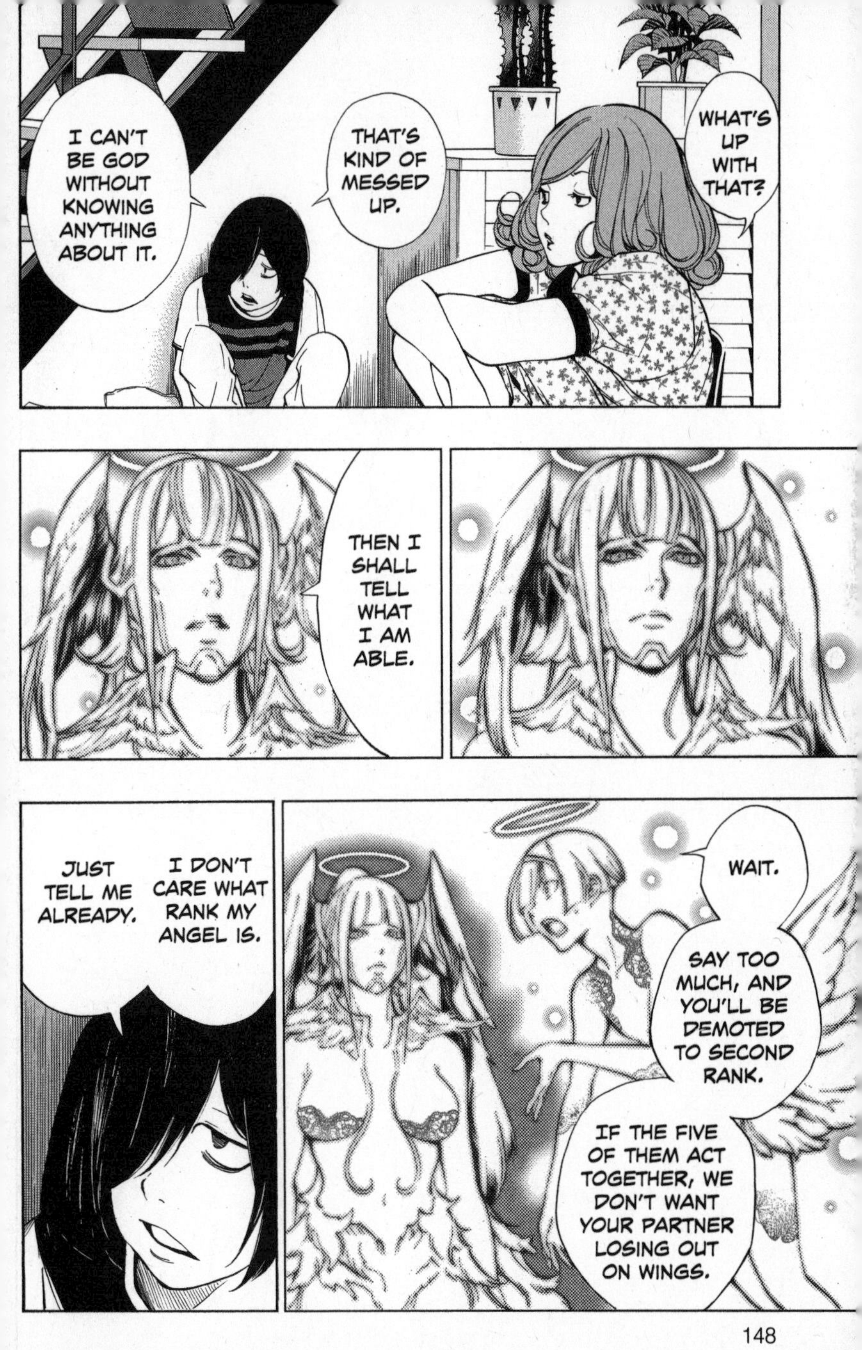
WHAT'S UP WITH THAT?
THAT'S KIND OF MESSED UP.
I CAN'T BE GOD WITHOUT KNOWING ANYTHING ABOUT IT.
THEN I SHALL TELL WHAT I AM ABLE.
WAIT.
SAY TOO MUCH, AND YOU'LL BE DEMOTED TO SECOND RANK.
IF THE FIVE OF THEM ACT TOGETHER, WE DON'T WANT YOUR PARTNER LOSING OUT ON WINGS.
I DON'T CARE WHAT RANK MY ANGEL IS.
JUST TELL ME ALREADY.

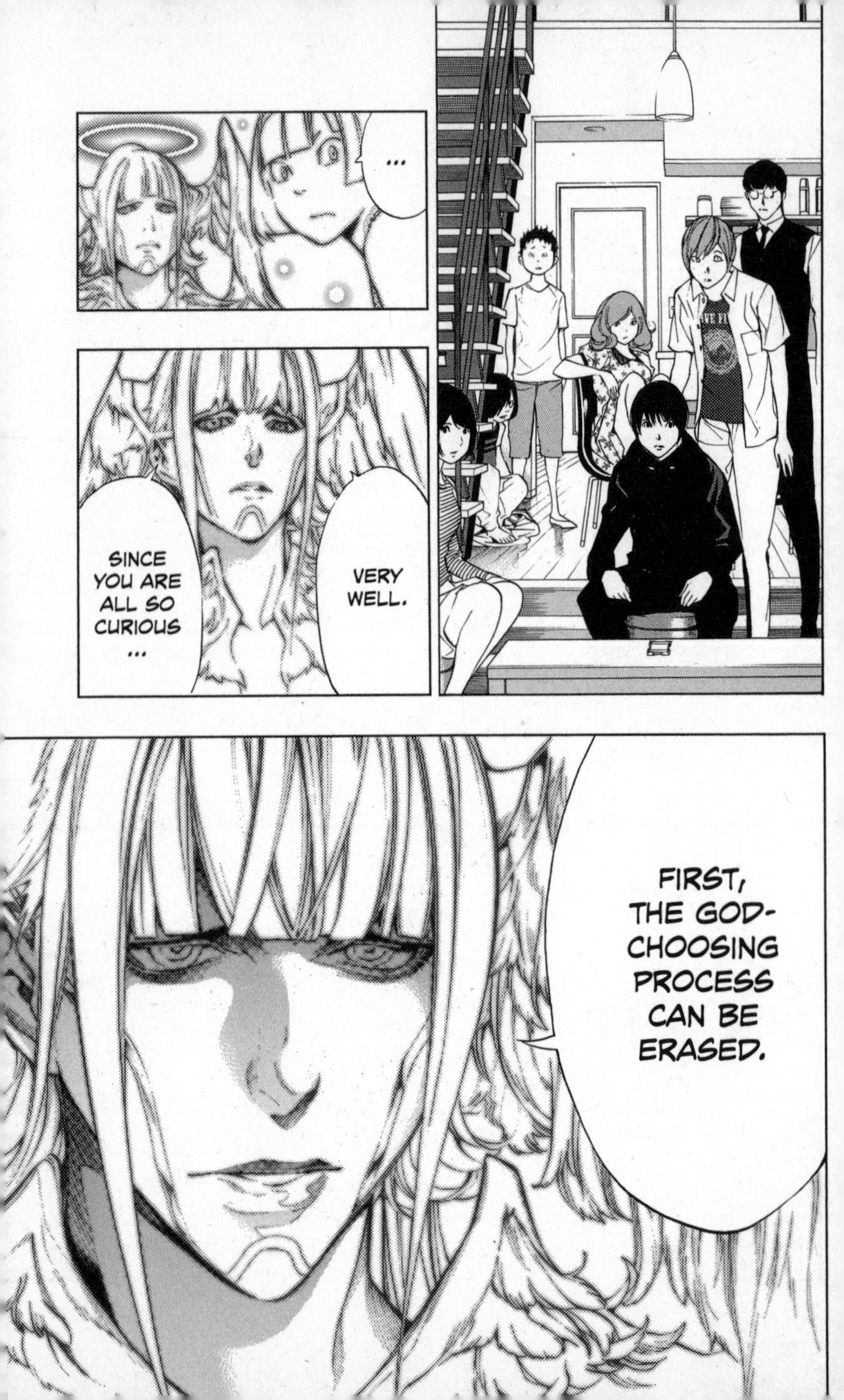
...
VERY WELL.
SINCE YOU ARE ALL SO CURIOUS ...
FIRST, THE GOD-CHOOSING PROCESS CAN BE ERASED.

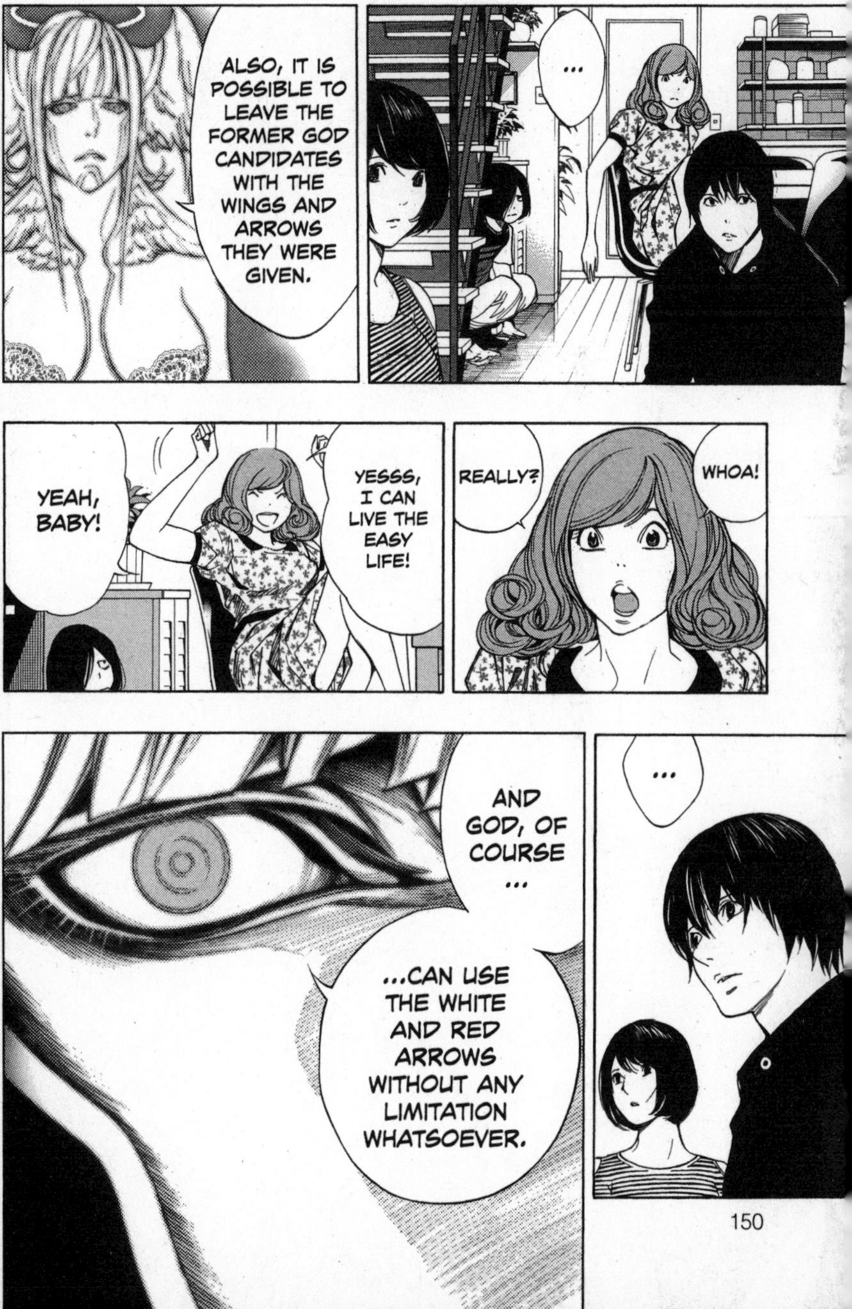
...
ALSO, IT IS POSSIBLE TO LEAVE THE FORMER GOD CANDIDATES WITH THE WINGS AND ARROWS THEY WERE GIVEN.
WHOA!
REALLY?
YESSS, I CAN LIVE THE EASY LIFE!
YEAH, BABY!
...
AND GOD, OF COURSE ...
...CAN USE THE WHITE AND RED ARROWS WITHOUT ANY LIMITATION WHATSOEVER.

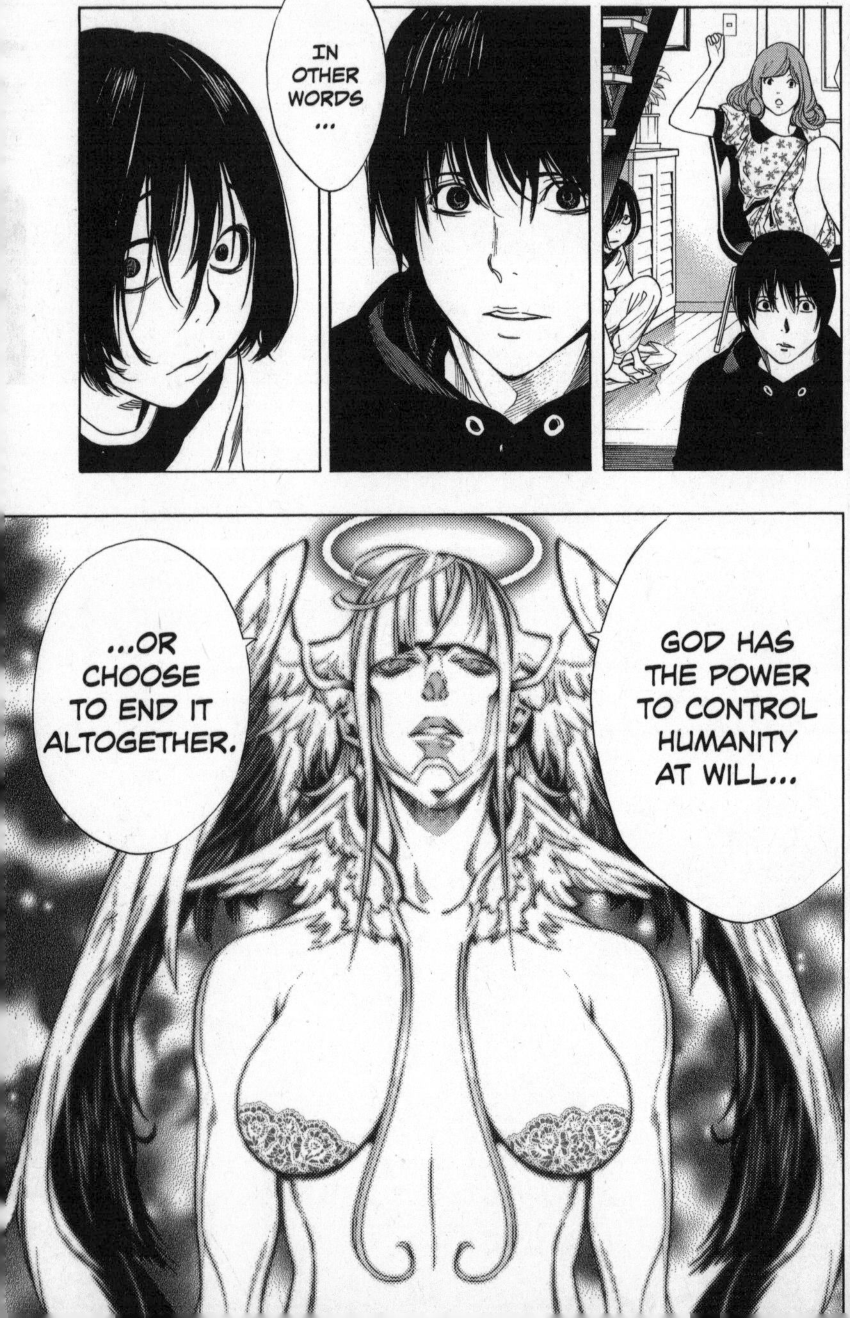
IN OTHER WORDS ...
GOD HAS THE POWER TO CONTROL HUMANITY AT WILL...
...OR CHOOSE TO END IT ALTOGETHER.

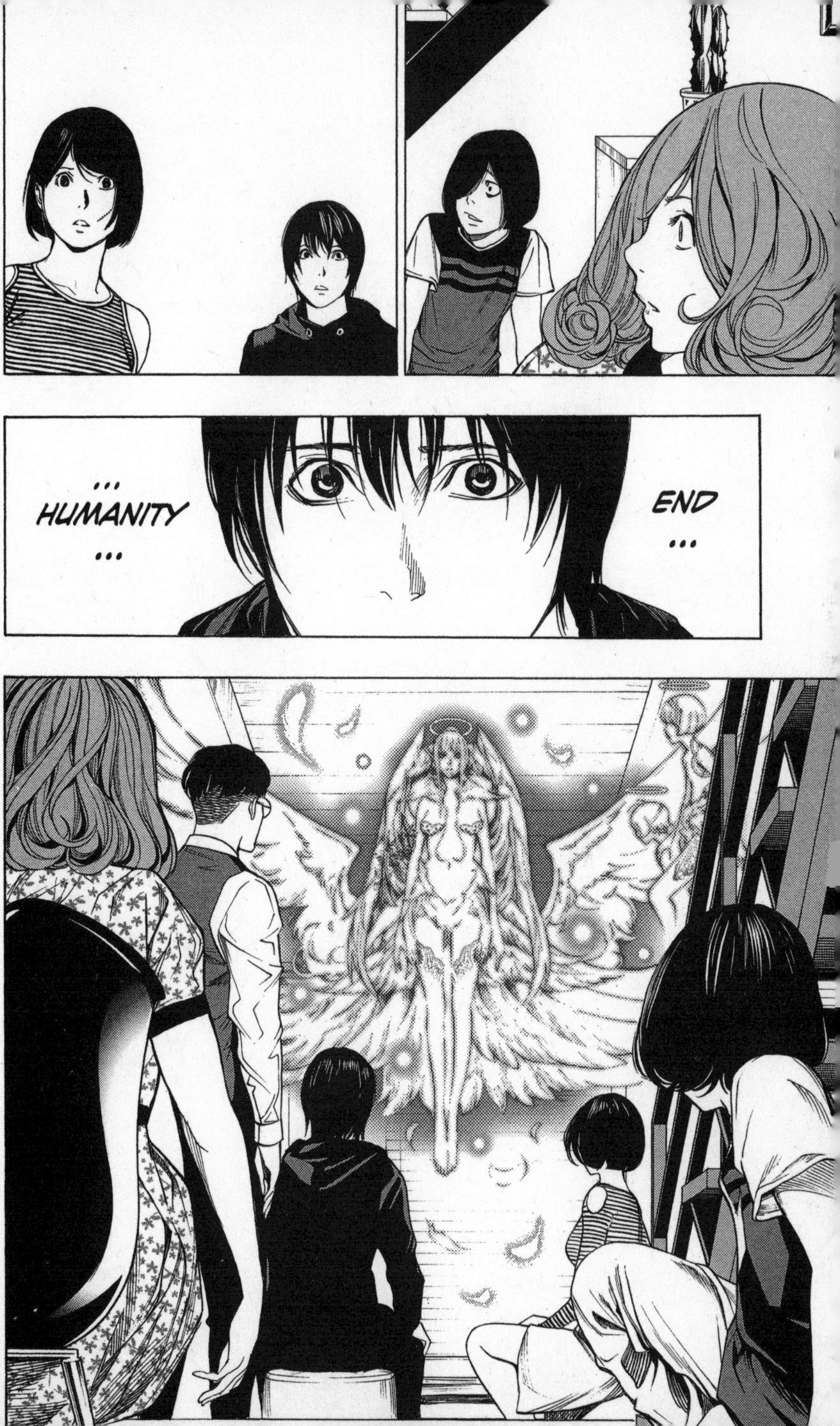
...
HUMANITY
...
END
...

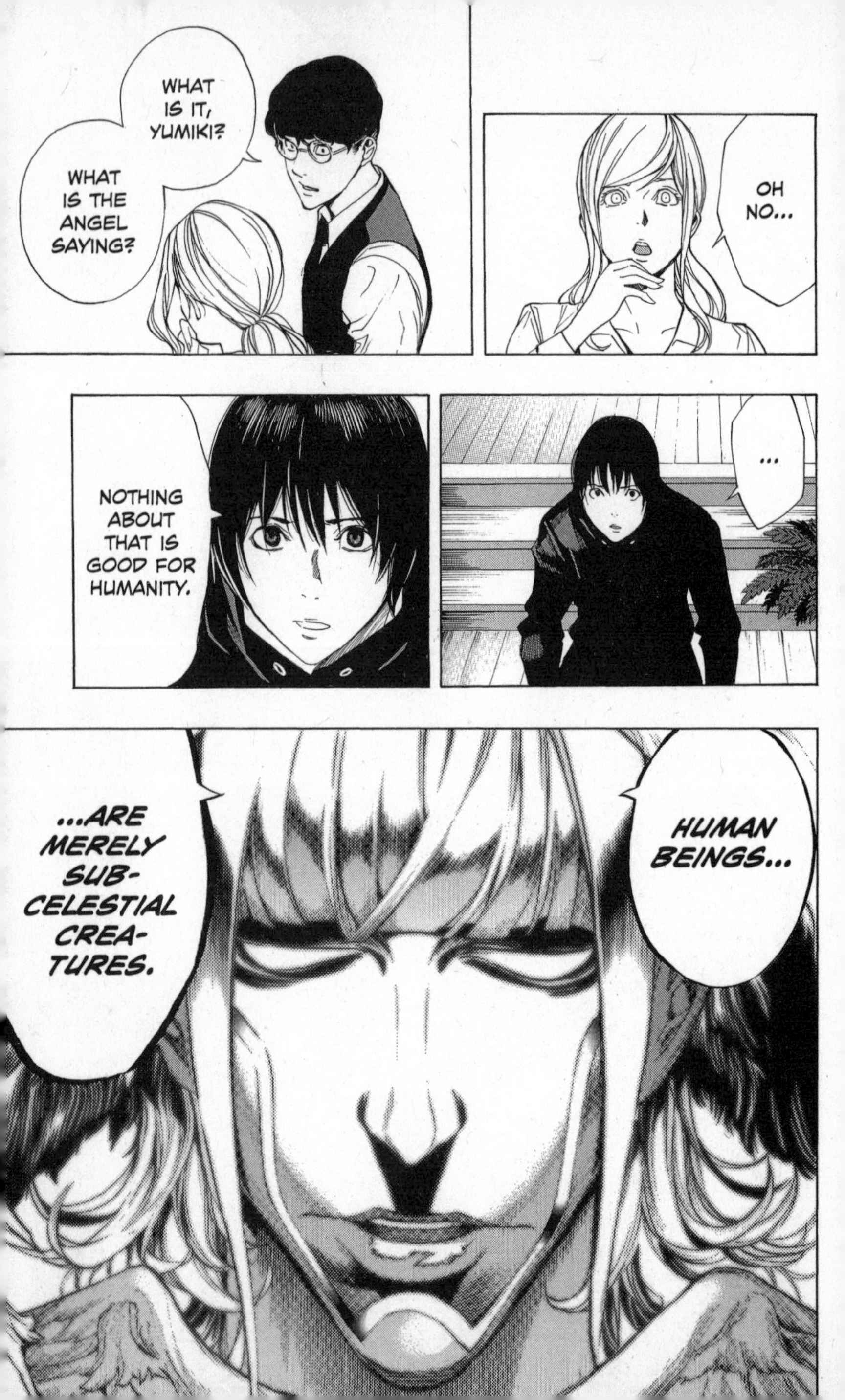
OH NO...
WHAT IS IT, YUMIKI?
WHAT IS THE ANGEL SAYING?
...
NOTHING ABOUT THAT IS GOOD FOR HUMANITY.
HUMAN BEINGS...
...ARE MERELY SUB-CELESTIAL CREATURES.

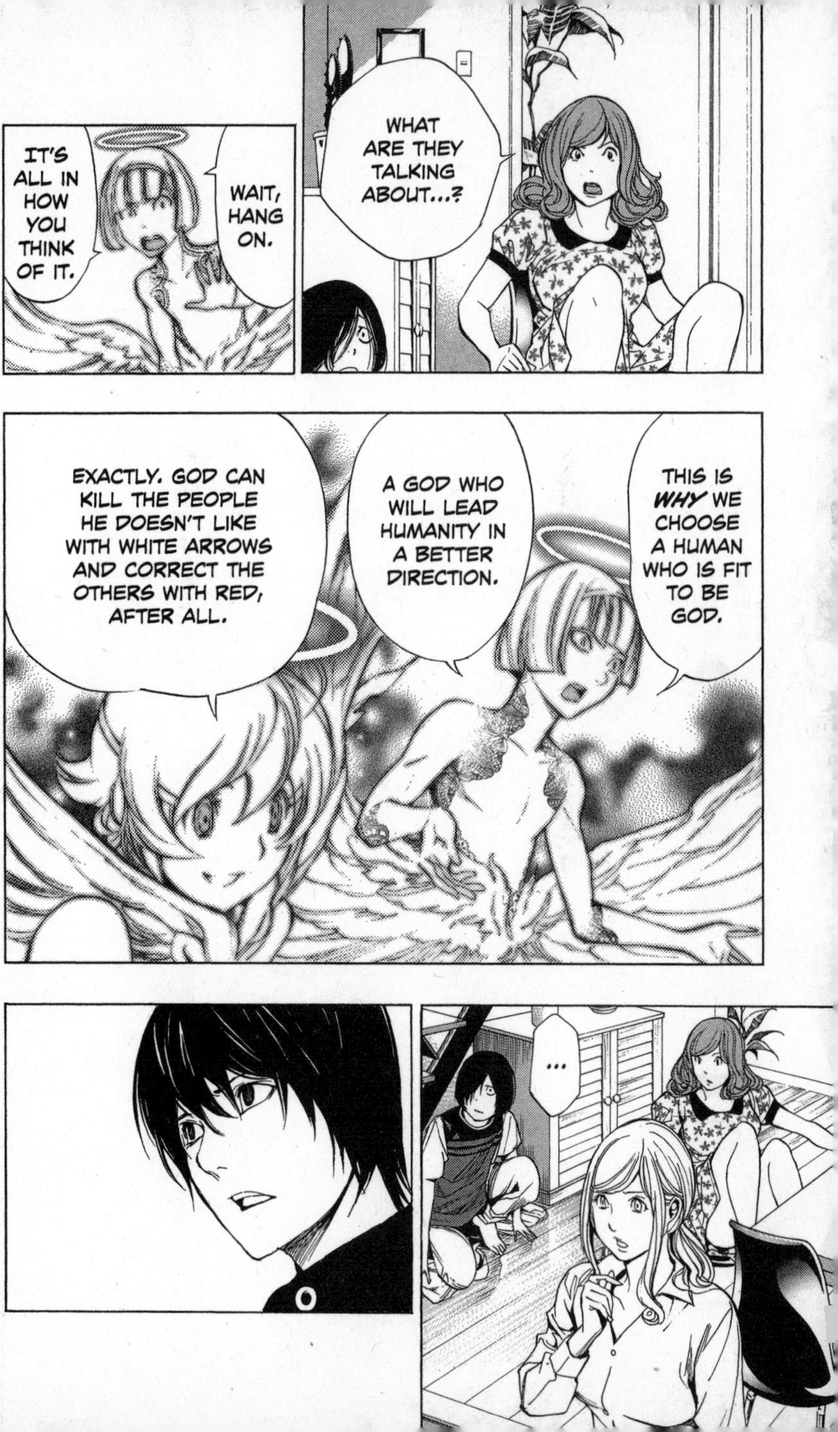
WHAT ARE THEY TALKING ABOUT...?
WAIT, HANG ON.
IT'S ALL IN HOW YOU THINK OF IT.
THIS IS *WHY* WE CHOOSE A HUMAN WHO IS FIT TO BE GOD.
A GOD WHO WILL LEAD HUMANITY IN A BETTER DIRECTION.
EXACTLY. GOD CAN KILL THE PEOPLE HE DOESN'T LIKE WITH WHITE ARROWS AND CORRECT THE OTHERS WITH RED, AFTER ALL.
...

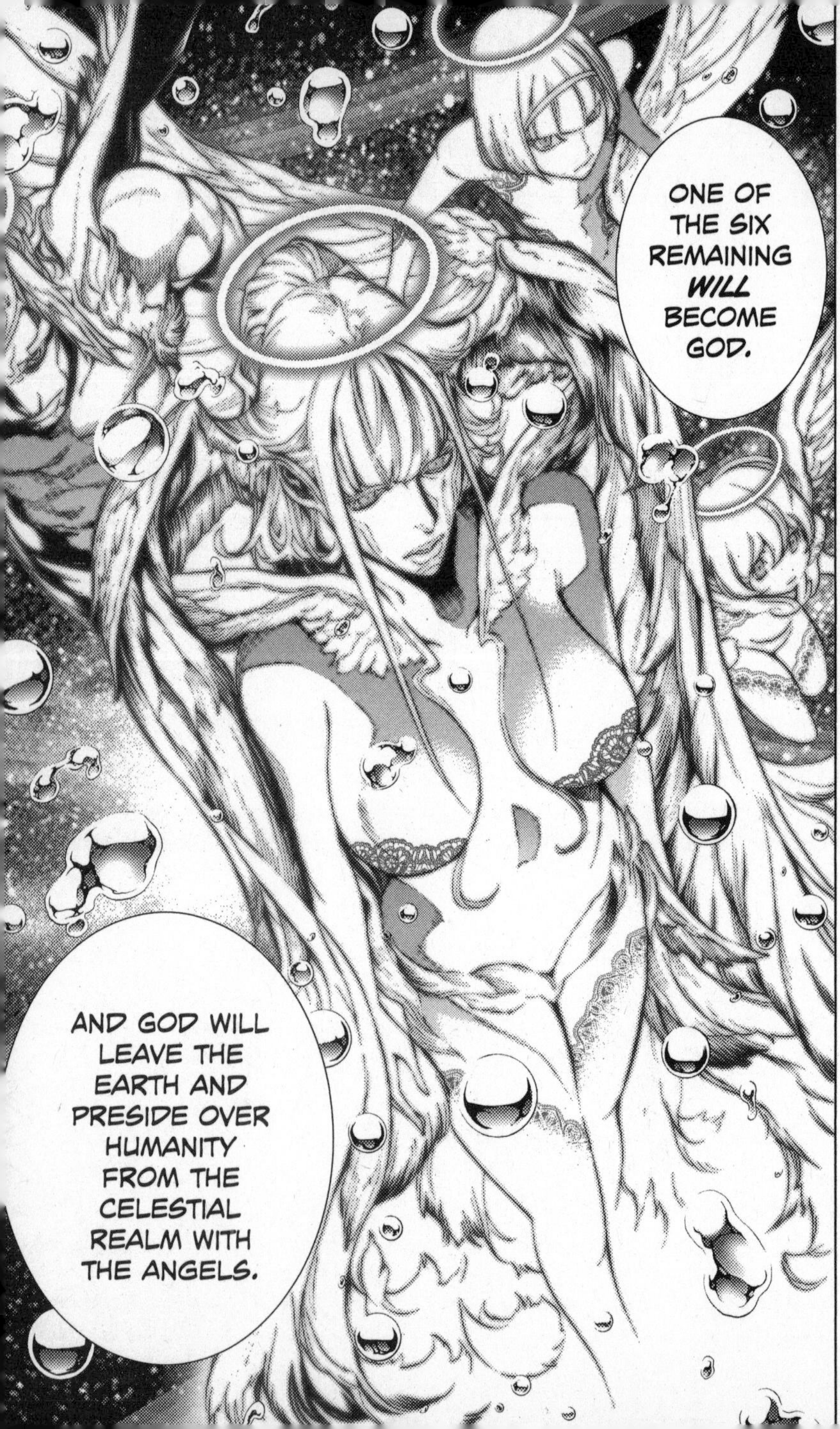
ONE OF THE SIX REMAINING *WILL* BECOME GOD.
AND GOD WILL LEAVE THE EARTH AND PRESIDE OVER HUMANITY FROM THE CELESTIAL REALM WITH THE ANGELS.

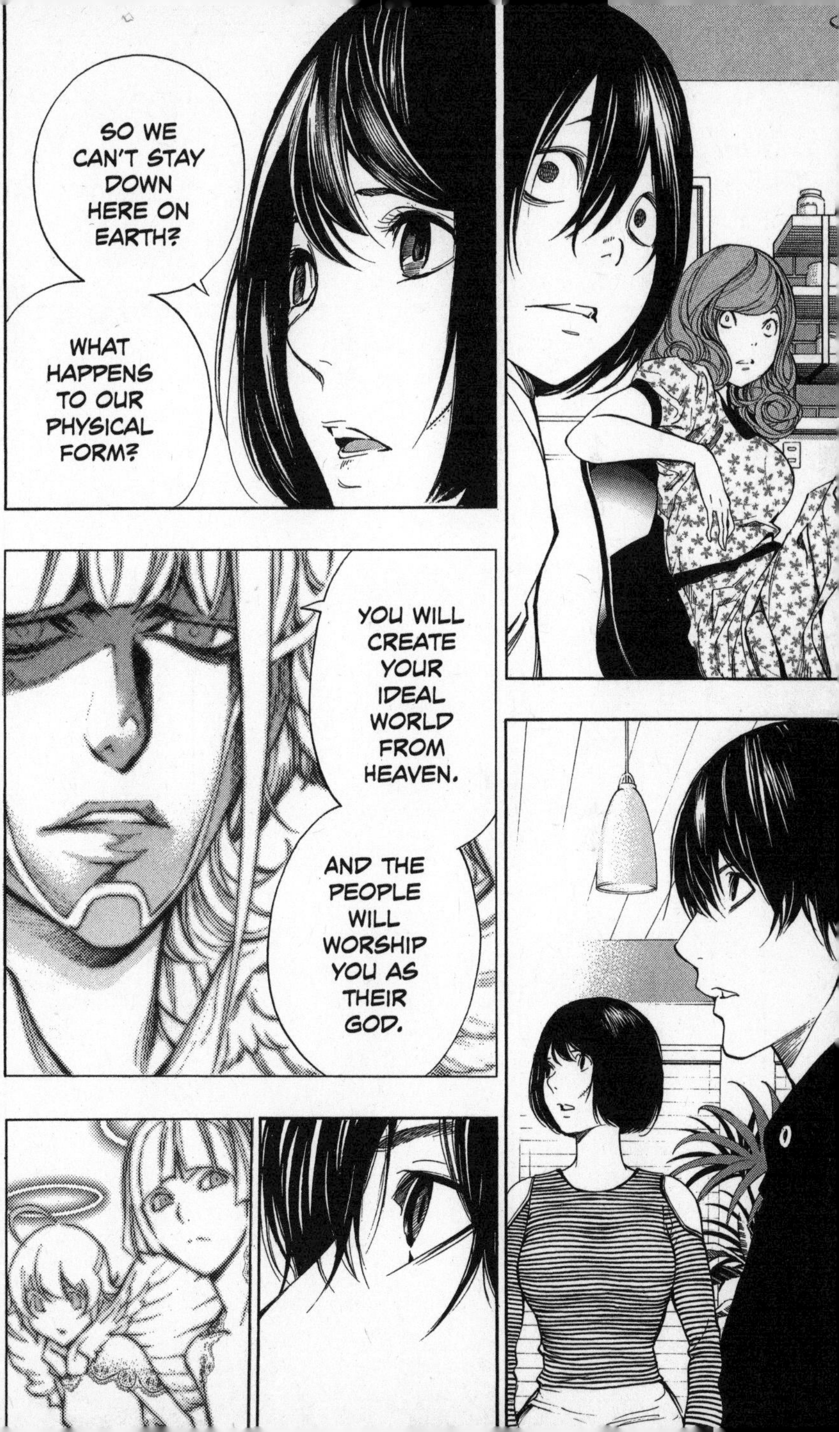
SO WE CAN'T STAY DOWN HERE ON EARTH?
WHAT HAPPENS TO OUR PHYSICAL FORM?
YOU WILL CREATE YOUR IDEAL WORLD FROM HEAVEN.
AND THE PEOPLE WILL WORSHIP YOU AS THEIR GOD.

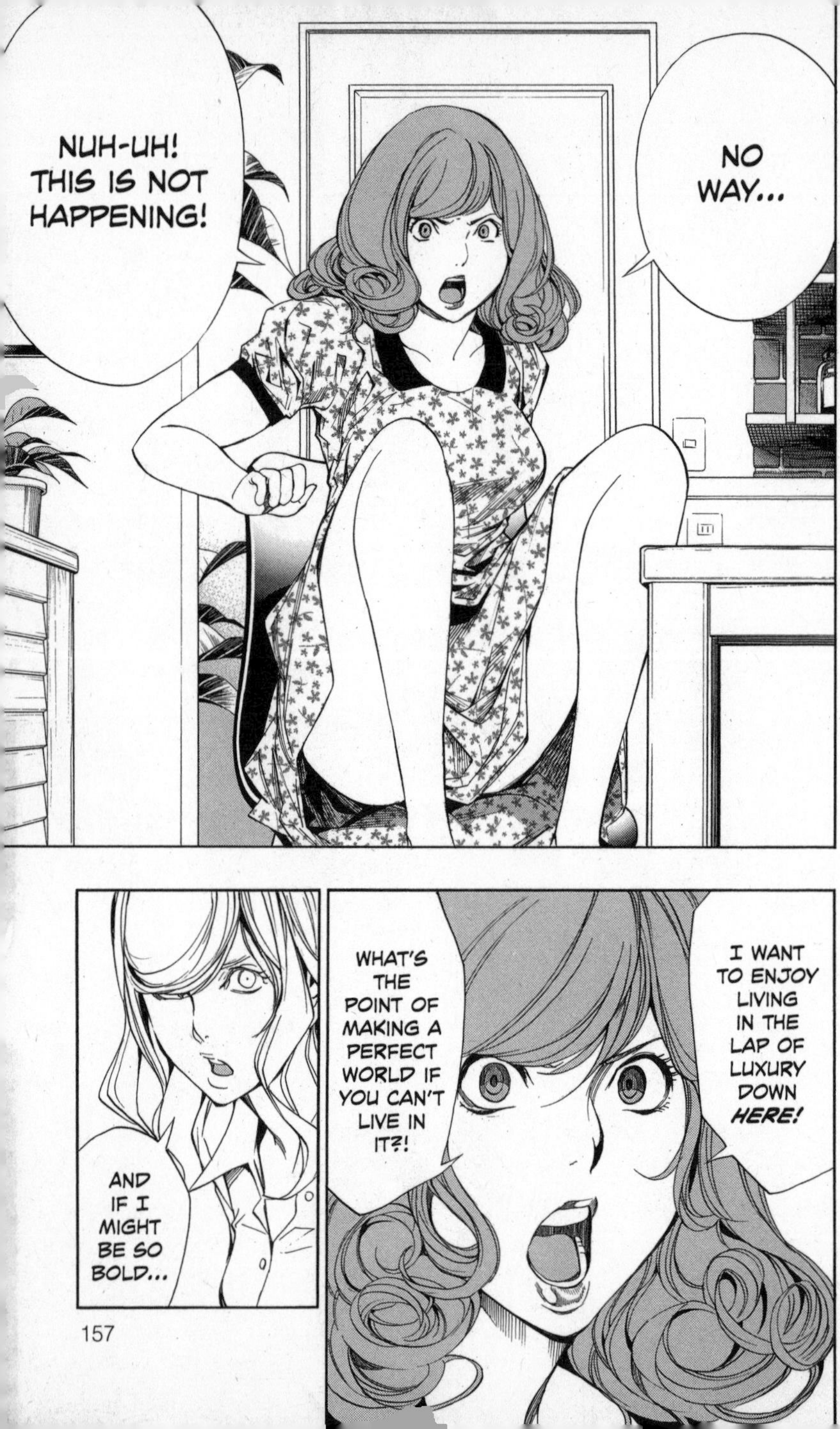
NO WAY...
NUH-UH! THIS IS NOT HAPPENING!
I WANT TO ENJOY LIVING IN THE LAP OF LUXURY DOWN *HERE!*
WHAT'S THE POINT OF MAKING A PERFECT WORLD IF YOU CAN'T LIVE IN IT?!
AND IF I MIGHT BE SO BOLD...

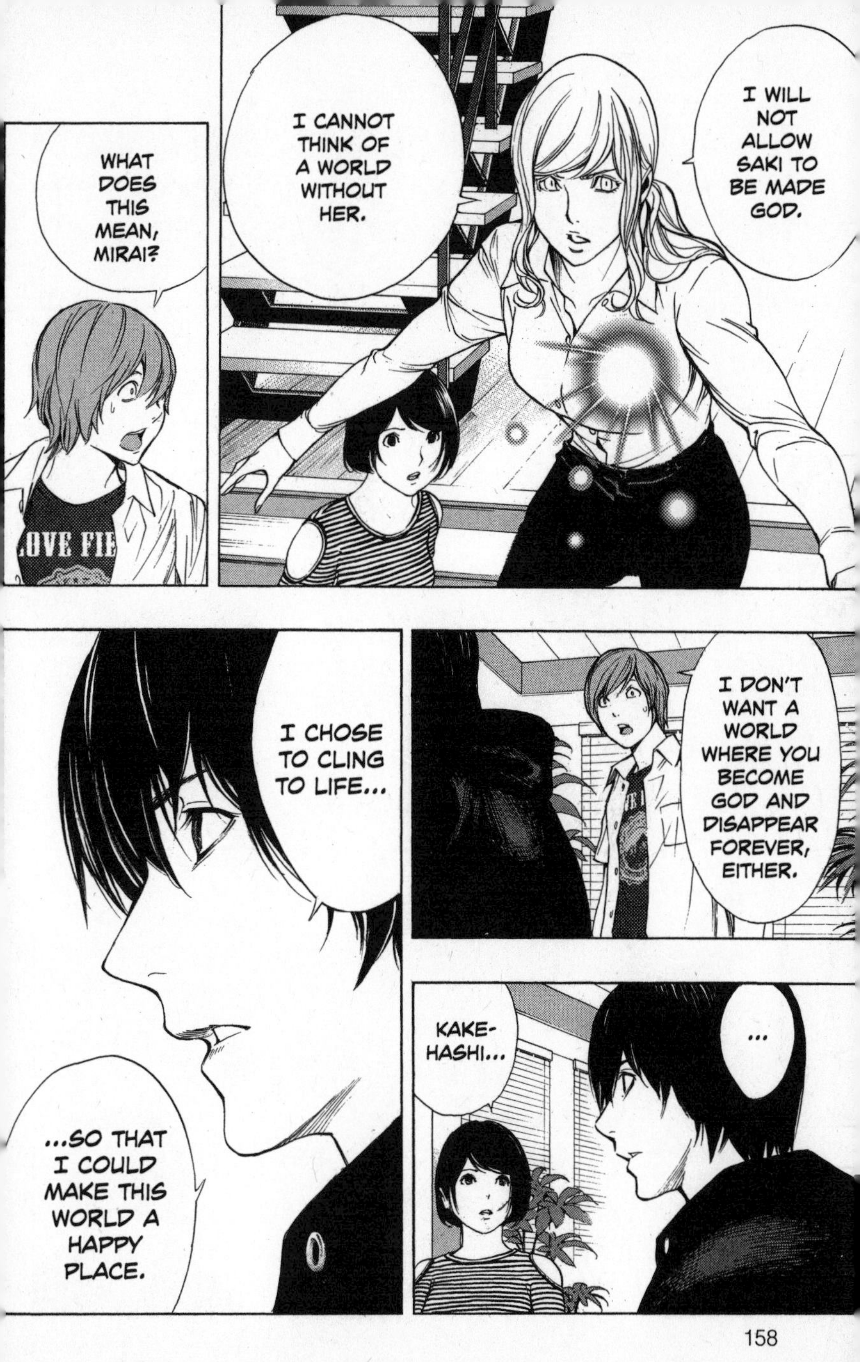
I WILL NOT ALLOW SAKI TO BE MADE GOD.
I CANNOT THINK OF A WORLD WITHOUT HER.
WHAT DOES THIS MEAN, MIRAI?
I DON'T WANT A WORLD WHERE YOU BECOME GOD AND DISAPPEAR FOREVER, EITHER.
...
KAKE-HASHI...
I CHOSE TO CLING TO LIFE...
...SO THAT I COULD MAKE THIS WORLD A HAPPY PLACE.

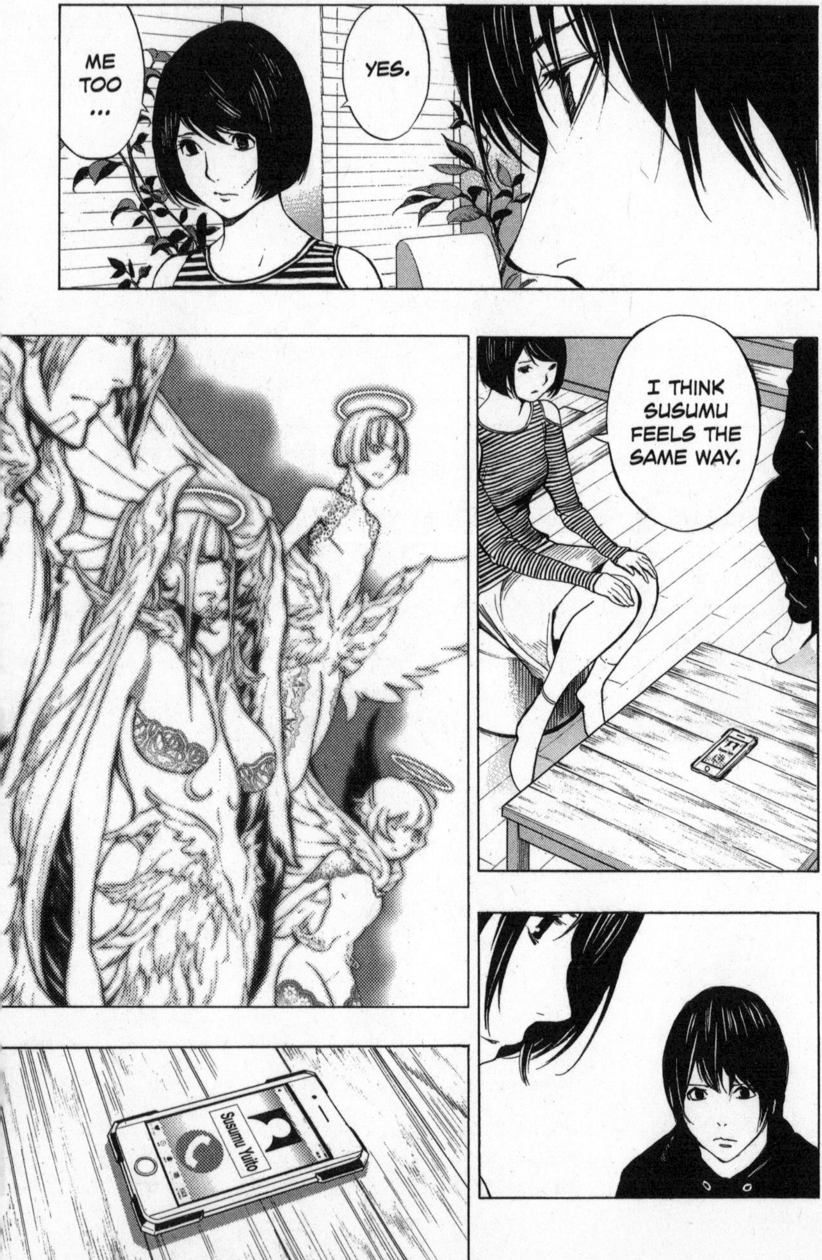
YES.
ME TOO ...
I THINK SUSUMU FEELS THE SAME WAY.
Susumu Yuito

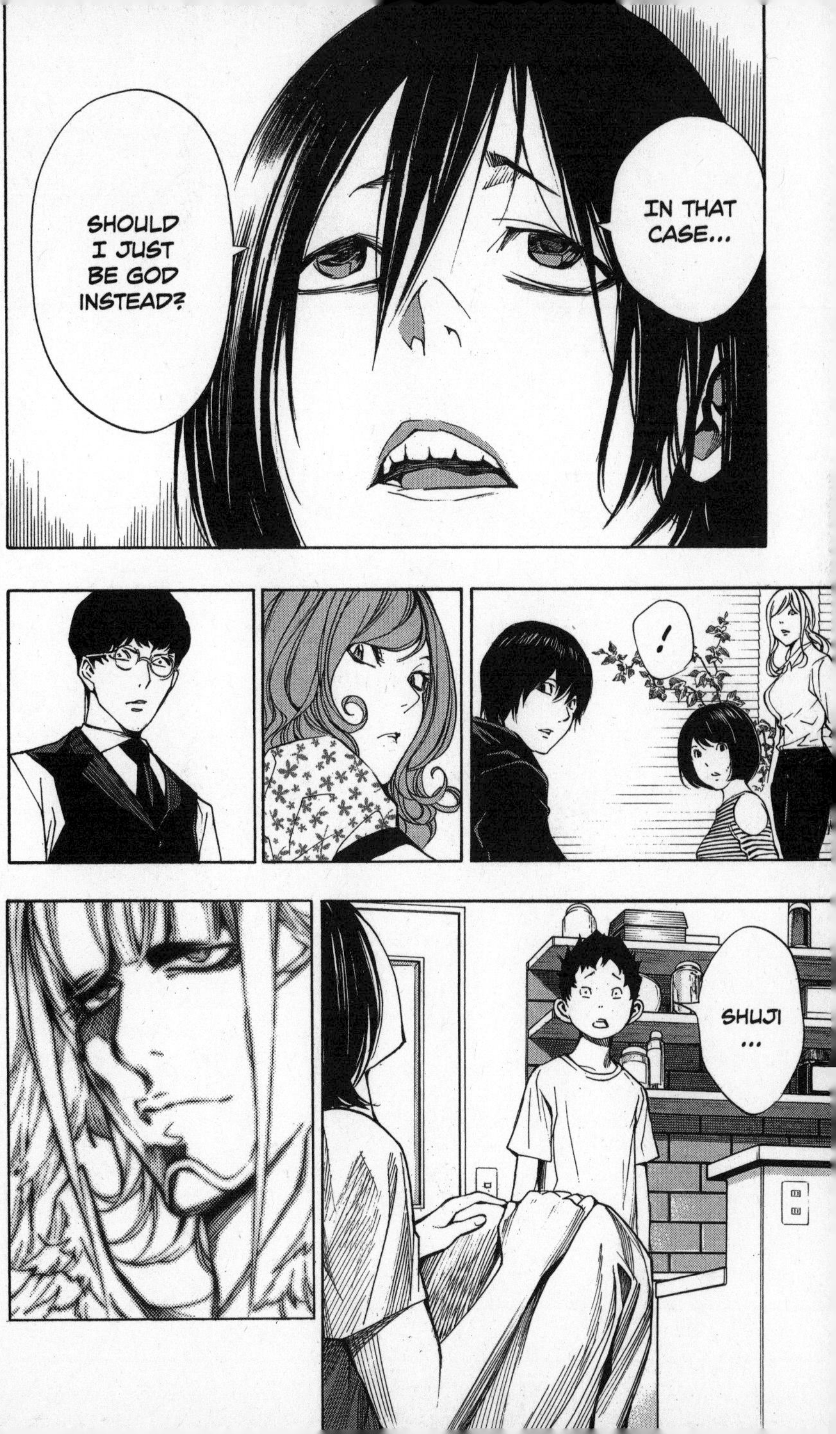
IN THAT CASE...
SHOULD I JUST BE GOD INSTEAD?
!
SHUJI ...

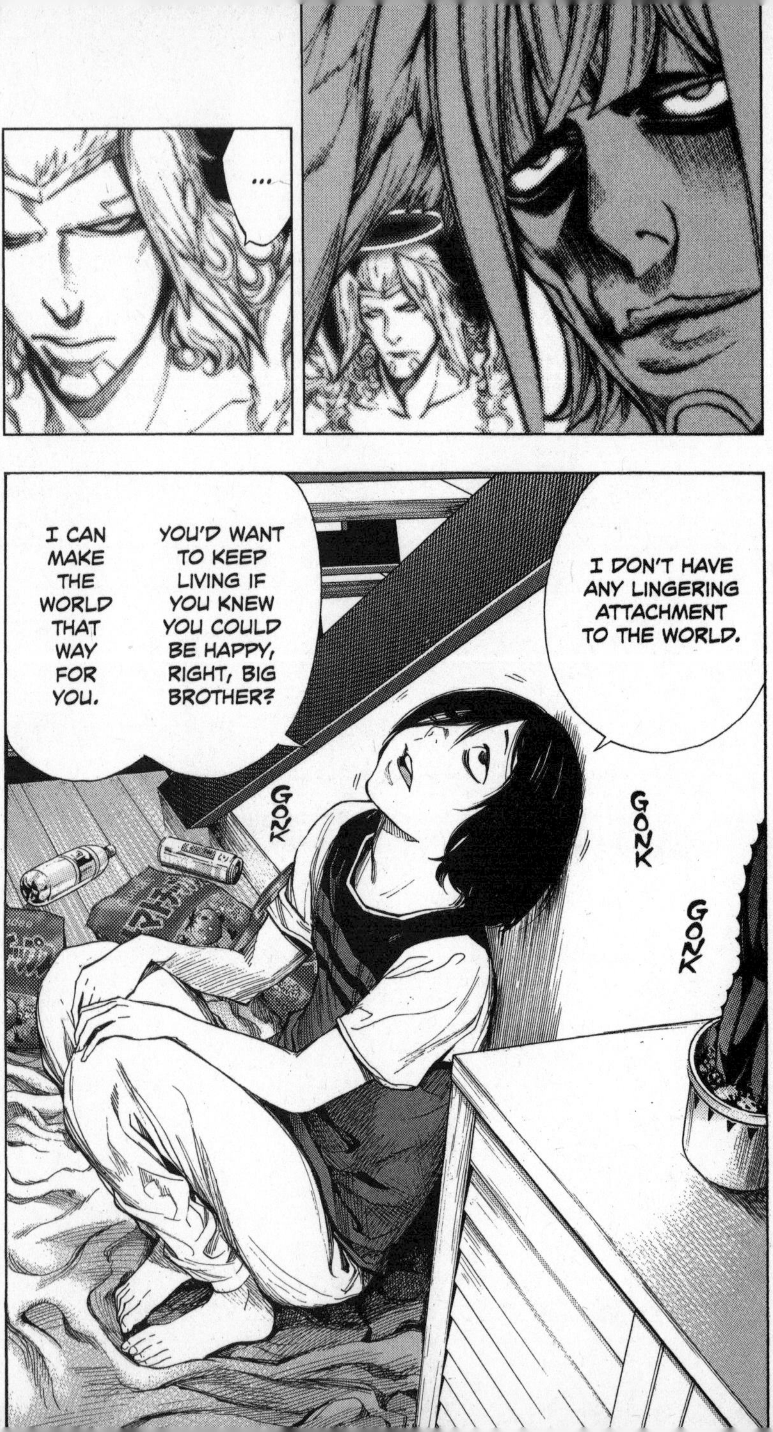
...
I DON'T HAVE ANY LINGERING ATTACHMENT TO THE WORLD.
YOU'D WANT TO KEEP LIVING IF YOU KNEW YOU COULD BE HAPPY, RIGHT, BIG BROTHER?
I CAN MAKE THE WORLD THAT WAY FOR YOU.
GONK
GONK
GONK

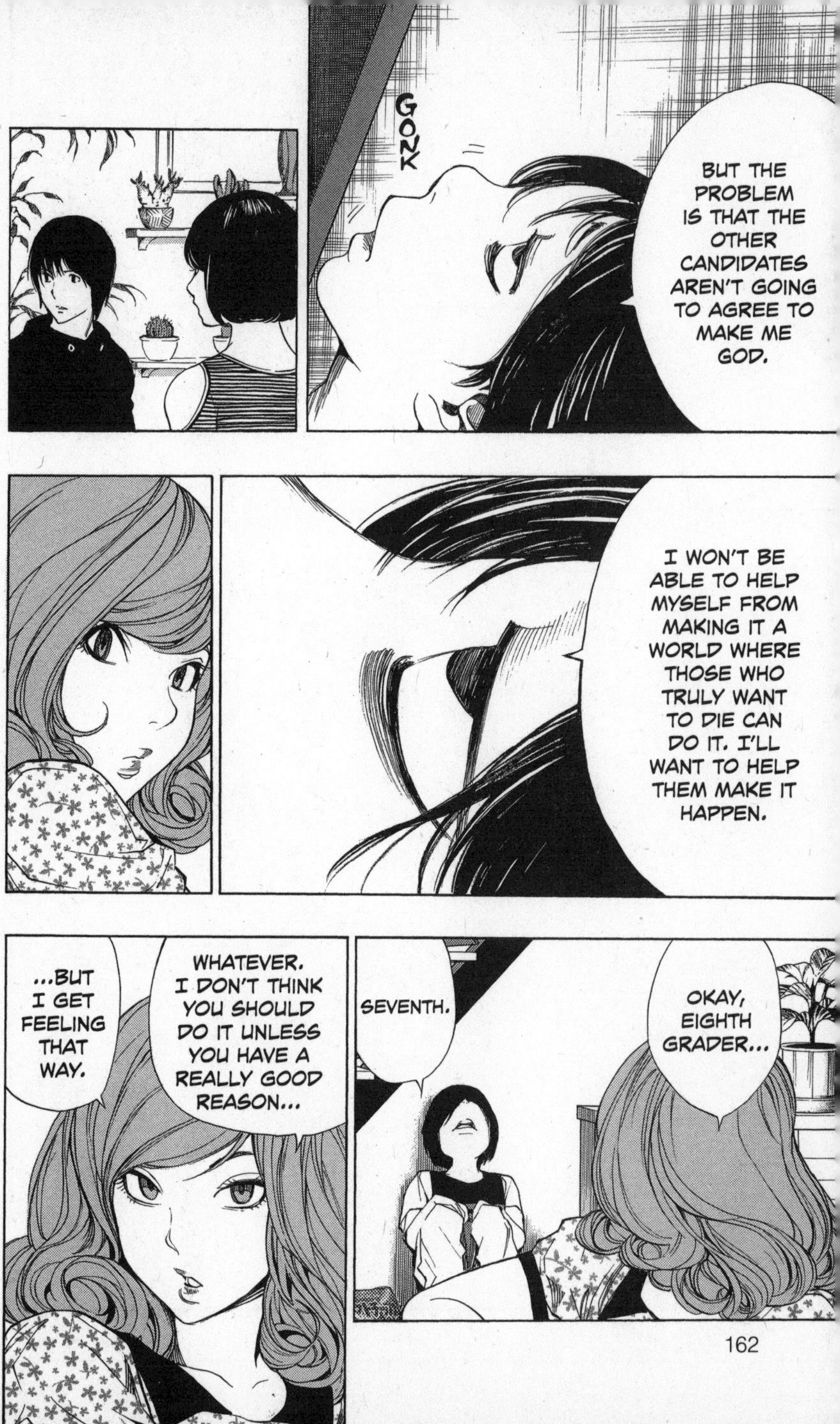
GONK
BUT THE PROBLEM IS THAT THE OTHER CANDIDATES AREN'T GOING TO AGREE TO MAKE ME GOD.
I WON'T BE ABLE TO HELP MYSELF FROM MAKING IT A WORLD WHERE THOSE WHO TRULY WANT TO DIE CAN DO IT. I'LL WANT TO HELP THEM MAKE IT HAPPEN.
OKAY, EIGHTH GRADER...
SEVENTH.
WHATEVER. I DON'T THINK YOU SHOULD DO IT UNLESS YOU HAVE A REALLY GOOD REASON...
...BUT I GET FEELING THAT WAY.

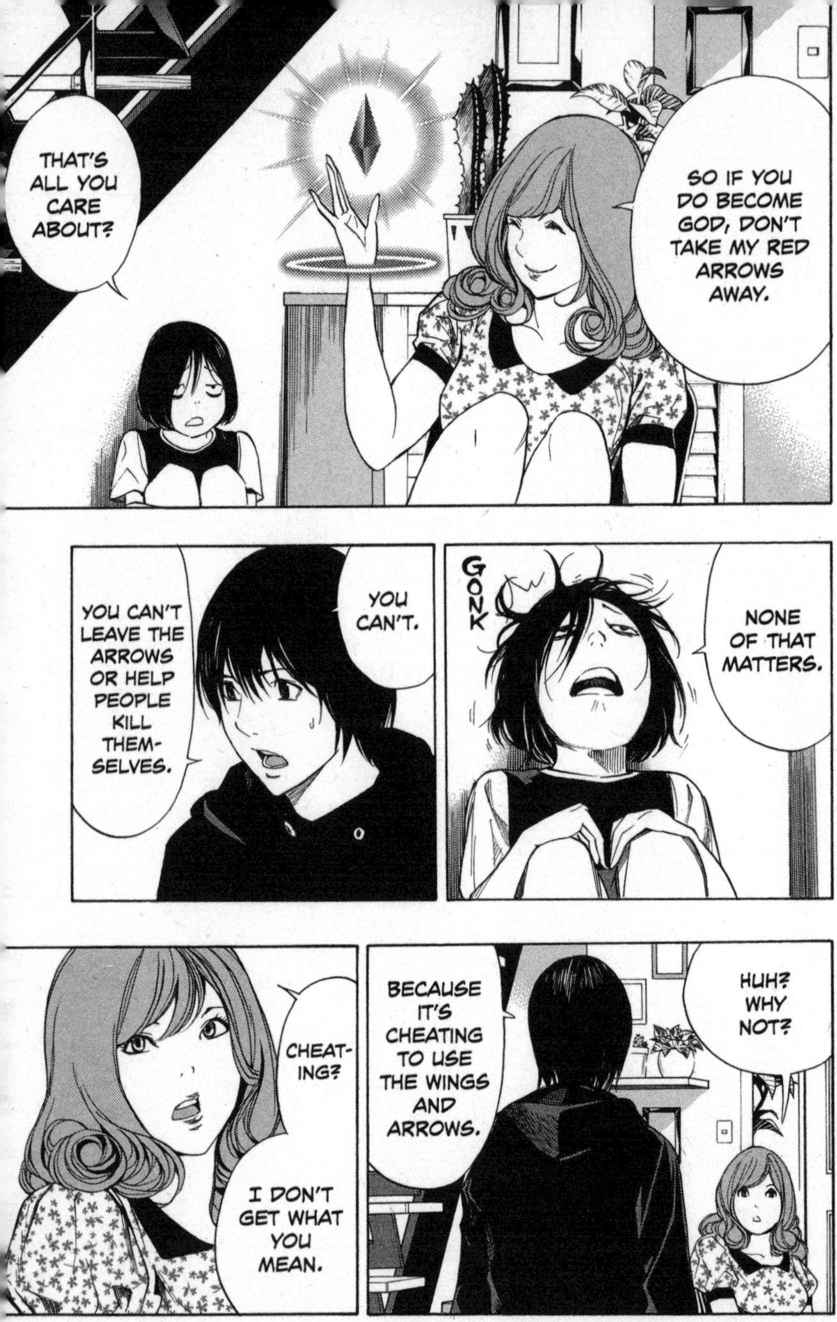
SO IF YOU DO BECOME GOD, DON'T TAKE MY RED ARROWS AWAY.
THAT'S ALL YOU CARE ABOUT?
NONE OF THAT MATTERS.
GONK
YOU CAN'T.
YOU CAN'T LEAVE THE ARROWS OR HELP PEOPLE KILL THEM-SELVES.
HUH? WHY NOT?
BECAUSE IT'S CHEATING TO USE THE WINGS AND ARROWS.
CHEAT-ING?
I DON'T GET WHAT YOU MEAN.

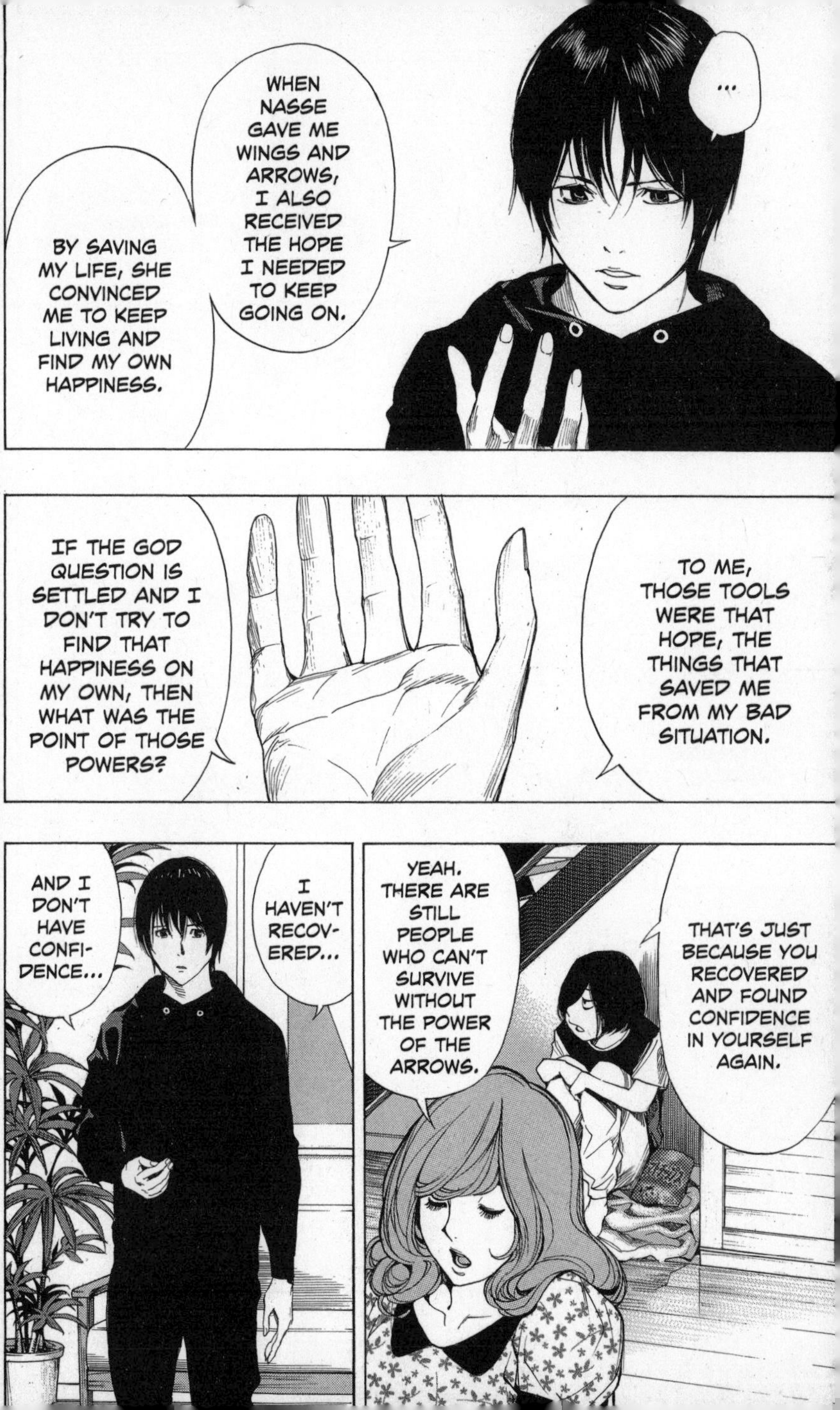
...
WHEN NASSE GAVE ME WINGS AND ARROWS, I ALSO RECEIVED THE HOPE I NEEDED TO KEEP GOING ON.
BY SAVING MY LIFE, SHE CONVINCED ME TO KEEP LIVING AND FIND MY OWN HAPPINESS.
TO ME, THOSE TOOLS WERE THAT HOPE, THE THINGS THAT SAVED ME FROM MY BAD SITUATION.
IF THE GOD QUESTION IS SETTLED AND I DON'T TRY TO FIND THAT HAPPINESS ON MY OWN, THEN WHAT WAS THE POINT OF THOSE POWERS?
THAT'S JUST BECAUSE YOU RECOVERED AND FOUND CONFIDENCE IN YOURSELF AGAIN.
YEAH. THERE ARE STILL PEOPLE WHO CAN'T SURVIVE WITHOUT THE POWER OF THE ARROWS.
I HAVEN'T RECOV-ERED...
AND I DON'T HAVE CONFI-DENCE...

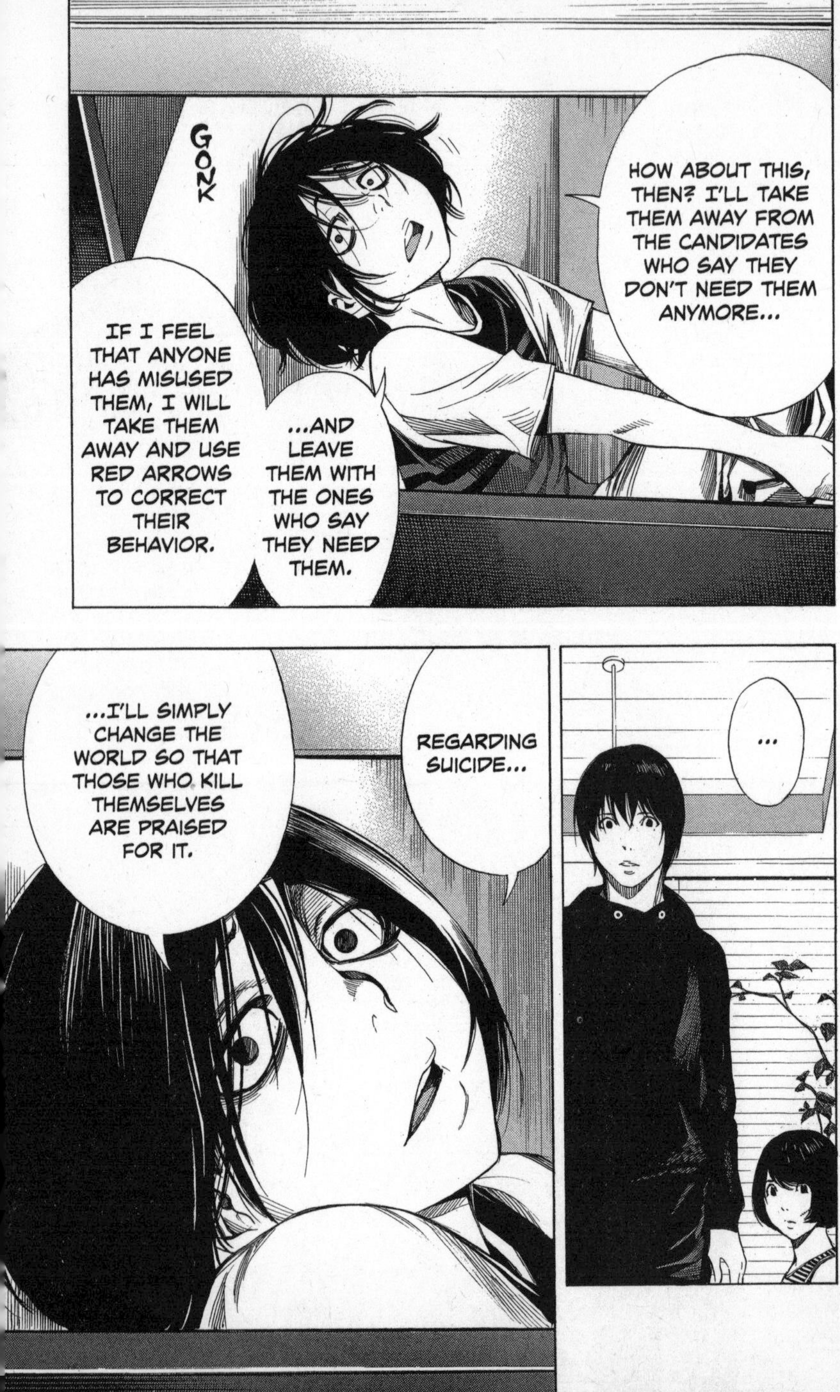
HOW ABOUT THIS, THEN? I'LL TAKE THEM AWAY FROM THE CANDIDATES WHO SAY THEY DON'T NEED THEM ANYMORE...
GONK
...AND LEAVE THEM WITH THE ONES WHO SAY THEY NEED THEM.
IF I FEEL THAT ANYONE HAS MISUSED THEM, I WILL TAKE THEM AWAY AND USE RED ARROWS TO CORRECT THEIR BEHAVIOR.
...
REGARDING SUICIDE...
...I'LL SIMPLY CHANGE THE WORLD SO THAT THOSE WHO KILL THEMSELVES ARE PRAISED FOR IT.

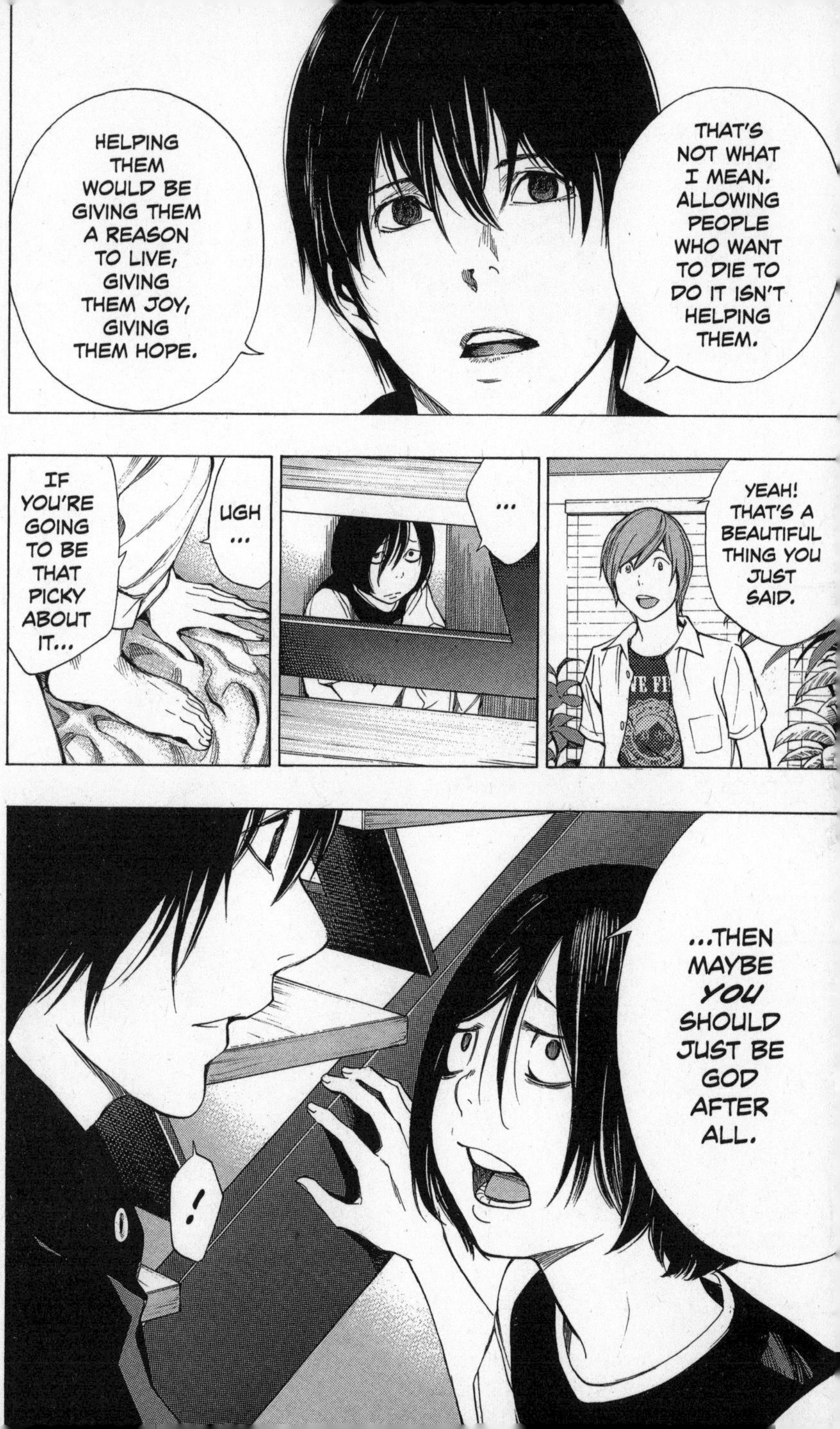
THAT'S NOT WHAT I MEAN. ALLOWING PEOPLE WHO WANT TO DIE TO DO IT ISN'T HELPING THEM.
HELPING THEM WOULD BE GIVING THEM A REASON TO LIVE, GIVING THEM JOY, GIVING THEM HOPE.
YEAH! THAT'S A BEAUTIFUL THING YOU JUST SAID.
...
UGH ...
IF YOU'RE GOING TO BE THAT PICKY ABOUT IT...
...THEN MAYBE *YOU* SHOULD JUST BE GOD AFTER ALL.
!

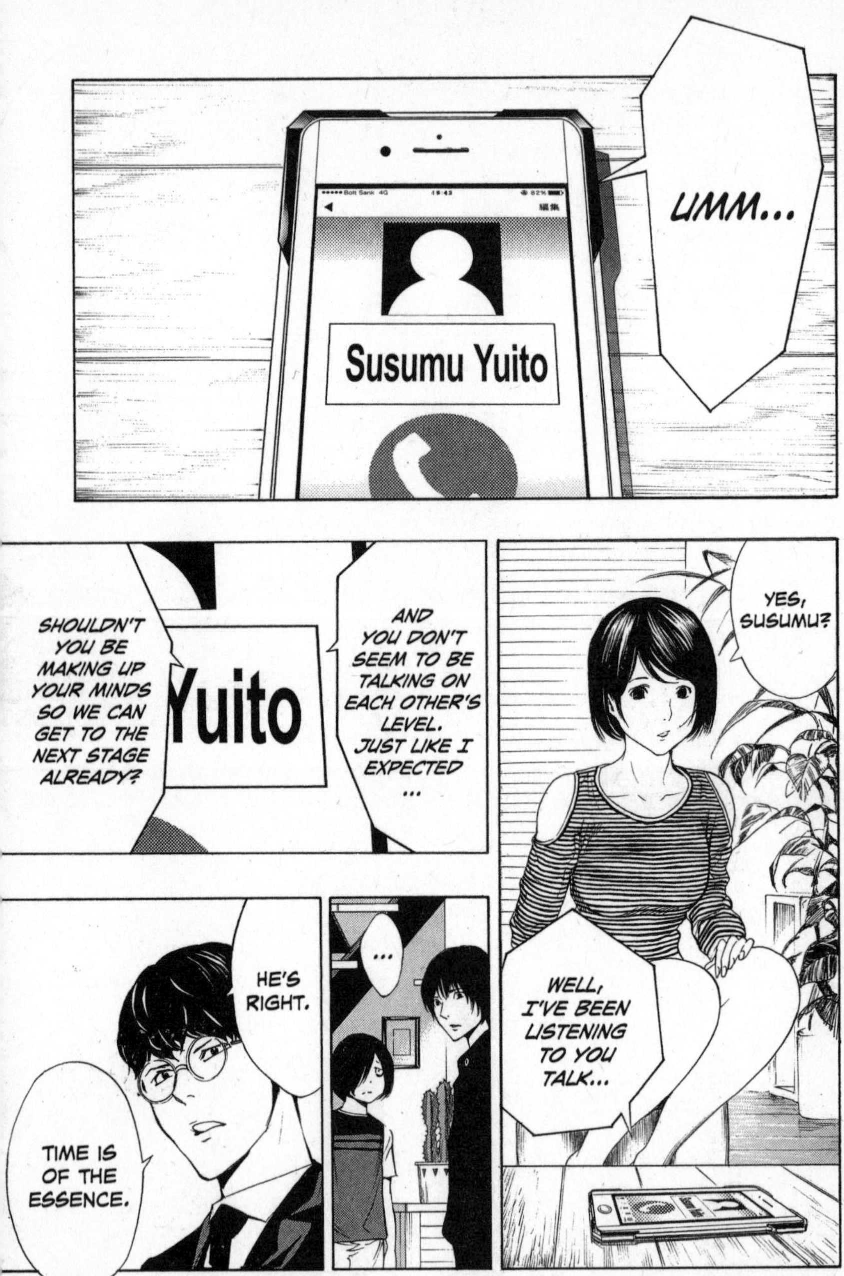
UMM...
Susumu Yuito
YES, SUSUMU?
WELL, I'VE BEEN LISTENING TO YOU TALK...
AND YOU DON'T SEEM TO BE TALKING ON EACH OTHER'S LEVEL. JUST LIKE I EXPECTED ...
Yuito
SHOULDN'T YOU BE MAKING UP YOUR MINDS SO WE CAN GET TO THE NEXT STAGE ALREADY?
...
HE'S RIGHT.
TIME IS OF THE ESSENCE.

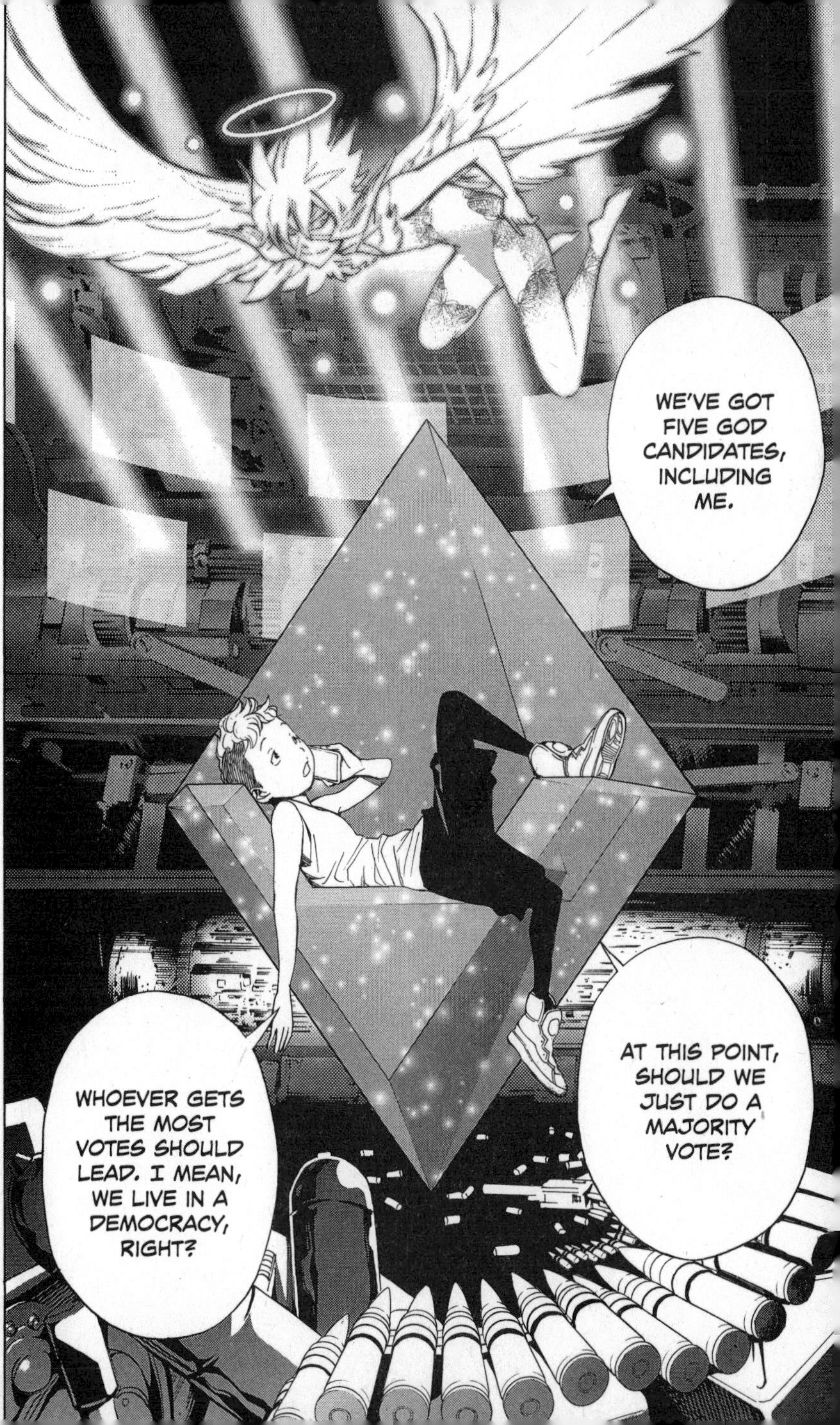
WE'VE GOT FIVE GOD CANDIDATES, INCLUDING ME.
AT THIS POINT, SHOULD WE JUST DO A MAJORITY VOTE?
WHOEVER GETS THE MOST VOTES SHOULD LEAD. I MEAN, WE LIVE IN A DEMOCRACY, RIGHT?

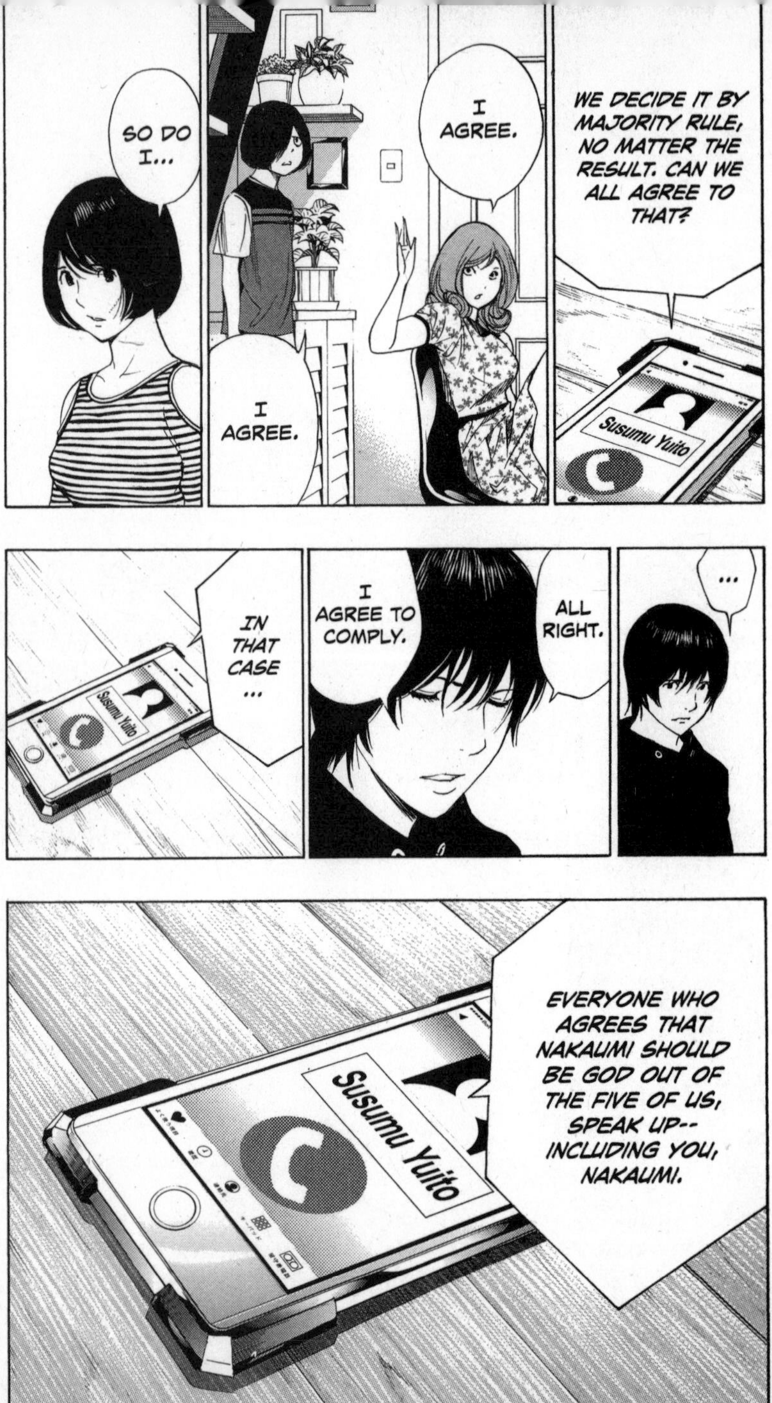
WE DECIDE IT BY MAJORITY RULE, NO MATTER THE RESULT. CAN WE ALL AGREE TO THAT?
Susumu Yuito
I AGREE.
I AGREE.
SO DO I...
...
ALL RIGHT.
I AGREE TO COMPLY.
IN THAT CASE ...
Susumu Yuito
EVERYONE WHO AGREES THAT NAKAUMI SHOULD BE GOD OUT OF THE FIVE OF US, SPEAK UP-- INCLUDING YOU, NAKAUMI.
Susumu Yuito

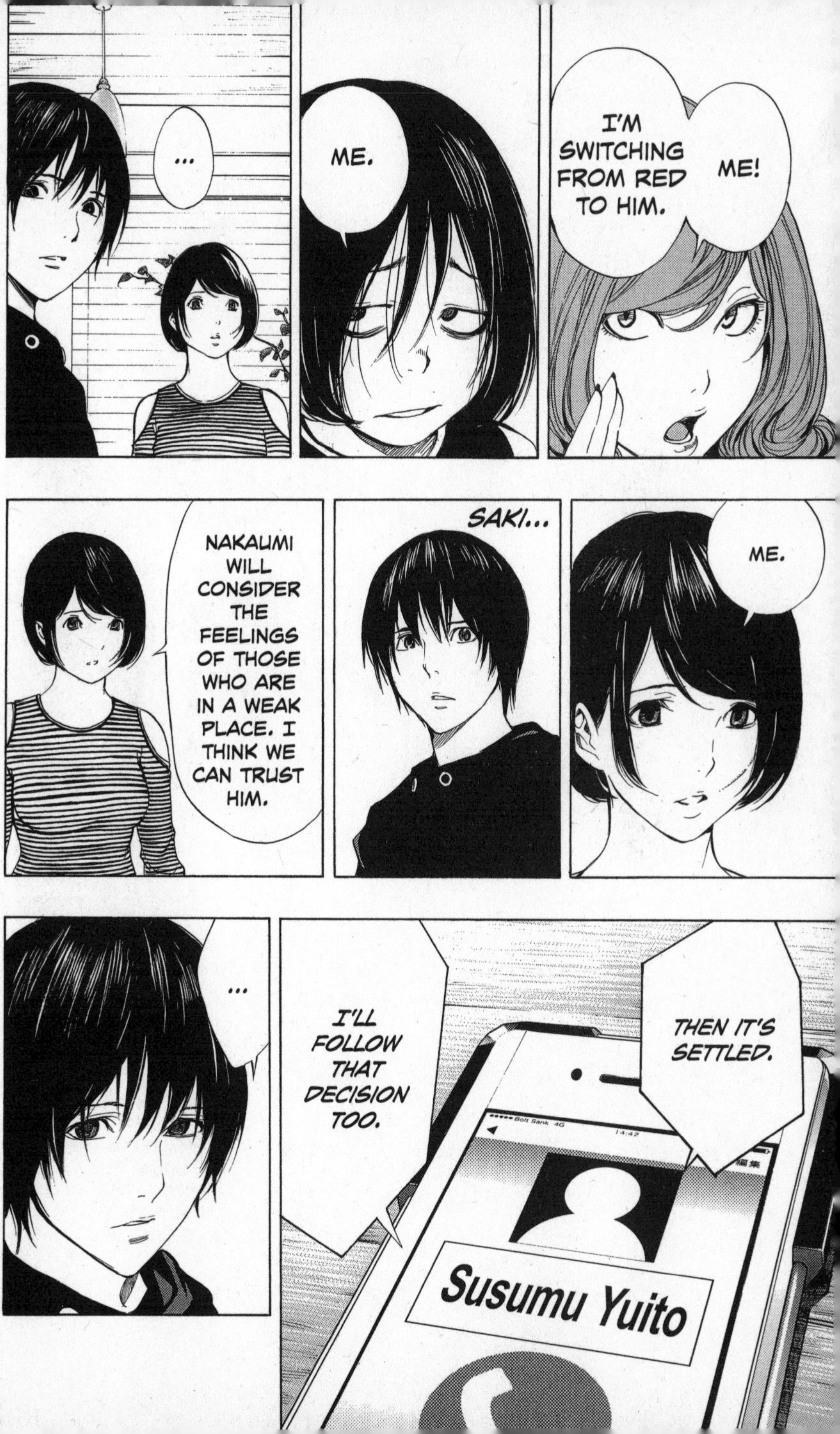
ME!
I'M SWITCHING FROM RED TO HIM.
ME.
...
ME.
SAKI...
NAKAUMI WILL CONSIDER THE FEELINGS OF THOSE WHO ARE IN A WEAK PLACE. I THINK WE CAN TRUST HIM.
THEN IT'S SETTLED.
Susumu Yuito
I'LL FOLLOW THAT DECISION TOO.
...

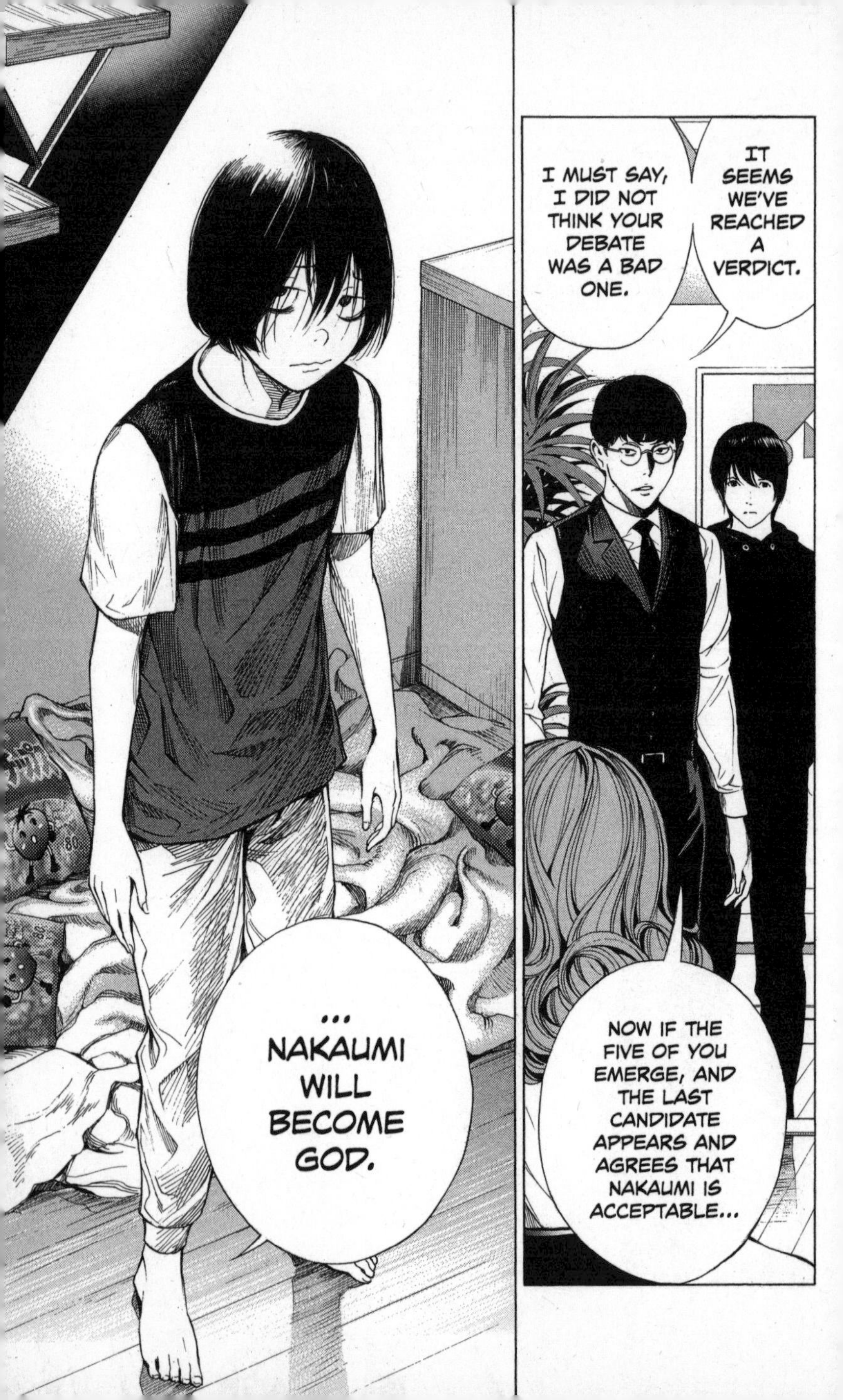
IT SEEMS WE'VE REACHED A VERDICT.
I MUST SAY, I DID NOT THINK YOUR DEBATE WAS A BAD ONE.
NOW IF THE FIVE OF YOU EMERGE, AND THE LAST CANDIDATE APPEARS AND AGREES THAT NAKAUMI IS ACCEPTABLE...
... NAKAUMI WILL BECOME GOD.

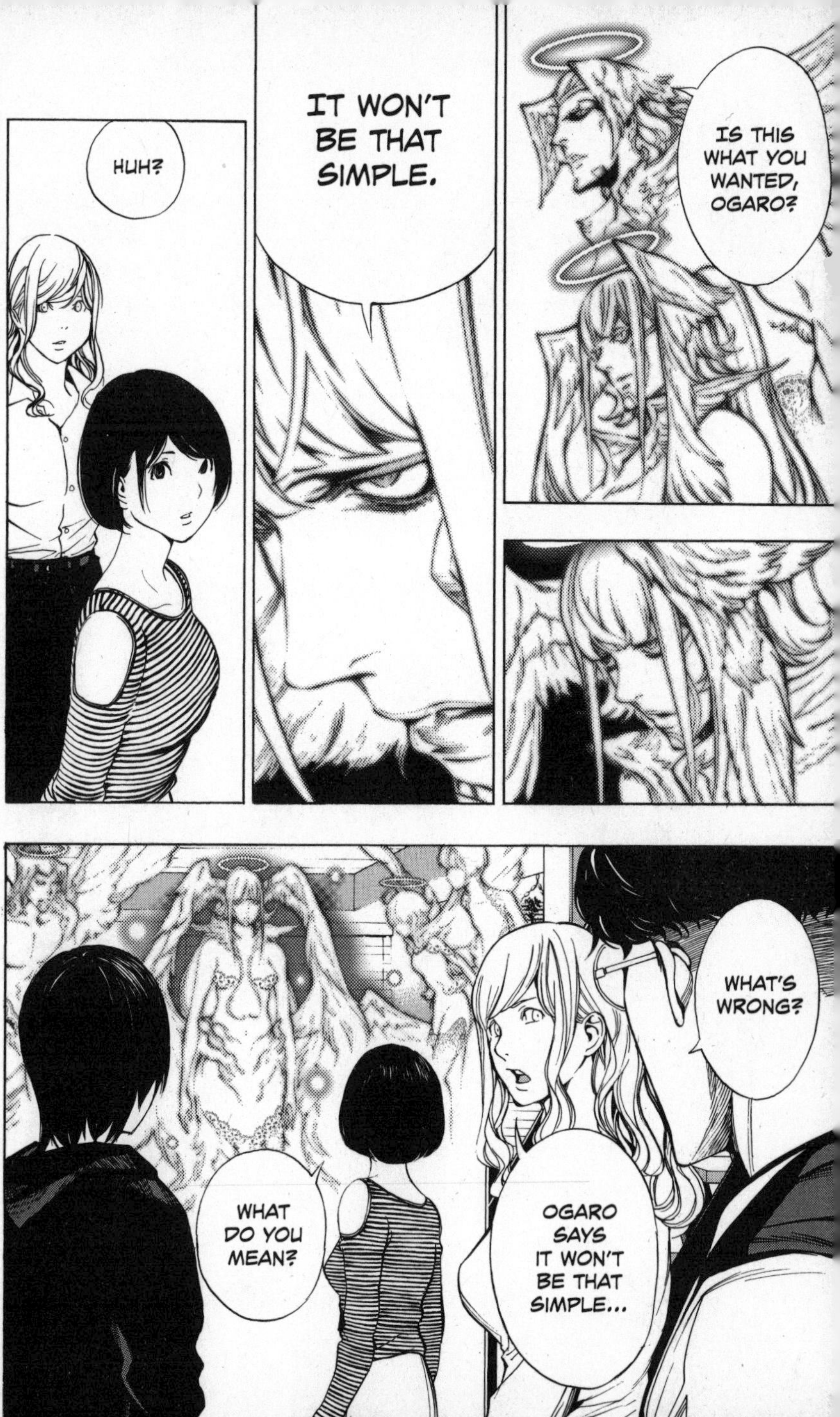
IS THIS WHAT YOU WANTED, OGARO?
IT WON'T BE THAT SIMPLE.
HUH?
WHAT'S WRONG?
OGARO SAYS IT WON'T BE THAT SIMPLE...
WHAT DO YOU MEAN?

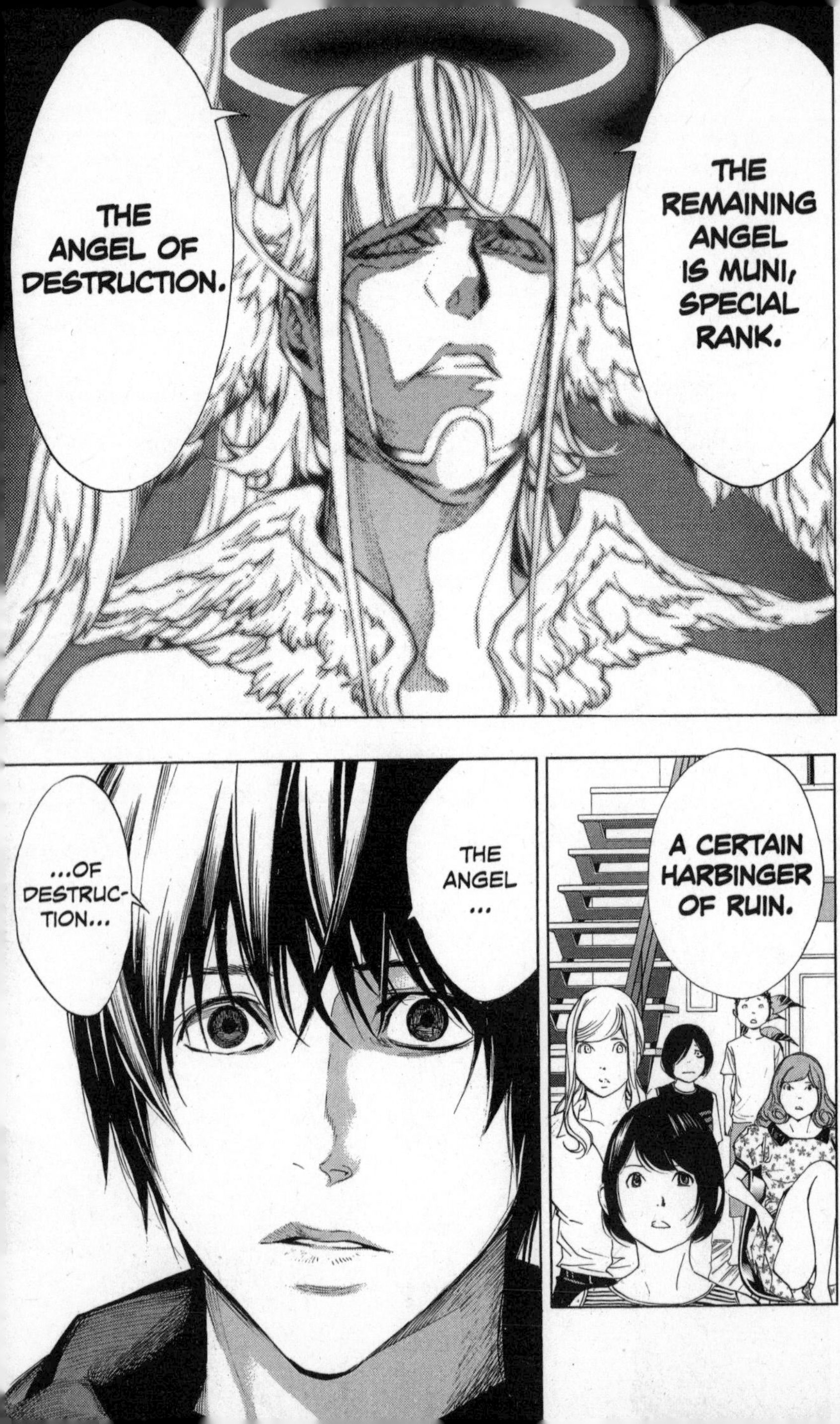
THE REMAINING ANGEL IS MUNI, SPECIAL RANK.
THE ANGEL OF DESTRUCTION.
A CERTAIN HARBINGER OF RUIN.
THE ANGEL ...
...OF DESTRUCTION...

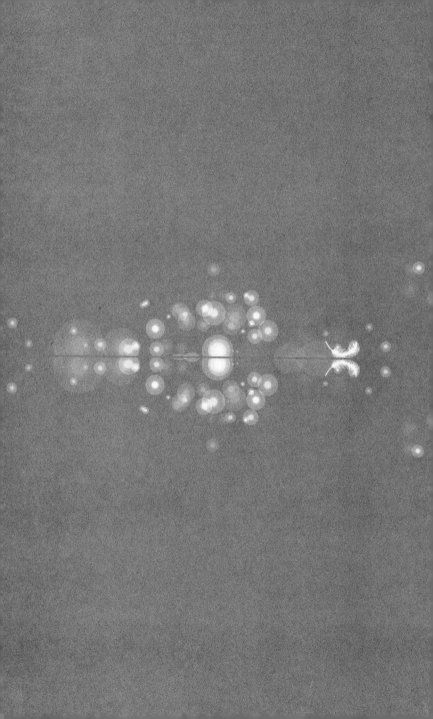

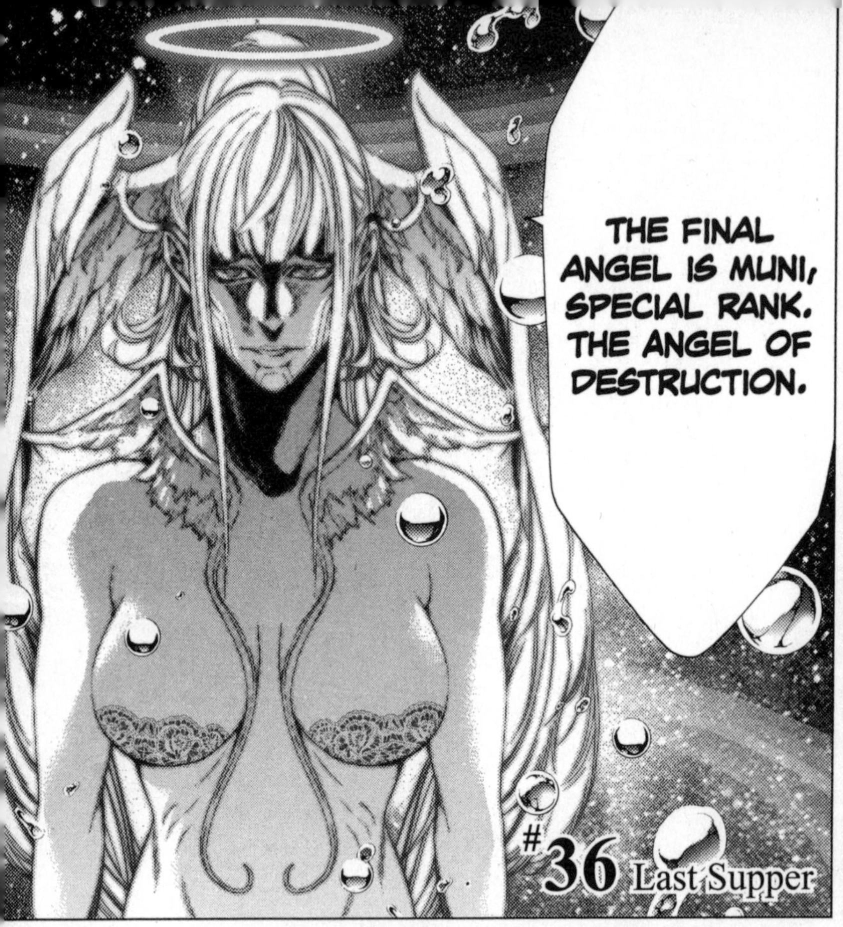
THE FINAL ANGEL IS MUNI, SPECIAL RANK. THE ANGEL OF DESTRUCTION.
#36 Last Supper

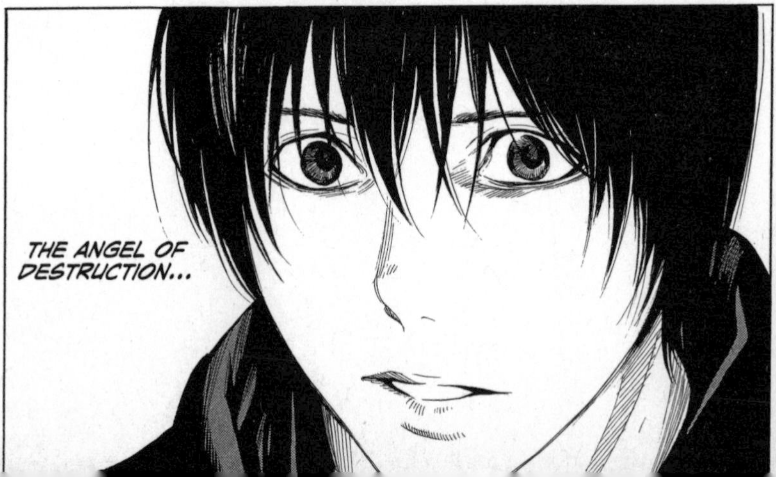
THE ANGEL OF DESTRUCTION...

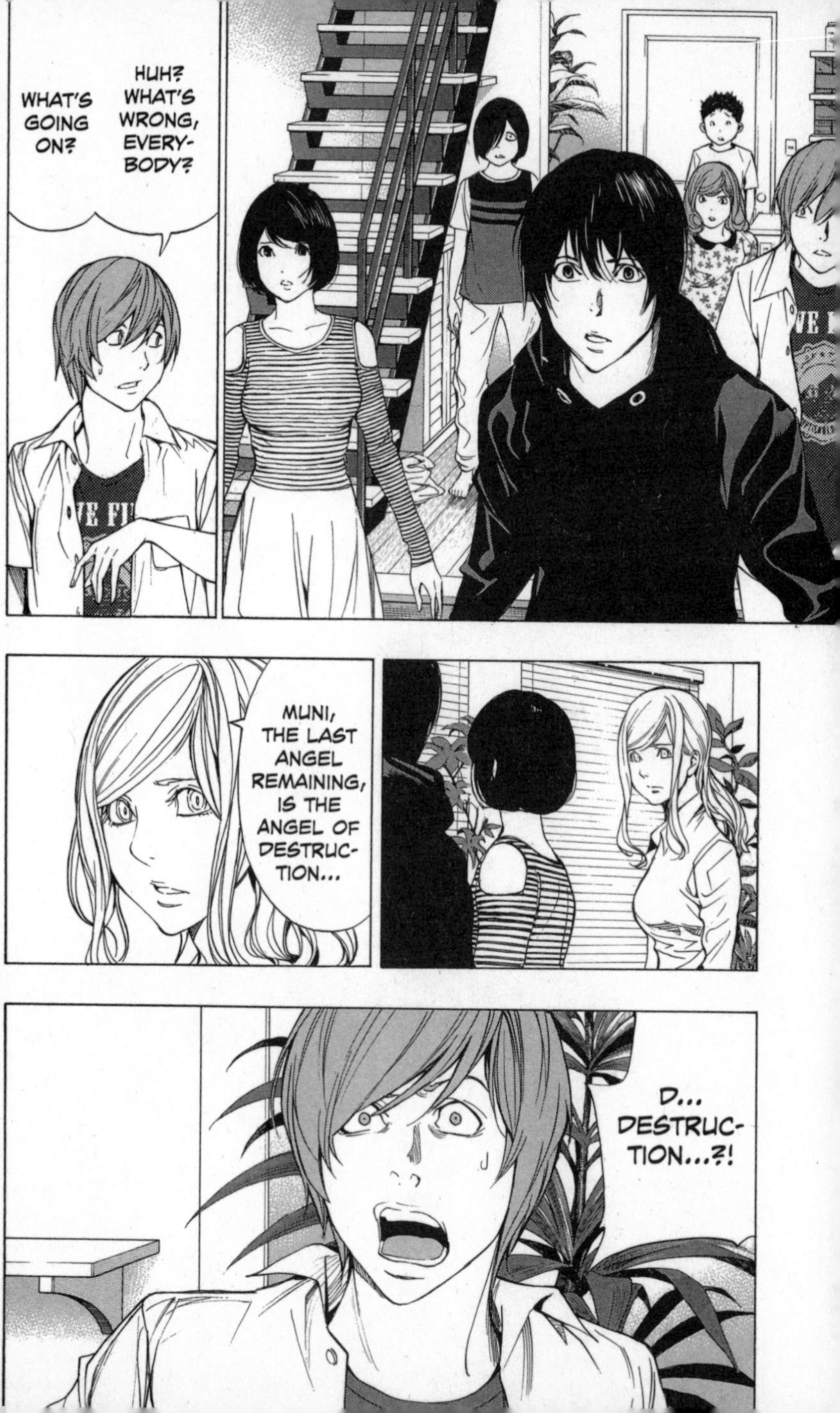
HUH? WHAT'S WRONG, EVERY-BODY?
WHAT'S GOING ON?
MUNI, THE LAST ANGEL REMAINING, IS THE ANGEL OF DESTRUC-TION...
D... DESTRUC-TION...?!

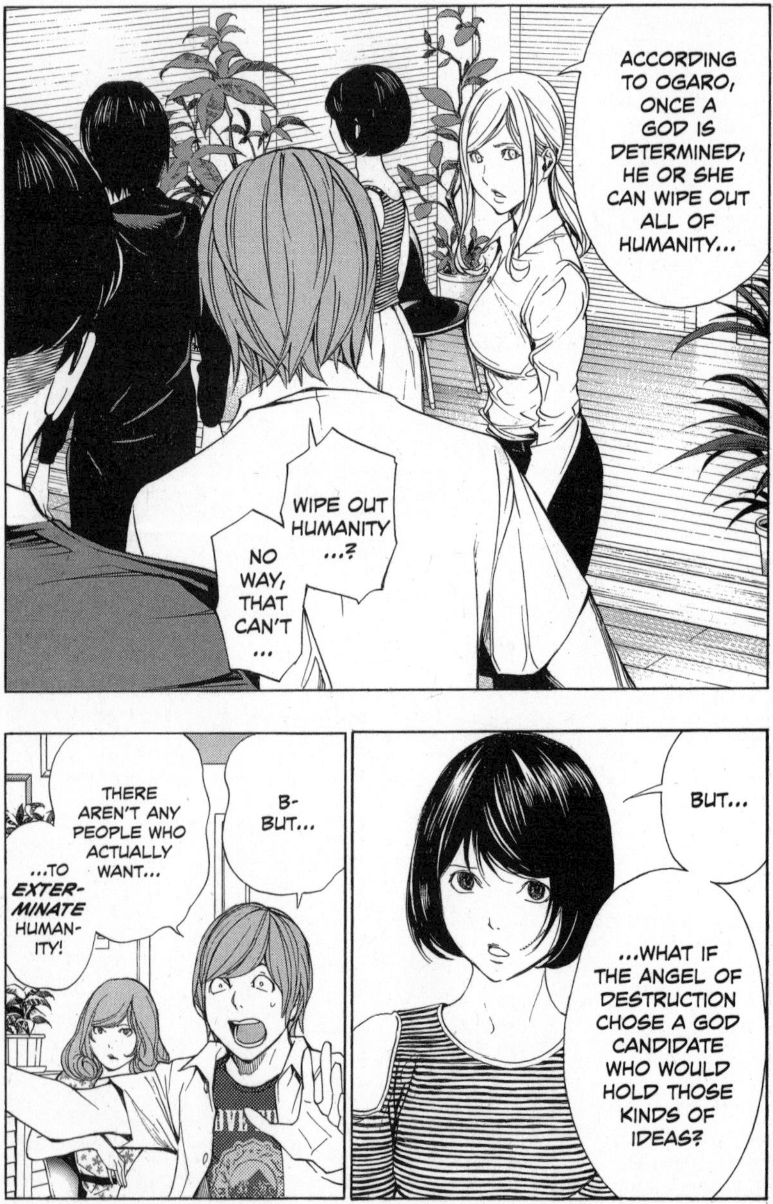

ACCORDING TO OGARO, ONCE A GOD IS DETERMINED, HE OR SHE CAN WIPE OUT ALL OF HUMANITY...
WIPE OUT HUMANITY ...?
NO WAY, THAT CAN'T ...
BUT...
...WHAT IF THE ANGEL OF DESTRUCTION CHOSE A GOD CANDIDATE WHO WOULD HOLD THOSE KINDS OF IDEAS?
B-BUT...
THERE AREN'T ANY PEOPLE WHO ACTUALLY WANT...
...TO *EXTERMINATE* HUMANITY!

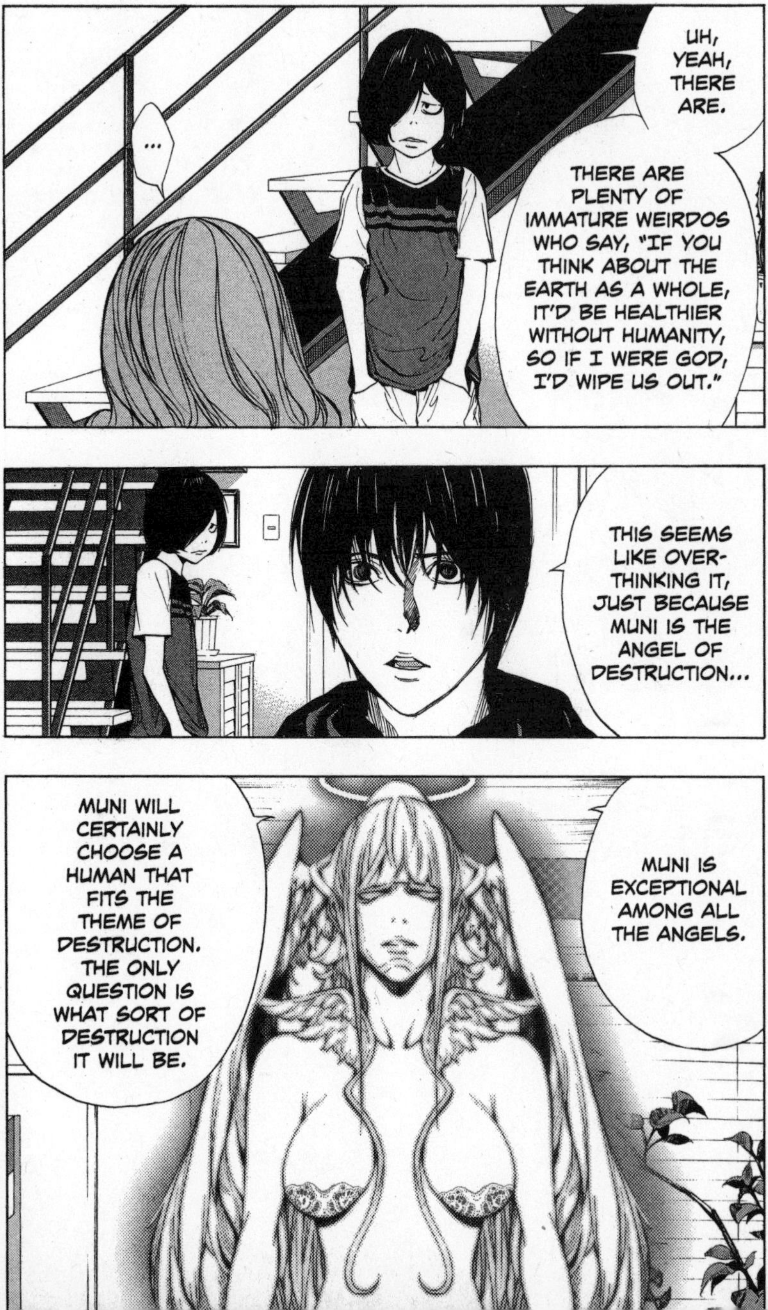
UH, YEAH, THERE ARE.
...
THERE ARE PLENTY OF IMMATURE WEIRDOS WHO SAY, "IF YOU THINK ABOUT THE EARTH AS A WHOLE, IT'D BE HEALTHIER WITHOUT HUMANITY, SO IF I WERE GOD, I'D WIPE US OUT."
THIS SEEMS LIKE OVER-THINKING IT, JUST BECAUSE MUNI IS THE ANGEL OF DESTRUCTION...
MUNI IS EXCEPTIONAL AMONG ALL THE ANGELS.
MUNI WILL CERTAINLY CHOOSE A HUMAN THAT FITS THE THEME OF DESTRUCTION. THE ONLY QUESTION IS WHAT SORT OF DESTRUCTION IT WILL BE.

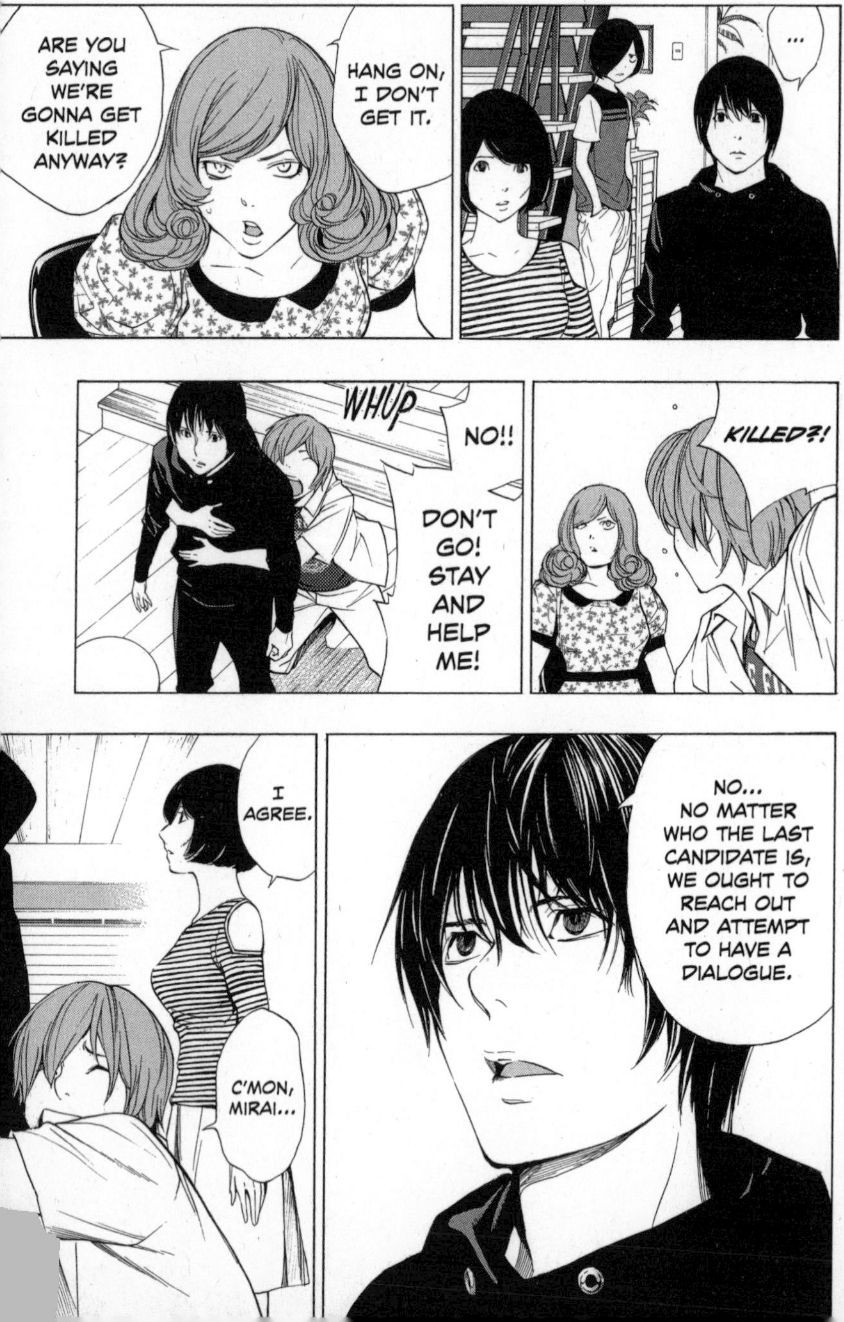
...
HANG ON, I DON'T GET IT.
ARE YOU SAYING WE'RE GONNA GET KILLED ANYWAY?
KILLED?!
WHUP
NO!!
DON'T GO! STAY AND HELP ME!
NO... NO MATTER WHO THE LAST CANDIDATE IS, WE OUGHT TO REACH OUT AND ATTEMPT TO HAVE A DIALOGUE.
I AGREE.
C'MON, MIRAI...

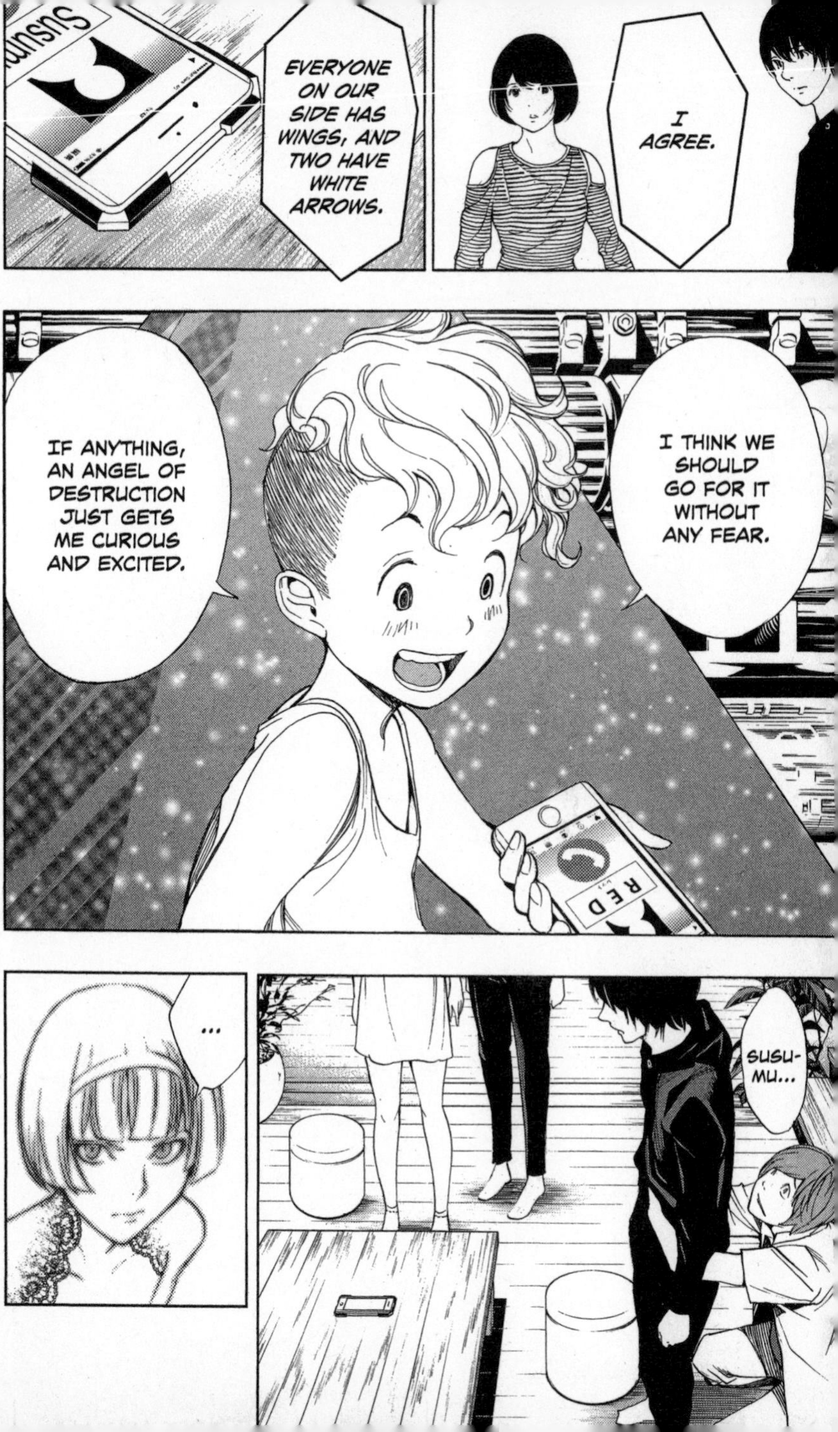
I AGREE.
EVERYONE ON OUR SIDE HAS WINGS, AND TWO HAVE WHITE ARROWS.
I THINK WE SHOULD GO FOR IT WITHOUT ANY FEAR.
IF ANYTHING, AN ANGEL OF DESTRUCTION JUST GETS ME CURIOUS AND EXCITED.
RED
SUSU-MU...
...

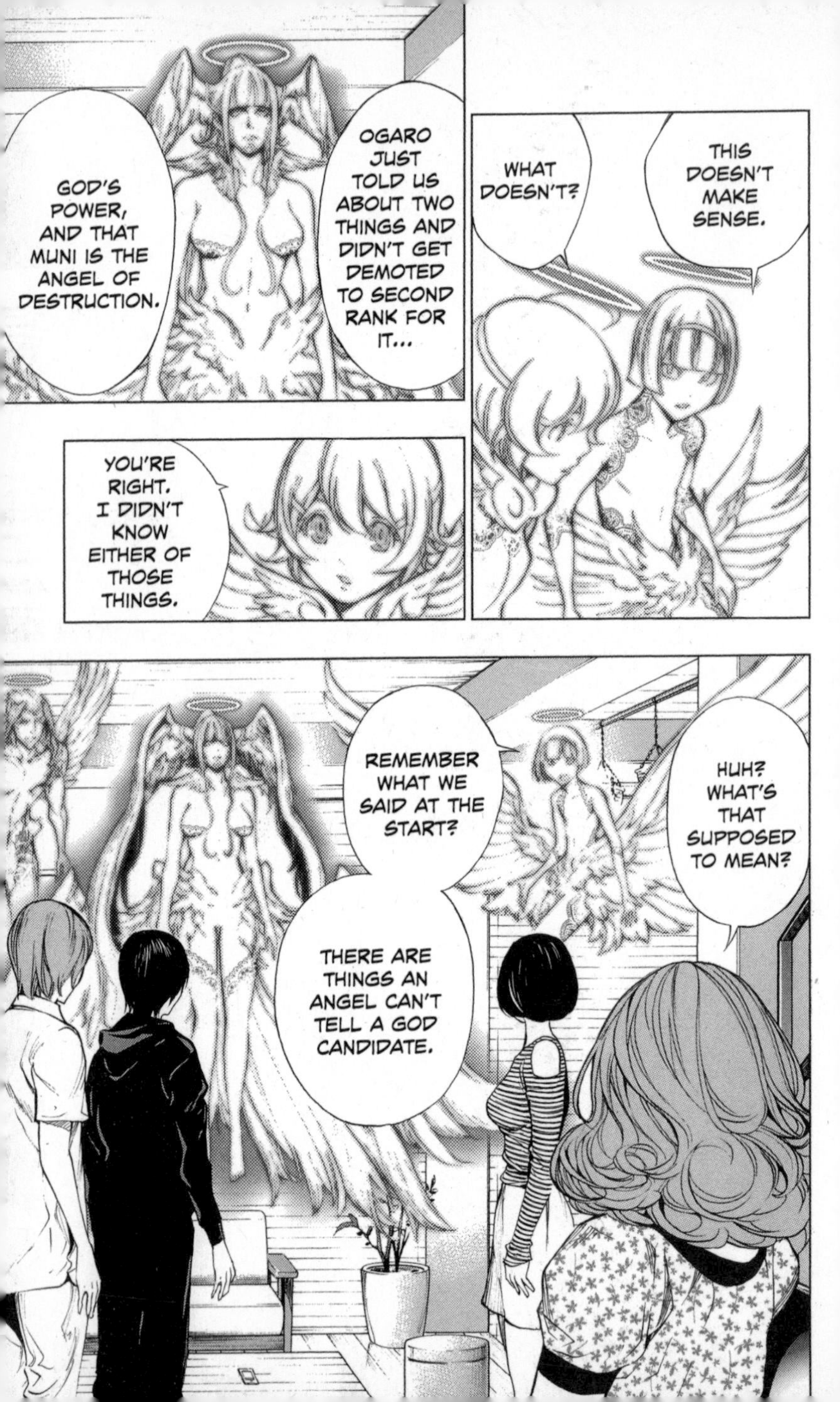
OGARO JUST TOLD US ABOUT TWO THINGS AND DIDN'T GET DEMOTED TO SECOND RANK FOR IT...
GOD'S POWER, AND THAT MUNI IS THE ANGEL OF DESTRUCTION.
THIS DOESN'T MAKE SENSE.
WHAT DOESN'T?
YOU'RE RIGHT. I DIDN'T KNOW EITHER OF THOSE THINGS.
HUH? WHAT'S THAT SUPPOSED TO MEAN?
REMEMBER WHAT WE SAID AT THE START?
THERE ARE THINGS AN ANGEL CAN'T TELL A GOD CANDIDATE.

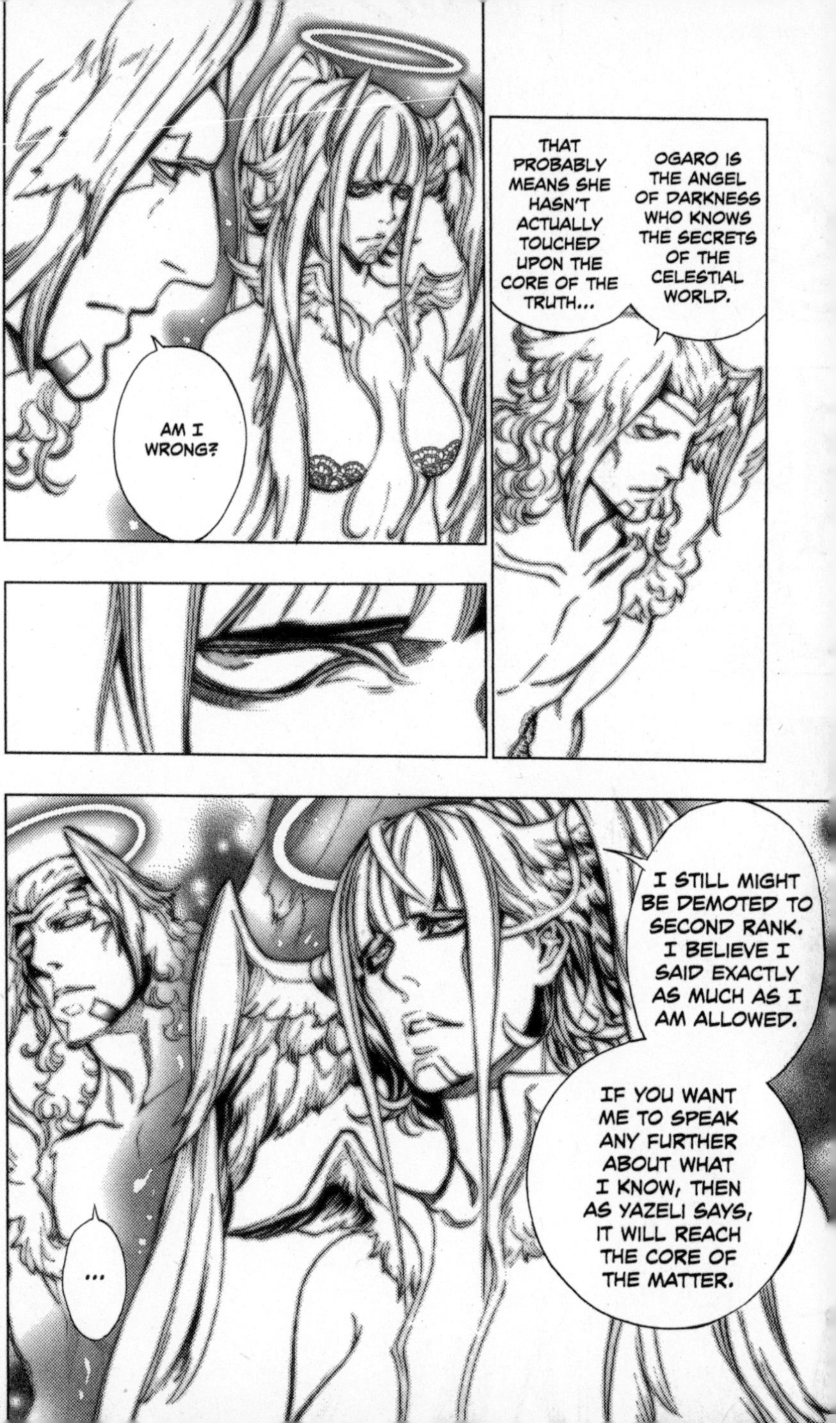
OGARO IS THE ANGEL OF DARKNESS WHO KNOWS THE SECRETS OF THE CELESTIAL WORLD.
THAT PROBABLY MEANS SHE HASN'T ACTUALLY TOUCHED UPON THE CORE OF THE TRUTH...
AM I WRONG?
I STILL MIGHT BE DEMOTED TO SECOND RANK. I BELIEVE I SAID EXACTLY AS MUCH AS I AM ALLOWED.
IF YOU WANT ME TO SPEAK ANY FURTHER ABOUT WHAT I KNOW, THEN AS YAZELI SAYS, IT WILL REACH THE CORE OF THE MATTER.
...

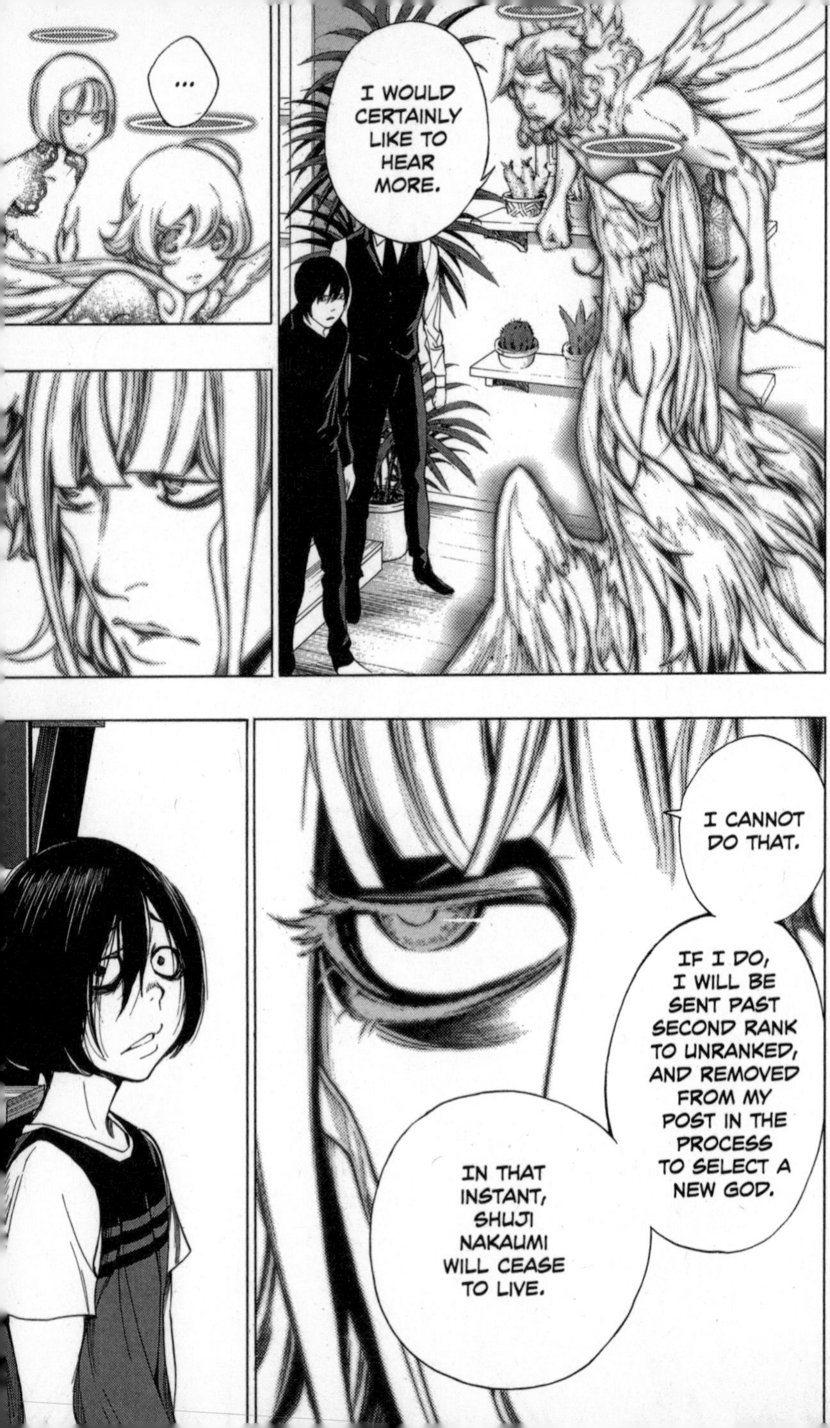
I WOULD CERTAINLY LIKE TO HEAR MORE.
...
I CANNOT DO THAT.
IF I DO, I WILL BE SENT PAST SECOND RANK TO UNRANKED, AND REMOVED FROM MY POST IN THE PROCESS TO SELECT A NEW GOD.
IN THAT INSTANT, SHUJI NAKAUMI WILL CEASE TO LIVE.

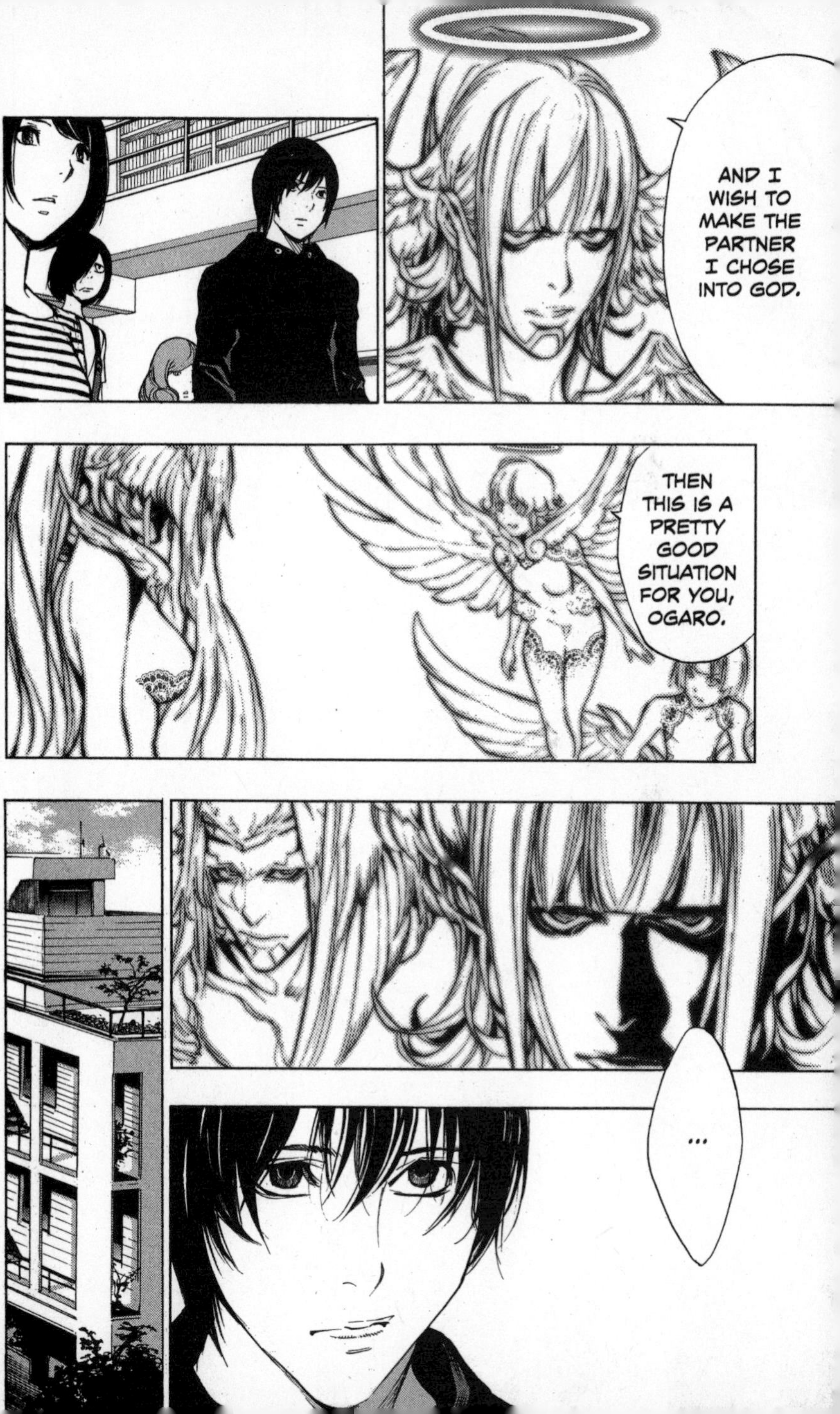
AND I WISH TO MAKE THE PARTNER I CHOSE INTO GOD.
THEN THIS IS A PRETTY GOOD SITUATION FOR YOU, OGARO.
...

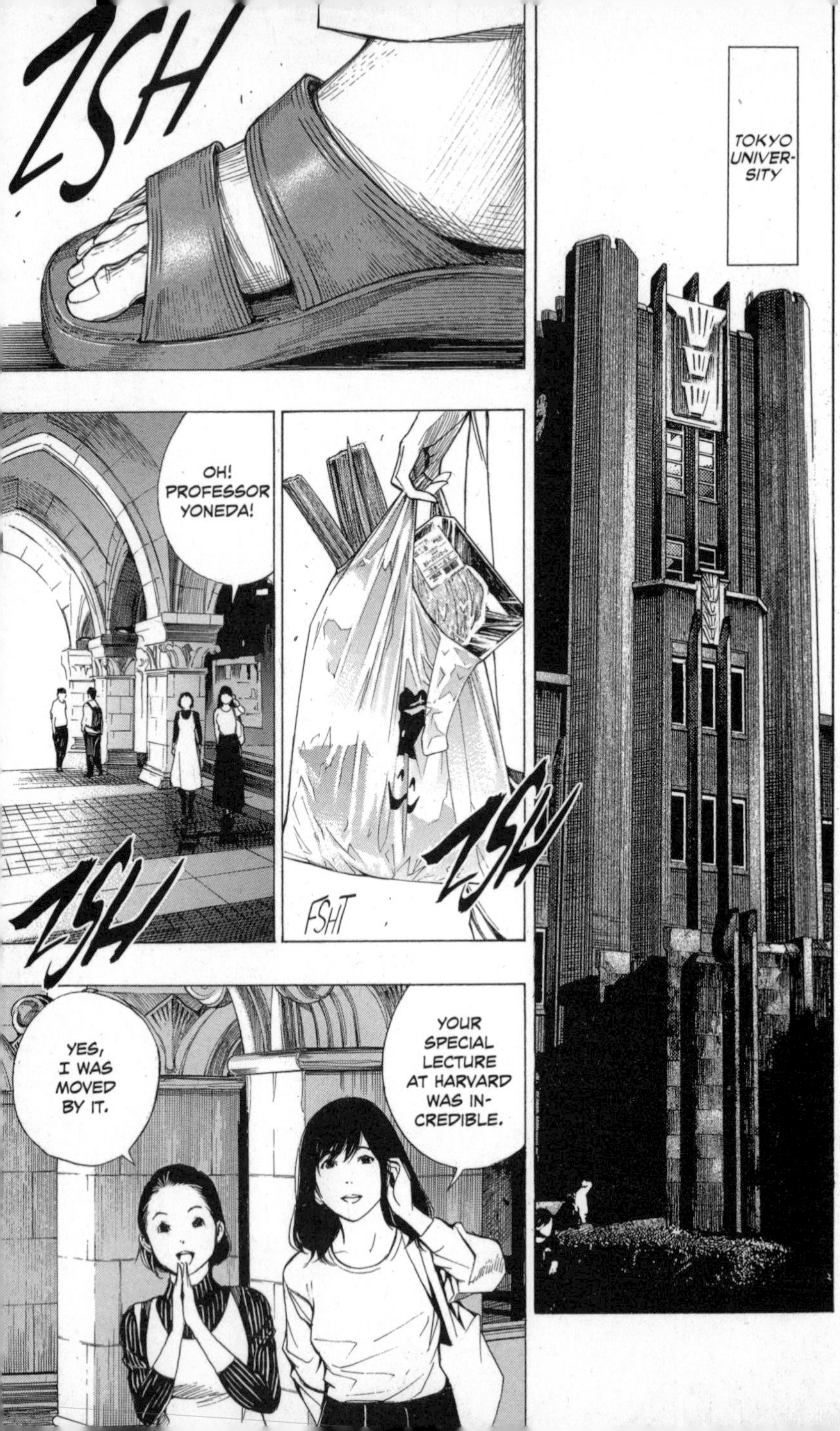
TOKYO UNIVERSITY
ZSH
ZSH
FSHT
OH! PROFESSOR YONEDA!
ZSH
YOUR SPECIAL LECTURE AT HARVARD WAS INCREDIBLE.
YES, I WAS MOVED BY IT.

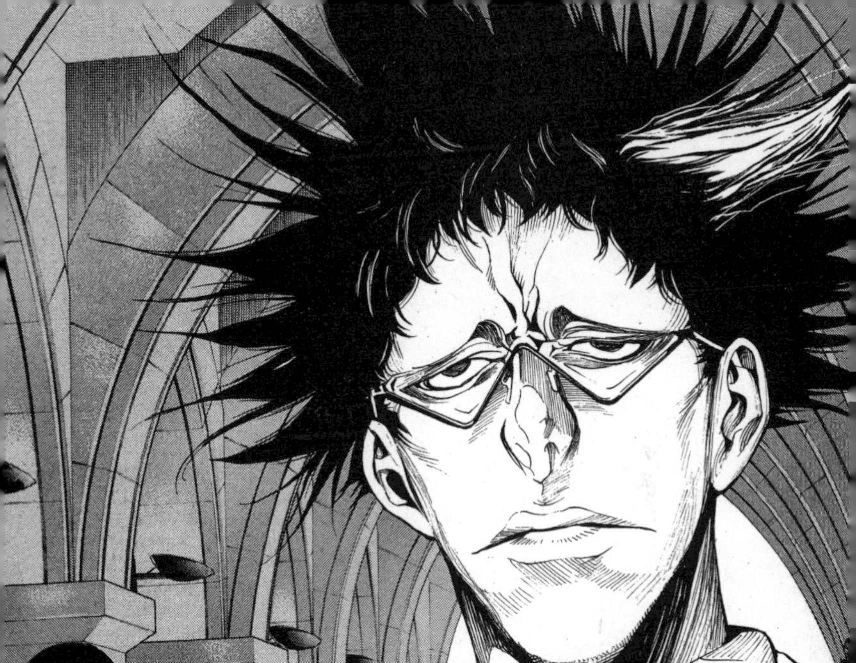

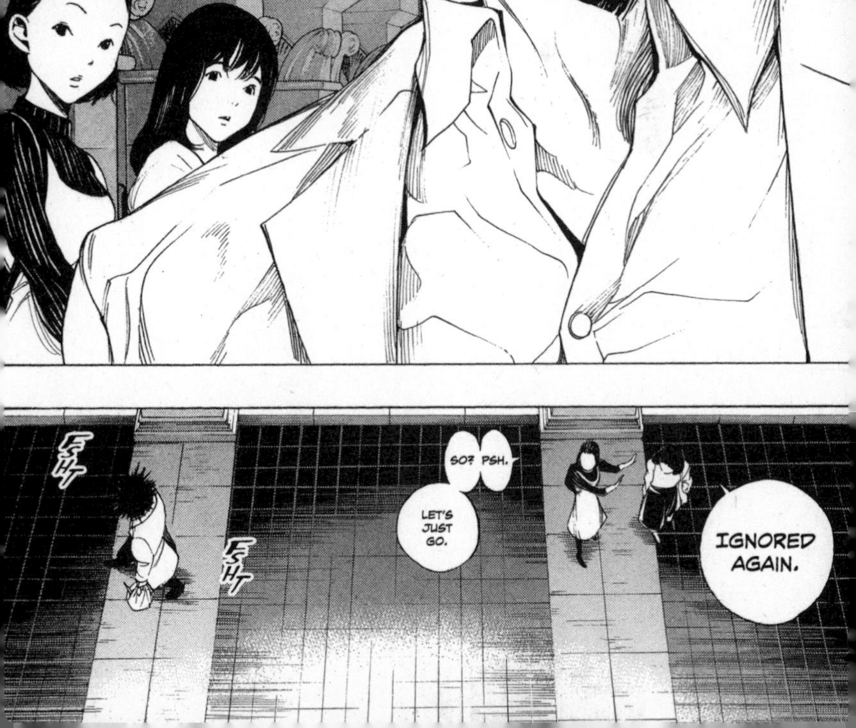
IGNORED AGAIN.
SO? PSH.
LET'S JUST GO.
FSHT
FSHT

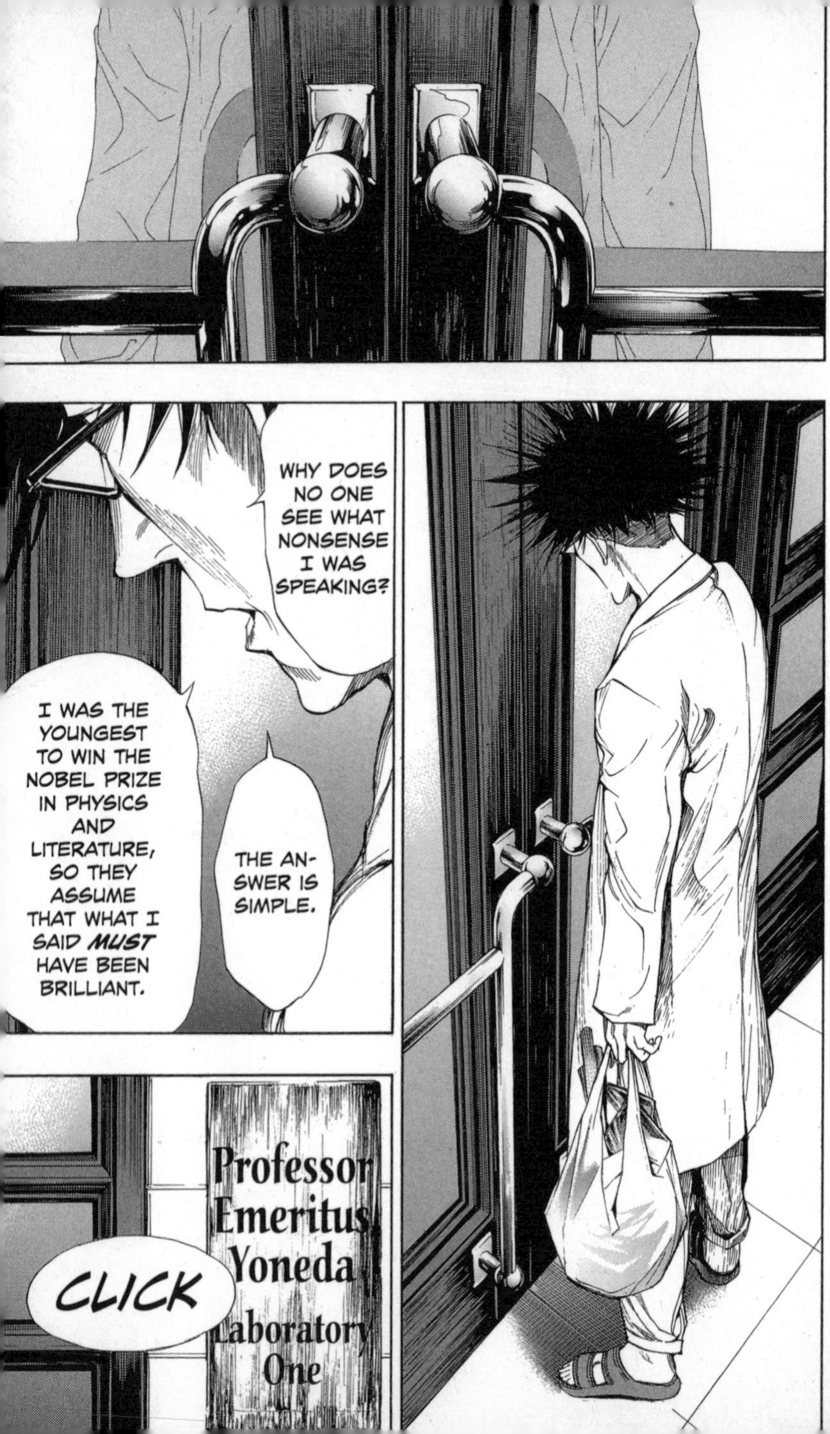
WHY DOES NO ONE SEE WHAT NONSENSE I WAS SPEAKING?
THE ANSWER IS SIMPLE.
I WAS THE YOUNGEST TO WIN THE NOBEL PRIZE IN PHYSICS AND LITERATURE, SO THEY ASSUME THAT WHAT I SAID *MUST* HAVE BEEN BRILLIANT.
Professor Emeritus Yoneda Laboratory One
CLICK

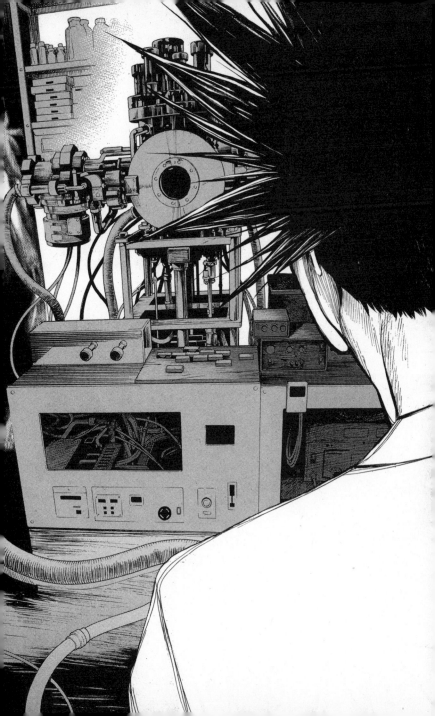

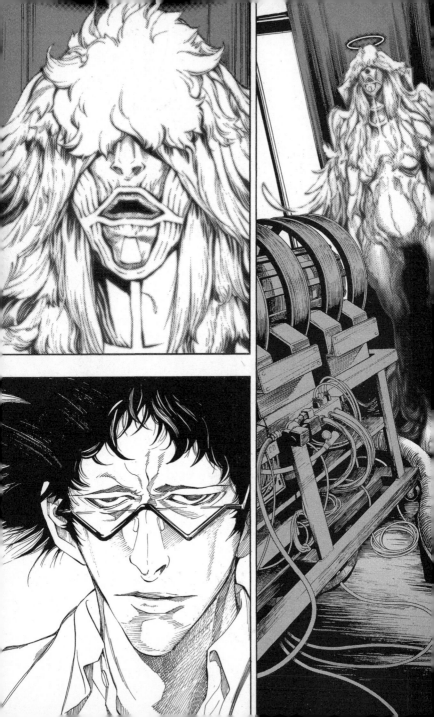

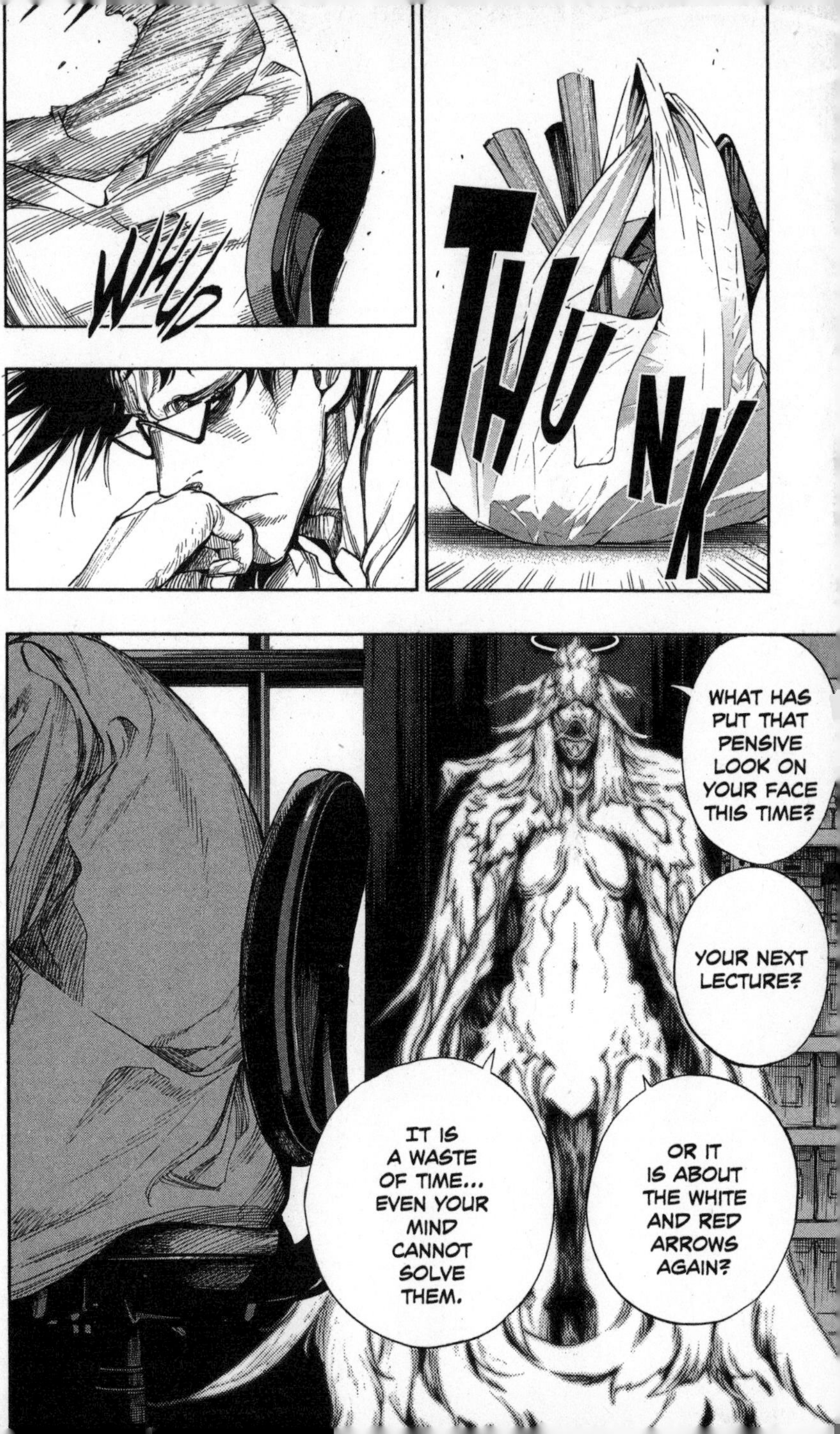
THUNK
WHUD
WHAT HAS PUT THAT PENSIVE LOOK ON YOUR FACE THIS TIME?
YOUR NEXT LECTURE?
OR IT IS ABOUT THE WHITE AND RED ARROWS AGAIN?
IT IS A WASTE OF TIME... EVEN YOUR MIND CANNOT SOLVE THEM.

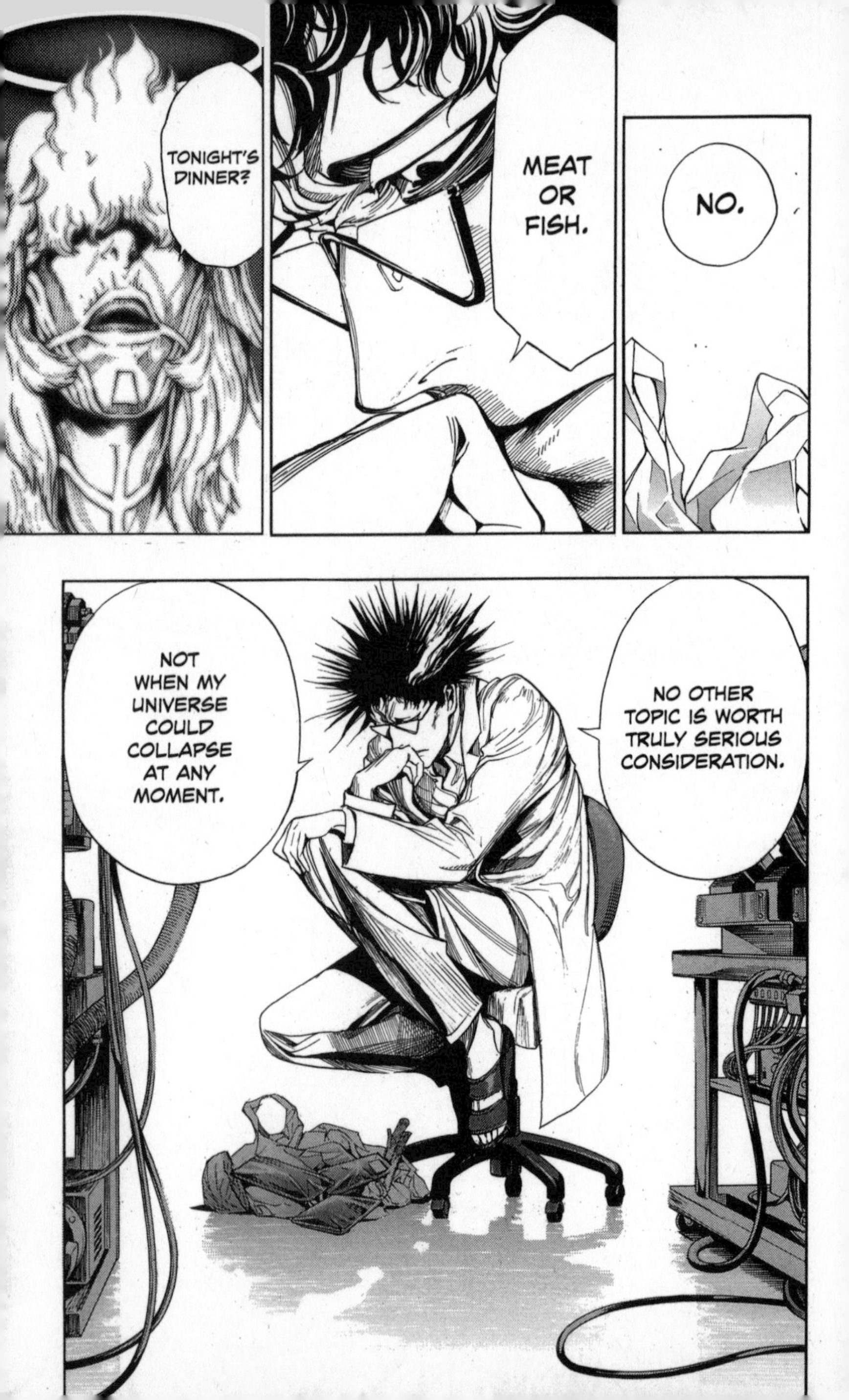
NO.
MEAT OR FISH.
TONIGHT'S DINNER?
NO OTHER TOPIC IS WORTH TRULY SERIOUS CONSIDERATION.
NOT WHEN MY UNIVERSE COULD COLLAPSE AT ANY MOMENT.

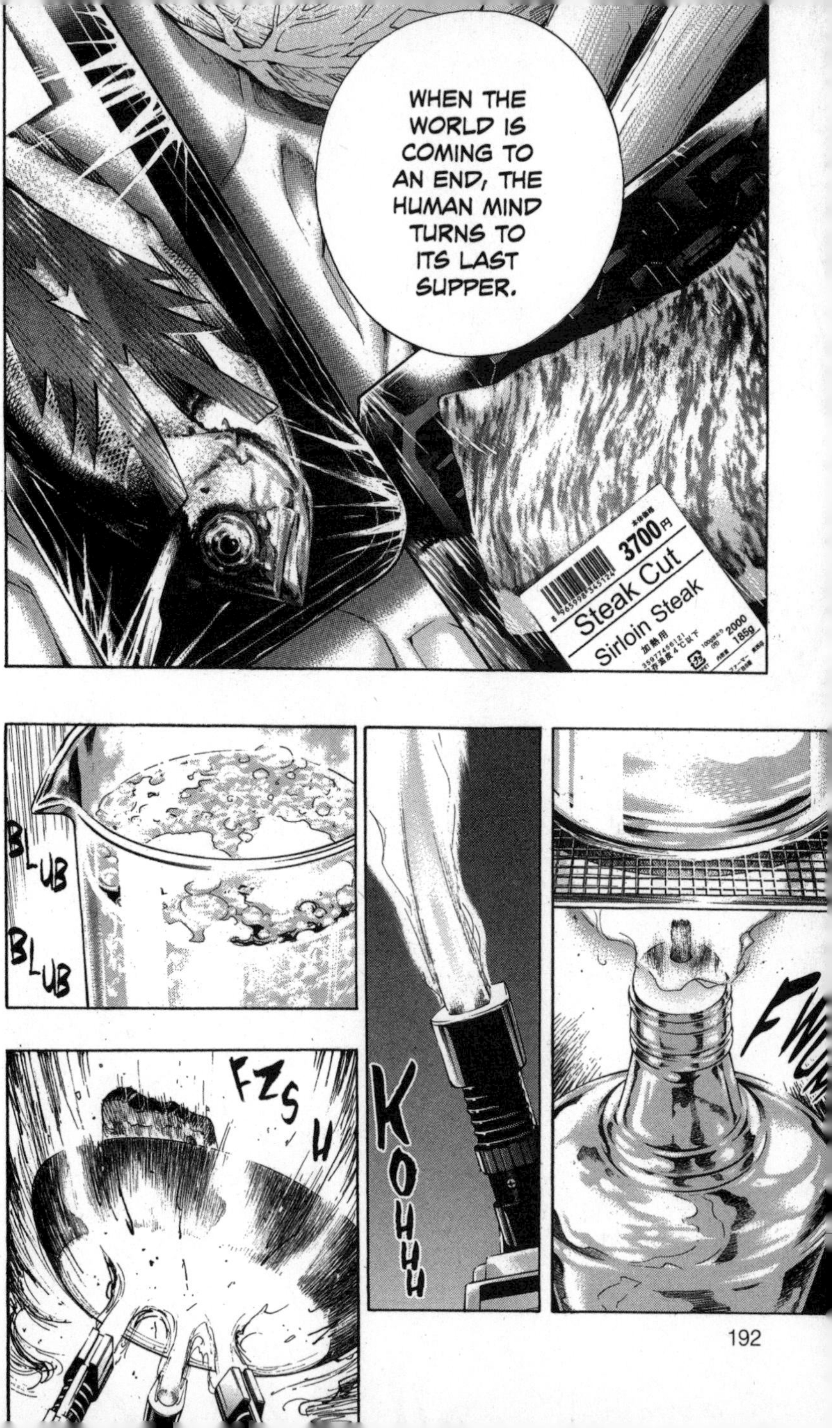
WHEN THE WORLD IS COMING TO AN END, THE HUMAN MIND TURNS TO ITS LAST SUPPER.
3700円
Steak Cut
Sirloin Steak
2000
185g
FWUM
KOHHH
BLUB BLUB
FZSH

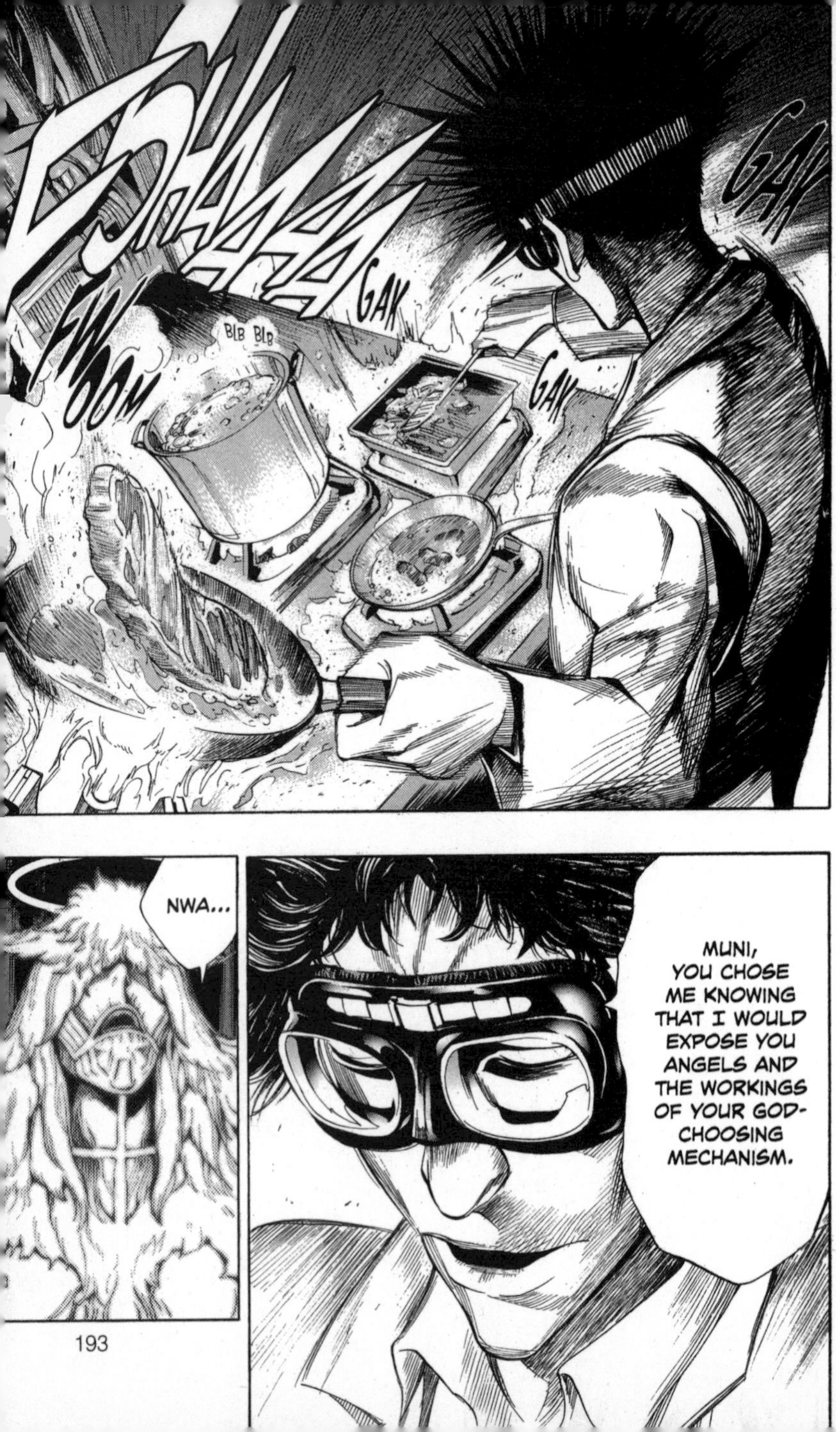
GAK
GAK
GAK
BLB BLB
FWOOM
MUNI, YOU CHOSE ME KNOWING THAT I WOULD EXPOSE YOU ANGELS AND THE WORKINGS OF YOUR GOD-CHOOSING MECHANISM.
NWA...

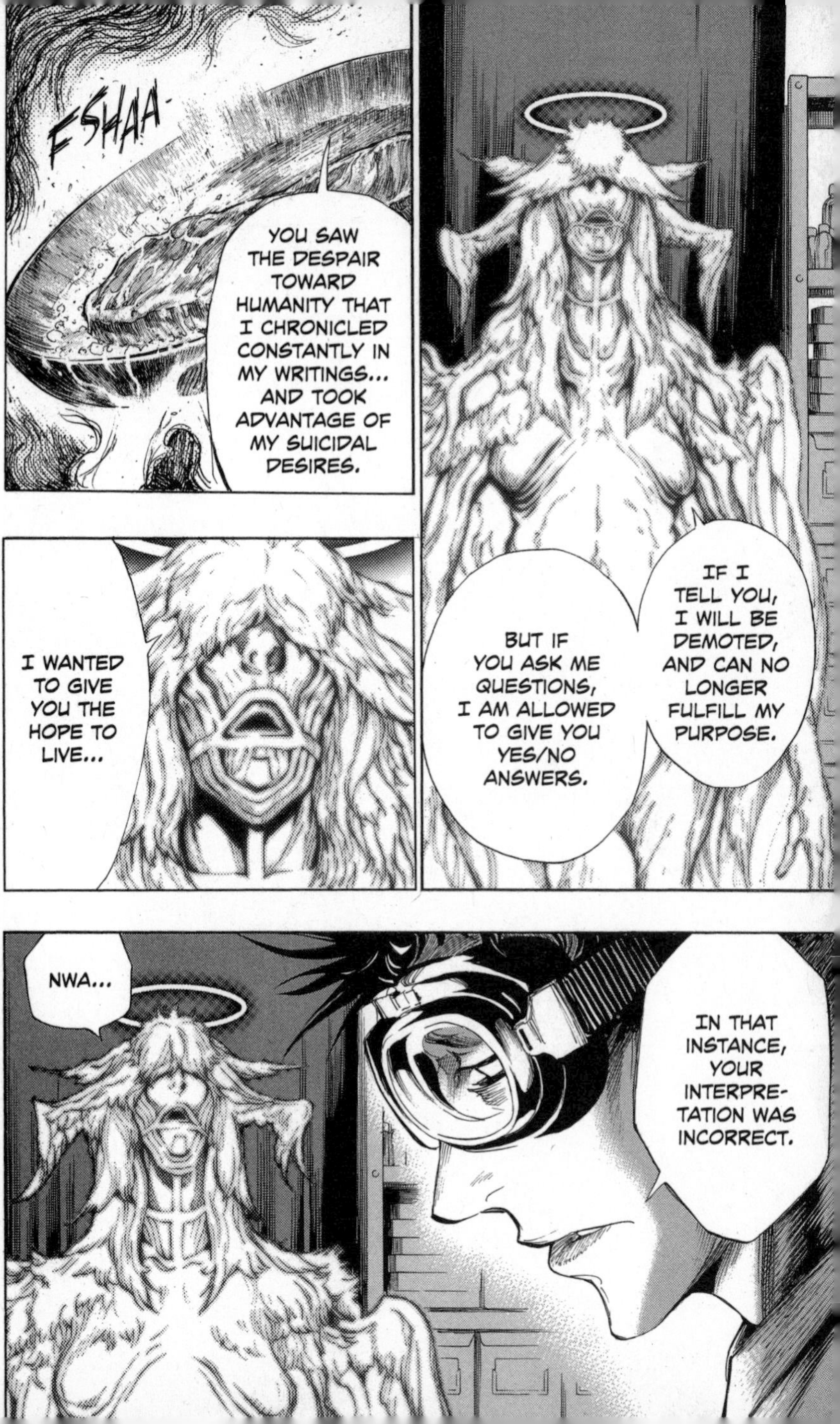
IF I TELL YOU, I WILL BE DEMOTED, AND CAN NO LONGER FULFILL MY PURPOSE.
BUT IF YOU ASK ME QUESTIONS, I AM ALLOWED TO GIVE YOU YES/NO ANSWERS.
FSHAA
YOU SAW THE DESPAIR TOWARD HUMANITY THAT I CHRONICLED CONSTANTLY IN MY WRITINGS... AND TOOK ADVANTAGE OF MY SUICIDAL DESIRES.
I WANTED TO GIVE YOU THE HOPE TO LIVE...
IN THAT INSTANCE, YOUR INTERPRE-TATION WAS INCORRECT.
NWA...

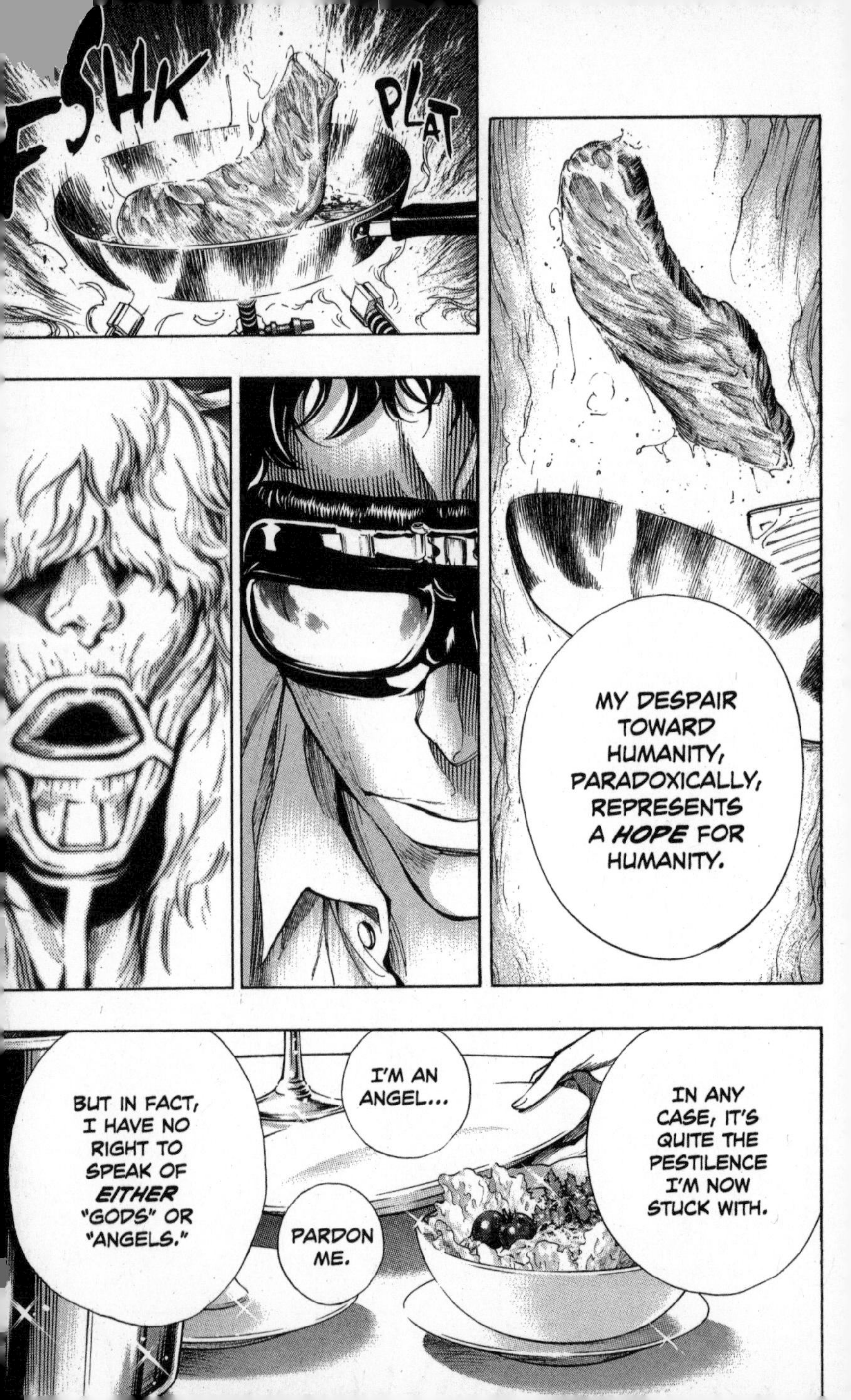
MY DESPAIR TOWARD HUMANITY, PARADOXICALLY, REPRESENTS A *HOPE* FOR HUMANITY.
FSHK
PLAT
IN ANY CASE, IT'S QUITE THE PESTILENCE I'M NOW STUCK WITH.
I'M AN ANGEL...
BUT IN FACT, I HAVE NO RIGHT TO SPEAK OF *EITHER* "GODS" OR "ANGELS."
PARDON ME.

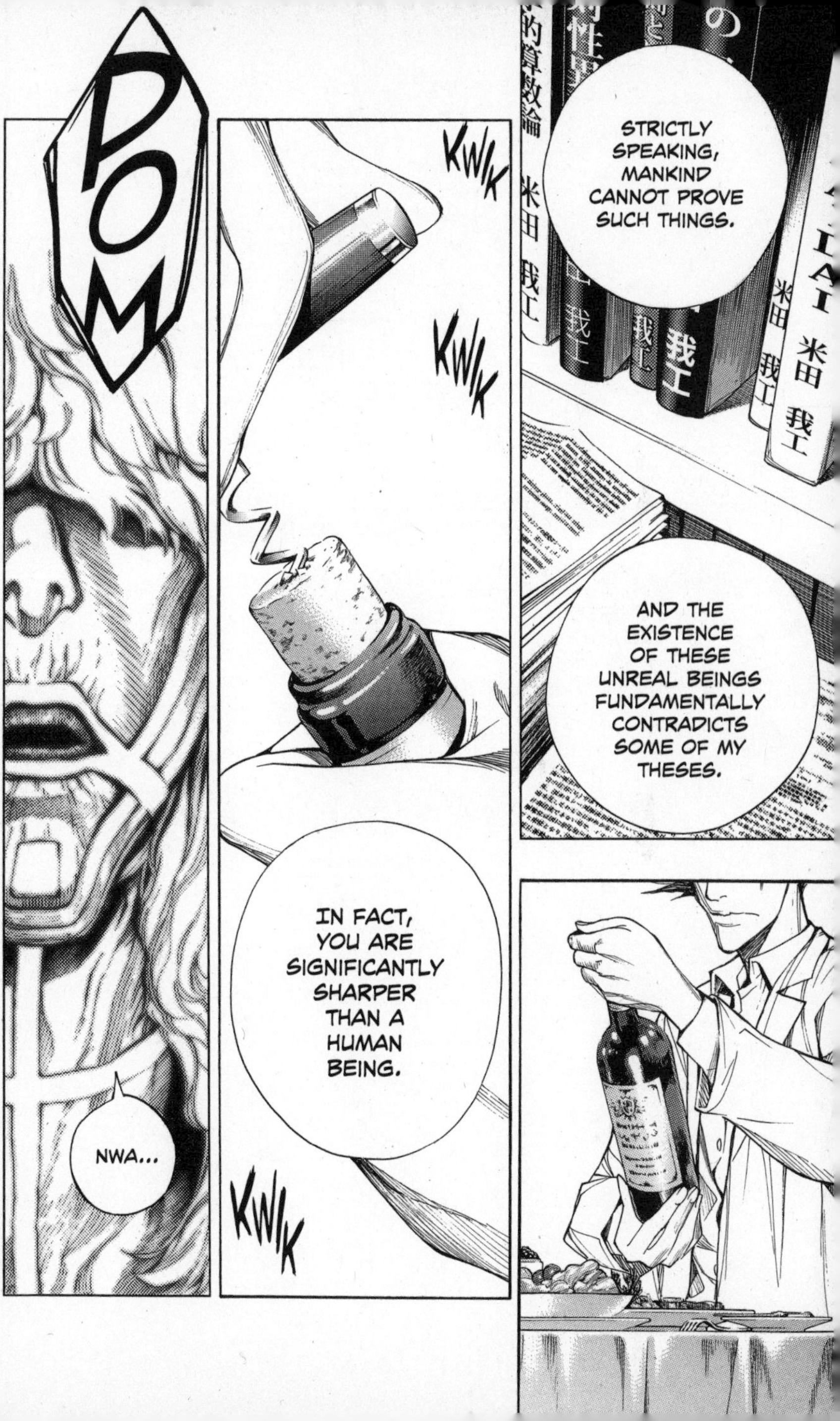
STRICTLY SPEAKING, MANKIND CANNOT PROVE SUCH THINGS.
AND THE EXISTENCE OF THESE UNREAL BEINGS FUNDAMENTALLY CONTRADICTS SOME OF MY THESES.
KWIK
KWIK
IN FACT, YOU ARE SIGNIFICANTLY SHARPER THAN A HUMAN BEING.
KWIK
POM
NWA...

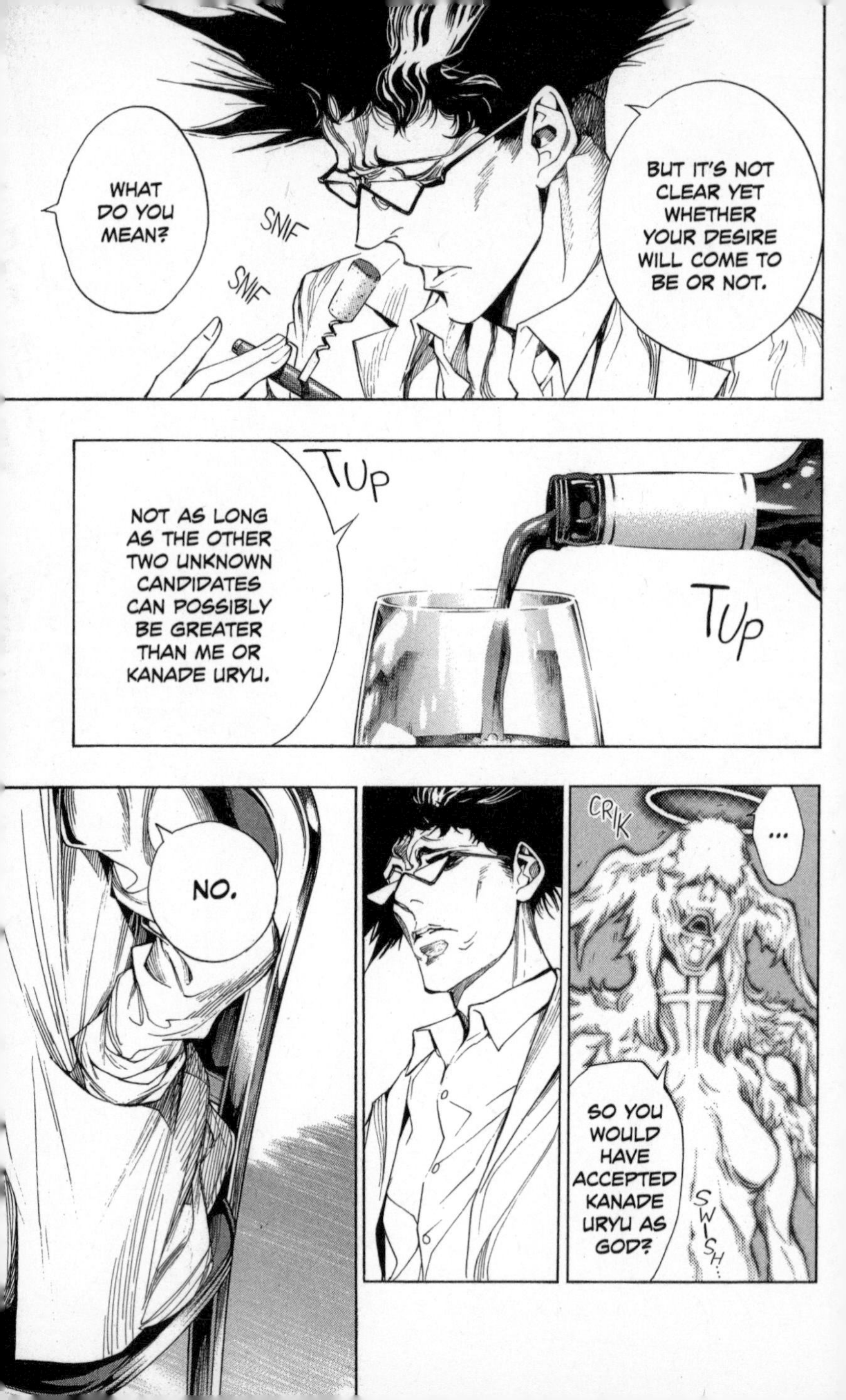
BUT IT'S NOT CLEAR YET WHETHER YOUR DESIRE WILL COME TO BE OR NOT.
SNIF
SNIF
WHAT DO YOU MEAN?
TUP
TUP
NOT AS LONG AS THE OTHER TWO UNKNOWN CANDIDATES CAN POSSIBLY BE GREATER THAN ME OR KANADE URYU.
CRIK
...
SO YOU WOULD HAVE ACCEPTED KANADE URYU AS GOD?
SWISH...
NO.

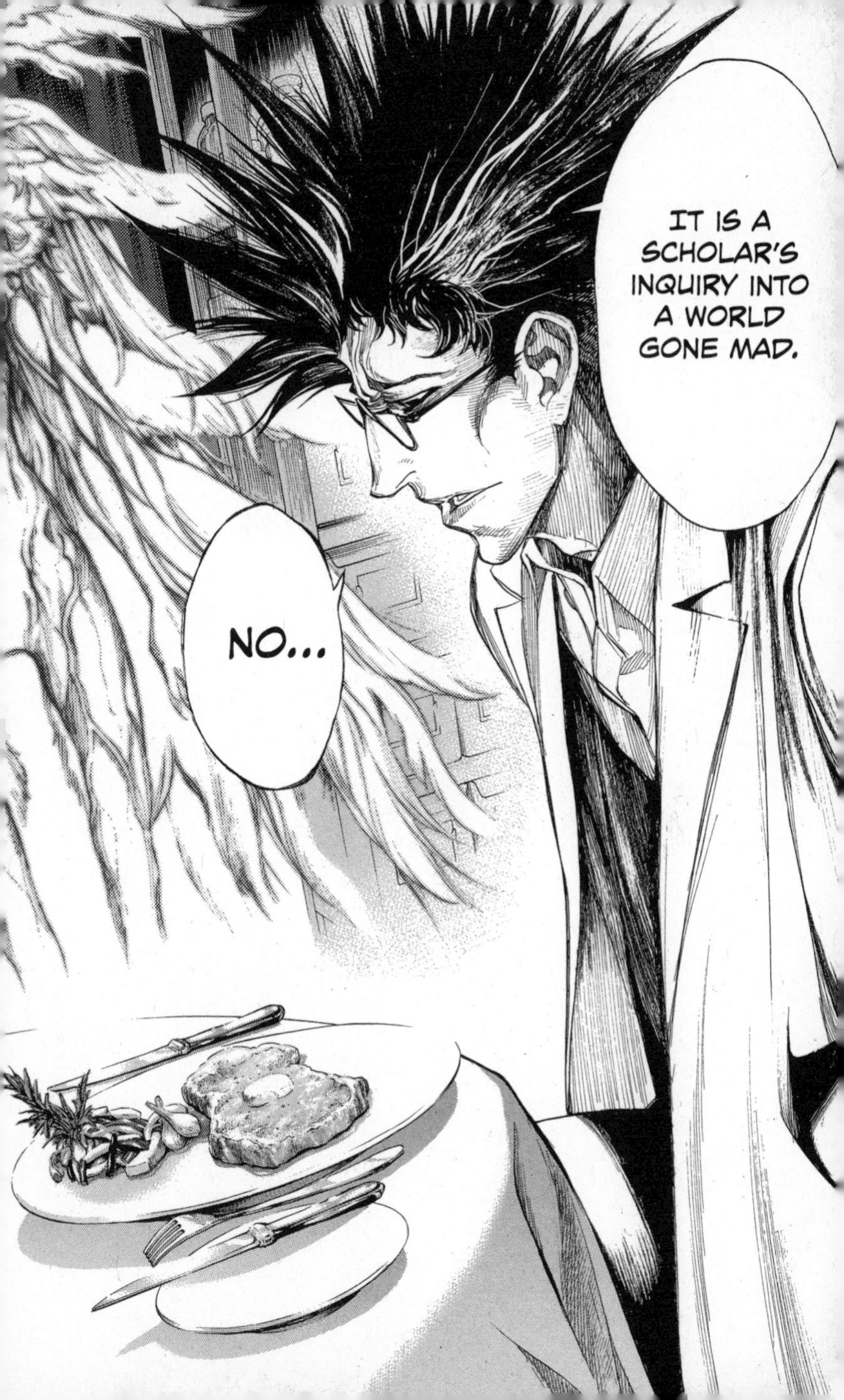
IT IS A SCHOLAR'S INQUIRY INTO A WORLD GONE MAD.
NO...

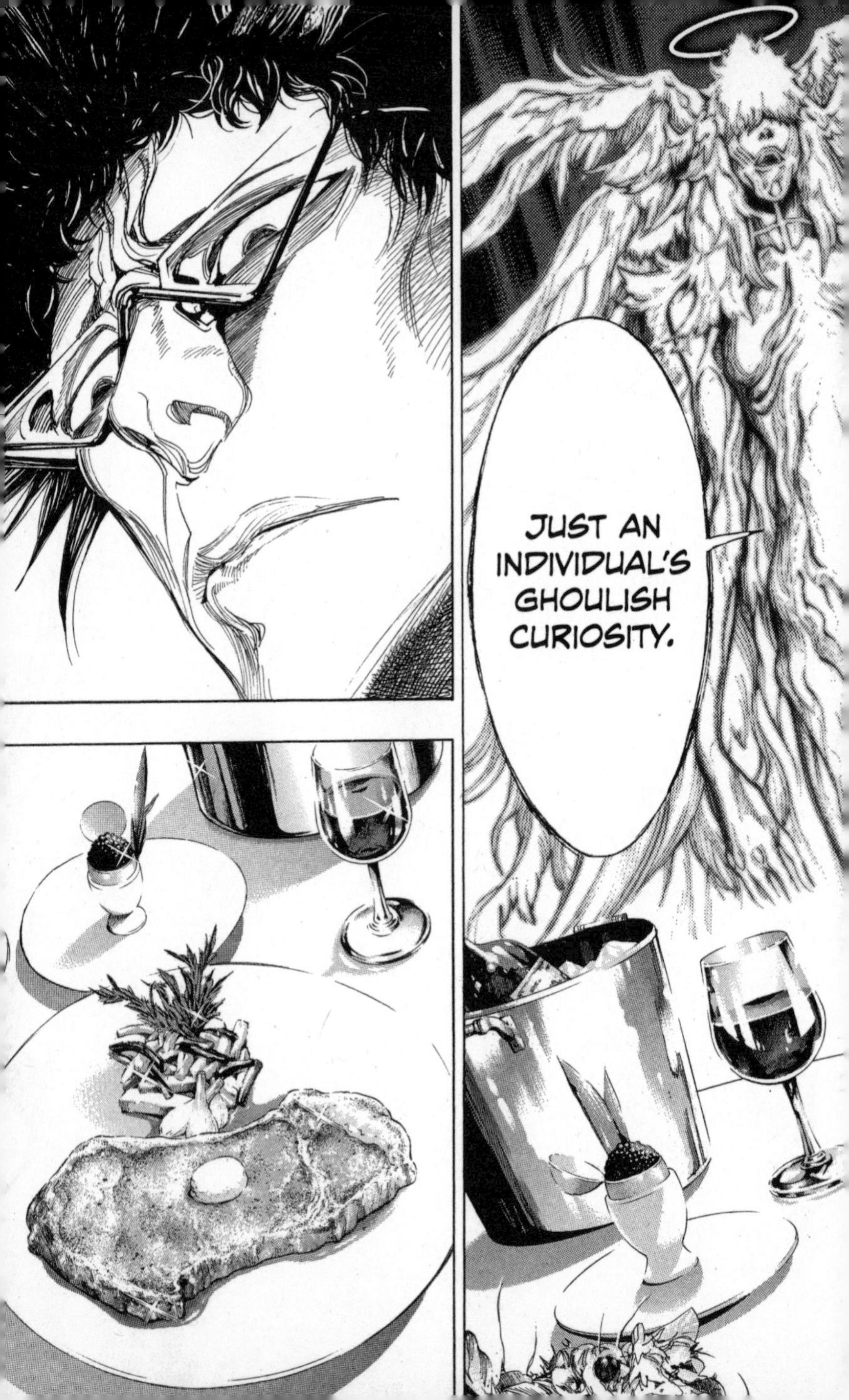
JUST AN INDIVIDUAL'S GHOULISH CURIOSITY.

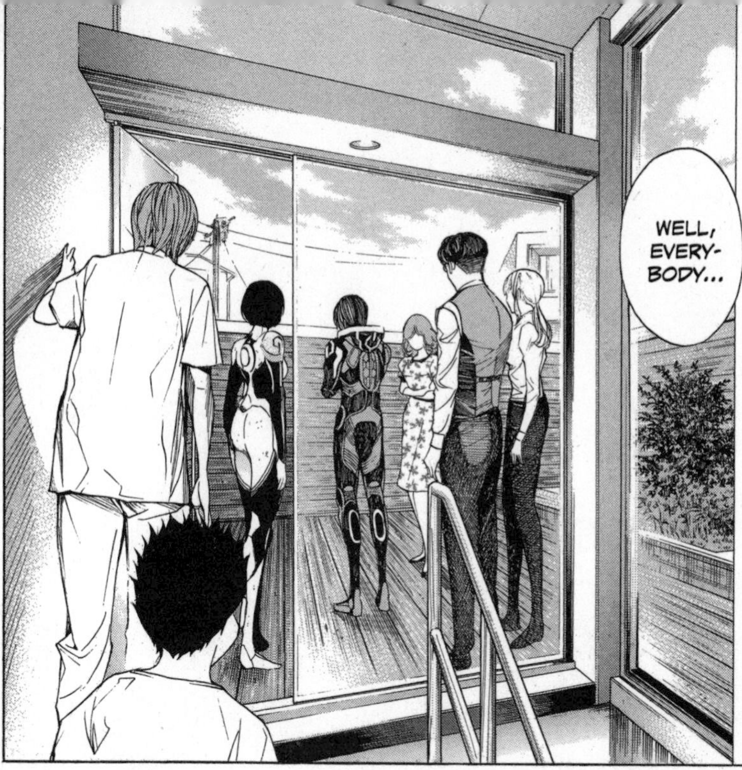
WELL, EVERY-BODY...
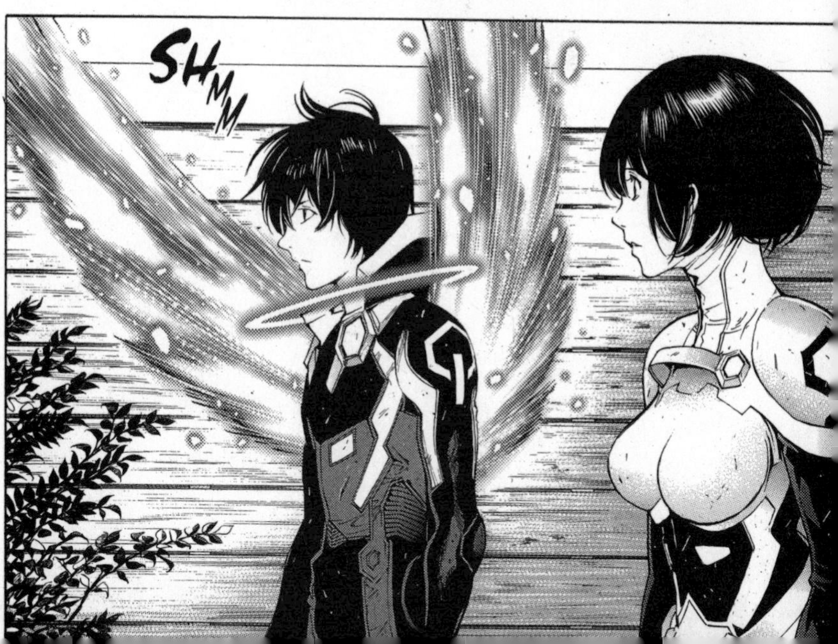
SHMM

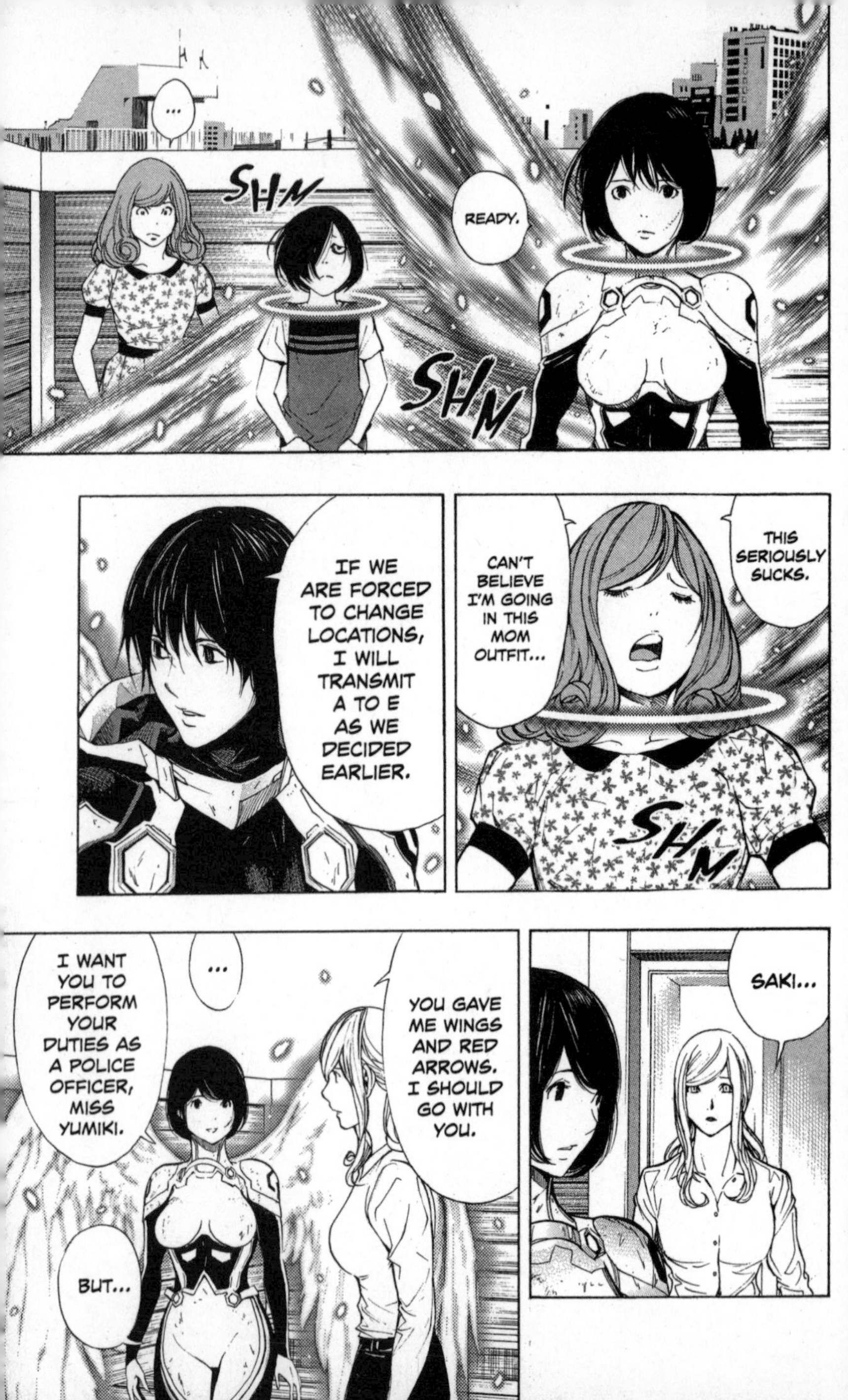
READY.
...
S-H-M
SHM
THIS SERIOUSLY SUCKS.
CAN'T BELIEVE I'M GOING IN THIS MOM OUTFIT...
SHM
IF WE ARE FORCED TO CHANGE LOCATIONS, I WILL TRANSMIT A TO E AS WE DECIDED EARLIER.
SAKI...
YOU GAVE ME WINGS AND RED ARROWS. I SHOULD GO WITH YOU.
...
I WANT YOU TO PERFORM YOUR DUTIES AS A POLICE OFFICER, MISS YUMIKI.
BUT...

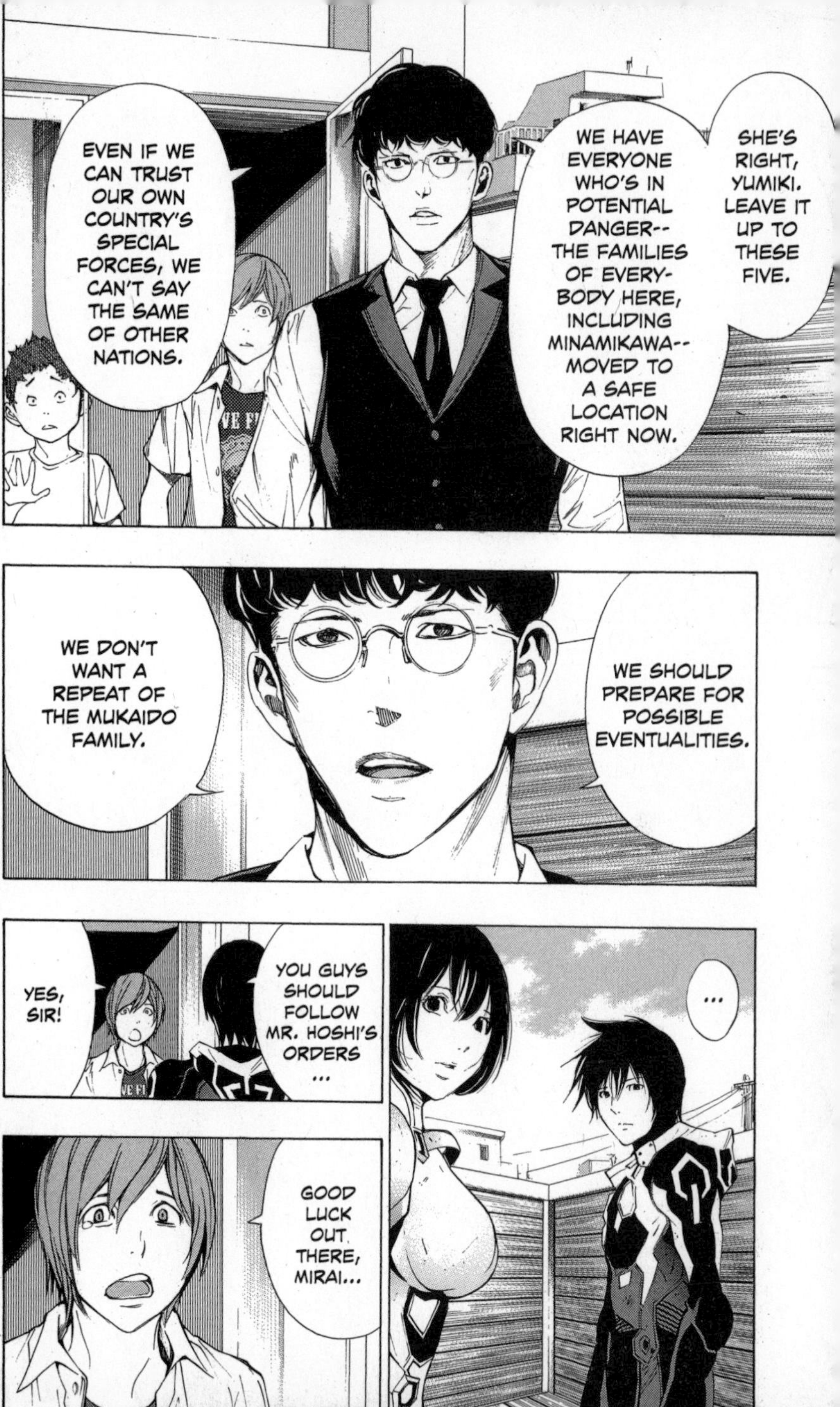
SHE'S RIGHT, YUMIKI. LEAVE IT UP TO THESE FIVE.
WE HAVE EVERYONE WHO'S IN POTENTIAL DANGER-- THE FAMILIES OF EVERYBODY HERE, INCLUDING MINAMIKAWA-- MOVED TO A SAFE LOCATION RIGHT NOW.
EVEN IF WE CAN TRUST OUR OWN COUNTRY'S SPECIAL FORCES, WE CAN'T SAY THE SAME OF OTHER NATIONS.
WE SHOULD PREPARE FOR POSSIBLE EVENTUALITIES.
WE DON'T WANT A REPEAT OF THE MUKAIDO FAMILY.
...
YOU GUYS SHOULD FOLLOW MR. HOSHI'S ORDERS ...
YES, SIR!
GOOD LUCK OUT THERE, MIRAI...

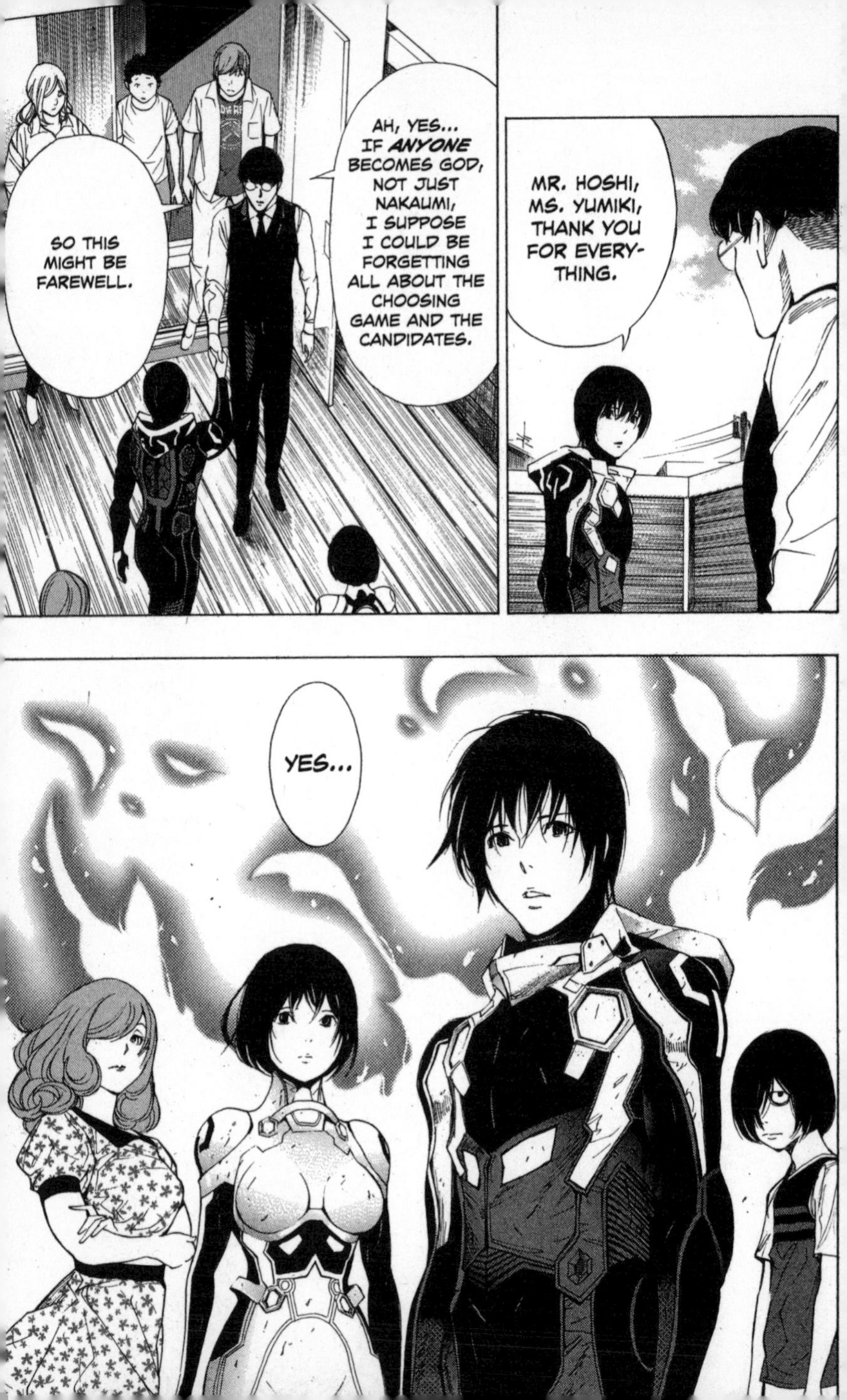
MR. HOSHI, MS. YUMIKI, THANK YOU FOR EVERY-THING.
AH, YES... IF *ANYONE* BECOMES GOD, NOT JUST NAKAUMI, I SUPPOSE I COULD BE FORGETTING ALL ABOUT THE CHOOSING GAME AND THE CANDIDATES.
SO THIS MIGHT BE FAREWELL.
YES...

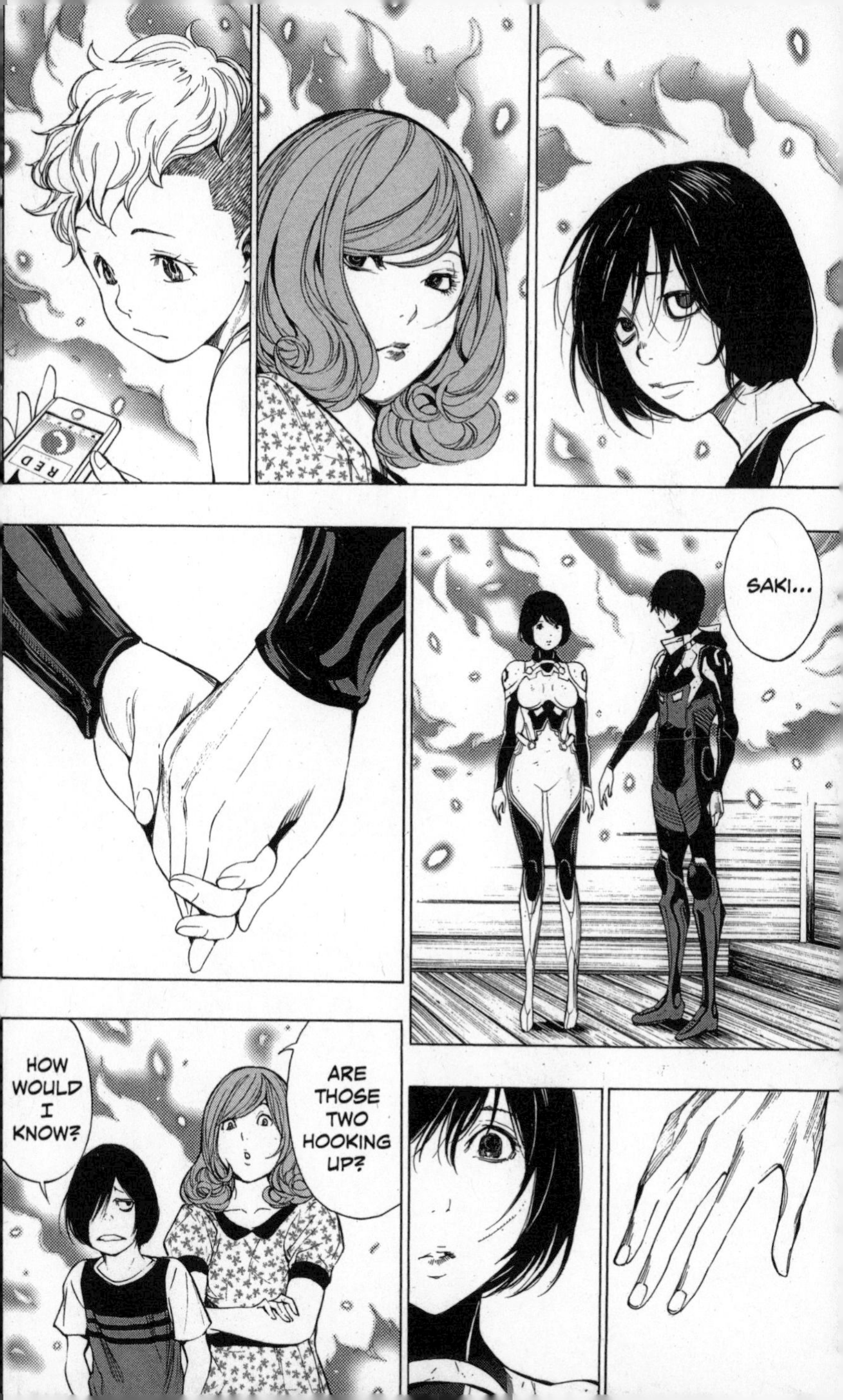
RED
SAKI...
ARE THOSE TWO HOOKING UP?
HOW WOULD I KNOW?

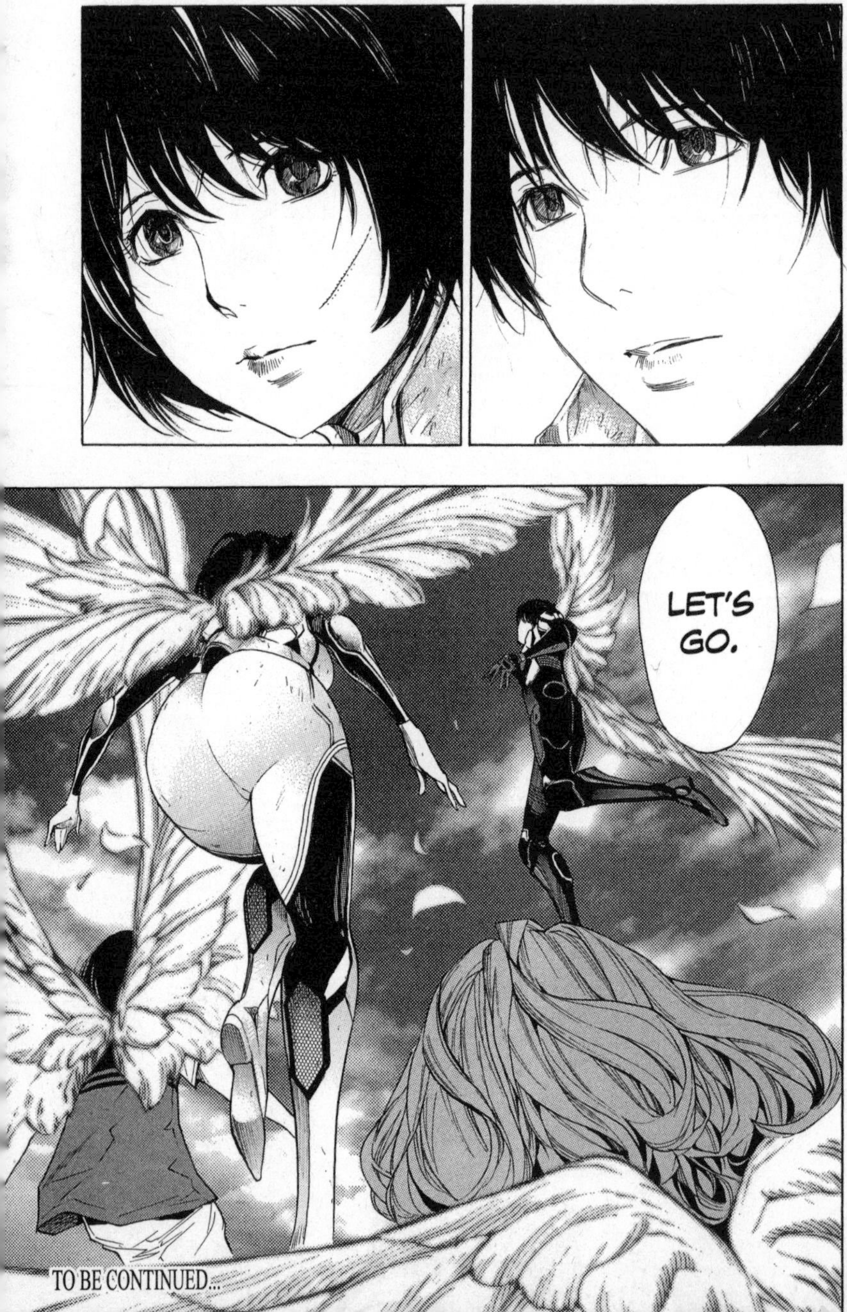
LET'S GO.
TO BE CONTINUED...

**T**sugu mi **O**h b **a**

Born in Tokyo, Tsugumi Ohba is the author
of the hit series *Death Note* and *Bakuman*。.

Ta **k** e s **h** i Oba **ta**

Takeshi Obata was born in 1969 in Niigata,
Japan, and first achieved international
recognition as the artist of the wildly popular
*Shonen Jump* title *Hikaru no Go*, which won the
2003 Tezuka Osamu Cultural Prize: Shinsei
"New Hope" Award and the 2000 Shogakukan
Manga Award. He went on to illustrate the smash
hit *Death Note* as well as the hugely successful
manga *Bakuman*。 and *All You Need Is Kill*.